THEMES IN VALUE AND DISTRIBUTION
CLASSICAL THEORY REAPPRAISED

THEMES IN VALUE AND DISTRIBUTION
CLASSICAL THEORY REAPPRAISED

Krishna Bharadwaj

Professor, Centre for Economic Studies and Planning,
Jawaharlal Nehru University, New Delhi

London
UNWIN HYMAN
Boston   Sydney   Wellington

© Krishna Bharadwaj, 1989

This book is copyright under the Berne Convention. No reproduction without permission. All rights reserved.

Published by the Academic Division of

Unwin Hyman Ltd
15/17 Broadwick Street, London W1V 3FP, UK

Unwin Hyman, Inc.
8 Winchester Place, Winchester, Mass. 01890, USA

Allen & Unwin (Australia) Ltd,
8 Napier Street, North Sydney, NSW 2060, Australia

Allen & Unwin (New Zealand) Ltd in association with the
Port Nicholson Press Ltd,
Compusales Building, 75 Ghunzee Street,
Wellington 1, New Zealand

First published in 1989

British Library Cataloguing in Publication Data

Bharadwaj, Krishna
  Themes in value and distribution: classical theory reappraised. —
  (Studies in international political economy).
  1. Economics. Classical theory, related to Marxism
  I. Title II. Series
  330.15'3
  ISBN 0-04-338148-0

Library of Congress Cataloging-in-Publication Data

Bharadwaj, Krishna.
  Themes in value and distribution: classical theory reappraised /
Krishna Bharadwaj.
     p. cm.
  Bibliography: p.
  Includes index.
  ISBN 0-04-338148-0
  1. Classical school of economics. I. Title.
  HB94.B53 1988
  330.15'3—dc19   88-18718
                                                              CIP

Typeset in 10/11 point Sabon
Printed in Great Britain by
Billing and Sons, London and Worcester

TO PIERO SRAFFA

Contents

	Acknowledgements	*page* ix
1	Introduction	1
2	Adam Smith's Political Economy	13
3	Ricardian Theory and Ricardianism	41
4	On a Controversy over Ricardo's Theory of Distribution	77
5	Sraffa's Ricardo	111
6	The Subversion of Classical Analysis: Alfred Marshall's Early Writing on Value	134
7	Marshall on Pigou's *Wealth and Welfare*	159
8	Maurice Dobb's Critique of Theories of Value and Distribution	176
9	On Certain Theoretical Issues in Classical Political Economy	204
10	Sraffa's Return to Classical Theory	222
11	On the Maximum Number of Switches between Two Production Systems	255
12	On Effective Demand: Certain Recent Critiques	275
13	Piero Sraffa: The Man and the Scholar – A Tribute	298
	Index	325

Acknowledgements

It is extremely difficult, if not impossible, to acknowledge by name those who have contributed to and aided the shaping of these essays which span a number of formative years of my research. Specific acknowledgements do occur in individual essays. However, I would like to mention here some of those who have given me constant encouragement and through their helpful and careful discussions have supported my endeavours. My greatest debt is to Piero Sraffa who initiated me into classical theory and whose scrupulous scholarship has set a goal, too difficult to attain I admit, which nevertheless continues to inspire. To Pierangelo Garegnani, I owe many stimulating discussions and shared interests and ideas over many years. Maurice Dobb, Nicholas Kaldor and Joan Robinson – no more with us now – provided the lively ethos, nurturing new explorations in theory and spearheading critiques of the mainstream economics in the Cambridge of the 1960s and 1970s when I was preparing the groundwork for these essays. Antonia Campus, John Eatwell, Geoffrey Harcourt, Donald Harris, Heinz Kurz, Barbara McLennan, Edward Nell, Luigi Pasinetti, Alessandro Roncaglia, Bertram Schefold, Ian Steedman, Sylos Labini and other friends in Cambridge, in Europe and America have read, commented and helped in this work and have actively collaborated in the recent revival and development of the classical theory.

In India, the resurgence of the classical and Marxian approach has had a significant impact on the analysis of development issues and policies. I have benefited from the keen and active interest taken by Amiya Kumar Bagchi, Amit Bhaduri, Nirmal Kumar Chandra, Sukhamoy Chakravarty, K. N. Raj and all my colleagues at the Centre for Economic Studies and Planning. With them I have shared my half-baked ideas, my enthusiasms and frustrations, my 'successes' and 'failures' and have received careful, critical and constructive responses. At the Centre for Economic Studies and Planning, my colleagues and students have provided considerable stimulus to combine theoretical interests with developmental issues so as to implant in my research a constant awareness of the requisites and tasks of economic theory. I have, over all these years of teaching, enjoyed a lively sense of active interaction with students which has not only stimulated ideas in fresh directions but also shaped them into an orderliness that pedagogy demands. Limitations, which these essays perhaps abound in, are entirely my own and remain despite all those who are acknowledged above.

During the course of this research I have received generous assistance and co-operation over different periods and durations, from the

Indian Council of Social Science Research, Clare Hall, Cambridge; the Universities of Manchester and of Rome; Trinity College, Cambridge; and Maison des Sciences de L'homme, Paris. The International Summer School held annually at Trieste by the Centro Intèrnazionale di studi di economia politica gave me the opportunity to interact with scholars drawn from various parts of the world. My short visits to the New School at New York provided very fruitful opportunities to interact with the young scholars.

I am grateful to the editors of the following journals for allowing me to republish my papers that originally appeared in their journals. These papers are presented in this volume with some modifications and revisions.

Australian Economic Papers for chapter 9: 'On Certain Theoretical Issues in Classical Political Economy'; *Cambridge Journal of Economics* for Chapter 4, 'On a Controversy over Ricardo's Theory of Distribution'; Chapter 5, 'Sraffa's Ricardo'; Chapter 6, 'The Subversion of Classical Analysis: Alfred Marshall's Early Writing on Value', and Chapter 8, 'Maurice Dobb's Critique of Theories of Value and Distribution'; *Economica* for Chapter 7, 'Marshall on Pigou's *Wealth and Welfare*'; *Economic and Political Weekly* for Chapter 13, 'Piero Sraffa: The Man and the Scholar – A Tribute'; *Political Economy: Studies in the Surplus' Approach* for Chapter 10, 'Sraffa's Return to Classical Theory *Schweizerische Zeitschrift für Volkswirtschaft und Statistik* for Chapter 11, 'On the Maximum Number of Switches Between Two Production Systems' and the Macmillan Press for Chapter 12, 'On Effective Demand: Certain Recent Critiques'.

To the former economics editor of this series, Walter Allan, as well as the present, Carolyn White, I express my grateful appreciation for having taken enthusiastic interest in the publication of the work. The job of editing has been rendered immensely difficult as it has involved bringing together writings spanning a long period and written and published at different places. The difficulty has been heightened by lack of access to libraries well equipped with classics. I am grateful to Sudhanshu Bhushan who assisted me ably and enthusiastically in the tedious and exacting tasks of reading the proofs and preparing the index: and to Juliet Aitchison, Carole Fries and Jayati Ghosh who have displayed considerable patience in prodding through the text with a watchful eye. I am highly obliged to Mr Yashwant Singh for his meticulous and patient typing of several drafts under severe time constraints.

Krishna Bharadwaj
Centre for Economic Studies and Planning
Jawaharlal Nehru University
New Delhi
December 1988

1
Introduction

In this book a selection of essays have been put together which were produced over several years and published at various points of time. Here, we provide a brief overview of the contents and the major thrust of the essays. Our treatment of the issues raised in the following is necessarily brief.

Although these essays engage in interpretations of the history of economic ideas with reference to particular author(s) or inquire into specific conceptual developments and connected controversies, their interest is not solely or even primarily exegetical or historiographical. They have an analytical core and an underlying unity of themes. They attempt to develop a critique of economic theory, seeking to bring out the distinctive differences in the methodological frameworks and theoretical approaches characteristic of the two broad streams in theories of value and distribution – one, the classical, or what we may call surplus-based, theories and the other, the demand-and-supply-based equilibrium (in short, DSE) theories. (The latter are commonly, but misleadingly, called neoclassical theories.)

The classical theory we here refer to had its beginnings in the works of William Petty in England and the Physiocrats in France. It advanced significantly through the contributions of Adam Smith and David Ricardo and found its comprehensive developments through radical reconstructions in Karl Marx. The DSE theories emerged in the third quarter of the nineteenth century, around the 1870s, spearheaded by the writings of Jevons, Menger and Walras. They rose to dominance eclipsing the classical approach not only for reasons of the logical and analytical hurdles the latter theory met with, but also because of the unacceptability of its sharp theoretical positions stressing the conflict-ridden dynamics of capitalist distribution and accumulation. The approach was prematurely abandoned and was superseded even while the logical problems remained insufficiently explored and hence unresolved.

While the theoretical critique suggested in these pages stresses the distinctiveness of the structures and approaches of the two streams in theory, it is not denied that there are differences among the proponents within each stream. In fact, the theory developed and was extended through debates and critical controversies among the proponents. It is possible, nevertheless, to suggest a broad dichotomy as there are basic unifying elements within each stream, and sufficiently significant distinctions demarcating the two, to postulate that a divide did occur in theory in the 1870s.

1 Accent on Themes of Value and Distribution

Our accent in this set of essays is on the theme of value and distribution as treated by the original proponents.[1] This is so for a number of reasons. First, the common or shared ground among Smith, Ricardo and Marx in this part of the theory is fairly substantial, notwithstanding critical modifications and refinements in theory that each successively brought in over his predecessor's. We take a similar view with regard to the DSE theorists, Jevons, Walras, Marshall and Wicksell who shared a common approach to the theory of relative prices and distribution despite differences in specifications of particular elements of their theory, like the 'primary resources', 'transformation possibilities' or 'structure of preferences'.

Secondly, the analysis of value and distribution has provided the foundation for the analysis of accumulation in both streams. The structural comparison between theories brings out precisely how they explain, in a different framework, the determination of prices and quantities in an interdependent economic system. Their differences in approach stand out clearly in the context of value and distribution which provides the scaffolding for other analyses.

Another, somewhat different, reason for focusing on the theory of distribution pertains to the historical process of the rise and decline of theories and the polemics surrounding it. The theory of distribution (and value) has played a critical role in determining the course of analytical history. The classical theory was prematurely abandoned mainly on the ground of the deficiency of the labour theory of value. Recent debates in the capital theory have questioned the logical consistency of the DSE's explanation of the rate of profit as determined by the equilibrium between demand for and supply of capital. (It has been demonstrated that the 'well-behaved' demand relation for capital, required by the theory, cannot be ensured consistently within the DSE theory.)

This is not to suggest that the critique proposed here is confined to the problems of value and distribution. It extends necessarily – and naturally – to the problems of accumulation,[2] particularly so, since in DSE theories all prices (including 'factor prices') *and* quantities (including 'factor-uses') are determined simultaneously within the same scheme of explanation. (See below, pp. 7–8.)

2 On the Analytical Divide around the 1870s

This position on the analytical divide, that it occurs around the 1870s, opposes the contrary view that economic theory advanced more or less unilinearly towards more rigorous, logically sounder and analytically more comprehensive (or, 'general') formulations – with Smith and Ricardo, in particular, being seen as the precursors of the DSE theories, and Marx being seen as an idiosyncratic ideologue outside the mainstream, even of the classical theory. Some Marxist commentators, while accepting the divide, suggest that the break occurs around the 1830s when Ricardian theory disintegrated so that Marx's critique of his predecessors amounts to a total refutation and a radical break with the past. As discussed in 'Ricardian Theory and Ricardianism' (Chapter 3 below), Ricardian theory indeed weakened and was eroded in the hands of his followers, strengthening thereby the trends towards consolidation of what Marx called the 'vulgar economy'. In the face of analytical difficulties, as well as the change in the political scene (with the emergence of sharp capital/labour conflicts and the opposition to Ricardian socialists), the Ricardians landed the classical theory into utter confusion through their attempts at modifications, extensions and at putting up a weak, non-viable defence of Ricardo's theory. However, no alternative theory was yet in sight in the 1830s. It is later, with Jevons, Walras and the Austrians, that a systematic, alternative theoretical structure arose. Marshall, despite his vociferous claims of continuity with the tradition of Smith and Ricardo, has to be counted as one among the influential progenitors of the DSE theories. (See 'The Subversion of Classical Analysis', Chapter 6 below.) This in no way minimizes the radical and original constructions of Marx, particularly in the domain of the theory of accumulation and his reconstitution of the surplus approach to distribution, threatened by its erosion in the post-Ricardo decline of 'scientific political economy'. It is for this reason, and for our purpose of constructing the critique in terms of the comparative structures of theories, that we take the 1870s as the line of divide and focus mainly on the value-distribution theme.

3 Themes in the Critique

The Basic Structure of Theories
The critique is advanced along three themes which appear singly or interwoven in these essays. One, is the attempt to delineate the shared basic elements in the analytical approach of the classical theory and to trace its development through the critical and constructive writings of Smith, Ricardo and Marx. We investigate the formation and evolution of the basic concepts and categories used in their analysis and identify the theoretical setting in which they analyse questions of value and distribution. Often the underlying structure of their theory is not explicitly formulated or laid out. Even when such explicit or complete statements are not present, it is possible to discern the 'rational foundation' of their theoretical propositions (as Piero Sraffa does in his well-known editorial introductions to Ricardo's works), by recognizing the peculiarities of the theoretical questions they sought to answer, the specific forms which logical difficulties assume in their theory, their own

perceptions regarding the nature of such difficulties, and their peculiar attempts at their resolution. The structure of their theory emerges through these investigations to provide a rationale consistent with their formulation of problems and pursuit of solutions. The rationale behind Smith's distinction between 'natural' and 'market' values, Ricardo's 'invariant standard' or Marx's 'transformation problem', for example, needs to be understood and interpreted in the context of their specific theoretical approach. Otherwise, neither the meaning nor the significance of such theoretical formulations or constructions can be appreciated. The temptation to judge the validity and usefulness of constructions such as Ricardo's 'invariant standard' in an alien structure (e.g. that of the DSE) has inevitably led the critics to conclude that the search for an 'invariant standard' is a chimera, invented by Ricardo, 'a profound but confused genius'. Similarly, Marx's 'transformation problem' has been viewed by Bohm Bawerk, among others, as his defensive, ill-conceived attempt to save the exploitation theory of profit, once he had realized, all too late, that prices deviate from labour values. In 'Adam Smith's Political Economy' (Chapter 2 below), we study Smith's conceptualization of the free, decision-making individual alongside notions such as 'effectual demand' which distinguish his theory of competitive value and distribution, so that we are forewarned against equating his 'invisible hand' with the DSE's Walrasian auctioneer. In 'On a Controversy over Ricardo's Theory of Distribution' (Chapter 4 below), we trace the development of Ricardo's theory of profit, paying close attention to the theoretical structure and the analytical core of his arguments as they move from the primitive corn-rate theory of profit to its generalized forms.

The problem of identifying the common basic structure is less difficult in the case of the DSE theories of value and distribution, as the structure is more explicitly and pointedly laid out even though there are differences in the specifications of 'given' primary resources, of 'technologically feasible sets', of the 'preferences' and of 'expectations', or in the 'methods' of analysis (static/intertemporal, short period/long period, etc.). The 'substitution' principle, however, remains the basic mainspring of change, whether in 'static' or 'dynamic' (or 'intertemporal') analysis. (See 'Sraffa's Return to Classical Theory', Chapter 10 below.)

Relativity of Concepts and Categories
The second strand in our critique is a critical scrutiny of attempts at assimilating and synthesizing the classical theory into the DSE stream. The attempts at such a synthesis, influenced to a great extent by Marshall's positions representing the classical writers as progenitors of the DSE approach, rest on picking out certain isolated elements in their analysis (such as their discussion of deviations of actual supplies from 'effectual demand' or of 'natural prices' from 'market prices') to argue that they are only primitive beginnings or partial anticipations of the later DSE theory. In 'Adam Smith's Political Economy' (Chapter 2 below) we examine such arguments which impute to Smith the notion of relative-price-guided, scarce-resource-allocational mechanisms.

Such interpretations are aided no doubt by the fact that, essentially, the same problems and similar concepts continue, although the methodological and analytical approaches of the theories may significantly differ. Individual concepts and notions, severed from their parent structures, when transplanted in a different analytical framework acquire very different connotations and roles. In 'Adam Smith's Political Economy' we suggest that the 'gravitation' of 'market' to 'natural prices' of his theory is different from the DSE theory's process of relating 'short-period equilibrium' to 'normal, long-period equilibrium' prices. In 'The Subversion of Classical Analysis' (Chapter 6 below) we discuss how Marshall, in gradual steps, translated the classical notion of 'market prices' into short-period equilibrium prices and used the idea of periodization to advance his 'Fundamental Idea' of continuity, namely, that all prices are determined by the same supply-and-demand equilibrium mechanism. See also 'Sraffa's Return to Classical Theory' (Chapter 10 below).

Further, an attempt recurrently made by those maintaining the 'continuity' thesis, is to treat the classical framework as a partial or incomplete scheme; or, as a subsystem of the more general DSE theory. Thus special assumptions are attributed to Smith and Ricardo: such as, uniformity of capital/labour ratios in all methods of production, or of constant returns to scale, or of 'extreme values' for the elasticity of demand in particular cases, or fixed factor-proportions in production, or of a single primary factor, labour or corn, etc. It is argued in such attempts that the classical theorists implicitly availed themselves of such assumptions in order to arrive at their peculiar special results or 'strong cases' (see, e.g., Hollander, 1979). By a strange twist of logic ('M. twist' we may call it, skilfully practised by Marshall) 'contradictions' and 'inconsistencies' are first attributed to the classical theorists whenever their observations or results deviate from those which the DSE theory would prompt us to expect; these are then shown to be reconcilable with the DSE theories by superimposing on the classical construction the assumptions necessary for such a reconciliation. With these twists and turns an attempt is then made to establish that the classical authors anticipated, although in primitive, and partial ways, the more rigorously theorized mechanisms of price-quantity relations of the DSE theory.

In the same spirit, considering the classical theory as a 'partial model' of DSE, appropriate 'closure conditions' are suggested. In the case of Ricardo, both Marshall (1920 [1961], Appendix I, pp. 813-21) and Samuelson (1959) have interpreted Ricardo as giving a role to 'demand' when he fixes the no-rent intensive margin on land. They have considered that a natural generalization of Ricardo's analysis would be an explicit supplementation of the 'demand' side to his 'cost of production' view of prices, particularly if wage is made flexible, and not determined by the iron necessity of a subsistence minimum. We have occasion to discuss some examples of such interpretations in 'On a Controversy over Ricardo's Theory of Distribution' (Chapter 4 below) and in 'Sraffa's Return to Classical Theory' (Chapter 10 below).

Not only do the original concepts, transplanted into a different theory, change their connotations, but, even more important, we find that the definitions and hence the content of concepts alter. These alterations have been introduced often to accommodate the concept consistently within the new theory. In 'Sraffa's Return to Classical Theory', we discuss how the classical notion of 'competition' (implying unrestrained mobility of outputs, capital and labour) developed into the notion of 'perfect competition' compatible with the new theory of price-quantity determination on competitive markets. We also discuss how the organizing concept of the 'natural position' of the classical theory was transformed into the notion of the 'long-period equilibrium', now explained by a different theory; at the same time, the classical distinction (which was a 'qualitative' one) between 'market' and 'natural variables' was reformulated as a distinction between 'short-period' and 'long-period' equilibria. These changes in the contents of the concepts were introduced in response to the requirements of the new theory in which they were now embedded, rather than to accommodate fresh observations of economic phenomena. A clear understanding of the differences in the structures and approaches of theories thus becomes essential for a careful interpretation of the apparently common concepts and theoretical propositions.

Juxtaposing Structures and Analytical Implications of Differences
The third strand in our critique is the juxtaposition of the two structures in order to derive their implications in terms of the strength and limitations of analysis flowing from their approach. The theme of juxtaposition of the classical and the DSE approach appears in various places and contexts in these essays.[3] Put briefly, it is maintained that the two theories have different explanations of prices and quantities and they deal with the problematic of changes (in prices and quantities) and of 'choice' (i.e., units of analysis, their decision-making behaviour and roles) in different methodological and theoretical frames.

The central concept in the classical theory is that of surplus whose production, appropriation, distribution and accumulation is the concern of analysis. An economy to be analysed is characterized as a circular system of reproduction. The mode of surplus generation and appropriation (i.e., the methods of production and the property/production relations), the mode of exchange/circulation and the mode of distribution of surplus among the revenue classes are stipulated, relevant to that social formation, on the basis of observed regularities. In particular, the competitive capitalist economy is characterized as the one where production is for exchange and is organized capitalistically on the basis of wage-labour. A tripartite division of revenues into wages, profits and rents corresponding to the revenue classes of labourers, capitalists and landlords is recognized, with competition affirming tendencies towards a uniform rate of profit and of wages.

This characterization of the competitive capitalist mode is common to both theories; so are the problems, namely, explaining competitive value and distribution. However, the *theory* determining prices, and consequently the role of prices, differ in the two theories. In the classical theory, given 'effectual demand' (or social outputs), given the methods of production (as observed and considered 'dominant') and given the wage (which is 'historically' determined), the 'natural prices' are defined as consistent 'exchange values' that render viable the circulation of commodities and the distribution of surplus in conformity with the rules of such circulation (a single price for a commodity) and distribution (uniform rate of profit and of wages). In such a theory, prices play the role of maintaining consistency of the conditions of reproduction of the production, exchange and distributive relations. The 'quantities' (social output, means of production, levels of utilization of labour, land and capital), as well as the wage, are determined separately from prices, in the sense that their explanation is not subsumed in the explanation of prices, and they are taken as the provisional data for deriving prices.

The perspective within which prices and quantities are analysed in the classical approach is one of circular reproduction of the system where commodities are produced by means of commodities, whether the economy itself is 'advancing', 'stationary', or 'retrograde'. The mutual interrelations between outputs, methods of production and wages are analysed in the context of surplus generation and accumulation. Thus, it is, that Adam Smith discussed the dynamic interaction between the division of labour and the extent of the market and considered the effects on wages of the growth of the economy. This view of the economic process is radically different from the 'one-way-avenue' of the DSE where the 'economic problem' is recognized, typically, as one of the optimum allocation of *given* resources.

The DSE theory visualizes the economy as an aggregate of atomistic individuals (producers and consumers) making their decisions autonomously, with no interference from the influence of 'externalities'. Relative prices and quantities are determined simultaneously in equilibrium as an outcome of the interplay of 'forces of demand and supply', generated by the optimizing behaviour of individuals subject to their resource constraints. A certain symmetry characterizes the behaviour of producers and consumers. Each producer, given the technological possibilities, chooses the profit-maximizing activities and outputs, at the going prices; each consumer, given his budget constraints and scales of preferences, maximizes satisfaction at the going prices. It is through the operation of the 'fundamental' and 'universal' principle of substitution that individuals adjust their chosen quantities in response to variations in the parametrically given prices. The relative prices formed on the market vary in response to excess demands or supplies in particular markets in such a way as to clear all markets in equilibrium. Thus the data for the theory of prices-and-quantity determination are the initial resource endowments and their distribution among individuals, the technological possibilities and the system of preferences.

Such a structure of explanation of relative prices and quantities has a number of analytical consequences. Stringent conditions need to be imposed on the feasible sets of choices in order to ensure that the price-quantity responses would be of appropriate magnitudes and directions so as to generate the 'well-behaved' demand-and-supply relations that make the existence of equilibrium possible. The progressive introduction of restrictive conditions and assumptions, such as the ruling out, a priori, of increasing returns or of externalities of all kinds, are discussed in 'Marshall on Pigou's *Wealth and Welfare*' (Chapter 7 below) and in 'Sraffa's Return to Classical Theory' (Chapter 10 below). Secondly, all prices including 'factor prices' and all quantities including factor-utilization are determined simultaneously in DSE. The first challenge came from Keynes when he questioned the presumed automatic tendency within the system to achieve full employment, with the rate of interest equilibrating savings and investment at full employment. The recent capital theory debate attacks the DSE's theory of profit directly. The assumption of given 'capital' (constituting heterogeneous produced means of production) militates against the fact that capital cannot be so measured independently of distribution, and if taken as a value-sum cannot necessarily yield the monotonic inverse relation between capital intensity and the rate of profit required in order to ensure a well-behaved demand function for capital. These are logical difficulties that violate the internal consistency of the theory.

Further, the notion of 'change' in the DSE theory gets restrictively predetermined by the theory in the following ways. First, all changes in quantities within the system are seen as the outcome of the ever-active principle of substitution. Thus the changes are primarily in relative quantities involving allocational variations. The role of prices as a scarce-resource allocator, given the resources, dominates the theory as contrasted with the resource-creational role of prices in classical theory (see Kaldor, 1972). Secondly, all changes are explained as induced by changes in relative prices and operate through the decisions of individuals who are only 'quantity-adjusters'; that is, all influences affecting quantities have to be necessarily mediated through relative prices or changes on the market and are outcomes of the atomistic responses of individuals. Thus relative prices acquire the all-powerful role of resource-allocation and the 'market' becomes the 'arena' of action.

4 The Significance of the Critique

The critique emphasizing the limitations of the theory flowing from its approach and logical structure lends accuracy and sharpness to the earlier critiques directed against the utilitarian or subjectivist basis of the DSE or against specific assumptions of the DSE, such as 'given preferences' or 'given distribution of resources'. These criticisms do contain more than a grain of truth. However, their thrust is not conclusively effective, and they need to be supplemented by a logical critique of the structure of the theory. For example, a philosophical viewpoint that an analyst holds may be defended as a matter of personal faith and belief. A criticism of particular assumptions may be countered by maintaining that all theorizing involves abstraction, which in turn involves seeking the aid of simplifying assumptions. A critique based on the methodological/philosophical position is strengthened when it can be shown that the position in question, as embodied in the approach and structure of the theory, restricts the capacity of that theory to handle certain significant questions or to interpret historical experience. Similarly, a critique of particular assumptions or postulates is rendered more effective if it is demonstrated that, within the theory, that assumption leads to internal inconsistency (such as, for example, the assumption of 'capital' as a 'given' resource independent of distribution), or that the theory based on a rather restrictive assumption cannot be consistently generalized through a process of 'successive approximation'. Such is the case of many DSE models where parables of one commodity-world, or a 'single-factor', or 'identical preferences' are constructed, presumably as a first step in analysis. (See, for example, Samuelson's [1962] attempt to construct a surrogate production function to validate the J. B. Clark parable and Garegnani's [1970] refutation of the attempt.) More often than not, these 'vehicles of thought', constructed for convenience, are too rickety to bear any forward movement. On such parables Joan Robinson (1977) remarks, 'A parable, in the normal sense, is a story drawn from everyday life intended to explain a mystery; in this case, it is the mystery which is expected to explain everyday life' (*Collected Economic Papers*, V, p. 63).

The early Marxist critiques of DSE were directed much more at the methodological and philosophical premises, or at the lack of realism of assumptions. Such criticisms, as noted above, would be more forceful if supplemented and extended by a structural critique. In 'Maurice Dobb's Critique of Theories of Value and Distribution' (see Chapter 8 below), we note a shift in his critique: in the earlier work Dobb regarded the classical theory and the DSE theories as being concerned with different *kinds* of problems. In his later work, particularly Dobb (1973), he emphasizes the different structures of theories of value and distribution and comes up with a clearer perception of the structure of classical theory. In the essay reviewing Ronald Meek's book [1977], 'On Certain Theoretical Issues in Classical Political Economy' (Chapter 9 below), we speak of the strength as well as some limitations of Meek's interpretations, particularly of Adam Smith.

5   Resurgence of the Classical Approach: Piero Sraffa's Contribution

The viewpoint emerging out of these essays has been greatly influenced by the work of Piero Sraffa. Sraffa's complete edition of Ricardo's *Works* (1951-5 and 1973) is a landmark in the interpretation of Ricardo and, through it, of the classical approach. The essay, 'Sraffa's Ricardo' (Chapter 5 below) evaluates the contribution that Sraffa makes to our understanding of Ricardo and in throwing new light on the classical approach. In 'Sraffa's Return to Classical Theory' (Chapter 10 below) are presented ideas on Sraffa's 'return' to the classical approach and an analysis of some aspects of the historical 'transition' to the alternative (DSE) theory – that is, the process by which radical departures constituting the subversion of classical theory occurred, though they were viewed as only modifications, extensions and generalizations by Marshall and others. The essay illustrates how similar notions and concepts, apparently shared by different theories, acquire different content and meaning in their particular context. The essay also points to certain misleading and erroneous interpretations of the classical theory arising from attempts at superimposing on it a DSE theory's viewpoint. This is illustrated with reference to certain misreadings of Sraffa's *Production of Commodities by Means of Commodities* (1960).

The essay 'On the Maximum Number of Switches between Two Production Systems' (Chapter 11 below), while focusing on a few technical points in the reswitching debate, brings out the significance of the basic/non-basic distinction between commodities, introduced by Sraffa – a distinction which has considerable significance within the classical approach. The essay on 'Piero Sraffa' (Chapter 13 below) is a tribute to the man and the scholar and gives a broad overview of his writings, along with some glimpses into his personality.

These essays are mostly concerned with the theme of value and distribution. However, as mentioned above, the critique of economic theory need not, and should not, be confined to these themes alone. As a matter of fact, the strength of the classical approach lies in its 'openness', that is, the possibility of allowing for a wide range of historical, socio-political factors to enter into the determination of 'quantities', that is, output, consumption, methods of production and wages (distribution). Also, various historico-specific patterns of interaction among these can also be envisaged, which indeed forms the crux of the theory of accumulation and analysis of 'historical change'. On the other hand, the simultaneous determination of quantities and prices *through the same mechanisms of supply and demand* in the DSE theories implies that a critique of their theory of value and distribution becomes simultaneously a critique of their theory of output and employment; the weaknesses of the structure of explanations of value and distribution, at the base, extend into the theories of output, employment and the dynamics of prices and quantities. The essay 'On Effective Demand: Certain Recent Critiques' (Chapter 12 below) attempts to provide a surplus-theoretic view on the post-Keynesian critiques of the theory of effective demand. It indicates the wider implications that the capital-theoretic debate has also for the theory of employment and output within the DSE theory, and discusses certain weaknesses of Keynes's critique of his predecessors, involving only a partial rejection of that theory.

These essays are more a record of an on-going exploration rather than reports of definitive results. They address different issues and have been written on different occasions. Inevitably, they reflect a process of understanding and, hopefully of learning. They share, however, a common endeavour: to clarify our understanding of economic theory and its formation, and to reappraise the classical approach in order to explore the possibilities of its providing a firmer foundation for economic theorizing. As in all analytical explorations, one cannot but feel humble when recognizing the difficulties of mapping a rugged and difficult terrain particularly with limited equipment and, then, to realize that 'a map is not a territory'.

Notes: Chapter 1

1. We do not enter into the neo-Marxian, neo-Walrasian or neo-Wicksellian formulations presently in vogue, because it would be possible to argue that, despite changes in methods and techniques, and shift of emphasis to short-period equilibria, intertemporal analysis, or non-competitive structures, the structure of the general theory of relative prices and distribution, as outlined in this section, remains fundamentally unaltered. (See 'Sraffa's Return to Classical Theory', Chapter 10 in the present volume.)
2. We hope to follow this set of essays with a sequel extending the critique to other domains of analysis.
3. A more comprehensive, although an early statement of the position, is contained in my *Classical Political Economy and the Rise to Dominance of Supply and Demand Theories* (R.C. Dutt Lectures, delivered in 1976; first edition, 1978, second edition, 1986. The 1978 edition is cited in the references throughout this volume). A shorter discussion is provided as a backdrop to the review of Dobb's position in 'Maurice Dobb's Critique of Theories of Value and Distribution' (Chapter 6 in the present volume). The distinction between the two approaches, on specific points, appears in the essay, 'Adam Smith's Political Economy' (first published as Chapter 2 in the present volume), and in 'Sraffa's Return to Classical Theory' (Chapter 10 in the present volume).

References: Chapter 1

Bharadwaj, K. (1978), *Classical Political Economy and the Rise to Dominance of Supply and Demand Theories* (Calcutta: Orient Longman); revised edition, 1986.
Dobb, M. H. (1973), *Theories of Value and Distribution Since Adam Smith: Ideology and Economic Theory* (Cambridge: Cambridge University Press)
Garegnani, P. (1970), 'Heterogeneous Capital, the Production Function and the Theory of Distribution', *Review of Economic Studies*, vol. 37, pp. 407–36.
Hollander, S. (1979), *The Economics of David Ricardo* (Toronto: Heinemann)
Kaldor, N. (1972), 'The Irrelevance of Equilibrium Economics', *Economic Journal*, December
Marshall, Alfred (1885) [1925, 1956] 'The Present Position of Economics', in A. C. Pigou (ed.) (1925) *Memorials of Alfred Marshall*, reprinted by Kelley & Miliman (1956) (New York)
Marshall, A. (1920) [1961] *Principles of Economics*, Ninth Variorum edition by C. W. Guillebaud (London: Macmillan)

Meek, R. L. (1977), *Smith, Marx and After* (London: Chapman and Hall).
Robinson, Joan (1977), 'The Meaning of Capital', *Collected Economic Papers*, V, pp. 59–70
Samuelson, P. A. (1959), 'A Modern Treatment of the Ricardian Economy', *The Quarterly Journal of Economics*, February and May
Samuelson, P. A. (1962), 'Parable and Realism in Capital Theory': The Surrogate Production Function', *Review of Economic Studies*, vol. 29, pp. 193–206.
Sraffa, P. (1950-55) (ed.) with the collaboration of M. H. Dobb: *The Works and Correspondence of David Ricardo*, 10 Vols (Cambridge University Press)
Sraffa, P. (1960), *Production of Commodities by Means of Commodities: Prelude to a Critique of Economic Theory* (Cambridge: Cambridge University Press)
Sraffa, P. (1973), *Works and Correspondence of David Ricardo: Index*, Vol. 11 (Cambridge: Cambridge University Press).

2
Adam Smith's Political Economy

Adam Smith's *An Inquiry into the Nature and Causes of the Wealth of Nations* (1776 [1937])[1], more than two centuries after its publication, continues to inspire controversial commentaries and interpretations. Smith's intellectual range and contribution was multifaceted. The recent collection of essays in critical assessments of Smith (Wood, 1984), spanning over a long period and running into four large volumes, indicates the breadth and depth of issues thrown up by Smith's work in philosophy, ethics, political economy, sociology and history. Our central concern in this essay is with Smith's contribution to political economy as a theoretical system and the diverse interpretations it has received from various scholars. It will be evident from our discussion below that Smith's theoretical system needs to be understood as being integrally embedded in a wider system of moral philosophy and a materialist notion of history to which he adhered. Smith can be placed indisputably among the pioneers of classical political economy, having first given a shape and direction to a number of questions that engaged the subsequent works in that tradition. He delineated concepts and categories within an analytical framework – which may broadly be termed the surplus approach – to analyse capitalist relations of production and accumulation. As Viner (1927 [1984]) puts it:

> There is much weight of authority and of evidence ... that Smith's major claim to originality, in English economic thought at least, was his detailed and elaborate application to the wilderness of economic phenomena of the unifying concept of a coordinated and mutually interdependent system of cause and effect relationships which philosophers and theologians had applied to the world in general.

Smith's doctrine that economic phenomena were manifestations of an underlying order in nature governed by natural forces gave to English economics, for the first time, a definite trend towards a logically consistent synthesis of economic relationships, towards 'system-building' (Wood, 1984, p. 143).

Interpretations of Smith's theoretical system have, however, widely differed: while Smith is counted among the founder-members of classical political economy, some proponents of the supply-and-demand-based equilibrium theories, that emerged in the last quarter of the nineteenth century (see Bharadwaj, 1978a) with altogether different analytical foundations, have equally claimed lineage from Smith.[2] The early commentators on Smith's *Wealth of Nations*, prominently David Ricardo and Karl Marx, both his admirers and successors in political economy, noted certain analytical inconsistencies and ambiguities. Later commentators (Dobb, 1973; Meek, 1977b, following Schumpeter, 1954) have seen the source of a dual development of theory in Smith. We shall attempt to examine the possible reasons for the apparently conflicting and divergent positions of Smith, viewed as providing links with diverse systems of economic theorizing. We maintain here that Smith's place as one of the originators and founder-scholars of the surplus-based theories is secure and that, despite common terminology and suggestive phrases carried over, the later demand-and-supply-based theories are founded on a distinctly different structure, not shared by Smith. Therefore, analogies drawn between certain parts of Smith's analysis and the later theories are misleading and inappropriate.

In order to appreciate the distinctiveness of Smith's theoretical system, we need to keep in mind his methodological stance and philosophical viewpoint. His analysis of society was inspired by a 'system of morality' – a theory maintaining that there exist propensities in human nature that incline and equip man for a social existence, or that man is endowed by the 'Author of Nature' with certain faculties and propensities which befit him to maintain viably his social state. This was combined with a historico-materialist view of the progress of society as a process through history – a process, embedded in nature and which has a discoverable pattern. The former view was developed in greater depth and consistency in the *Theory of Moral Sentiments* (1759 [1966]), while the latter was explored more intensively in the *Wealth of Nations*. It was within these twin perspectives that he sought to discuss the individual in society and to discover the *modus operandi* of a particular system, that is, to build an analytical engine to theorize about the 'commercial society'.[3]

The simultaneous reliance on both 'moral' and 'materialist' approaches is in no way a singular peculiarity of Smith. It was shared by a number of contemporary philosophers in Scotland and France, known for their 'materialist historical sociology'.[4] This concurrence in approach to social analysis appears not to be accidental, but reflects the fast-changing economic scene – a period of rapid transformation from feudalism and mercantalism to an incipient capitalism (to a 'commercial society', as Smith calls it). The period had seen an intellectual confrontation with the ecclesiastical authority: efforts were directed towards the construction of new philosophical systems appropriate for the emergence of the *free* individual, viewed as a moral being governed by a rational plan, inherent in 'nature'. It had also experienced simultaneously the accentuation of conflicts of interests, as well as a forward thrust of technological possibilities and achievements, so that the 'natural order' needed to be recognized and discovered out of an apparently chaotic, conflict-ridden reality.

In Section 1 below, we shall briefly sketch those ideas of Smith on philosophy and history that appeared to have spurred his conceptualization in political economy. In Section 2 we shall present briefly the analytical framework constructed by Smith to characterize the commercial society and analyse its *modus operandi* in the *Wealth of Nations*. While presenting Smith's ideas, we shall draw attention to the differences between his conceptualization and that of the later supply-and-demand-based equilibrium theories, and point to instances where similarities have been superimposed, suggesting therefrom false parallels. In Section 3 we shall examine the 'ambiguities' and 'inconsistencies' perceived by Smith's successors, in particular Ricardo and Marx, in order to suggest that these critiques do not reflect radical differences in terms of the fundamentals and of the basic structure of their theory, and that, despite their differences in problematics and on many particular propositions, they share, at their roots, a common basis and approach to political economy.

1   The Social Philosophical Perspective of Smith

The 'Natural Order' and the System of Morality
Smith was among those eighteenth-century philosophers who presented a stadial view of the development of society, occurring through successive stages, each characterized by a specific mode of subsistence.[5] Smith upheld the concept of an underlying order – a 'natural order' that manifests itself through the operation of material forces, as well as individual psychology. It was Smith's remarkable achievement that he attempted to apply the scientific method to the analysis of the economic process, with the purpose of discovering 'the nature of order which underlay the surface chaos'. Smith adopted a method – characterized as 'theoretical history' or 'conjectural history' by Dugald Stewart (1793 [1858]) or as 'philosophical history' by Skinner (1979, p. 68) – which, following a Newtonian viewpoint, attempted to account for observed phenomena in terms of 'a small number of basic principles and familiar ideas'. The method rested on the belief that there is a 'rational plan' or 'natural order' that binds phenomena in terms of interdependent cause/effect relations. The historical-analyst's task was to discover these regularities and cause/effect nexuses in the observed world. Each such social formation characterized by the mode of subsistence was associated with its own social, political, legal and moral structures which would give the mode a viable social existence. Thus, parallel to the material forces and their advances, there was also a system of morality: a parallel theory concerning the existence of certain propensities in human nature and their evolution that incline man to a *social* existence. It argues that at each stage of social existence, a corresponding moral system evolves which endows individuals with propensities and codes of conduct that

befit them to maintain the social state. Society as a collectivity can thus become viable through the progress of morality, and a harmonious 'natural order' can exist where the propensities of the individual befit the social processes. This rather idealized and optimistic, as well as universalist, vision of an evolution of harmonious order predominated in Smith's *Theory of Moral Sentiments*. Although it spoke of harmony, we note already in the conceptualization of the socio-historical evolution, the interaction between the individual's instinctive drives and passions, on the one hand, and the needed 'social morality', on the other. In the *Theory*, Smith appeared to be more sanguine regarding the eventual harmony and hence the progressive evolution of society.

'Theoretical History' of Smith

The basic propositions, held in common with the Scottish School of Theoretical History,[6] related much more to the material base and the institutional forms corresponding to the modes of subsistence and may be put as follows:

(a) The mode of subsistence that unites men into collective social existence determines the nature of the society with its particular structure of property, and correlated social 'orders' and 'classes'.
(b) There is a close relation between the type of property relations established and the juridical and political system that supports it.
(c) The society has continuously advanced through successive stages, the transition arising through changes in conditions of production and exchange.

These materialist principles were applied to the analysis of the progressive movement of the economy through four successive stages: in his *Lectures on Justice, Police, Revenue and Arms* (1762 [1896]), Smith identified these stages as hunting, pasturage, agriculture and commerce. Each stage is defined in terms of its mode of collective subsistence and the property relations, appropriate to it, are traced. In the first stage of hunting, there is a virtual absence of private property and hence of formal government. 'Till there be no property, there can be no government, the very end of which is to secure wealth and to defend the rich from the poor' (p. 15). In the second stage of pasturage, with private ownership of flocks and herds, the inequality of fortune arises and so does a system of power and subordination, necessitating a formal government. It is in the third stage of agriculture that the notion of property is fully extended and the system of government altered in form and scope. In the stage of commerce, there is progressive commercialization, production being increasingly geared to specialization and exchange. While commerce acts as a stimulant to production through making possible division of labour, the growing productive powers of labour through the division of labour in turn expand the arena of exchange.

To Smith, while the transition is gradual it is born out of the changing economic conditions themselves and is not due to 'accidental causes' and historical personages. For example, the change from agriculture to commerce is not only induced by expanding commodity production and markets, with the accompanying commercialization and extension of the cash nexus, but it is also due to the political instability, inherent in the encouragement given by the monarchy to the formation and development of towns as alternative centres of power to counter the feudal authority. That is, the conflict among different 'orders' of the society could be a potent cause for change.

Modes of Subsistence and Transitions
Thus Adam Smith attempts to correlate the mode of subsistence, the property relations, and the structure of institutions and of political authority.[7] In the *Wealth of Nations*, Smith focused particularly on the relations between the constituent 'orders' of a capitalist society and the constant interaction between their interests. Smith recognizes that the movement from one stage to another in social development is not caused by sheer accident, but the transition is 'natural'. For example, the passage from agriculture to commerce is partly described thus: 'As men could not confine themselves to one species of labour, they could naturally exchange the surplus of their own commodity for that of another of which they stood in need' (*Lectures*, 1762 [1896], p. 108). In the *Wealth of Nations*, Smith very often relates the conditions of labour, the mode of distribution of surplus among classes, and the ensuing conflicts of class interests to the state of the progress of society.[8] (See Section 2 below.)

The System of Natural Liberty:
Harmony and Conflicts in a Commercial Society
In the *Theory of Moral Sentiments*, as well as the *Wealth of Nations*, Smith's focus is on analysing the conditions of a 'commercial society' – his contemporary reality in England. However, in the *Theory* Smith spells out the system of morality compatible with a social existence of the individual in much more abstract and universal terms. He speaks of the innate propensity of human beings towards the pursuit of self-interest that is the propelling force in all social advances. Smith is abundantly aware that the reckless pursuit of self-regarding activities may produce undesirable effects on others. But, in the *Theory*, Smith evinces the Scottish optimistic theism in believing that the 'Author of Nature' had endowed other faculties and propensities that qualify the individual for social existence, such as his faculties of sympathy, of judging himself as much as others, based upon imagination and reflection. The spectator inside each individual helps the latter to place himself in the position of others and to extend sympathetic imagination and understanding. Further, there is the innate urge for social distinction and approbation. Thus, on the moral and ethical plane, there is the balancing of two sets of propensities, 'selfish' and 'social'. It is through the dictates of moral faculties that the 'natural principles' establish themselves in practice. It is due to their proven usefulness in a society that man is led, as if

by an invisible hand, to promote ends which may not be part of his original intentions. The *Theory* thus reflected Smith's optimistic faith in the possibility of the evolution of a harmonious natural order which would be independent of individual volitions,[9] an idealized outcome.

In the historical context of the commercial society, the pursuit of self-interest as the basic and dynamic faculty of the individual was to acquire the status of a moral principle providing the foundation of the system of natural liberty. The latter was deemed 'natural and obvious', as though managed by an invisible hand which renders individuals' actions, propelled by the pursuit of self-interest, conducive to collective welfare. This provided the philosophical basis for *laissez-faire* and the rationale for a virulent opposition to mercantilist and other interventionist policies that interfered with the individual's freedom. In the *Theory* the harmonious social (or collective) outcome of the individual's pursuit of self-interest, even while unintended by him, was presumed to be an *obiter dictum*. The countervailing interest, 'benevolence', acted as a modifier, taming the aggressive spirit of self-aggrandizement.

In the *Wealth of Nations*, where Smith turned to a more concrete description of 'the anatomy of civil society', he retained the importance of self-interest as an innate faculty of the individual reflected in 'a uniform, constant and uninterrupted effort to better his condition'. This - together with the other 'axioms' (a) that every individual in his own 'local situation' is a better judge of his economic interest than even a 'sagacious' statesman, and (b) that the income of the whole nation is the aggregate of incomes of individuals – suggested to some (see, e.g., Mitchell, 1967, pp. 51–5) that Smith arrived at his vociferous defence of the system of natural liberty (or, of *laissez-faire*) by arguing syllogistically. However, while Smith's attack on the mercantilist and state interventionist policies was acute and vigorous (wherein he emphasized not only the compatibility of the pursuit of self-interest with social well-being, but even its essentiality for opulence), he enlisted an equal number or more of cases when the pursuit of self-interest would not necessarily ensure natural harmony. Viner (1927) observes:

> In the *Theory of Moral Sentiments*, this harmony ... is represented as universal and perfect. In the *Wealth of Nations* the harmony is represented as not extending to all elements of the economic order, and often as partial and imperfect when it does extend. Where harmony does prevail, it is as a rule as a sort of average or statistical harmony, revealing itself only in the general mass of phenomena and leaving scope for the possibility that natural processes whose general effect is beneficial may work disadvantageously in individual cases or at particular moments of time. (pp. 149–50)

Further, Viner makes the significant observation that

> though Smith in the *Wealth of Nations* frequently makes general statements intended apparently to apply to the entire universe, he has

always before him for consideration some concrete problem, or some finite section of the universe. In no instance does Smith rely heavily upon his assertions as to the existence of harmony in the natural order at large to establish his immediate point that such harmony exists within the specific range of economic phenomena which he is at the moment examining. p. 151)

In the *Theory* the argument was based on philosophical speculation where the premises 'were all drawn from a peculiar class of axioms which urgently require, but are incapable of proof'. In the *Wealth of Nations* on the other hand, Smith attempted to build up his argument that the system of natural liberty led to natural harmony in the economic order, with reference to specific problems. In particular, he attempted to propose an extensive programme for the extension of natural liberty through the eradication of existing mercantilist and state regulations. While advocating some central programmes of policy action for such an extension, he was not shy to acknowledge exceptions to the doctrine of 'natural harmony' which persisted even without interventions of the kind distorting the natural course of the economy. Adam Smith would have, in fact, considered necessary a large number of functions for the government, apart from the well-known list of 'appropriate' minimal ones, the list depending upon the particular institutional environment of the economy and polity. (see Rosenberg, 1960; Viner, 1927).

Smith's 'Individual in the Society' and the Doctrine of laissez faire
It appears that Smith's advocacy of *laissez faire*, as well as the prescription of 'natural liberty', as conducive to social well-being, needs to be understood within a more complex formulation of the individual in society. The system of natural liberty advocated freedom of the individual and the directive principle of leaving the system alone to take its natural course through actively opposing the prevalent system of interventions and restrictions imposed by the operation of monopoly privileges and government policy. In particular, restraints on the movement of commodities (through trade), of labour (the guild system and administrative restrictions) and of capital were opposed, so that the conception of 'free competition' in the market was associated with free mobility of commodities, labour and capital. Smith advocated that the initiative to make decisions should be left to the individual. However, it would be too simplistic to presume that Smith arrived at his conclusions by mere syllogism, that atomistic competition and the mobility of resources were sufficient to guarantee a harmony between social well-being and the unhampered pursuit of self-interest. As Rosenberg (1960) rightly points out, such an interpretation of Smith's position ignores the fact that Smith presented a much more complex conception of the motivation of individuals who were propelled by conflicting and countervailing interests and passions (see also Hirschman, 1977). Further, Smith was fully aware that the individuals' actions, as well as their welfare consequences, were shaped and mediated through 'institutional arrangements' – or,

if we may use a Marxian phrase, through 'production and exchange relations'. In the *Wealth of Nations*, Smith specifically attempted to discuss institutions which harmonize or hinder the pursuit of self-interest leading to collective well-being. He critically attacked institutions and policies such as monopoly cliques, landlordism, laws of primogeniture, mercantilist restrictions on trade and investment, and viewed the actions of individuals in the context of specific institutions and contexts within which they functioned.

The Invisible Hand and the Walrasian Auctioneer
The modern argument that under atomistic competition, competitive markets achieve resource-allocational efficiency conducive to maximum welfare – an argument used in defence of *laissez-faire* – rests on a different conception of the individual agent (a producer or a consumer) as a decision-maker. Competition in this later (neoclassical) theory is identified not only with the unrestrained mobility of commodities, capital and labour, but also includes conditions regarding uniform and equal access to markets, equal information and independence from 'externalities'. Each agent, it is presumed, makes quantity-adjustments in response to changes in relative prices, given to him parametrically, without the direct influence or intervention of others or others' decisions. What is remarkable about Smith's producers or consumers is that their behaviour and decisions are hardly discussed in the *Wealth of Nations* as atomistic actions. It is more importantly, as members belonging to 'classes' or 'ranks' or 'groups' that their activities are analysed. The constraints that operated on the individual decision-maker were, no doubt, the physical and material resources at his command, but the feasibility and the efficacy of the decisions also depended on the institutional environment in which the individual is situated. Thus there were constraints which emanated from the macro-system. Its rate and pattern of progress influenced the environment, as well as the objective conditions in which individual decision-makers operated. Moreover, the process of accumulation and growth had differential consequences on the various orders and classes who were certainly not equally or symmetrically placed in terms of the power to take decisions or the feasible options accessible to them individually. Not only this, but the objectives pursued by the different decision-makers belonging to their respective 'class' or 'order' differed. Smith, in the *Wealth of Nations*, pointed attention to the role that various classes played, and explicitly recognized the asymmetries of relations between manufacturers and labourers, tenants and landlords, manufacturers and merchants and customers, etc. Thus Smith's individual is neither 'atomistic', nor is the domain and arena of his actions circumscribed and isolated, as is presumed in the later equilibrium theories through *ex hypothesi* negation of 'externalities'. These actions are determined by, are located in and play themselves out in the specific institutional environment, and the individual acts as one situated in the particular class of decision-makers, within that 'environment'.

Further, as we shall see in Section 3, the modern argument concerning the efficiency of the market, achieved by the 'Invisible Hand', rests on a theory of price formation and quantity-determination which is radically different from that of Smith, giving to the problematic of 'resource-allocation', and the consequent argument regarding 'efficiency' a different context and content. Smith's conceptualization of political economy, as we shall see in the next section, was developed explicitly in the context of growth and accumulation – with problems relating to the creation and mobilization of resources rather than resource-allocation of the extant resources. His analysis of the individual's decisions regarding resource-use and allocation was conducted in this context of specific historical situations and environments, and the ongoing economic processes he observed in the economy of his times. Thus, while Smith believed and advocated that the self-interest of individuals could, in a system of natural liberty, lead to greater wealth and prosperity as against the then-existing system of restrictions and unfreedom, he was equally aware of, and analysed, concrete situations wherein an unrestrained pursuit of self-interest may lead to inequities and have deleterious consequences on the growth of the economy. He was interested in analysing 'the anatomy of civil society', so the constraints on the individual emanating from the developments in the macro-system, as well as the effects of the individual's decisions on the 'natural' course of the economy, were studied by him with reference to concrete historical observations. Just as the pace and nature of progress affects the different 'orders' of the society and their 'decision-making' capacities as well as decisions, Smith fully recognized that the influence which individual decisions have on the path and pace of accumulation are not uniform or equal. He was much concerned with identifying the influential investors, and took specific note of the class of merchants, manufacturers, landlords, tenants and their specific economic decisions and actions. It was thus that the dynamics of 'commercial economy' were analysed. The growth process widened the feasible sets of options for individuals along with extending their access/command over resources. However, these effects of the growth process, as well as the influence that different decision-makers can exercise on this process, are not uniform between individuals and hence there are conflicts of interests and contradictions. However, Smith appears to have had sufficient optimism to believe that, given the conducive environment of the system of natural liberty, the dynamic pace of accumulation, working through the powerful mutuality of interaction between the 'division of labour' and the 'extension of market', would lead to a situation of general progress and well-being. This was particularly true of the working classes who would stand to gain from the dynamics of accumulation. Smith was, however, aware that the course of accumulation would have to be guided by an evolution of a consistent morality and the creation of supporting institutions. While noticing conflicts of interests and contradictions in the system, he appears to have treated them more as aberrations, rectifiable through judicious policies.[10]

2 Political Economy of Smith

Surplus, Basis of Analysis

To Smith the question that was of primary importance was: wherein does the wealth of a nation lie and what determines its extent and growth? As the very opening paragraph of the *Wealth of Nations* states, it was in production – in the allocation of labour to productive uses and the development of the productive powers of labour – that Smith saw the sources of real opulence, thus shifting the focus away from exchange relations that had been at the centre of mercantilist doctrines and policy. Commerce and 'profit upon alienation' (as Steuart, 1767 [1966] called profits generated through trade – i.e., 'selling dear and buying cheap') had been looked upon then as the most potent source of enrichment for a nation and, so long as attention was fixed upon exchange and on wealth in the form of the accumulation of specie, what went on within the real sphere of production seemed of secondary importance. However, with master-craftsmen gaining ground over merchants and the industrial capital asserting itself over merchant capital, with rapid improvements in techniques, the expansion of markets (and the opening of new ones) and, most importantly, the emergence of 'free labour' as the foundation for expanding production, the real conditions of production as the basis of surplus generation acquired prominence. Smith was to open his *magnum opus* with a discussion of the dynamic interaction between the division of labour and the extent of the market.

Impelled by the inquiry as to what determines opulence, Smith identified it with the 'annual' produce of a nation, 'or what is purchased with it' and, further, maintained: 'According therefore, as this produce ... bears a greater or smaller proportion to the number of those who are to consume it, the nation will be better or worse supplied with all the necessaries and conveniencies for which it has occasion' (*Wealth of Nations*, 1776, p. lvii).[11] The per capita annual produce is, in turn, seen as being regulated by two factors: (a) the productivity of labour, or, 'the skill, dexterity and judgement with which labour is applied', and (b) the proportion of those who are employed in 'useful labour'. It is the dynamic movement of these two factors that leads to a growth of the produce. Smith's focus was on the accumulation process in a commercial economy, and he devised categories of analysis and framed the questions for inquiry in the context of this accumulation process as it would take place in 'a system of natural liberty', that is, in the setting of a competitive capitalist economy.

Smith advanced the central concept of surplus much beyond the Physiocrats, in the context of a commercial society where production for exchange and exchange of commodities was much advanced. Smith acknowledged that surplus arose not only in agriculture (as was the view of the Physiocrats in France), but also in manufactures. Smith gave the first conceptual form to a competitive capitalist system, by recognizing the emergence of 'abstract labour' as a source of wealth and by identifying the tripartite division of revenue-sharers (capitalists, wage-earners and rentiers) with their respective returns, each determined along different principles.[12] He characterized the competitive system – a 'system of natural liberty' – as one of free mobility of capital and giving rise to a tendency towards the equalization of rates of profits and wages.

The 'Natural State' of the Economy
Central to the analysis of the generation and accumulation of surplus was the conception of an economy in its 'natural state'; the belief being that every economy as a social formation is governed by certain regularities, and these could be discovered and conceptualized in the form of certain stable tendencies and mechanisms at work in the process of surplus generation (and its accumulation), its appropriation as well as its distribution. Each social formation can thus be studied as a concatenation of cause/effect relationships that prevail in the 'natural state'. The real history was one of a complex web and flux of events, but the analyst could use his analytical intuition and discrimination to separate out permanent causes and effects from those that are transitory and accidental.[13] Thus the 'natural state' of the economy is analytically constructed on the basis of historical observation. Smith characterized the 'commercial economy' (i.e., the capitalist economy), with competition or the natural system of liberty at work, using the following as data: the state of 'effectual demand' (i.e., the average state of social demand), the methods of production that stipulate how material means of production are combined with labour to produce outputs, and the rules for distributing this net produce among the revenue-sharers (as wages, profits and rents). The 'commercial economy' is based on the exchange of commodities produced by means of other commodities, and the rules of exchange need to be such as to allow the economy to be reproduced in its productive and distributive relations. It was the behaviour of such an economy in its generation, distribution and accumulation of surplus that Smith seeks to discover and analyse – to discover the 'natural order' in the apparent complexity and chaos of reality.

The Measure of Surplus and Explanation of Value
As we saw above, Smith's concern was to explain how surplus originates and is accumulated in the 'commercial economy'. Once he rejected both the mercantilist conception of surplus as an accumulation of monetary specie and the drastic simplification of the Physiocrats that the net produce consists of agricultural produce alone, Smith needed to develop an analytically satisfactory measure of surplus which constituted heterogeneous commodities. This brings Smith to the question of the determination of the exchange value of commodities, primarily as an upshot of the complex problem of measuring the real produce. What is the 'real money' in terms of which the 'surplus' of a nation, with varying composition, can be compared over different periods? Or, how can the surpluses of two countries be compared? Thus he inquires into the 'real basis' of value and proceeds to search for a stable 'invariant' standard.

In proposing labour as 'real money', Smith appears to acknowledge the importance of labour both in the explanation of exchange value and as a means of measuring the productive potential of surplus (see below). As is well known, he suggests a 'labour-embodied explanation' of exchange value (i.e., commodities exchange in proportion to the labour embodied in their production) only to confine it to the 'early and rude state of society which precedes both the accumulation of stock and the appropriation of land'.[14] Instead he proposes the 'labour-commanded measure', that is, he suggests that the value of a commodity be measured in terms of labour that it can purchase. Analytically the shift to the 'labour-commanded' in the context of the *explanation* of value had deficiencies which Ricardo was to criticize (see below). Smith, in discarding the 'labour-embodied explanation' in the event of the 'appropriation of land and accumulation of capital', did indeed point to a problem arising from a historical transition in the relations of production from pre-capitalist to capitalist ones. With capitalist production, the produce of labour belongs to the capitalist and, as Smith saw it, 'the value which the workmen add to the materials, therefore, resolves itself in this case into two parts, of which the one pays their wages, the other the profits of their employer upon the whole stock of materials and wages which he advanced' (*Wealth of Nations*, p. 54). The 'labour-commanded measure' was no explanation of value and, as a measure, was no more 'invariant' than were 'corn' or 'gold' which Smith himself had opposed. The notion of 'labour-commanded' bore, however, a significance with regard to the process of accumulation. Smith perceived the growth process in terms of the rising numbers of 'productive labour' employed through the redeployment of 'surplus' and its rising productivity through the expanding 'division of labour'. Indeed, Smith distinguished the 'productivity' of different sectors in terms of their potential to generate productive employment or to command labour (see pages 27–9 below on the resource-allocational analysis of Smith).

'Natural' and 'Market' Price
Smith's contribution to the problem of value was his clear formulation of the 'natural price' and the distinction he maintained between 'natural' and 'market' price.[15] The 'natural price' is one that 'is sufficient to pay the rent of the land, the wages of the labour, and the profits of the stock employed in raising, preparing and bringing it to market, according to their natural rates' (*Wealth of Nations*, p. 55). While the actual or 'market prices' could be 'below' or 'above' the 'natural prices', the latter is 'as it were, the central price, to which the prices of all commodities are continually gravitating', and 'whatever may be the obstacles which hinder them from settling in this center of repose and continuance' – so that the 'natural price' may never be actually observed – 'they are constantly tending towards it' (*Wealth of Nations*, p. 58).

The 'natural price', however, is not an empirical or purely statistical average; it is a 'theoretical price' to the extent that it requires a natural position (the long-run position) of the economy to be postulated so that the 'natural prices' are the set of exchange values that render viable reproduction of the 'natural state'. The basic elements defining the 'natural state' and hence the 'natural prices' compatible with its reproduction are: (a) the 'effectual demand', or the level and composition of social output, (b) the methods of production, and (c) the wages.[16] Given these 'quantities', the 'natural prices' are calculated so as to make reproduction of the outputs and the distribution of surplus compatible with the competitive norms of the uniformity of the rates of wages and profits. Since the 'quantities' – 'effectual demand', methods of production and wages – were derived as 'average characteristics' of the economy, on the basis of observations, the 'natural prices' are rooted in historical experience and are not entirely 'abstract'.

Smith's Theory of Value-determination: Some Distinctive Features
Some of the peculiarities of the structure of Smith's theory of value determination which continue to feature in the classical theory after Smith and distinguish it from the later supply-and-demand equilibrium theories may be noted here. The 'given quantities' in the classical structure were derived from observations pertaining to the economic system. 'Effectual demand' was a position, a vector of social outputs that would be demanded by those 'who are willing to pay the natural price of the commodity'. This was thus the 'average' or 'central' position of demands which, in turn, were explained by a whole set of social and economic factors, such as distribution of incomes, habits, social conventions, class-based influences on consumption, availability of commodities, demonstration effects, etc. Smith, in common with the Physiocrats, proposed the notion of 'average wage' or the 'natural price of labour'[17] – a 'pricce' which is historically determined. He observed forthrightly that the level of the wages may be determined by the bargaining between the workers and the employers, and that the latter are in an advantageous position to force the workers into compliance – a position strengthened further by their 'tacit but constant and uniform combinations'.[18] The pace of accumulation also affects the wages positively (see below).

In Smith and the classical theories – unlike in the equilibrium theories wherein the prices of commodities and factors, as well as all the quantity (commodity output and factor-utilization) levels, are determined simultaneously within the same scheme of determination – the dynamics of quantities are analysed separately, not coterminus with the analysis of prices. Significantly, Smith began his analysis with the interaction between the division of labour (or 'methods of production') and the expansion of markets (or of 'effectual demand'). He saw the close connection between the pace of accumulation and wages:

> There is in every society or neighbourhood an ordinary or average rate both of wages and profit in every different employment of labour and stock. This rate is naturally regulated ... partly by the general circumstances of the society, their riches or poverty, their advancing,

stationary or declining condition; and partly by the particular nature of each employment. (Wealth of Nations, p. 55)

Moreover, an important distinctive feature of the theory is the determination of wages outside the scheme of price determination. In the equilibrium theories, factor prices are determined along with the commodity prices by the same mechanism of equilibrium between demand and supply.

Quantity Dynamics and the Role of Relative Prices
The quantity variations in the equilibrium theories are also explained in a specific model of change and choice, whereby the relative prices and changes therein become all-determining and the role of relative prices as the resource-allocating device is all-powerful. The role of relative prices, the problematic of 'resource-allocation', and the mediation of the 'Invisible Hand' of the market in achieving maximum welfare, acquire a very different content and meaning in the neoclassical (equilibrium) theory.[19] The equilibrium theories take as their data: (a) the primary factor endowments and their distribution among individual agents, (b) the technological possibilities depicting feasible activities for each agent, and (c) the preferences of the agents. Under competitive conditions, with free and equal access to and unfettered mobility across markets for all transactors, each agent (as a producer or consumer) maximizes his return (profits or satisfaction), applying his given scarce resources to alternative uses by choosing such options as would yield the optimum return. The agents are thus 'quantity-adjusters' while, at the collective market, where all the individual quantity signals are aggregated, relative price movements follow excess supplies or demands so that, in equilibrium, all markets are cleared.

Certain peculiarities of such a theory of quantity variations need to be remarked upon: the changes are in *relative quantities*, brought about through the universal application of 'the substitution principle' *in response to changes in relative prices*. The relative prices, in turn, respond to these quantity variations. The price-quantity responses therefore need to be not only sufficiently flexible but, in order that equilibrium be attained, the substitution effects also need to act appropriately so as to bring about quantity variations in the right direction. Only then are the supply-and-demand relations 'well behaved'. The model of 'choice' for the individual is also specifically constrained. The individual acts atomistically, in the sense that all 'externalities' are assumed away. In other words, no 'external' influences act on his quantity-determining decisions except those which are mediated through the market in the form of the price signals. As to the price adjustments, the equilibrium theorists themselves have raised the question as to who is the Walras 'auctioneer' who initiates these (see Arrow and Hahn, 1971.)

Thus, in the equilibrium theory, where the economic process is a one-way avenue, from *given* endowments to final consumption, the relative prices perform the role of allocating the given scarce resources to alternative ends and thus determine the relative and absolute levels of quantities. The role of prices is different in the classical theory, which perceives the economy as a circular process and where the problem is not only one of the allocation of *given* resources, but of generating, mobilizing and creating resources through *'production of commodities by means of commodities'*. The *role* that prices play is one of establishing conditions of exchange that make the circular movement of commodities in production and distribution viable. The dynamics of quantities, of social consumption, of technology, of distribution (or wages) and their interaction is analysed in a separate domain than that for price determination.

This is not to say that there are no influences that flow from prices to quantities. However, these are analysed in specific cases and no universal patterns on price-quantity responses are imposed (such as the slope and curvature conditions) as in the case of the well-behaved demand-and-supply relations in the equilibrium theories.

Whereas the 'natural prices' were so determined as 'central prices', Smith did consider the 'market or actual price', falling either *below* or *above* the 'natural price', as a more likely event, and these he explained in terms of the actual supply falling either above or below the 'effectual demand', or the actual demand itself falling short of, or exceeding, 'effectual demand'. While the *level* of the 'natural price' was thus determined by the methods of production and wage, the deviations were seen as arising from the demand or supply divergencies. Therefore, it has been usual in the literature to deduce from Smith's propositions on the 'market prices' that he propounded a theory of the supply-and-demand-determined equilibrium price. Attempts are also made to analyse the 'gravitation' around 'natural prices' in terms of the supply-and-demand mechanisms on the analogy of similar mechanisms conceived in equilibrium theories. While the exact manner in which the 'centrality' of the 'natural price' and the 'oscillations around it' may be rigorously interpreted in the Smithian analysis needs yet to be explored, the difference between the Smithian approach and the supply-and-demand mechanism in the equilibrium theory needs to be noticed. First, Smith considers 'effectual demand' as a position and not as a 'demand schedule' of the equilibrium theory. The deviations of supply from 'effectual demand' (the excesses or shortfalls) are discussed in terms of each individual sector or commodity and the 'market price' of every particular commodity is regulated by 'the proportion between the quantity which is actually brought to market, and the demand of those who are willing to pay the natural price of the commodity (*Wealth of Nations*, p. 56). Secondly, there is very little *general* discussion or a universal theory about the operation of the substitution principle, whereby relative commodity proportions vary in response to changes in relative prices.

The Notion of Effectual Demand and Resource Allocation in Smith
On the basis of a misleading comparison, Smith is often charged with neglecting 'demand' in explaining 'natural price'. It is the absence

of the 'demand schedule' in Smith which is the source of this criticism because, in delineating the accumulation process, Smith indeed placed considerable importance on demand forces as explanatory variables. Rosenberg argues quite convincingly that 'Smith has a fairly well integrated view of the nature and formation of human tastes and the manner and direction in which human wants develop over time. This view is an essential part of his conception of economic growth' (1968, pp. 222–33). Smith discusses historically the evolution of needs and the factors that influence preferences, such as 'rank and order', desire for distinction, the introduction of new commodities and of the division of labour and trade. The division of labour and the extension of the market constantly interact throwing up new commodities and new possibilities of consumption. Smith discusses the natural progress of society, from agriculture into manufacture and commerce, in terms of this evolution of the commodity world (see Rosenberg, 1968). The 'effectual demand' notion needs, therefore, to be clearly distinguished from the 'demand schedule' in equilibrium theories.

The role which relative prices play in allocating the given scarce resources and the resource-allocational efficiency attributed to the 'market' forces in the equilibrium theory is contingent upon the particular modelling of the choice and change in that theory. We have, in the previous section, noted the difference in conceptualization of the decision-makers in Adam Smith ('individual in the society') and the atomistic transactor of the equilibrium theories. It is also clear that the equilibrium theories determine variations in quantities in response to variation in relative prices, and it is through the specific theory in which the price-quantity responses are conceived of that the 'market' is shown to establish the optimum position.

Smith's theory of output is developed in the context of accumulation wherein forces of technology (division of labour) and of trade ('extent of the market') interact in a perpetual movement (see Adolph Lowe, 1954 and 1975; Thweatt, 1958; Eltis, 1975). An analysis of 'resource-allocation' (i.e., of the different 'employment of capitals' and their consequences on growth) occurs in Smith, which leads him to note the different progress of opulence in different nations (*Wealth of Nations*, pp. 341-55) and to suggest 'the natural course of things' as being 'first agriculture, then manufactures and finally, foreign commerce' (ibid., p. 360). Smith writes:

> Though all capitals are destined for the maintenance of productive labour only, yet the quantity of that labour, which equal capitals are capable of putting into motion, varies extremely according to the diversity of employment; as does likewise the value which the employment adds to the annual produce of the land and labour of the country. (*Wealth of Nations*, p. 347)

Thus, in comparing alternative activities, Smith considered the differing capacity of an investment to generate productive employment and to add to annual produce. He discusses four different ways of employing capital:

> first, in procuring the rude produce annually required for the use and consumption of the society; or, secondly, in manufacturing and preparing that rude produce for immediate use and consumption; or, thirdly, in transporting either the rude or manufactured produce from the places where they abound to those where they are wanted; or, lastly, in dividing particular portions of either into such small parcels as suit the occasional demands of those who want them [i.e., in short, agriculture, manufactures, wholesale trade and retail trade]. (*Wealth of Nations*, p. 341)

He observes further:

> Equal capitals, however, employed in each of these different ways, will immediately, put into motion very different quantities of productive labour, and augment too in very different proportions the value of the annual produce of the land and labour of the society to which they belong. (ibid., p. 343)

On this criterion, Smith regarded agriculture as of primary importance since 'no equal capital puts into motion a greater quantity of productive labour', and 'they regularly occasion the reproduction of the rent of the landlord' (ibid., p. 344).[20] Smith was to view the progress in the sequence, agriculture to manufacture to trade to commerce, as the 'natural course of things'. We shall not stop here to inquire into the historical or analytical validity of Smith's position on the 'natural course' of the sequential growth of the economy. We only note that this problematic of resource-allocation is different in method, context and approach from that of the equilibrium theories. In Smith the context is of surplus accumulation, while in the latter theories it is allocation of given scarce resources by individuals to maximize their returns.

3 Critical Advances in Surplus-based Theory

Ricardo's Critique of Smith

Even while building upon the foundations that Smith provided, Ricardo began his *Principles of Political Economy* as a critique of Smith's position, particularly on the determination of profit. Although Ricardo picked upon certain inconsistencies in Smith, he shared with Smith the basic framework and approach to theory. In the *Theories of Surplus Value*, Marx, too, speaks of 'the vulgar elements' in Smith's theory (1862–3 [1963–8], II, p. 89), his 'dual views' of the relationship between value and revenue (ibid., I, p. 95), 'contradictions' and 'inconsistencies' (ibid., I, p. 97), but he also gives him fulsome praise for his successful attainment of the task of founding a theoretical system which his successors could build upon (ibid., II, p. 165).

Primarily, it was Smith's proposition that the rate of profit is determined by 'competition of capitals' that Ricardo began to question in the course of his generalization of the theory of profit from the *Essay on the Influence of a Low Price of Corn on the Profits of Stock* (1815 [1951, IV]) to the *Principles of Political Economy* (1817 [1951, I]). Smith's view that 'as soon as stock has accumulated in the hands of particular persons' and 'as soon as the land of any country has all become private property', the price of commodities is arrived at by a process of *adding up* the wages, profits and rents, induced him to seek *independent* explanation of the rates of wages, rents and profits. Ricardo looked upon this as 'the original error' of Smith which inclined Smith to argue as if the movements of the rate of profit could be independent of those in wages, while Ricardo himself argued that 'profits depend upon wages'.

As Sraffa (1951, I, p. xxxiii) remarks, Ricardo had initially subscribed to the Smithian view, which was also the one generally accepted, that a rise in corn prices, through its effect on wages, would be followed by a rise in all other prices. 'He had not regarded this view as inconsistent with his theory of profits so long as the latter had been expressed in its primitive "agricultural form"', although in the *Essay*, Ricardo repudiated this view in a footnote. A systematic theory of value – the labour theory of value – was presented by Ricardo in the *Principles*, where he contested Smith's view that after stock was accumulated and land appropriated, with the consequent division of produce into wages and profits, the values of commodities were no longer regulated by the quantity of labour necessary to their production. Ricardo explained to Mill his difference with Smith (letter dated 28 December 1818, *Works*, VII, p. 377):

> In opposition to him [Smith], I maintain that it is not because of this division into profits and wages – it is not because capital accumulates, that exchangeable value varies, but it is in all stages of society, owing only to two causes: one, the more or less quantity of labour required, the other, the greater or less durability of capital – that the former is never superseded by the latter.

It is not our purpose here to pursue Ricardo's trail; we note that Ricardo's difference with Smith was on the evaluation of the labour theory of value as a general theory. Ricardo was to criticize Smith for considering the 'labour-commanded measure' as 'invariant', arguing that it was variable, as was 'corn' or 'gold' which Smith himself had disfavoured on the ground of their variability.

Smith's theory of distribution remained a weaker part of his analysis and Ricardo was to focus on these themes. While Smith clearly recognized the 'components' of price and the tripartite division of revenues, as well as their different origins, the adding-up view inclined him to explain the factors determining these revenues separately and independently for each category. The 'inner connection' between wages and profits was thereby lost. While Smith's analysis of distribution abounds in extremely interesting and rich insights, his diverse views were not always mutually consistent. For example, Smith viewed rent both as a monopoly price, landed property being concentrated in the hands of a few landlords, and also as arising in the form of 'differential rents'; and he maintained, at times, without sufficient distinction of the two rents, that rent does not enter price while, at the same time, he defined natural price by including in it the rent at the natural rate. Ricardo inferred logically from the theory of differential rents that rent does not enter price – an argument that he forcefully used to discuss the effects which taxation and restrictions on corn imports had on rents and other incomes.

Marx's Critique of Smith

Marx was to see 'dual aspects' of Smith's analysis leading to apparent inconsistencies and contradictions at times. He notes:

> Smith himself moves with great naïveté in a perpetual contradiction. On the one hand he traces the intrinsic connection existing between economic categories or the obscure structure of the bourgeois economic system. On the other, he simultaneously sets forth the connection as it appears in the phenomena of competition and thus as it presents itself to the unscientific observer just as to him who is actually involved and interested in the process of bourgeois production. One of these conceptions fathoms the inner connection, the physiology, so to speak, of the bourgeois system, whereas the other takes the external phenomena of life, as they seem and appear and merely describes, catalogues, recounts and arranges them under formal definitions. (*Theories of Surplus Value*, II, p. 165)

It would seem, therefore, that when Smith analysed the material processes of production, accumulation and distribution, he described, as it were, the 'inner physiology' of the system, the 'objective' mechanisms and forces at work. Whereas, alongside, Smith also recognized and identified and 'gave a nomenclature' in terms of concepts and categories to the subjective perceptions of the actors in the bourgeois system. Marx justifies this dual approach, although he notes that the two methods (namely, 'esoteric' that deals with the 'inner connections' and 'essence', and the 'exoteric' that deals with 'appearances') were so intermingled in Smith as to create inconsistencies and contradictions.

For example, while Smith defined, as we have seen, the concept of 'natural price' as price consistent with reproducibility of the natural state (i.e., the 'costs' needed to be paid out by the producer), he interpreted its components, wages, profits and rents, not only as sources of revenue but also as independent sources of value.[21] Having faced a problem with the labour-embodied theory of value, he set out to discuss these three components of price. First, he assumes erroneously that 'the whole price of any commodity must still finally resolve itself into some one or the other, or all of the three parts' (*Wealth of Nations*, 1776 [1961], p. 52), and, likewise, the whole annual produce of the labour of the economy resolved into wages, profits and rents. Second, Smith rightly identifies the original revenue-recipient classes and their revenues, but as Marx points out: 'They are sources of revenue for their owners in so far as they are titles to a certain quantity of surplus-labour which the labourer must perform over and above the labour-time required to replace his wage.' (*Theories of Surplus Value*, I, p. 93). However, if profits and rents are taken as 'deductions' from produce, as Smith did, at places in *Wealth of Nations*, they cannot all be regarded simultaneously as original *sources* of value.[22]

It was this 'analysis of components of value' presenting value as a sum of wages, profits and rents paid at their 'natural' rates that provided later economists with the basis to argue that Smith treated the trinity – land, labour and capital – as 'factors of production' on symmetrical terms. Further, having presented price in this additive fashion with the 'natural' rates of wages, profits and rents variously and inadequately explained, Adam Smith could not analyse in a logical and coherent fashion the crucial question regarding the relation among different distributive shares – a question that was left to Ricardo. Smith did, however, broadly comment on the varying effects on the fortunes of these classes as accumulation proceeds. For example, he argued, on the one hand, that a rise in wages will be passed on to consumers in terms of rising prices (this was in keeping with his 'adding-up' view), while, on the other, he also suggested that a rise in wages causes a decline in the rate of profit. Similarly, generalizing from the case of an individual commodity, he maintained that the falling rate of profit was to be ascribed to the competition of capitals, while attributing it, at times, to a rise in wages.

Similarly, Smith, on the one hand, looked upon wages as the material requirements of sustaining labour (i.e., as a 'productive consumption') – a material necessity of production; while, on the other, he also reckoned them to be the compensation for the 'toil and trouble'. This slender piece of evidence was to provide Marshall with the basis for the development of his 'real-cost analysis' – an analysis based on 'measurable motives' which treated wages as an outcome of balancing the utility of income against disutility of effort.[23]

Again, while Smith unambiguously talked of rents and profits as 'deductions' from the produce of labour, he also said that the capitalist 'could have no interest to employ them [the workers], unless he expected from the sale of their work something more than what was sufficient to replace his stock to him' (*Wealth of Nations*, p. 54). Now, as Marx points out, this is quite correct when seen from the viewpoint of the capitalist. It is true that the capitalist is not interested in the use-value of what he produces but merely in appropriating the surplus. But this does not explain the *existence* or the level of surplus value. However, later interpreters of Smith were quick to read such statements as implying that the existence and level of profits are to be *explained* by the 'interest' of the capitalist and his 'willingness' to advance stock (analytically representable in the concept of the 'supply price'). Such interpretations were further strengthened by statements such as: '... he [capitalist] could have no interest to employ a great stock rather than a small one, unless his profits were to bear some proportion to the extent of his stock' (*Wealth of Nations*, p. 48). Adam Smith would seem to suggest here that it is the volume of capital stock that directly determines profit.[24]

It would seem from the above that the 'esoteric' aspects of Smith's analysis concerned the relations at the material base of the economy, while the 'exoteric' aspects related to the perceptions of the individuals – the surface phenomena. The former dwell on the 'inner connections' (the real relations of production), and the latter appear as their manifestations in circulation. To the individual capitalist, profits are a payment, an inducement to carry on investment or a recompense for frugality, and Smith recognized them as such. From the production point of view, they appear as a 'deduction' from the produce of labour. To the wage-earner, his income appears as a reward for 'toil and trouble', while it is 'productive consumption' when viewed from the circular process of production. Price, in exchange, appears definitionally as a sum of various 'factor payments' paid out to bring the commodity to the market and wherein the 'factor payments' to the producer all seem to be independently derived. Viewing the explanation of prices within the surplus structure, on the other hand, we note that, once methods of production are known, either the rate of profit or wages, *but not both*, can be taken as *independently* determinable – a point rightly stressed by Ricardo in insisting that 'profits depend upon wages'. Thus the 'exoteric' elements within Smith's analysis seem to arise as a description of the 'appearances', of the phenomena as they appear in circulation and as they appear in the perception of the individual participants. Smith did not always integrate the 'esoteric' categories with the 'exoteric', but both, in fact, are important and necessary for the analysis of capitalist relations. As Marx acknowledges:

> ... his task was indeed a twofold one. On the one hand he attempted to penetrate the inner physiology of bourgeois society but on the other, he partly tried to describe its externally apparent forms of life for the first time, to show its relations as they appear outwardly and partly he had even to find a nomenclature and corresponding mental concepts for these phenomena. (*Theories of Surplus Value* (1862–3[1963–8], II, p. 165)

4   Conclusion

Despite 'inconsistencies' and 'contradictions' noticed by Smith's successors in political economy, in particular by Ricardo and Marx, Smith is undoubtedly one of the founder-members of the classical school. Through their critiques, both Ricardo and Marx extend an elemental basic structure of theory constructed by Smith to analyse production and the accumulation of surplus. The 'inconsistencies' and 'duality' in Smith's analysis reflect, as Marx argued, perceptions of the same abstracted reality from different sides. One focuses on the objective, material relations in production, the other provides 'the corresponding mental concepts' and the categories of circulation. In Marx, we find a rigorous attempt to relate coherently the 'esoteric' and the 'exoteric' elements in a comprehensive characterization and analysis of the capitalist mode of production. Ricardo directed his attention intensively – almost exclusively – to the theory of distribution. Notwithstanding the original and insightful descriptions, Smith's treatment of the theory of distribution lacked internal coherence. Ricardo constructed a consistent theory of distribution within the surplus approach. Nevertheless, the basic categories of distribution and the forces that influenced their determination were charted out in a masterly account by Smith which has remained a classic to this day. We may add a word of caution here. First, this sharing of the elemental basic structure of the surplus approach does not connote that there are no differences between Smith and Ricardo or Ricardo and Marx; nor does it diminish the originality of the critiques, the novelty of the reconstructions and radical departures, particularly of Marx which, indeed, in many respects not only regenerated but also revolutionized scientific political economy. Secondly, the significance of the shared elements in the theoretical structure is prominently highlighted here to focus sharply on their contrast with the structure of the supply-and-demand based theory, since such a juxtaposition is one of our main purposes here.

We argued in the above that Smith's advocacy of free markets and the role of the 'individual' needs to be interpreted in the light of his comprehensive theoretical and philosophical system. The contemporary theoretical defence of markets as efficient resource-allocators and of the 'optimality' of the competitive system governed by optimising decisions of individual agents rests on a particular theory of 'choice' and 'change' specific to the supply-and-demand-based equilibrium theories. The underlying theory of choice pertains to decision-making by atomistic agents relying on their optimizing behaviour with rather stringent conditions placed upon the feasible sets of choices and on their interaction with other agents and with the market. Changes in prices and quantities are also explained on the basis of a specific theory of price formations on markets and of quantity-determination. In the above we have attempted to bring out the different theoretical context and content of Smith's concept of the 'free individual' ('individual in the society') and his perception as to how the individual's positioning in the social structure affects his choice-domain as well as how the choices of different individuals influence differently the progress of the society. We have noted the dynamic, accumulation-oriented perspective of Smith and have attempted to bring out the distinctiveness of the theoretical structure of Smith's explanation of prices and quantities. In particular, we have indicated the different connotations that concepts such as 'resource-allocation', 'supply and demand' and 'effectual demand' have in his theory. We need to be forewarned against drawing parallelisms between Smith's political economy and the demand and supply-based equilibrium theory, or reading into Smith anticipations of results arrived at in the altogether different framework of that theory.

Notes: Chapter 2

An earlier version of this essay was presented at a seminar celebrating the bicentennial anniversary of the publication of the *Wealth of Nations* in December 1976 at Madras and was published in that version under the title 'The historical conditioning of theory: A study of Adam Smith's political economy', in *Studies in History*, vol. 1, no. 1 (1979). In the process of revising the article many substantive changes have been introduced. I have benefited from very detailed and perceptive comments by Prue Kerr. I am grateful also to G. C. Harcourt, Jayati Ghosh, Deepak Nayyar, C. P. Chandrashekhar and Arun Kumar for their helpful comments.

1 All quotations from the *Wealth of Nations* are taken from the 1937 Modern Library edition cited in the references at the end of this chapter.
2 An important claim to this effect was made by Alfred Marshall in his 'The present position of economics' (1925). Hollander (1973) has strongly advocated this view in his *The Economics of Adam Smith*. See also Meek (1977b) where he reports (p. 3) the genial, proprietorial remark of George J. Stigler at the bicentennial celebration of *Wealth of Nations* at Glasgow University: 'I bring you greetings from Adam Smith who is alive and well and living in Chicago.' See Bharadwaj (1980), Chapter 9 in the present volume.
3 Smith, an eclectic scholar, drew upon previous intellectual advances and his originality lay in weaving together different influences into a theoretical system to interpret the concrete economic experience of advancing capitalism in England. As Viner (1927) [1984] p. 144 remarks: 'The Roman *jus naturale*, through Crotius and Pufendorf, strongly influenced Smith's thinking. The Renaissance emphasis on the individual, the materialistic philosophy of Shaftsbury, Locke and Hume, Hutcheson, the optimistic theism of the Scotch philosophers, the empiricism of Montesquieu were the more immediate and more powerful of influences.'
4 Deriving inspiration from Montesquieu, Newton, Bacon and Locke, the Scottish School of Philosophy and Historical Sociology developed in the hands of David Hume, Francis Hutcheson, Adam Smith, George Turnbull, Adam Ferguson, Dugald Stewart and John Millar, to cite the more prominent members. Across the channel, in France, where the influence of the *économiste* was strong in intellectual circles, similar efforts were seen in the works of the Physiocrats, more prominently in those of Quesnay and Turgot, to combine 'social moralism' with a certain brand of 'historical materialism'. For a detailed discussion, see Meek (1976, 1977a, and 1977b).

5   See A. S. Skinner (1979, 'Historical theory', Ch. 4, pp. 68–103). According to the account rendered by John Millar, a part of the lectures delivered by Adam Smith proceeded on the following plan: 'Upon this subject [that branch of morality which relates to justice] he followed the plan that seems to be suggested by Montesquieu; endeavouring to trace the gradual progress of jurisprudence, both public and private, from the rudest to the most refined ages, and to point out the effect of those arts which contribute to subsistence, and to the accumulation of property, in producing correspondent improvements or alterations in law and government' (quoted in Skinner, 1979, p. 68).
6   The lead in this direction may be said to have been given by Montesquieu. Smith's own efforts are described in the memoir on him by Dugald Stewart (1793 [1858]). Smith's own efforts were followed by his notable pupil, John Millar. For focusing on the Scottish School see Meek (1977a and 1977b, ch. 2).
7   A formulation along Smith's ideas occurs in John Millar's *The Origin of the Distinction of Ranks* (1779) from which the following excerpt is drawn: 'In searching for the causes of those remarkable systems of law and government which have appeared in the world, we must undoubtedly resort, first of all, to differences of situations which have suggested different views and motives of actions to the inhabitants of particular countries. Of this kind are the fertility or barrenness of soil, the nature of its productions, the species of labour requisite for procuring subsistence, the number of individuals collected together in one community. The variety that frequently occurs in these, and other particulars must have prodigious influence on the great body of a people, as by giving a particular direction to their inclinations and pursuits, it must be productive of correspondent habits, dispositions and ways of thinking ... There is, in man a disposition and capacity for improving his condition by the exertion of which he is carried on from one degree of advancement to another; and the similarity of his wants, as well as faculties by which those wants are supplied, has everywhere produced a remarkable uniformity in the several steps of its progression. By gradual advances in rendering their situation more comfortable the most important alterations are produced in the state and condition of people ... The distribution of property among any people is the principal circumstance that contributes to reduce them under civil government and to determine the form of their political constitution' (quoted in Lehmann, 1952).
    It is known that Smith stimulated and shared these ideas with his pupil and, among his projected plans, which he could not execute, were the writing of a philosophical history of literature and a theoretical history of law and government. Thus Smith had a unified approach to all knowledge about human societies.
8   The Scottish materialist interpretations of history differed from the later approach to the dialectical historical materialism of Marx in important respects. In the latter, 'the primacy of production relations' was more consistently – and insistently – worked out. In the Scottish School, the role of nature, of geographical factors, of 'communications and transport', of 'education', etc. was given prominence, suggesting a multiplicity of independent causations. The human propensities and behavioural characteristics were often treated as if they were universal, innate and immutable and, as such, autonomous forces determining actions. Secondly, while the transition was considered as 'natural' and not accidental, the Scottish School did not see the dynamics in the form of internal contradictions in their dialectical movement. The conflict of interest was often attributed to the abuse and

misdirection of authority and privilege that rank and distinction bestowed on individuals in society, and therefore eliminable through recourse to the right moral principles and the conflicts resolvable through the evolution of a system of morality. Thirdly, the state of 'commerce' was treated by the Scottish School as if it were the ultimate stage of social development, as if history stopped with the present. In Marx capitalism was also a transient phase in social development. Marx himself wrote to Weydemeyer on 5 March 1852 (*Selected Correspondence*, 1942, p. 57), drawing out how he differed from his predecessors: 'No credit is due to me for discovering the existence of classes in modern society nor yet the struggle between them. Long before me bourgeois historians had described the historical development of this class struggle and bourgeois economists the economic anatomy of the classes. What I did that was new was to prove: (i) that the existence of classes is only bound up with particular historical phases in the development of production, (ii) that the class struggle necessarily leads to the dictatorship of the proletariat, (iii) that this dictatorship itself only constitutes the transition to the abolition of all classes and to a classless society.'

9 He shared this vision of a society with its innate natural order and laws of functioning, as if of a 'mechanical system', with David Hume, George Turnbull and Francis Hutcheson, his contemporaries. The underlying 'plan' was not a conscious one, but was revealed only through its functioning and grasped through imaginative speculation. Smith also appears to have relied at times on the optimistic theism current in Scottish philosophy, where ultimate governance is perceived to be exercised by the 'Author of Nature', 'Providence', the 'Invisible Hand', 'the final cause', the 'Divine Being', or some such proxy for 'beneficient Nature'.

10 As discussed in note 8 above, Marx's view of the dialectical progress through history was markedly different from Smith's.

11 Smith, in his Introduction and plan of the work, sets out the central features of his approach quite remarkably: 'The annual labour of every nation is the fund which originally supplies it with all the necessaries and conveniencies of life which it annually consumes, and which consists always either in the immediate produce of that labour or in what is purchased with that produce from other nations.' (*Wealth of Nations*, p. vii) The economy is here looked upon as one generating surplus annually and the surplus is regarded in 'real terms' produced or purchased by labour. We may note also the accent here on 'labour' as the source of surplus.

12 The parallel to the recognition of labour in the social abstract form was that of the role of capital as advances, and profits as a category of income, distinct from wages, rents and interest; it was neither a 'superior wage' for superintendence or management nor rent, and was instead perceived clearly as a *rate* of return on the amount of capital.

13 The permanent causes are the ones that affect the 'natural state' in a way which displaces the components of the 'natural state' from their central values, and therefore the natural position needs to be reconstituted. The latter, as 'temporary' causes, may not have permanent effects on the natural position so that the position is not altered. This is best illustrated by the distinction between 'natural price' and 'market price' (see p. 24 above).

14 His argument is: 'In this state of things, the whole produce belongs to the labourer; and the quantity of labour commonly employed in acquiring or producing any commodity, is the only circumstance which can regulate the quantity of labour which it ought only to purchase, command, or exchange

for ... As soon as stock is accumulated in the hands of particular persons, some of them will naturally employ it in setting to work industrious people, whom they will supply with materials and subsistence, in order to make a profit by the sale of their work, or by what their labour adds to the value of their materials' (*Wealth of Nations*, pp. 47–8.) This views profits as 'leavings of wages' and makes way for the surplus-based explanation of the rate of profit, fully developed in Ricardo.

15 Smith's discussion of value, like many other writers, is not original, but he draws upon the ideas of predecessors, such as Cantillon, and synthesizes these into a coherent system of analysis.

16 Smith, taking the 'adding-up' view of natural prices, not only treated the average rates of wages, profits and rents as component elements of prices but also considered all the three as 'original sources of value'; in the sense that each of these rates was determined independently of each other. (See also Section 3 in the present essay.)

17 'A man must always live by his work, and his wages must at least be sufficient to maintain him' (*Wealth of Nations*, p. 67). Further, following Cantillon, he adds, 'They must even upon most occasions be somewhat more, otherwise it would be impossible for him to bring up a family' (ibid.).

18 'What are the common wages of labour, depends everywhere upon the contract usually made between those two parties, whose interests are by no means the same. The workmen desire to get as much, the masters to give as little as possible. The former are disposed to combine in order to raise, the latter in order to lower the wages of labour.

It is not, however, difficult to foresee which of the two parties must, upon all ordinary occasions, have the advantage in the dispute, and force the other into a compliance with their terms ... In the long run the workman may be as necessary to his master as his master to him but the necessity is not so immediate' (*Wealth of Nations*, p. 66).

19 A contrary view is held by Hahn (1981, p. 123), for example, when he writes: 'In decentralized economies a large number of individuals make economic decisions which, in the light of market and other informations, they consider most advantageous. They are not guided by the social good nor is there an overall plan in the unfolding of which they have preassigned roles. It was Adam Smith who first realized the need to explain why this kind of social arrangement does not lead to chaos ... *Smith not only posed an obviously important question but also started us off on the road to answering it. General Equilibrium Theory as classically stated by Arrow and Debreu (1954) and Debreu (1959) is the near end of that road*' (Italics added). While Smith does enunciate the problem, it is arguable whether the road he started upon, and the one traversed by Arrow and Debreu, is the same.

20 With a vestige of Physiocratic thinking, Smith attributes an additional productivity to land since it yields rent. This is disputed by Ricardo.

21 'Wages, profits and rents are the three original sources of all revenue, as well as of exchangeable value' (*Wealth of Nations*, p. 152).

22 'In so far as they are titles (conditions) for the appropriation of a part of the value, that is, of the labour materialised in the commodity, they are sources of income for their owners. But the distribution or appropriation of value is certainly not the source of the value that is appropriated' (*Theories of Surplus Value*, 1862-3 [1963–8], I, p. 94). Moreover, it is *labour* and not *wages* which, according to Marx's view, created value.

23 Marshall attributed the idea of 'measurable motives' to Adam Smith: 'A point of view was conquered for us by Adam Smith, from which a commodity is regarded as the embodiment of measurable efforts and sacrifices' ('Mill's Theory of Value' [1876], in Pigou, 1925, p. 126).
24 This is also the implication drawn from Smith's statement: 'They [profits of stock] are, however, altogether different [from wages and], are regulated by quite different principles, and bear no proportion to the quantity, the hardship, or the ingenuity of this supposed labour of inspection and direction. *They are regulated altogether by the value of the stock employed, and are greater or smaller in proportion to the extent of this stock*' (*Wealth of Nations*, p. 48; italics added).

References: Chapter 2

Arrow, K. J., and Debreu, G. (1954), 'Existence of an equilibrium for a competitive economy', *Econometrica*, 22, 265–90
Arrow, K. J. and Hahn, F. (1971), *General Competitive Analysis* (Edinburgh: Oliver and Boyd)
Bharadwaj, K. (1978a), *Classical Political Economy and the Rise to Dominance of Demand and supply Theories* (Calcutta: Orient Longman)
Bharadwaj, K. (1978b), 'The subversion of classical analysis: Alfred Marshall's early writing on value', *Cambridge Journal of Economics*, vol. 2, no. 3 (September), pp. 253–71: 2nd edition 1986; Chapter 6 in the present volume.
Bharadwaj, K. (1980), 'On certain theoretical issues in classical political economy: a review article', *Australian Economic Papers*, Vol. 19 (December); Chapter 9 in the present volume
Cantillon, R. (1755 [1931]), *Essay on the Nature of Trade in General*, ed. Henry Higgs, reprinted 1964 (New York. M. Kelley)
Debreu, G. (1959) *Theory of Value* (New York: Wiley)
Dobb, M. H. (1973), *Theories of Value and Distribution since Adam Smith* (Cambridge: Cambridge University Press)
Eltis, W. A. (1975), 'Adam Smith's theory of economic growth', in Skinner and Wilson (eds) (1975) *Essays on Adam Smith* (Oxford: Clarendon Press)
Hahn, F. (1981), 'General equilibrium theory', in D. Bell and I. Kristol (eds), *The Crisis in Economic Theory* (New York: Basic Books)
Hirschman, A. O. (1977) *Passions and the interests: political arguments for capitalism before its triumph*. (New Jersey: Princeton University Press)
Hollander, S. (1973), *The Economics of Adam Smith* (London: Heinemann)
Lehmann, W. H. (1952), 'John Millar, historical sociologist', *British Journal of Sociology*, Vol. III, No. 1 (March), pp. 30–46
Lowe, A. (1954), 'The Classical Theory of Economic Growth', *Social Research*, xxi
Lowe, A. (1975), 'Adam Smith's system of equilibrium growth', in Skinner and Wilson (eds), op. cit. pp. 415–25
Marshall, A. (1925), 'The present position of economics', in A. C. Pigou (ed.), *Memorials of Alfred Marshall* (London: Macmillan)
Marx, Karl (1862-3 [1963–71]), *Theories of Surplus Value*, 3 parts (Moscow: Progress Publishers)
Marx, Karl (1942), *Selected Correspondence, 1846–1895* (New York: International Publishers)

Meek, R. L. (1954) [1977a], 'The Scottish contribution to Marxist sociology', in John Saville (ed.), *Democracy and Labour Movements* (London)

Meek, R. L. (1973), *Turgot on Progress, Sociology and Economics* (Cambridge: Cambridge University Press)

Meek, R. L. (1976), *Social Science and the Ignoble Savage* (Cambridge: Cambridge University Press)

Meek, R. L. (1977b), *Smith, Marx and After* (London: Chapman & Hall)

Millar, John (1799), *The Origin of the Distinction of Ranks*, 3rd edn (Edinburgh)

Mitchell, W. (1967), *Types of Economic Theory* (New York: Augustus M. Kelly)

Ricardo, D. (1810–23 [1951–73]), *Works and Correspondence of David Ricardo*, ed. by P. Sraffa, with the collaboration of M. H. Dobb, 10 vols and *Index* (Cambridge: Cambridge University Press)

Ricardo, D. (1817 [1951]), *Principles of Political Economy*, Vol. I of *Works and Correspondence*, op. cit.

Ricardo, D. (1815 [1951]), 'An Essay on the Influence of a Low Price of Corn on the Profits of Stock', in P. Sraffa (ed.), with the collaboration of M. H. Dobb, *Works and Correspondence* of David Ricardo, Vol. IV (Cambridge: Cambridge University Press)

Rosenberg, N. (1960), 'Some institutional aspects of the *Wealth of Nations*', *Journal of Political Economy*, vol. 18, no. 6, pp. 557–70

Rosenberg, N. (1968), 'Adam Smith, consumer tastes and economic growth', *Journal of Political Economy*, vol. 76, no. 2, pp. 361–74, May-June 1968

Schumpeter, J. A. (1954), *History of Economic Analysis* (London: Allen & Unwin)

Skinner, A. S. (1979), *A System of Social Science: Papers relating to Adam Smith* (Oxford: Clarendon Press)

Skinner, A. S., and Wilson, T. (eds) (1975), *Essays on Adam Smith* (Oxford: Clarendon Press)

Smith, Adam (1759 [1966]), *The Theory of Moral Sentiments* (New York: A. M. Kelley reprint)

Smith, Adam (1762 [1896]), *Lectures on Justice, Police, Revenue and Arms*, ed. by E. Cannan (Oxford: Clarendon Press)

Smith, Adam (1776 [1937]), *An Inquiry into the Nature and Causes of the Wealth of Nations*, 2 vols, ed. by E. Cannan (New York: The Modern Library)

Spengler, J. (1975), 'Adam Smith and society's decision-makers', in Skinner and Wilson (eds), op. cit. pp. 390–414

Sraffa, P. (1951), Editorial introduction to *Works and Correspondence of David Ricardo*, Vol. I (Cambridge: Cambridge University Press)

Stewart, Dugald (1793 [1858]), *Account of the Life and Writing of Adam Smith, LLD*, in *Works*, ed. by W. Hamilton (Edinburgh)

Steuart, Sir James (1767 [1966]), *An Inquiry into the Principles of Political Economy*, A. S. Skinner (ed.) (Chicago)

Thweatt, W. D. (1958), 'A growth equation analysis of the Ricardian and Marxian theories of growth', *International Economic Review*, vol. 4, no. 1 (February), pp. 227–30

Viner, J. (1927), 'Adam Smith and laissez faire', *Journal of Political Economy*, vol. 35, no. 2, reprinted in Wood (ed.), op. cit., Vol. I, pp. 143–67.

Wood, John Cunningham (ed.) (1984), *Adam Smith: Critical Assessments*, 4 vols (London: Croom Helm).

3
Ricardian Theory and Ricardianism

This essay examines one strand in the analytical developments that occurred in political economy during Ricardo's lifetime and immediately after his death.[1] It is attempted here to illustrate the manner in which Ricardo's surplus approach to distribution was gradually but effectively eroded in the hands of the 'Ricardians'; focus being on the positions taken by James Mill, J. R. McCulloch, De Quincey and John Stuart Mill, the more prominent among the followers of Ricardo. It will emerge from the discussions below that the Ricardians introduced conceptual and other modifications in their attempts to reinterpret, recast and extend Ricardo's results, especially on the theory of profit. Ricardo's basic theoretical structure was thereby obfuscated, paving the way for its ultimate abandonment.

Despite John Stuart Mill's well-known confident posture (1848 [1965], p. 436), a state of theoretical confusion arose. While Ricardian theory, particularly the theory of distribution, was substantively eroded, no alternative theory was in sight until the emergence of the new marginalist theory in the 1870s. This state of affairs is important for understanding subsequent, seemingly paradoxical, developments; such as Marshall claiming a continuity in tradition and approach while replacing the classical theory by a new marginalist theory (see Bharadwaj, 1978b, Chapter 6 in the present volume). Marx, on the other hand, forewarned by the confusions Ricardo's theory had given rise to and alerted by the deviant directions it was taking in the hands of Ricardo's 'disciples', restated the surplus approach in clearer terms by drawing out its fuller implications, and extending it in new directions; whilst emphasizing his differences with a number of features of the 'classical political economy' of his predecessors.

1 Ricardo's Theory of Profits

As is well known, Ricardo's major preoccupation was to arrive at a consistent theory of distribution – the most challenging part of which was the determination of the rate of profit and its relation to rents and wages. The following main propositions emerge as central to his theory:

(a) The rate of profits is constrained by the conditions of production, so that profits cannot originate in circulation. That is, under competition, the rate cannot be raised permanently by marking up prices above the 'natural price'.
(b) 'Profits depend upon wages' – a phrase which, we shall see, lent itself to confusing interpretations. The statement is best understood to mean that, once methods of production and the wage are known, the rate of profit cannot be determined independently of the wage level. A corollary that followed pertains to the inverse relation between the share of wages in net product (or 'the value of wages') and the rate of profit.

While these propositions remained Ricardo's central concern, his arguments developed in phases: the first was that of the *Essay on the Influence of a Low Price of Corn on the Profits of Stock* (1815)[2] (*Works*, IV, pp 1–41), followed by the second, of the *Principles of Political Economy* (1817), (*Works*), I. While the surplus approach is adopted throughout, the form it takes changes substantively from the *Essay* to the *Principles* as the basis of the arguments moves from corn quantities to a fully fledged value-based analysis.[3] We may even talk of subphases within the latter, purely for expository purposes in the present essay: the first stage covering the first two editions of the *Principles* (1817 and 1819) and the second, focusing on the analysis in the third edition of Principles (1821), and, particularly the unfinished manuscript on 'Absolute Value and Exchangeable Value' (1823), (Works, IV, pp. 357–442). The subphasing may appear useful in clearly identifying the deviations which the Ricardians introduced when confronted with theoretical difficulties which Ricardo attempted, unsuccessfully, to resolve.

In the *Essay* the focus was on the agricultural sector; with the agricultural rate of profits determining the general rate of profits. The characteristic features of the *Essay* which we may note are: (a) with the adoption of the theory of differential rent advanced by West (1815), Torrens (1815), and Malthus (1815a, b), and with simplifications such as capital consisting entirely of wages (and the latter consisting of corn) Ricardo was able to perceive clearly and to insist upon the inverse relation between rents and incomes, and between the rate of profits and the share of wages; (b) no rigorous theory of exchange value was yet formulated, although the later theory of the *Principles* was foreshadowed in certain aspects; (c) a sketch of an accumulation process, employed more for polemical purposes,[4] was outlined to highlight the logical consequences of restrictions on corn imports; (d) the focus was on the rents versus profits *and* wages (or, correspondingly, the interests of the landlords versus those of other social classes in agriculture – the sector within which the determination of the distributive shares was resolved). At this stage, Ricardo regarded the theory of rent as a central aspect of the analysis, though his theory of profit was worked out *prior* to the pamphlets on rent by Torrens, West and Malthus (see Sraffa's editorial note on the *Essay*, *Works*, IV, 3–8).

The *Essay* had an immediate impact and Ricardo's ascendancy in intellectual circles was quite remarkable. His success and the acceptance of his theory may be ascribed to a number of factors. First, the Corn Law debate being a topical and controversial issue at that time, Ricardo's contribution was bound to attract wide attention. Secondly, his theory was built upon the two major concerns of the period: rising corn prices attributed to declining productivity of extended agriculture and the spectre of population boom. Both were accepted as more or less well founded empirically, so that the rent theory and the population doctrine had won intellectual support (see Blaug, 1958). Lastly, and perhaps most important of all, was the fact that Ricardo's conclusions had appeared to be politically acceptable. The clashes among classes – mainly between the landed and the manufacturing interests – were within the reasonable constraints of parliamentary debate and had not yet passed into the hands of the 'mob'. The class issues, it appeared, were amenable to amicable settlement through timely legislation.[5]

The second phase is marked by the publication of the *Principles*. As a result of the post-*Essay* discussions, especially with Malthus, Ricardo recognized the prime need for a theory of relative prices to resolve the problem of distribution in a general setting. Ricardo, armed with the labour theory of value, could generalize the surplus approach of the *Essay* to a general determination of the rate of profits: he could now allow for wages to be composed of commodities apart from corn and could consider heterogenous compositions of capital. Of course, while the corn calculation of the rate of profits was superseded, the notion that the rate of profits was determined on no-rent land was preserved. In so far as corn remained a major and stable component of wage goods, the state of cultivation continued to play a significant role in Ricardo's analysis. Moreover, while the 'modifications' to the labour theory of value occasioned by the variations in the wage having differential effects on prices of commodities were discussed by Ricardo, he deemed them 'as not superseding' (or, as 'exceptions' to) the labour-embodied principle of relative value determination (*Works*, VII, p. 377).

Ricardo then sought to derive an unambiguous relation between the share of wages and the rate of profits by suggesting the use of an 'invariant standard' in terms of which net output and other aggregates entering the profit determination could be measured so as to circumvent variations in their values arising solely because of the change in the value of the standard due to the same change in wage (Garegnani, 1960).

In the first two editions of *Principles* (1817 and 1819), the property of 'invariance' that the standard was required to meet was the one corresponding to a simple labour theory of value; namely, that the commodity so chosen required the same amount of labour embodied at all times and places. In the third edition of the *Principles* (1821), and the unfinished manuscript, 'Absolute Value and Exchangeable Value',

Ricardo made an effort to handle with greater rigour the 'modifications' in the labour theory of value arising from different proportions of means of production to labour in different commodities. Ricardo's method of determining r, the rate of profit (once rent is 'got rid of') was by taking the following relation, defined, say, on an annual cycle:

$$r = \frac{\text{Social (Net) Product} - \text{Wages}}{\text{Social Capital}}$$

As long as the three aggregates on the right-hand side constituted homogenous quantities (as in the case of the 'corn' simplification) or were reducible to homogenous magnitudes (labour, under the rule of the simple labour theory of value), the resolution of the rate of profits by this 'surplus approach', of distributing profits as social surplus net of wages over social capital, posed no problem. The 'inverse' relation between the share of wages in net product and the rate of profit was straightforward. However, once Ricardo recognized that a change in the wage brought about variations in relative prices, even when the methods of production remained the same, a problem of simultaneity – the value of the aggregates depending on the rate of profit itself – arose; a problem seen by Ricardo as one of circularity. Ricardo's search was now directed towards finding out ways and means of keeping the social net product to be divided between wages and profits invariant in value with respect to changes in distribution (*Works*, I, p. xlviii). Furthermore, as Sraffa remarks (*Works*, I, p. xlix):

> This function of the theory of value of making it possible, in the face of changes in distribution, to measure changes in the magnitude of aggregates of commodities of different kinds or, what is even more important, to ascertain its constancy, appears once more in connection with the measurement of the quantity of capital.

Ricardo now attempted to redefine the properties of the 'invariant standard': money, 'produced with such proportions of the two kinds of capital (fixed and variable) as approach nearest to the average quantity employed in the production of most commodities' (*Works*, I, p. 45). Measured in such a standard, 'those commodities on one side of this medium, would rise in comparative value with it, with a rise in the price of labour, and a fall in the rate of profits; and those on the other side might fall from the same cause (*Works*, VIII, p. 193). Ricardo did not succeed in discovering such a standard and his theory of profit and the 'inverse relation' remained adequately and satisfactorily demonstrated only within the labour theory. Nevertheless, in his last paper, on 'Absolute Value and Exchangeable Value', Ricardo had set out the direction in which a solution could be sought. As key analytical notions, he focused attention on the ratio of means of production to labour, or alternatively a conception, which, following Sraffa (1960), we may call the 'reduction to dated labour'. Lacking the tools to handle simultaneity, Ricardo's attempts to transcend the difficulties did not succeed. It was left to Marx to restate the problem of transforming labour values into prices of production, having first defined the notion of 'prices of production' in clearer terms and distinct from 'values'. The Ricardians failed to advance upon Ricardo's efforts and, in the process, gave up certain substantive results of Ricardo, eroding his surplus approach. In particular, they failed to appreciate the logical basis of Ricardo's efforts to grapple with the characteristic of 'capitals' as produced commodities by means of other commodities, with heterogeneous structure of production. This, Ricardo identified as the main difficulty in reducing 'cost of production' to labour alone.

In anticipation of our discussion, we may note here some features of Ricardo's theory which were either missed out or not adequately grasped by his followers:

(a) The search for the 'invariant standard', in Ricardo, was prompted by his theory of profits and the difficulty that his surplus-based theory faced when the social net product (and social capital) could not be evaluated independently of the rate of profits.

(b) The question of discovering a 'standard' was not merely a practical or 'empirical' problem for Ricardo. He was primarily interested in enunciating the theoretical properties such a standard would have to possess. These properties themselves varied with the *theory* of relative values he proposed.

(c) To Ricardo the search for these properties of the standard was coterminus with the explanation of the relative values itself: 'Is it not clear then that as soon as we are in possession of the knowledge of the circumstances which determine the value of commodities' he asks McCulloch, 'we are enabled to say what is necessary to give us an invariable measure of value'? (*Works*, IX, p. 358). Ricardo insisted on this search even when realizing that, of such a standard, 'we have no knowledge'. He proceeded in the first and second editions of the *Principles* to add: 'It is, however, of considerable use towards attaining a correct theory, to ascertain what the essential qualities of a standard are, that we may know the causes of the variation in relative value of commodities' (*Works*, I, p. 17, n. 3). The Ricardians, as we shall see, tended however to separate the discussion of exchange value from that of the influence of a change in wages on relative prices, treating the latter as a peripheral addendum. More particularly the 'measure' of value, considered as a 'chimera', is disassociated from the theory of profits.

Certain conjunctural factors, as well as analytical difficulties, appear to have turned against the acceptance of Ricardo's theory. Increasingly, the centre of class conflict which, in Ricardo, had remained more prominently focused upon the landlord versus the rest and within parliamentary confines was shifting to a more open confrontation between labour and capital. Even during Ricardo's lifetime, his altered position on the machinery question had been opposed vigorously by McCulloch, not only on analytical grounds, but also because of the fear that it may have unintentionally provided an implicit support to the Luddites. We shall also note the shift of positions by De Quincey on Ricardo's conclusions on distribution. It is also known that Ricardo's labour theory and his emphasis on the inverse relation between wages and the rate of profits had provided the backdrop for the 'Ricardian Socialists' to advocate radical organizational reforms.[6]

In short, the Ricardian results were feared to have 'mischievous' implications. Other factors added to the growing reaction. First, the Malthusian theory of population in its earlier strict, uncompromising version was meeting resistance and being replaced by 'neo-Malthusianism'. 'Prudential Checks' were advocated, albeit indirectly, in intellectual circles. The statistical basis of the theory was under debate, although the principle of demographic variations continued to play a predominant role in policy matters and as long-range theory. Analytically, the important consequence appears to be that this provided one of the grounds for replacing the notion of a 'customary' wage by the wage-fund theory. Although Ricardo did not require a fixed subsistence wage – 'given' wage should not be confused here with 'fixed' wage – and adopted Malthus's theory of rents, the attack on both these led the Ricardians, especially John Stuart Mill, to advocate the wage-fund doctrine. Secondly, the period that followed Ricardo was one of rapid increases in agricultural productivity and Ricardian theory, erroneously interpreted as implying a pessimistic view, was attacked on empirical grounds.[7] As we shall see, the Ricardians obfuscated the *theoretical* wage/profit relation by not separating the relation under *given* methods of cultivation from the case where methods change. With shifts in productivity occurring simultaneously with a change in the wage, the rate of profits need not necessarily move inversely to the wage. Ricardo was himself aware of this.[8] In viewing how the Ricardian theory fared in the hands of the Ricardians, we concentrate on their analysis of value and distribution.

2 James Mill's Elements of Political Economy[9]

Composed by the author as a 'school book of political economy', 'to detach the essential principles of the science from all extraneous topics', Mill's *Elements* attempted to 'state the propositions clearly and in their logical order'. In presenting Ricardo's theory in a 'systematic' form and in abstract but elementary outlines, James Mill tends to bypass or reduce to triviality the terse – but often crucial – parts of the theory. On the other hand, his 'sense of order' extends beyond the bounds of logic when he attempts to prove that the real contradictions in capitalist society are only apparent ones (see, e.g., Marx, 1862–3 [1971], III, pp. 84–5). Despite emphasis on *logical order*, for example, it is striking that Mill discusses production and distribution prior to 'exchangeable value' and treats the latter in a rather cursory and simplistic manner, explaining (away) the difficulties posed for the labour theory of value. These unresolved analytical difficulties reappear in his presentation of the theory of profits and the wage/profit inverse relation.

James Mill on 'Exchangeable Value'
Mill does not explicitly distinguish between 'market prices' and 'natural prices' as Ricardo does. However, he presents the familiar Smith–Ricardo position that behind exchange lie the laws according to which 'supply is furnished to demand' (1824, p. 87). Demand provides the necessary condition for occasioning supply but it is the cost of production which 'ultimately' and 'entirely' regulates the exchange value. The cost of production is then variously resolved into 'capital' or 'labour'. Mill first takes up the former 'opinion' – that is, to resolve costs into capital – since wages form a part of the capital advanced, capital is defined so as to include labour. Here Mill evidently has Torrens's (1815) proposition in mind: that commodities are valuable according to the value of the capital employed in their production. He objects to such a view, without explicit reference to Torrens, as containing one of the most obvious of all absurdities: 'capital is commodities. If the value of commodities then depends upon the value of capital, it depends upon the value of commodities; value in short depends upon value. It is an attempt clearly and completely abortive' (1844 [1965], p. 98). Mill argued further that 'the value of all capital must be determined by labour', as all capital is produced ultimately by labour. He concludes: 'It thus appears, that quantity of labour, in the last resort, determines the proportion in which commodities exchange for one another' (ibid., p. 98).

To the assertive statements of Mill on the determination of exchange value by 'quantity of labour' in the first edition of *Elements* (1821), Ricardo had commented (letter to Mill, dated 18 December 1921, *Works*, IX, p. 127):

> I see the same difficulty, in this section, that I have seen in my own, on the same subject, of laying down a general and positive rule with respect to quantity of labour realised in commodities as being the rule and measure of their exchangeable value. The exceptions will be opposed to you as they have been to me.

What Ricardo himself referred to as 'exceptions' or 'modifications' arose from the significant difficulty which differences in the proportions of means of production to labour (and, the different composition of the means of production) in the production of commodities created for relative value determination. However, James Mill retained the arguments in his successive editions although he elaborated further, particularly in the third edition, on the difficulty introduced by the presence of 'fixed capital' and the 'element of time'.

Bailey (1825) [1931]), referring to the second edition of *Elements* (1824), had objected to Mill's criticism of Torrens, mentioned above.

> The value of commodities may not be capable of depending on itself, but the value of one commodity, which is one thing, may very easily depend on that of another, which is a different thing; and if it did not in point of fact, there would be no logical absurdity in asserting it. He who maintains that the mutual value of two commodities is chiefly determined by the comparative quantity of capital extended in their production, undoubtedly maintains that it is determined by the value of preceding commodities; and this is quite consistent with the value of those preceding commodities having been determined by their comparative quantities of producing labour, or by any other cause. (pp. 203–4)

With hindsight, we may sort out the issue better: James Mill's hurried and simplistic refutation of Torrens purely on the basis of 'circularity' is not adequate since the problem is one of simultaneous determination of relative values (as probably Bailey hints, although circuitously). Simultaneity, by itself, is no reason for rejection. Ricardo was to raise the pertinent difficulty encountered in Torrens' formulation of value as determined by 'capitals', in a letter to McCulloch, dated 21 August 1823 (*Works*, IX, pp. 359–60):

> I would ask what reasons you have of ascertaining the equal value of capitals ... These capitals are not the same in kind ... and if they themselves are produced in unequal times they are subject to the same fluctuations as other commodities. Till you have fixed the criterion by which we are to ascertan value, you can say nothing of equal capitals.[10]

That James Mill did not comprehend this line of Ricardo's thought is clear from the fact that a difficulty arising from the same source in reducing capital to labour is also 'resolved' by him only superficially,[11] as in the following: 'Commodities exchange according to labour time embodied', and since 'the first capital must have been the result of pure labour', he infers: 'It thus undeniably appears, that not only the value of the first capital, but, by equal necessity, that of the commodities which are produced by the first capital, is determined by quantity of labour', and following the same reasoning in successive productions, the value of all commodities must be determined by labour (1824, pp. 93–4; 1844 [1965], pp. 97–8).

James Mill was to deal rather cursorily with the difficulty created by capital – the 'one phenomenon which is brought to controvert these conclusions', although he elaborated his argument slightly from the second to the third edition. 'It is said that the exchangeable value of a commodity is affected by time, without the intervention of labour; because, when profits of stock must be included, so much must be added for every portion of time beyond that of another' (1824, pp. 94–5; 1844 [1965], pp. 98–9). He argued that the objection 'is founded upon a misapprehension with respect to the nature of profits. Profits are, in reality, the measure of quantity of labour'. This is explained by treating capital as hoarded labour, and 'what is called by time ... is the mere computation of annuity' (1824, p. 99). This is illustrated by an example: 'A portion of capital produced by 100 days labour is 100 days hoarded labour ... If capital, paid for by an annuity, is paid for at the rate of 10 percent one-tenth of the hundred labour may be correctly considered as expended in one year'. In the second edition, taking the problematic case of wine, he had disposed of the difficulty by a mere tautology: 'If the wine which is put in the cellar is increased in value one-tenth by being kept a year, one-tenth more of labour may be correctly considered as having expended upon it' (ibid., p. 97–8). In the same edition Mill had concluded: 'It has been most pertinently and conclusively remarked by Mr McCulloch, that time does nothing. How then can it create value? Time is a mere abstract term' (ibid., p. 99). The main problem was thus only superficially resolved. Mill did not explain – and did not realize that it needed an explanation – how the 'annuity' was to be computed. The 'rate of ten per cent' was taken as given but this rate would be none other than the rate of profit *to be explained*. His wine example in the 1824 edition cited above demonstrated the principle only by definition.

It was probably Bailey's attack on the wine example (1825 [1931], p. 219) pointing out that the increase in value takes place without additional labour that prompted Mill to elaborate the example in the third edition (1826, reissued 1844). Profits, he claimed,

> are the remuneration for labour; labour not applied immediately to the commodity in question but applied to it through the medium of other commodities, the produce of labour. And if you may measure the amount of immediate labour by the amount of wages, you may measure the amount of secondary labour by that of the return of capitalist'. (1844 [1965], p. 104)

This, he contended, applied to wine as to other cases and further that 'the return which is made to capital employed upon the land, is that which determines the rate of annual profit from all other employments of capital, and, of course, for that which is employed in ameliorating wine in a wine-cellar' (ibid., p. 104). Writing in 1826, it is surprising that Mill reverts to Ricardo's early, pre-*Principles*, theory of profits, attributing a determining role to agricultural profits! This need had arisen as Mill had no explanation for the determination of the general rate of profits.

Wage Variations and Relative Prices
That apart, Mill's solution does not satisfactorily resolve the Ricardian question: how to explain changes in relative prices when a change occurs in wages, methods of production remaining the same. (If the labour theory of value were to hold strictly no such change from such a cause should arise.) Continuing to treat 'capital' and 'labour' as different species of labour – the former as hoarded or secondary and the latter

as 'immediate' or 'primary', Mill first notes that 'they are not always paid according to the same rate; that is, payment of the one does not rise when that of the other rises or fall when that of the other falls. And secondly, that they do not always contribute to the production of all commodities in equal proportion' (ibid., p. 105). Treating capital as 'another species of labour' was tantamount to treating capital as a homogeneous unit with its own measure, independent of distribution. On this premise, Mill proceeded to rank commodities according to the proportion of labour to capital, independently of any given wage level and to infer that, with a rise in the wage, those commodities with a relatively greater labour to 'capital' ratio would rise in relative value. The analysis is simplified as the ranking of these commodities according to the proportion of capital to labour is taken to be independent of the variation in the wage. Also, while the discussion of the chapter begins by treating labour and capital as two species of labour, the wages of which did not rise and fall in the same proportion (thus keeping the wage/profit relation rather vague) Mill presumes the inverse relation in the later part of the chapter (ibid., p. 107).

It is also surprising that the chapter tracing the effect of a change in the wage on exchange values is treated as if it is only an appendage to the issue of relative values, the latter being already settled on the basis of labour values. *What is more, it is associated with the problem of finding a 'measure' which itself is viewed as a distinct problem from that of the value determination and the theory of profits.* This is absolutely at variance with Ricardo's own perception. Mill states: 'Though we can by strict analysis discover, that exchangeable value is proportioned to a quantity of labour expended in production yet there are two reasons why we cannot have recourse to this as the measure of value'[12] (1824, p. 110). These were made into 'three circumstances' in the third edition of 1826 (reissued 1844 [1965], p. 115). The first was 'the different proportions of the two kinds of labour' in commodities which is responsible for the produce being shared in different proportions between labour and capital; secondly, that there are no practical means of ascertaining the quantity of hoarded labour 'since the only measure we have of its quantity is the price which it brings'. Both these difficulties, we knew from Ricardo, are not peculiar to the problem of a measure, as distinct from that of value-determination. The third reason – added in the third edition (probably the influence of Bailey) – is that, 'labour is not constant in its productive powers' (ibid., p. 116). Again, we know that if productivity of labour is uniform in all productions, labour embodied could be an unexceptionable explanation of relative prices. It is all the more surprising that James Mill continued to hold these views given the fact that he was aware of Ricardo's unfinished manuscript on 'Absolute Value and Exchangeable Value' (*Works*, IV, p. 376), where Ricardo had asked: 'How can Mill then be right in saying that the value of wine is regulated by the quantity of labour worked up in cloth', when, even though there is no change in the mode of producing cloth, wages change bringing about a change in the price of cloth?

James Mill on Production and Distribution

As earlier remarked, James Mill treats production and distribution prior to exchange value. Under production, he introduces the mutual convertibility of capital and labour: 'in the idea of labour, the idea of subsistence is included and capital, as including means of subsistence, includes labour'. On the other hand, capital is a product of labour. Further, as means of subsistence advanced by the capitalist, 'capital' is seen by Mill as a direct result of, and hence identified with, savings. The implications of symmetry drawn between labour and capital and the identification of the latter with savings, emerge in Mill's outlook on distribution.

First, Mill tends often to identify capital with 'wages or subsistence advanced to the worker', thus, as Marx comments (1862–3 [1971], III, p. 85) he identifies surplus value with profits. While Ricardo tended to take for granted the existence of a positive rate of profits, Mill attempts to provide a logical basis for the emergence of profits. He visualizes the capital/labour relationship as one between the buyer and seller of labour. The share in the produce is received by the workers in advance 'to suit much better their convenience', whereby they avoid waiting till the commodity is produced and hence also avoid delays and uncertainties. The capitalist, through the advance, buys the share of the labourer gaining a full claim on produce. Moreover, these bargains are determined by competition. He thus reduces the transaction between capitalists and labourers into a common transaction between commodity owners, both owners of materialized labour. But the transaction is supposed not to be ordinary, as one party, the capitalist, pays the share 'in advance'. However, as Marx reminds us (ibid., p. 91): 'The worker who, for example, is paid weekly, "advances" his labour and produces the share of the weekly product which belongs to him ... before he receives "payment" from the capitalist'. Moreover, 'the capitalist can advance the worker nothing except what he has taken previously from the worker, i.e. what has been advanced to him by other people's labour' (ibid., p. 93). That Mill seeks to find in the transaction a harmonious co-operation between labour and capital, 'convenient for all parties', becomes even more evident when he visualizes a sanguine society where births are limited to a number only necessary to keep up population; the reward of the labourers is ample and a greater part of this net produce finds its way into the hands of persons 'exempt from the necessity of labour, and placed in the most favourable circumstances both for the enjoyment of happiness and for the highest intellectual and moral attainments' (1844 [1965], p. 66).

It is striking that James Mill makes no reference to a distinction, important in Ricardo, between natural and market wage. No reference is made to 'natural wage' as customary wage. Instead he proposes that the rate of wages depends upon the proportion between capital and labour. But having used the expression 'the rate of wages' in the section title, he proceeds in the text to discuss the determination of the *share* of the labourer, or the proportion in which the commodity, or its worth, is divided between him and the capitalist, and curiously the 'bargain' between the parties occurs in terms of the *'shares'*. No explanation is provided either as to the basis in practice of this form of bargain or its theoretical connotation. Further, Mill states: 'All bargains, when made in freedom, are determined by competition and the terms alter according to the state of supply and demand' (ibid., p. 42). Interestingly, Mill illustrates the principle of supply and demand by starting from an initial situation wherein 'the proportion in which commodities produced are divided between them [capitalists and workers] has fixed itself at a particular point'. It is the changes from this fixed level as occasioned by relative changes in population and means of employment that he discusses. But no explanation is given of the initial fixed 'proportion'. Mill's emphasis on the relative interplay of population and 'means of employment' at the cost of neglect of the concept of natural wage was probably the embryonic idea that was finally systematized by John Stuart Mill into the wage-fund doctrine.

James Mill on the Determination of Profits
When we examine Mill's views on profits we must note that he does not confront the question of exchange value which is treated only later. Mill begins with the view of profits and wages as shares out of net produce remaining after deduction of rent; and, since 'the active principle of change is on the side of population, and consequently wages, as the regulator', he affirms that wages determine profits (1824, pp. 72–3; 1844 [1965], pp. 70–1). James Mill elaborates considerably the explanation of profit in the third edition taking into account specifically the various meanings of Ricardo's proposition 'profits depend upon wages' including the relation between the share of wages and the *rate* of profits (and not merely as shares) and elaborating a little on the relation in terms of values, although essentially no new principle is introduced.[13]

James Mill, expounding the various meanings of the relation between wages and profits, first enunciates it as between 'share of wages and that of profits'. The inverse relation follows, although it is then a vacuous one as James Mill does not raise any question about valuation or as to how the net product is to be defined. Implicitly, it appears that Mill assumes that wages, profits and product are all homogeneous aggregates. Mill proceeds to discuss the relation in terms of 'quantities' and then denies the necessity of the inverse relation between wages and profits, if productivity of labour changes along with a change in the wage. In the third edition Mill was to introduce value, distinguishing between 'value-in-exchange' (i.e., purchasing power over other commodities) and 'cost of production' (which, referring to Ricardo, was taken as labour required for production). Mill also refers to the wage/profits relation in 'another sense' – that is, share of wages and the rate of profits, which incidentally was the one Ricardo is concerned with. He denies the necessity of the inverse relation in this case (as well as in terms of 'quantities' as above) when commodities are reckoned at value-in-exchange. His reason, however, is that productivity of labour may change due to changes in methods of production – and not with reference to the difficulty that Ricardo himself faces; which arises because of the change in the value of aggregates entering the profit-rate determination, due to a change in wage, even when methods of production remain the same. We have noted how this problem of changes in exchange value, as well as Ricardo's search for 'invariant standard', appear to have been separated from the theory of profits in Mill.

What is evident in the muddled discussion of James Mill is that he had supported the inverse relation 'in terms of proportions'; but so stated, it was a vacuous proposition. He had virtually abandoned the proposition in its meaningful and more general form because of his inadequate analysis of the question of value. It is possible that Bailey's attack on Ricardo had struck more deeply at his theory of profits so that even when James Mill continued to assert the labour theory, in parts, and rather mechanically, he had failed to follow Ricardo in his attempts to accommodate the 'modifications' required by the presence of means of production in heterogenous proportions and durabilities. The introduction of the notion of 'exchangeable value', without any deeper analysis, and of productivity changes, not only obfuscated the inverse relation but led virtually to its abandonment. The reference to productivity changes, his wage doctrine, the mutual convertibility of labour and capital, the weakening – to the point of negation – of the inverse relation between wages and the rate of profits, all tended to obfuscate the 'inner connections' of the system as analysed by Ricardo.

3   McCulloch on Value and Distribution

Despite the common impression that McCulloch was more Ricardian than Ricardo and indeed repeated a number of Ricardian tenets, we see that in his works[14] the many important features of Ricardo's analysis were eroded and some even abandoned entirely.[15]

On value, McCulloch persisted in repeating his adherence to a simple labour theory of value, while at the same time trying to imbibe the views of opponents like Malthus and Bailey, not sufficiently recognizing the contradictions that he was thus harbouring. As early as 1822, on reading some lectures by McCulloch, Ricardo was to caution him (letter dated 19 March 1822, *Works*, IX, p. 178):

> You go a little farther than I go in estimating the value of commodities by the quantity of labour required to produce them: You admit of no exception or qualification whatever, whereas I am always willing to allow that some of the variations in the relative value of commodities may be referred to causes distinct from the quantity of labour necessary to produce them.

Ricardo was to point out that apart from the first cause for variation of relative values (quantity of labour embodied), there was another; namely, a change in the wage and to add further: 'To this second cause, I do not attach near so much importance as Mr Malthus and others but I cannot wholly shut my eyes to it' (*Works*, IX, p. 178). McCulloch, who in his reply (*Works*, IX, p. 185) justified the 'simplification' for popular exposition continued in his later work the enunciation of the simple labour theory, probably for similar purposes.

What must be noted is McCulloch's notion of labour, which he invariably elaborates as 'sweat or toil' whether in his early review of Ricardo's *Principles* in the *Scotsman* where he interpreted Ricardo's theory of value in similar terms,[16] his article in the *Encyclopaedia Britannica* (1825) or in *Principles of Political Economy*, where he harked back to Locke and Hobbes for the idea that labour was the only scarce factor and hence the only source of wealth (1825, p. 41; 1864, p. 5). His notion of labour verges close to suggesting 'disutility of labour'.[17] We may contrast this with Ricardo's insistence on the distinction between wealth and exchange value (*Works*, I, pp. 273–8). McCulloch skirts round the entire question of comparabilities of different 'sacrifices' by asserting:

> But however the same amount of labour may be laid out, and whatever may be its produce, it unavoidably occasions the same sacrifice to those by whom it is performed; and hence it follows, that products of equal quantities of labour or of toil and trouble, how greatsoever the differences amongst them, are identical in their cost and consequently, also in their real value. (1864, pp. 239–40)

In this, McCulloch was not far different from Smith. But what is material is that this attempt to look at labour as a 'sacrifice' or 'force' led McCulloch to enunciate 'real cost' and to extend the concept, as we shall see, to include work done by 'natural agents' as another species of labour.

McCulloch on Ricardo's Absolute Value

McCulloch while asserting the simple labour theory of value attempted to accommodate the contrary points of view of Malthus and Bailey and also handle the problem created by capital without recognizing the deeper contradictions that remained unresolved[18] by his superficial attempts. In his *Principles*, McCulloch enunciates a distinction between 'real value' and 'exchangeable value', probably under the influence of Malthus and Bailey. (The distinction continues in all editions but the former term acquires a different connotation in later editions.) The 'exchangeable value' was first defined (1825, p. 114), 'in relation to the power or capacity which it [the commodity] possesses of exchanging for, or purchasing certain quantities of labour, or other commodities obtainable only by means of labour', while the 'real value' was defined as the 'quantity of labour that has been expended in its appropriation or production'. As Marx points out (1862–3 [1971], III, p. 170), Ricardo realized that the quantity of labour embodied in a commodity (i.e., 'real value') necessarily deviated from the power of a commodity to purchase labour. Hence he

> excluded the exchange of commodity and labour from the relative value of a commodity. For, if a commodity is exchanged for a commodity, equal quantities of labour are exchanged; but if a commodity is exchanged for labour, unequal quantities of labour are exchanged, and capitalist production rests on the inequality of this exchange.

McCulloch, on the one hand asserts: '... the quantity of labour required to produce commodities is at once the only determining principle and measure of their real and, generally speaking, also of their exchangeable value' (1825, p. 131; also 1864, p. 242). Nowhere does he indicate that his notion of exchange value, involving power to purchase labour comes essentially into conflict with this. On the other hand, he explicitly states:

> It is material, however, to observe that, speaking generally, commodities uniformly exchange for or buy more labour, or the produce of more labour, than was required for their production. And unless such were the case, a capitalist would have no motive to lay out a stock on the employment of labour; for his profits depend on his getting back the produce of a greater quantity of labour than he advances. (1864, pp. 240–1; also for similar statement, 1825, p. 120 n)

The 'exchangeable value', this would suggest, depends upon the wage since the power to purchase labour would so depend. McCulloch adds, however:

> But the cost, and, in all ordinary states of the market, the exchangeable value of commodities is not affected by these variations. The change is not in the principle that regulates and determines value – that is, in the physical exertion or sweat and toil of the labourer – but in what he obtains for it. (1864, p. 241)

McCulloch thus moves between two very different explanations of value, without confronting their distinctiveness. Also, he gives what appears as a hint that profits are to be explained on the ground of 'motive' of the capitalist. Here a distinction needs to be drawn: classical economists, including Ricardo, considered a positive rate of profit to be a precondition for viability of capitalist production, providing the 'motive'. However, the explanation of the level of profits was another matter. For Ricardo, 'profits depend upon wages' and taking the wages as customarily given, he presumed positivity of the rate of profits without proceeding to explain it. McCulloch attempts both: providing a rationale for the existence of profits and explaining its level. On the first account, he argues: 'Profits depend on his [the capitalist's] getting back the produce of a greater quantity of labour than he advances. When he buys labour, he gives the produce of that which has been performed for that which is *to be* performed' (1864, p. 241; also, for similar views, 1825, p. 120). This argument is similar to James Mill's and encounters similar difficulties. Furthermore, McCulloch extends a parallel logic even to wages, when he constructs a symmetry between capital and labour and correspondingly, between profits and wages:

> A labourer is himself a portion of the national capital and may, without impropriety be considered ... in the light of a machine which it has required a certain outlay of labour to construct; the wages which he earns are a remuneration for his services, and if we may so speak, yield him, at an average only the common and ordinary rate of profit on his capital, exclusive of a sum to replace its wear and tear. (1864, pp. 294–5; also in 1825, p. 120)

McCulloch does not show how he can reconcile this view of wages and profits with the simple labour theory of value that he upholds. Nor does he indicate how this cost-of-production view of wages is to be reconciled with the determination of the level of wages that he proposes:

> It is obvious, too, in as much as there is no fund except capital, or the commodities already produced and actually existing in a country, to feed and support the labourers, ... that the quantity of produce they receive in exchange for their labour, or their wages, must vary according to the variations in the amount of capital and in their number. (1864, p. 241; also for a similar statement, 1825, p. 120)

That is, the level of the wage is explained in terms of the size of the capital fund relative to population. Ricardo had treated these factors basically as determining the variations of the market price of labour around the natural wage.

Probably under the influence of Bailey,[19] McCulloch was to change somewhat his position on the determinants of exchange value in later editions of *Principles*. He divides commodities into two kinds: 'freely produced commodities' whose 'supply brought to market were uniformly such as could be taken off by those who were desirous of obtaining them and willing to pay the cost of their production', and another class of commodities which 'exist in limited quantities, and are, consequently subject to a natural monopoly' (1864, p. 237). In the case of the first class of commodities, allowing for accidental variations, 'there is nothing that could affect the value of commodities, except the labour expended upon them', while the exchange value of commodities in the second class 'bears no definite proportion to their cost or real value, but varies in every different degree, according to the closeness of the monopoly, and the competition for them' (1864, p. 237).

In two respects McCulloch's position on the value question stands in sharp contrast to Ricardo.

Ricardo had used 'absolute' or 'real' value to mean exchange value expressed in terms of an 'invariant standard' (see *Works*, IV, 'Absolute Value and Exchangeable Value', pp. 358–412). McCulloch was to contest not only the existence of Ricardo's 'invariant standard' but question its usefulness, even were such a standard to be found.[20] Following Bailey, whom he quotes approvingly (1864, p. 236 n) as the first to point out clearly the conditions essential to an invariable measure of 'exchangeable value', McCulloch argues that 'Exchangeable value being the power which a commodity has of exchanging for other commodities, or for labour, it follows that the exchangeable value of no single commodity can vary without occasioning a simultaneous variation in the exchangeable value of those with which it is compared'. Under these conditions, he adds 'no commodity can be constant or invariable, in its exchangeable value unless it will at all times exchange for, or purchase, the same quantity of all other commodities and of labour' (1864, p. 235). McCulloch failed entirely to appreciate Ricardo's conception of 'invariance' and its relation to his theory of exchange value and to the theory of profits. The above objection, repeating the position of Bailey was trivial, and precisely it was the 'relativity' in the exchange-value variations that prompted Ricardo to search for a standard that would enable him to locate the source of changes in value, when they occur. Moreover, McCulloch appears to have considered the issue of the 'invariant standard' as not being relevant to the issue of exchange value. He writes to Ricardo (letter dated 11 August 1823, *Works*, IX, p. 344):

> There is a radical and essential difference between the circumstances which determine the exchangeable value of commodities, and a measure of that value, which I am afraid is not always kept sufficiently in view ... as the circumstances under which every commodity is produced must always be liable to vary. None can be an invariable measure, though some are certainly much less variable than others and may, therefore, be used as approximations. It is evident I think that there neither is nor can be any real and invariable standard of value; and if so it must be very idle to seek for that which can never be found.

Ricardo was to point out (letter to McCulloch dated 21 August 1823, *Works*, IX, p. 358): 'Is it not clear that as soon as we are in possession of the knowledge of the circumstances which determine the value of commodities, we are enabled to say what is necessary to give us an invariable measure of value?'; if so, the problem of determination of exchange value and that of the 'invariant standard' were closely linked.

McCulloch on the Labour Theory of Value
The controversy concerning the measure also brought out another point of difference between McCulloch and Ricardo. The 'modifications' in the simple labour theory of value were considered essential by Ricardo due to the different composition of the means of production and labour

in different commodities. McCulloch's positions changed in his attempts to validate the labour value theory by redefining 'labour'. In a letter to Ricardo (dated 5 December 1819, *Works*, VIII, pp. 137–9), McCulloch briefly indicated his view that was later to be elaborated in his review of Malthus's *Principles* (1820) contained in a letter of 29 April to the *Scotsman*. Criticizing Torrens, McCulloch states

> the other cases [of Torrens] all proceed on the mistaken hypothesis that it is required in your theory that labour should be applied by the instrumentality of workmen; while it is altogether immaterial, provided the quantities be the same, whether it is by human hands, by machine for making beef, or by the action of natural juices in the process of fermentation.

Ricardo probably was not entirely convinced even at this stage about McCulloch's comprehension of the measure problem as he went on to describe at length to McCulloch the difference between himself and Malthus on the question (letter dated 2 May 1820, on receipt of McCulloch's review of Malthus's *Principles, Works*, VIII, p. 180). Ricardo also indicates his own hesitation, probably in reaction to Mc-Culloch's over-confident posture:

> You, I know, understand me, but I fear that I have not been particular enough in shewing the various bearings of this question. After the best consideration that I can give to the subject, I think that there are two causes which occasion variations in the relative value of commodities – 1. the relative quantity of labour required to produce them. 2-ndly the relative times that must elapse before the result of such labour can be brought to market. All the questions of fixed capital come under the second rule...

This was to be followed by the oft-quoted statement in the letter of 13 June (*Works*, VIII p. 194) where Ricardo speculated about acknowledging the *two* causes – relative labour quantity and 'the rate of profit for the time that capital remained dormant' instead of only one, the former, but feared equal difficulties in this approach. In fact, he returned to his earlier position, relying again on an appropriate choice of standard[21] which also shows the importance Ricardo attached to that choice, as part and parcel of a consistent explanation of exchange value.

McCulloch, as we have seen earlier, adhered to a simple labour theory of value in his exposition (see above for Ricardo's remark on his lecture). Much later, in 1823, he was to restate his peculiar views on the issue of capital in a letter to Ricardo, dated 11 August:

> were it not for the doubts which you entertain I should myself have none respecting the proposition that it is by the *quantity of labour* only

that all exchangeable value is to be estimated. I do not exclude all reference to time; but I refer to it only in order to assist me in discovering the quantities of labour which have been actually expended on or worked up in the commodities whose value is to be measured ... time of itself produces no effect whatever; it only affords space for really efficient agents to produce effects. But whether these agents be men, or the processes which nature herself carries on in the production of commodities seems to me to be wholly immaterial provided it require *equal capitals to set them in motion*. (*Works*, IX, pp. 342–3).[22]

In the *Scotsman* of 1 February 1824, he voiced again his disagreement with Ricardo on the same issue, and while maintaining his *result* to be the same as Ricardo's as far as the law of profits is concerned, he considered his own method superior in leading to the result 'in a much more simple and direct manner and without engaging in the enquiry respecting the effects of that rise of wages which is caused by the increased value acquired by raw produce in the progress of society'. This response of McCulloch is striking, for Ricardo had pointed out to him the cardinal error in this construction which McCulloch in fact shared with Torrens. McCulloch, however, had maintained his own method to be different from Torrens's. 'You explain', Ricardo writes to McCulloch (21 August 1823)

that you estimate the labour bestowed on a commodity by the labour bestowed on the capital or agent by which the commodity is produced. This I think is Torrens' mode of estimating value, for it is in fact saying that commodities are valuable according to the value of the capital employed on their production, and the time for which it is so employed. This is a different thing from saying that the commodities are valuable according to the quantity of labour worked up in them. I do not, however, agree with either proposition, and I would ask what means you have of ascertaining the equal value of capitals? ... These capitals are not the same in kind – what will employ one set of workman is not precisely the same as will employ another set, and if they themselves are produced in unequal times they are subject to the same fluctuations as other commodities. (*Works*, IX, pp. 359–60)

McCulloch showed little appreciation of Ricardo's criticism in his *Principles* (1825). He not only continued to treat capital as 'nothing more than the accumulated produce of '*anterior labour*' and the value of commodities as regulated by 'the total quantity, as well of immediate as of accumulated labour', – 'a sum of the two' and as such, held that employment of capital cannot affect the principle determining exchange value. The effect of a change in wages on price was treated until the last edition as if it were an addendum and as if it concerned only the question of an appropriate measure.[23] Further, he specifically referred to Ricardo's inclination to modify 'his grand principle of value' (meaning the labour theory of value) to allow for the effect of profits on capital and stated his difference. Illustrating with the case of wine, he maintained that the additional value acquired by wine during the period it has been kept in the cellar is not a compensation in return for time, but 'for the effect or change that has been produced on it' (1825, p. 166) and repeated over again his statement about 'efficient causes' (cf. letter of August 1821 above). The quantity of capital 'sets agents in motion' and 'there is not at bottom a shadow of difference in the nature of the operations effected by the aid of the machinery, from those of fermentation, and the other processes carried on inside a cask, except that they are visible to the eye, and the others are not' (ibid., p. 168). With this wholesale extension of the concept of labour to all processes including those operating through natural agents, McCulloch gets into a contradiction: he, like Ricardo, had elsewhere maintained a difference between wealth and exchange value – the natural forces do not add to exchange value,[24] and now natural agents appeared to be not dissimilar to labour.

In the second edition of *Principles*, however, McCulloch revised his position, where, acknowledging the contribution of natural agents to production, he added, 'it is, as I formerly stated, the peculiar and distinguishing feature of the natural agents, or powers, that they render their services gratuitously' (i.e. add nothing to value) (1830, p. 332).[25] Also, he explicitly pointed out that it was a mistake to contend that labour and natural agents are productive of value, in the case of wine. He does not mention, however, that this was indeed his own earlier view. His altered position in the fifth edition was that

> the producer of wine would not ... employ his capital in this way, unless it were to yield him the same return that is derived from the capital employed in other business ... the additional value which it acquires being a consequence of the profit accruing on the capital required to enable the process to be carried on. [There is a similar argument in the last edition, 1864, p. 294]

We may note that *this is no determination of the rate of profit but only elaboration of the principle of the uniformity of the rate of profit*. At the same time, McCulloch continued to maintain that the value of all non-monopolized commodities 'may be traced' solely to the quantity of labour required for their production.

McCulloch on Wages
While McCulloch does refer to the difference between 'natural' and 'market' wages he considers the former as a necessary wage stipulated only as the minimum. The actual wages, as in James Mill, are determined by the amount of capital relative to labour[26] From this McCulloch was to conclude that 'the well-being of the labouring classes is essentially dependent on the relation which they bear to capital'. The inferences drawn were two. First, the onus of determining 'their weal and their woe' rested upon the restraint applied to population. Secondly, the view that the interests of the capitalists are frequently opposed to that of the

workers was groundless: 'Labour and capital are alike dependent upon, and necessary to each other' (1864, p. 317). He argues further that the not-so-desirable state of the working classes is not to be ascribed to the capitalists' endeavouring to reduce wages but that the capitalists themselves are subject to competitive bidding and it is the relative abundance of capital to labour that decides the level of wages (ibid., pp. 318–19).

An issue on which McCulloch was vociferously to oppose Ricardo was the machinery question. Ricardo, in the third edition of his *Principles* (1821), had altered his view on the effect of introduction of machinery on employment, suggesting that consequent upon such an introduction, the level of employment could be permanently lowered and hence was injurious to the interests of the workmen. McCulloch was evidently agitated by Ricardo's stand and opposed it in no uncertain terms (see *Works*, VIII, pp. 381–6; letter dated 5 June 1821), not only on theoretical grounds but for the encouragement it would give to the Luddites. In later editions of *Principles*, McCulloch spent considerable space on elaborating how the introduction of machinery served the interests of labour – arguing in fact that the interests of capital and labour were identical.[27]

McCulloch on Profits

McCulloch sees profits, on the one hand, 'as excess of the produce realised over and above the produce necessarily expended on production'; on the other hand, as a return on advances of capital with capital itself being viewed as a product of 'the principle which prompts to save and amass, which leads man to sacrifice an immediate gratification for the sake of increased security, or of greater enjoyment at some future date' (1864, p. 54). McCulloch tended to emphasize the latter in his zeal to establish the harmony of interests and did not recognize that the two views may lead to very different explanations of profit.

McCulloch's discussion of the average rate of profit, like Mill's, does not enter into the intricacies of value theory. He approaches it by considering factors determining *proportions* in which the produce of the industry, after deduction of rent, is shared between wages and profits and accepts, as does James Mill, that 'the portion falling to either party would vary inversely as the portion falling to the other'. He questions, however, the inverse relation between the rate of profit and the share of wages in the produce on the grounds that:

(a) the productivity of industry may change; and
(b) the burden of taxation and of such other deductions from gross produce may change.

It is to be remembered, however, that Ricardo's inverse relation was proposed in the context of 'given methods of production' and the second qualification (b) pertains to the distinction between gross profits and net, post-tax profits. Finally, the inverse relation is abandoned as McCulloch sees 'innumerable exceptions to Ricardo's theory' (1864, p. 455).

4 Thomas De Quincey

Although not personally acquainted with Ricardo, De Quincey appears to have been so deeply impressed by the theoretical power of Ricardo's work[28] that he unequivocally advocated Ricardo's labour theory of value in the 'Dialogues of three templars' (1824). Written in a polemical form soon after Ricardo's death, this work earned him a place among the Ricardians. He was uncompromisingly Ricardian in the 'Dialogue' as he himself acknowledges[29] in *The Logic of Political Economy* (1844). Despite Bailey's criticism, De Quincey continued to hold his original ideas on 'various aspects of this embarrassing doctrine' (i.e., labour theory of value), although he introduced, in this later work, a number of important innovations that proved to be significant deviations. These were with regard to the definition of 'use-value', its relation to exchange value, the notion of 'market value' and his attack on Ricardo's conclusions on the distributive implications of the rent doctrine. He continued to treat prices as proportional to labour values, setting aside, rather summarily, the problem created by different compositions of the means of production as not suitable in a work dealing with 'separate principles which happen to be fundamental'. He does recognize, in passing, that this part of Ricardo's theory requires 'a more searching consideration' (1844 [1863], p. 335). He considered the search for a *measure* of value as a chimera which could never be realized and which had no practical benefit. He maintained in *Logic of Political Economy* (as well as in the 'Dialogues') that a general confusion had pervaded political economy between two ideas – a measure of value and a *ground* of value and that only the last was indispensable for analysis (1844, p. 275).

De Quincey on Value
De Quincey attributes two meanings to 'value-in-use'. One, referring to 'useability' which is essentially a qualitative notion and cannot be 'compared' with exchange value, a quantitative notion reflecting 'difficulty in production'. Possessing 'use-value' in this sense is a necessary characteristic of an article to become an object of exchange. He also defines 'use-value' in another, 'purely teleological' sense, meaning the utility of a commodity to an individual in his own estimation and proposes a measure of 'teleological value', namely, the sum which the individual considers justifies the intrinsic value of the commodity to him and would be ready to pay to obtain it rather than go without. *So defined, the 'use-value' can be put on the same quantitative scale as the exchange value.* De Quincey criticizes Adam Smith's water/diamonds paradox (namely, that a commodity with high 'use-value' may have very low exchange value and contrary wise), arguing that the exchange value can never exceed 'use-value' (in the 'teleological value' sense; for, it will then not be produced). Smith's casting the paradox in comparative terms of 'high and low levels', no doubt, lends itself to the attack. De Quincey's interpretation, however, opens up a new line of reasoning. The idea of

subjective estimation of 'use-value' by an individual and its measure in terms of the maximum price he is willing to pay rather than forego its use, was adopted later by John Stuart Mill and was fully developed in the marginalist theory of Marshall (see Bharadwaj, 1978b, Chapter 6 in the present volume).

De Quincey also discusses the distinction between 'market price' and 'natural price' which he believes is not adequately treated by Ricardo. He emphasizes the importance of this distinction to Ricardo, which induced him to write a separate, short chapter on it, as 'he would be eternally crossed by and thwarted by one and the same form of objections; viz. by those which are drawn from market value' (1844 [1863], p. 337). De Quincey, in fact, supports Ricardo further, arguing that 'the modifications to value, arising out of accidental disturbances in the market, out of casual excesses or casual defects in the supply, are in fact no objections at all' (ibid., p. 337). He also strongly opposes the idea that 'price is, or can be, determined by the relation between supply and demand'[30] his argument being; what is determined by supply relatively to demand is the deviation from natural value and it cannot fix independently the *level* itself. However, he accuses Ricardo and Smith of confounding 'market price' with 'actual price' (i.e., 'market value as a fact'), arguing that the 'market' value is a *'technical concept'* – it points to a law modifying the price, and derived from the market' (ibid., p. 237). Although De Quincey himself does not clearly formulate the distinction between 'market price' and 'actual price', it is possible that John Stuart Mill was prompted to develop the 'technical concept' into a *Law of Value* itself (see below).

De Quincey on Distribution

When De Quincey comes to the theory of distribution – wages, rents and profits – his objections appear not to be so much analytically founded as against the practical operations of the distribution relations and their political implications. Under wages, he does not distinguish between 'market' and 'natural' wage but puts down 'four elements' which govern wages: the rate of movement in the population, the rate of movement in national capital, the fluctuations in the price of the necessaries, and the traditional standard of living. Further, given that the movements in population and capital act slowly, 'by degrees fine and imperceptible', he regards the fourth element as the primary determinant of the level of wage. However, he finds fault with Ricardo's emphasis on food and denounces 'the habit of' estimating the labourer's expenses by the cost of his diet ('nay – exclusively by one item of his diet – bread') as 'radically false', although, of that, Ricardo is aware. De Quincey is particularly troubled by the use made of the proposition by the 'corn-law incendiaries' (ibid., p. 363).

It is when he comes to *Rents* that De Quincey states his reservations on Ricardo's conclusions in no uncertain terms. On analytical grounds, De Quincey upholds Ricardo's theory – arguing against a number of counter-positions.[31] While agreeing with the theoretical demonstration of Ricardo that rent arises due to extension of cultivation to lands of different fertilities, he raises objections on two grounds. One, mainly based on extant institutional arrangements: that rents may be paid from diverse sources and the surplus-sharing arrangements could be so variegated that the actual distribution between rents and profits may turn out differently than theoretically supposed. Also in actual practice, the profit and the rent elements may be intermixed, so that 'the constant excesses arising through the development of the land scale may be divisible upon any mixed principle'. Secondly, De Quincey argues that with expanding outputs, as 'rents become developed upon the land, a perpetual change is going on derivatively in the shares allotted to labourers and farmers' (ibid., p. 391). However, he does not provide any analysis of these possible derivative changes. In his commentary on Ricardo's Table of the *Essay* he takes exception to Ricardo's choosing a priori a certain level of wage which is not particularly high. He blames Ricardo for keeping 'studiously out of sight that eternal counter-movement, by an equivalent agency, to redeem the disturbed balance among the revenue-shares'. However, no alternative theory is proposed of these 'counter-movements'. What is interesting and new in this position is that changes in wages are, it is suggested, linked with changes in output.

De Quincey, while on the subject of rent, carries out a rhetorical attack on the implications of Ricardo's doctrines. Referring to a 'dreadful class' forming itself in France, Germany and England, 'of systematic enemies to property' he writes:

> It happens (though certainly not with any intentional sanction from so upright a man as David Ricardo) that in no instance has the policy of gloomy disorganizing Jacobinism, fitfully reviving from age to age, received any essential aid from science, excepting in this one painful corollary from Ricardo's triad of chapters on Rent, Profit and Wages. A stress lies on this word *triad*, for it is not from insulated views of rent that the wicked inference arises: It is by combined speculations upon the three. Separate, the doctrine of rent offers little encouragement to the anarchist, it is in connection with other views that it ripens into an instrument of mischief the most incendiary (1844 [1863], p. 397).

and so on. His own view – the more 'harmonious' – of the distributive relation was: 'The evil generates its own check ... Every fresh pulse of rent causes a new arrangement even for that which rent leaves behind, and this new arrangement more and more favours wages at the expense of profits' (ibid., p. 400).

In dealing with determination of profits, De Quincey follows Ricardo in a simple formulation. 'Profits', he declares, 'are the leavings of wages; so much will the profit be upon any act of production, whether agricultural or manufacturing, as the wages upon the act permit to be left behind' (1844 [1863], p. 407). Although he immediately raises the valid and more complex question of valuation, De Quincey falls back upon the labour theory of value to assert the inverse relation between wages and profits. Further, to the extent that 'the change that can disturb the existing relations must originate in wages', it is to wages that we turn for the determination of profits. He repeats the idea that the rate of profit in agriculture determines that in manufacturing, although we know that Ricardo himself had moved away from the position. His objections to Ricardo's results rest more on practical grounds: that, with extended cultivation, the rate of profit in agriculture may not tend to decline, in so far as there are productivity gains in agriculture due to improvements in cultivation.

5 John Stuart Mill: 'The Last of The Ricardians'

John Stuart Mill on Wages and Profits

As Ashley (1909 [1973]) remarks in his introduction to Mill's *Principles* (1871 edn): 'For good or for ill ... John Mill's economics remained those of his father down to the end of his life' and 'it may possibly be open for discussion how far James Mill was a trustworthy interpreter of Ricardo' (p. vii). While a number of Ricardian ideas make a prominent appearance in Mill, he introduced important deviations that paved the way for a transition to a new marginalist theory (for a detailed discussion see Bharadwaj, 1978a; also Marx, 1862–3 [1971], III, pp. 190–237; Schumpeter, 1954, pp. 529–30; Dobb, 1973, pp. 121–222).

John Stuart Mill follows the 'logical order' of his father's *Elements* in discussing first production and distribution prior to value and consequently his discussion, particularly of the theory of profit, remains inadequate, although he shows, in this respect, better grasp than others. In the discussion of exchange value, however, John Stuart Mill was to introduce a number of new ideas which were disruptive of the Ricardian approach. As discussed elsewhere (Bharadwaj, 1978b, Chapter 6 in the present volume) Mill was to accept, *in toto*, De Quincey's amendment of 'use-value' and its relation to exchange value; formulate, for the first time, demand as functionally dependent upon price and enunciate a 'cost of production' view of the prices, wherein both the rate of wages and profits (the latter themselves viewed as a recompense for abstinence) were considered *independent determinants* of value. Further, Mill, probably influenced by Bailey (see de Vivo, 1981), identified classes of commodities with their own separate laws of value and formulated for the first time an explicit connection between cost of production and output, hence introducing the incipient idea of varying returns, linking unit costs with variations in output. The full implications of these innovations may be seen in the contributions of Marshall towards an early formulation of the marginalist theory (see Bharadwaj, 1978b, Chapter 6 below).

On the distribution front, the incipient ideas of Mill and McCulloch on wage determination on the basis of the relative magnitudes of capital stock and population, were formalized by John Stuart Mill into the wage-fund doctrine:

> Competition ... must be regarded in the present state of society as the principal regulator of wages, and custom or individual character only as a modifying circumstance, and that in a comparatively slight degree ... wages not only depend upon the relative amount of capital and population, but cannot under the rule of the competition, be affected by anything else. (1871 [1973], p. 344)

He proceeded on this ground to refute the general idea that wages rest upon the price of food and denied the ultimate effectiveness of wage increases through bargaining or of other interventionist policies.[32] Mill formally retracted from the wage-fund doctrine in a review of Thornton's book *On Labour*, in the *Fortnightly Review* of May 1869. He accepted that the premise of a fixed wage fund 'unconditionally devoted to workers, the wages of each depending solely on the divisor, the number of participants', was wrong and hence also the doctrine regarding the futility of wage struggles. The doctrine, however, lurked in subsequent works in altered forms.[33]

As to profits, John Stuart Mill was to incorporate formally the 'abstinence' principle to justify profits: 'As the wages of the labourer are the remuneration of labour, so the profits of the capitalists are properly according to Mr Senior's well-chosen expression, the remuneration for abstinence.' Profits were only, in part, 'a recompense for forebearance'. The remuneration for mere abstinence is measured by the current rate of interest, while the surplus (profit) accruable to the capitalist is also, in part, a compensation for risk and also 'the remuneration for superintendence' (1871 [1973], pp. 405–6). On the other hand, J. S. Mill continued to adhere to the Ricardian refrain: 'The cause of profit is that labour produces more than is required for its support ... profit arises not from the incidence of exchange, but from the productive power of labour' (ibid., pp. 416–17).

J. S. Mill then turns to the question of the relation between wages and the rate of profit. His treatment in *Principles* is very brief. However, he, unlike the other Ricardians, explicitly treats the Ricardian result as referring to the share of wages in net product, after deduction of rent, and the *rate of profit*. In *Principles*, he discusses the simple case where he presumes that all advances – inclusive of materials, implements and buildings – are reducible to wages; so that,

> the two elements on which, and which alone, the gains of the capitalists depend, are, first the magnitude of the produce, in other words, the productive power of labour; and secondly, the proportion of the produce obtained by the labourers themselves. These two things form the data for determining the gross amount divided as profit among

all the capitalists of the country; but the *rate* of profit ... depends only on the second of the two elements, the labourer's proportional share, and not the amount to be shared. (ibid., p. 419)

It is in this form that J. S. Mill defends the Ricardian conclusion that the rate of profit depends upon wages and moves inversely with it. He also reformulates the Ricardian proposition, substituting 'cost of production of wages' in place of proportion of wages.

It was, however, in his essay 'On Profits and Interest' (written between 1829 and 1830 – perhaps his best work), published in *Essays on Some Unsettled Questions of Political Economy* (1844 [1967]) that J. S. Mill expresses his views at greater length and with clarity. Therein he clarifies the sense in which Ricardo's wage/profit relation is to be understood: First, that it is the rate of profit and not gross profits that Ricardo is concerned with and secondly, the rate of profits depends not upon absolute or real wages but upon 'the value of wages', where value of wages is the quantity of labour required to produce the wage goods.

> A rise of wages, with Mr Ricardo, meant an increase in the cost of production of wages; an increase in the number of hours labour which goes to produce the wages of a day's labour; an increase in the *proportion* of the fruits of labour which the labourer receives for his own share; an increase in the ratio between the wages of his labour and the produce of it. (1844 [1967], pp. 96–7)[34]

Or in other words, J. S. Mill clarifies that when all capital was reducible to wages (and the simple labour theory of value was applicable), Ricardo's position was easily demonstrable. Proceeding further Mill recognized the difficulties that Ricardo's theory would meet.[35] He recognized that the *whole* of the values (meaning, price) of the means of production which are themselves produced commodities, cannot be entirely resolved into wages. His dilemma was that there entered an element of profit into the outlay of the capitalists as the means of production themselves afforded profits to their producers.

> If any contrivance, therefore, were devised by which that part of the outlay which consists of previous profits could be either wholly or partially dispensed with, it is evident that more would remain as the profit of the immediate producer; while, as the quantity of *labour* necessary to produce a given quantity of the commodity would be unaltered, as well as the quantity of produce paid for that labour, it seems that the ratio between the price of labour and its produce would be the same as before; that the cost of production of wages would be the same, proportional wages the same, and yet profits different. (ibid., p. 99)

Here, what J. S. Mill is encountering, to put it in Marxian terms, is the difference between the rate of surplus value and the rate of profits, when constant capital is involved. In fact, Ricardo encountered the same problem in somewhat different terms: the value of the aggregates entering the determination of the rate of profit changed with a change in distribution. Mill, recognizing the difficulty, adds, 'The conclusion, then cannot be resisted that Mr Ricardo's theory is defective', but considers that

> those political economists ... who always dissented from Mr Ricardo's doctrine, or who, having at first admitted, ended by discarding it, were so far in the right; but they committed a serious error in this, that, with the usual onesidedness of disputants, they knew no medium between admitting absolutely and dismissing entirely. (ibid., p. 101).

J. S. Mill himself suggested a 'very slight' modification which he thought would suffice to render Ricardo's theory completely true. He proposes substituting '*cost of production of wages*' in place of value of wages, the cost of production of a commodity including not only the wages of the labour directly employed but also 'profits of those who, in any antecedent stage of production, have advanced any portion of those wages'. Mill, then constructs an example of corn, assuming that wages are paid in terms of corn and means of production measured in corn and shows that 'the variations ... in the rate of profits and those in the cost of production of wages go hand in hand and are inseparable'. He generalizes to conclude: 'Mr Ricardo's principle that profits cannot rise unless wages fall, is strictly true, if by low wages he meant not merely wages which are produce of a smaller quantity of labour, but wages which are produced at less cost, reckoning labour and previous profits together.' Mill's illustration implicitly relied upon the homogeneity of the produce, the means of production and wages, and he did not recognize – as Ricardo did – that once the composition of these aggregates would be diverse, the problem of valuation would need to be squarely confronted: a change in the cost of production of wages (reckoning labour and '*previous profits*') could not be given a meaning without referring to the entire system of relative prices.[36] Mill's attempt to rescue the Ricardian results in his early work was not strong and conclusive enough to battle the mounting opposition. His own statements in *Principles* on this issue were much more muted and confused. At the same time, he had unwittingly introduced a number of modifications in other parts of theory – particularly in value theory – that, despite his confident posture on its contemporaneous state, the theory was suffused with unresolved contradictions which were already moving towards 'settling the questions' in the 'marginalist' direction. It is striking to note that in the last edition of *Principles* which appears, coincidentally in 1871, Mill writes in the preface that

> since the publication of these, there has been some instructive discussion on the theory of Demand and Supply, and on the influence

of strikes and trade unions on wages, by which additional light has been thrown on these subjects; but the results, in the author's opinion, are not ripe for incorporation in a general treatise on Political Economy. (1871 [1973], p. xxxi)[37]

6 Summing Up

We may note the following features concerning the theoretical picture emerging from the works of the Post-Ricardians. Ricardo had carried forward the surplus approach to distribution and had succeeded in establishing his explanation of profit and its relation with wages in the simpler cases of the labour theory of value and all capital reducible to wages. He had recognized, however, the problem of 'capital' in a particular form, namely, in terms of deviations that occur in relative prices arising solely from a change in distribution. His attempts at solutions were not entirely successful and remained in a rather uncertain state. Ricardo had, however, indicated the direction in which he would search for a resolution of the problem: his efforts were directed towards a search for an 'invariant standard', in the course of which he had analysed relative price movements and sought to define the theoretical properties required by that standard. He indicated two alternative ways of specifying the standard: in terms of a commodity with an average composition of means of production to labour, or a commodity in which labour was invested over an average period. He did not succeed in arriving at definitive results in either case while recognizing the source of the difficulty for each of the suggested solutions. The 'inverse relation' therefore remained established unambiguously in the simple case of prices proportional to labour values.

Ricardo's followers, on the one hand, appear to have resorted to a more simplistic assertion of labour theory; while doing so, they, however, appear to have sought to reduce its possible anti-capitalist implications by suggesting mutual convertibility of capital and labour and by referring to a symmetry between profits and wages. Inevitably a problem was faced, both in explaining exchange value and the rate of profit when 'capital' was involved in production. However, the link between value and distribution was not adequately brought out. In fact, the problem of value was discussed by the two Mills, *after* discussing the 'inverse relation'. James Mill and McCulloch denied the inverse relation except in a vacuous fashion when it was stated in terms of 'proportions'. J. S. Mill, who stated the inverse relation correctly as one between wages as a proportion of net product and the rate of profits, gave a different interpretation of the inverse relation but did not succeed in establishing it in those terms. Consequently, the 'inverse relation' stated in general terms, involving prices or 'heterogenous quantities', was abandoned altogether. It is clear that the Ricardians had by-passed entirely the attempts of Ricardo in his last phase and had not tried to carry forward his reasoning. Further, the inverse relation was obfuscated by bringing in considerations of productivity changes. This shows that Ricardo's method was either not grasped or, due to conjunctural factors, not pursued. That they did not comprehend Ricardo's method is also evident from their treatment of the 'invariant standard' question. It is either ignored or its 'meaningfulness' denied (McCulloch) or when referred to, the standard is defined, as in early Ricardo, in terms of a commodity with the same amount of labour embodied in all places at all times (McCulloch; J. S. Mill). Both McCulloch and James Mill were aware of Ricardo's last paper on 'Absolute Value and Exchangeable Value' but they nowhere refer to it. (See Sraffa's comment on the paper, *Works*, IV, pp. 358–89; James Mill was to consider it not suitable for publication and McCulloch to have dropped the only reference he had made to it in his writings.) It is possible that Ricardo's terse pursuits were considered too abstruse to be followed and particularly so in popular writings. The analytical difficulties, too, appeared insurmountable. It is also significant to note that when, indeed, the question of changes in relative prices due to changes in wages was brought in and Ricardo's 'curious effects' referred to, the discussion is not linked with the question of distribution at all. Treated in a section or chapter appended to the central theme, almost as an afterthought, this discussion presupposed the inverse movement of the rate of profits with change in wages as already established and ignored the difficulties Ricardo recognized in the 'measure' of capital. Analytical difficulties apart, it would seem that the 'inverse relation' was no more expedient while the 'many exceptions' to it were.

In short, the important conclusions of Ricardo on the distributional relations were being effectively abandoned quite rapidly. While the labour theory of value was advocated, its connection with the theory of distribution was rendered tenuous. On the question of exchange value, however, Bailey's influence was creeping in. A compromise was sought in various ways, not yet consistently developed: by separating cost of production from prices or by suggesting that both *profits* and *wages* were determinants of prices, being components of cost of production (J. S. Mill). The adding-up view was coming to the forefront in different ways, amidst the confusions following the technical difficulties that the labour theory was facing. This was so even *while the specific nature of these difficulties* (in terms of deviations of prices of production from labour values) *was not cogently formulated or rigorously analysed by advancing upon Ricardo's efforts*. The scene was set for a premature abandonment of the surplus approach. One can say that while the Ricardians continued to propound certain propositions from Ricardo and the analytical questions were still being posed as Ricardo had shaped them, the *structure* of the surplus theory was already eroded. No new theory was yet in sight but enough ambiguities and confusions had been generated so that, on the one hand, the surplus approach had to be restated in clear terms by Marx and, on the other hand, the ground had been made fertile (with already some seeds sown in) for the emergence of an alternative theory.[38]

Notes: Chapter 3

This essay was first published in *Contributions to Political Economy* (1983, vol. 2, pp. 49–77) and is reprinted here with minor modifications. For very helpful suggestions, I am grateful to the editors of *Contributions*, John Eatwell, Murray Milgate and the participants at the seminars at Modena, Milan and Perugia where this paper was presented in its formative stage in May 1980.

1. Two other strands, equally significant and related to the theme of the essay, namely, the works of the 'Ricardian Socialists' who used the labour theory of value and its theoretical conclusions on distributional relations, and those of the 'dissenters' who foreshadowed certain elements of the later marginalist theories, are not discussed here.
2. All references to the *Works and Correspondence of David Ricardo* (1810-23) [1951–73] (hereafter *Works*) are indicated by volume number in roman numerals, followed by page numbers.
3. For an ongoing controversy on this interpretation, see: Sraffa (1951), Hollander (1975, 1979, 1982), Eatwell (1975), Garegnani (1982) and Bharadwaj (1983, Chapter 4 in the present volume).
4. Undue emphasis and attention has been placed on Ricardo's brief deductions by later writers. Described as 'magnificent dynamics' (Baumol, 1959, 2nd ed.), Ricardo is ascribed a dynamic model of capital accumulation, relying on the law of diminishing returns in agriculture and the Malthusian law of population, so presenting a pessimistic vision of the economy.
5. McCulloch, for example, believed that with 'fair' legislation allowing corn imports the conflict among classes would be resolved.
6. Although not all the 'Ricardian Socialists' (Godwin, Hall, Gray, Bray, Thompson and Hodgskin) use the labour theory rigorously, Ricardo's influence is noted by Foxwell (1899) in unqualified terms. Foxwell also coined the phrase 'Ricardian Socialists'.
7. See Mallet's diaries (1823 [1921], p. 253).
8. See his letter to Malthus dated October 1814, in *Works*, VI, p. 145, and Bharadwaj (1983a Chapter 4 of the present volume) for comments.
9. First published in 1821, its second edition of 1824 had no substantive changes; the third edition of 1826, reissued 1844, however, carried significant alterations particularly in sections on value and profits.
10. See Sraffa's comment (*Works*, I, p. xlix) on this issue: 'This function of the theory of value of making it possible, in the face of changes in distribution, to measure changes in the magnitude of aggregates of commodities of different kinds or, what is even more important, to ascertain its constancy, appears once more in connection with the measurement of the quantity of capital'.
11. It is also evident in the defence provided by the author of the review of Bailey's book (attributed to James Mill (1826) in *Westminster Review*) where considerable verbal play is made on the circularity of explaining value by value. Also the resolution of cost of production into labour is there considered fully satisfactory as against Bailey's argument that cost cannot be resolved into simpler elements. It may, however, be pointed out that when Bailey identifies 'cost' as if it were a homogenous quantity, he is confronted with the very same difficulty that Ricardo faced, although he, unlike Ricardo, appears to be unaware of it.

12 It is interesting to note that Mill, in the second edition, having asked 'how it [time] creates value?' (1824, p. 99) (quoted above) had proceeded thus: 'Time is a mere abstract term. It is a word, a sound and it is the very same logical absurdity, to talk of an abstract unit measuring value, and the time creating it'. Bailey (1825 [1931], p. 204) had admonished Mill for confounding 'cause' and 'standard' of value (1825 [1931], p. 204). In the review of Bailey attributed to James Mill cited earlier, Mill indicated that he had made no such error, adding; '... it is very evident from Mr Mill's language, that by standard he means cost of production'. However, in the 1824 and also the third edition of 1826, reissued 1844, he maintained that 'From the explanations here afforded, it will be easy to see what is meant by the term 'measure of value' and wherein it differs from that which we have already endeavoured to explain, the 'regulator of value'.

13 A statement appearing in the second edition (1824, p. 78) concerning the diminishing return on land leading to similar diminution in 'manufacturing and all other species of industry' is dropped in the third edition.

14 McCulloch is considered the more persistent and aggressive popularizer of Ricardo's doctrines. He was the most prolific among the Ricardians – noted also for frequent self-plagiarism (see O'Brien, 1970). His *Principles of Political Economy* which is his more substantial work was enlarged from his essay in the *Encyclopaedia Britannica* (1824, 4th to 6th Editions) and was first published in 1825, with editions following in 1830, 1843, 1849 and 1864.

15 Comparing the first with last edition of his *Principles*, we note that references to Ricardo recede: in the former, apart from the commendatory remarks, the grounds of his dispute with Ricardo on the questions of machinery and profits are expressly brought out. In the 1864 edition, McCulloch presents only his own views, not much altered, as established truths.

16 'Mr Ricardo has set out from the same premises with Dr Smith', writes McCulloch, quoting from Adam Smith: 'The real price of everything is the toil and trouble of acquiring it. What everything is really worth to the man who has acquired it, and who wants to dispose of it, or exchange it for something else, is the toil and trouble which it can save himself and which it can impose on other people' (*Scotsman*, 3 May 1817, pp. 19–20).

17 O'Brien (1970) stresses the real-cost view implicit in McCulloch but recognizes that he did not sufficiently elaborate the notion of individual disutility schedules and hence the idea remained more on a suggestive plane.

18 Marx, quoting Malthus, writes (1862–3 [1971], III, p. 168). 'Mr McCulloch, unlike other exponents of science, seems to look not for *characteristic differences*, but only for *resemblances*; and proceeding upon this principle, he is led to confound material with immaterial objects; productive with unproductive labour; capital with revenue; the food of labour with the labourer himself; production with consumption; and labour with profits' (Malthus, 1827 [1971], pp. 69–70).

19 Bailey (1825 [1931]) talked of different classes of commodities and the influence of the monopoly element on their valuation.

20 McCulloch considered the 'invariant standard' a chimera and thought it was 'entitled to no more respect, and we believe, will be crowned with no better success than the search after the philosopher's stone. (*Principles*, 1825, p. 340).

21 'I am not satisfied, as I have often told you, with the account I have given of value, because I do not know exactly where to fix my standard. I am fully persuaded that in fixing on the quantity of labour realised in

commodities as the rule which governs their relative value we are in the right course, but when I want to fix a standard of absolute value I am undetermined whether to chuse labour for a year, a month, a week, or a day' (*Works*, VIII, p. 344).

22 'In both cases [when you give them a fluid or a capital in the shape of a fluid, to turn it into wine] you employ certain capitals, that is certain quantities of labour to produce certain effects; and if the capitals be equal and the times in which the effects have been produced be different, it is at once a proof that more labour has been required to produce the one effect than the other, and an exponent of that greater quantity (*Works*, IX, p. 343). McCulloch thus defines 'quantity of labour' only circuitously to be equivalent to the value of capital.
23 The related issues were dealt with in a separate chapter indicating at the close of the previous one that 'all really important practical questions were exhausted and the following chapter, 'intended for the use of the scientific reader ... may without impropriety, be passed over by others' (1864, p. 274).
24 A full discussion of the twists and turns that McCulloch has to engage in, is in Marx (1862–3 [1971], III, pp. 180–5).
25 See O'Brien (1970), pp. 141–2.
26 '[It is] on the amount of its capital applicable to the employment of labour, and on the disposition of the owners of capital so to apply it, that the capacity of a country to support work-people at any given period, and the amount of their wages wholly depend' (1864, p. 316).
27 The following comment of Ricardo on the article of McCulloch on Corn Laws is interesting: quoting the latter's statement, 'The interests of individuals is never opposed to the interests of the public', Ricardo observes: 'In this I do not agree. In the case of machinery the interests of master and workmen are frequently opposed. Are the interests of landlords and those of the public always the same? I am sure you will not say so' (*Works*, IX, p. 194).
28 See, David Masson's editorial preface to De Quincey's *Political Economy and Politics* (1897 [1970]).
29 'The purpose of this fragment was to draw into much stronger relief than Ricardo himself had done, that one radical doctrine as to value, by which he (Ricardo) had given a new birth to Political Economy' (1844 [1863], p. 235).
30 'A [this] crazy maxim has got possession of the whole world' (p. 343). He writes in the introduction, 'Within a few moths this monstrous idea has been assumed for true by Colonel Torrens, in an express work on Economic Politics; by Lord Brougham, in relation to foreign corn trade; and by almost every journal in the land that has fallen under my own eye' (1844 [1863], pp. 237–8).
31 De Quincey clarifies a number of aspects of rent theory: the rent emerging due to 'differential' product on different qualities of land and hence a 'transfer', and as well as the issue of 'no rent' land (whether the *existence* of land paying no rent is essential for the validity of the theory). These basically go to support the Ricardian propositions.
32 He writes (1871 [1973], p. 350): 'The condition of the class can be bettered in no other way than by altering the proportion [of population to the wage fund] to their advantage; and every scheme for their benefit, which does not proceed on this as its foundation, is for all permanent purposes, a delusion.'

33 Cairnes in his *Leading Principles* (1874) attempted a reformulation. Marshall considered Mill's concession to Thornton excessive and the idea of 'subsistence fund' in the Austrian theory was given currency by Böhm-Bawerk as an important element in an alternative theory of distribution.
34 So conceptualized, profits are identical with Marx's surplus value.
35 'We have now arrived at a distinct conception of Mr Ricardo's theory of profits in its most perfect state. And this theory we conceive to be the basis of the true theory of profits. All that remains to be done is to clear it from certain difficulties which still surround it, and which, though in a greater degree apparent than real, are not to be put aside as wholly imaginery' (1844 [1967], p. 98).
36 While Mill's demonstration remained inadequate, later works of Sraffa (1960) and Garegnani (1960) have shown that Mill's conclusion, 'the rate of profit cannot fall unless concurrently with one of two events: first an improvement in the labourers condition; or secondly an increased difficulty of producing or importing some article which labourer habitually consumes', has substantive content.
37 The reference is to the debate in the *Fortnightly Review* following J. S. Mill's review of Thornton's *On Labour* in May and June 1869 and Thornton's reply included in the second edition of his book. Marshall's early formulation of his theory was to be stimulated by this controversy (see Bharadwaj, 1978b, Chapter 6 in the present volume).
38 This assessment is close to that of Marx (1862–3 [1971]), Meek (1950) and Dobb (1973). A very different position is taken by Hollander (1977) in denying a decline in Ricardian theory and the related notion of a 'dual' development in economic theory. Fetter (1969) offers a review of views concerning the essence of the Ricardian contribution and finds, given their spectrum, the dating of the decline a hunt for a 'will-o-the wisp'.

References: Chapter 3

Ashley, W. (1909 [1973]), Editorial introduction to J. S. Mill, *Principles of Political Economy*, 1871 edn (New York: A. M. Kelley reprint)

Bailey, S. (1825 [1931]), *A Critical Dissertation on the Nature, Measure and Causes of Value* (London: London School of Economics Reprints of Scarce Tracts, no. 7)

Baumol, W. J. (1959), *Economic Dynamics*, second edition (New York)

Bharadwaj, K. (1978a), *Classical Political Economy and the Rise to Dominance of Supply and Demand Theories* (Calcutta: Orient Longman); Revised edition, 1986

Bharadwaj, K. (1978b), 'The subversion of classical analysis: Alfred Marshall's early writing on value', *Cambridge Journal of Economics*, vol. 2, no. 3 (September), pp. 253–71; Chapter 6 in the present volume

Bharadwaj, K. (1983), 'On a controversy over Ricardo's theory of distribution', *Cambridge Journal of Economics*, vol. 7 (March), pp. 11–36; Chapter 4 in the present volume

Blaug, M. (1958), *Ricardian Economics* (New Haven)

Cairnes, J. E. (1874), *Some Leading Principles of Political Economy Newly Expounded* (London)

De Quincey, T. (1824), *Dialogues of three templars on political economy*, *London Magazine* (April/May)

De Quincey, T. (1844 [1863]), *The Logic of Political Economy*, in *Collected Works*, Vol. XIII (Edinburgh: Adam & Charles Black)

De Quincey, T. (1897 [1970]), *Political Economy and Politics*, in *Collected Works*, Vol. IX, ed. by D. Masson (New York: A. M. Kelley reprint)
de Vivo, G. (1981), 'John Stuart Mill on value', *Cambridge Journal of Economics*, vol. 5 (March), pp. 67–9
Dobb, M. H. (1973), *Theories of Value and Distribution since Adam Smith* (Cambridge: Cambridge University Press)
Eatwell, J. L. (1975), 'The interpretation of Ricardo's *Essay on Profits*', *Economica*, vol. 42, No. 166 (May), pp. 182–7
Fetter, F. W. (1969), 'The rise and decline of Ricardian economics,' *History of Political Economy*, 1, (Spring) pp. 67–84
Foxwell, H. S. (1899), *Introduction* to Menger Anton's *Right to the Whole Produce of Labour* (London)
Garegnani, P. (1960), *Il capitale nelle teorie della distribuzione* (Milan: Giuffre)
Garegnani, P. (1982), 'On Hollander's interpretation of Ricardo's early theory of profits', *Cambridge Journal of Economics*, vol. 6, no. 1 (March), pp. 65–77
Garegnani, P. (1984), 'Value and distribution in the classical economists and Marx', *Oxford Economic Papers*, vol. 36, pp. 291–325
Hollander, S. (1977), 'The reception of Ricardian economics', *Oxford Economic Papers*, vol. XX (July), pp. 221–57
Hollander, S. (1975), 'Ricardo and the Corn Profits Model and Reply to Eatwell', *Economica*, vol. 42
Hollander, S. (1979), *The Economics of David Ricardo* (Toronto: Heinemann)
Hollander, S. (1982), 'A Reply (to Roncaglia, 1982)', *Journal of Post-Keynesian Economics*, vol. IV
Mallet, J. L. (1823 [1921]), 'Diaries', in *Centenary Volume of the Political Economy* (London: Macmillan)
Malthus, T. R. (1815a), *The Grounds of an Opinion on the Policy of Restricting the Importation of Foreign Corn* (London: Murray)
Malthus, T. R. (1815b), *An Inquiry into the Nature and Progress of Rent* (London: Murray)
Malthus, T. R. (1827 [1971]), *Definitions in Political Economy* (New York: A. M. Kelley reprint)
Malthus, T. R. (1920), *Principles of Political Economy*, first edn (London: John Murray)
Marshall, A. (1890 [1961]), *Principles of Economics*, 9th Variorium edn, ed. by C. W. Guillebaud, 2 vols (London: Macmillan)
Marx, K. (1862–3 [1971]), *Theories of Surplus Value*, Part III (Moscow: Progress Publishers)
McCulloch, J. R. (1817), 'Review of Ricardo's *Principles*', *Scotsman*, 3 May, pp. 119–20
McCulloch, J. R. (1818), 'Ricardo's political economy', *Edinburgh Review*, XXX, no. LIX, June, pp. 59–87
McCulloch, J. R. (1820),'Review of Malthus's *Principles*, *Scotsman* (29 April), p. 143.
McCulloch, J. R. (1824), 'Political economy', supplement to 4th and 6th edns of *Encyclopaedia Brittanica* April; first appearing as an article in the supplement to the fourth and fifth edition, dated April.
McCulloch, J. R. (1825), *Principles of Political Economy*, 1st edn (Edinburgh: A. & C. Black).
McCulloch, J. R. (1830), *Principles of Political Economy*, 2nd edn (Edinburgh: A. & C. Black).
McCulloch, J. R. (1859), *Treatises and Essays* (Edinburgh: A. & C. Black)

McCulloch, J. R. (1864), *Princilpes of Political Economy*, 6th edn (Edinburgh: A. & C. Black)
Meek, R. L. (1950), 'The decline of Ricardian economics in England', *Economica*, Vol. 17, No. 1 (February), pp. 43–62, in Meek, R. L. (1967), *Economics and Ideology and Other Essays* (London)
Mill, James (1821), *Elements of Political Economy*, 1st edn (London: Bohn)
Mill, James (1824), *Elements of Political Economy*, 2nd edn (London: Bohn)
Mill, James (1826), *Elements of Political Economy*, 3rd edn revised and corrected, reissued 1844 (London: Bohn)
Mill, James (1826 [1967]) 'On the Nature, Measures, and Causes of Value', *Westminster Review*, V, No. IX, January, 157–72, reprinted in Cass (ed.), Bailey's *Critical Dissertations*, London, 1967
Mill, James (1844 [1965]), *Elements of Political Economy*, reissue of 3rd edn of 1826 (New York: A. M. Kelley reprint)
Mill, J. S. (1844 [1967]), *Essays on Some Unsettled Questions of Political Economy*, in J. M. Robson (ed.), *Collected Works*, Vol. IV (Toronto: Toronto University Press)
Mill, J. S. (1848 [1965]), *Principles of Political Economy*, ed. by W. J. Ashley (New York: A. M. Kelley reprint)
Mill, J. S. (1869), 'Thornton's *Labour*', *Fortnightly Review*
Mill, J. S. (1871 [1973]), *Principles of Political Economy*, ed. by W. J. Ashley (New York: A. M. Kelley reprint)
O'Brien, D. P. (1970), *J. R. McCulloch: A Study in Classical Economics* (London: Allen & Unwin)
Ricardo, D. (1810–23 [1951–73]), *Works and Correspondence of David Ricardo*, ed. by P. Sraffa with the collaboration of M. H. Dobb, 10 vols and Index (Cambridge: Cambridge University Press)
Schumpeter, J. (1954), *History of Economic Analysis* (New York: Oxford University Press)
Sraffa, P. (1951–73), Editorial introductions to *Works and Correspondence of David Ricardo*, Vols I–X, op. cit.
Sraffa, P. (1960), *Production of Commodities by Means of Commodities: Prelude to a Critique of Economic Theory* (Cambridge: Cambridge University Press)
Torrens, R. (1815), *An Essay on the External Corn Trade* (London: Longman)
West, E. (1815), *Essay on the Application of Capital to Land* (London: Underwood)

4
On a Controversy over Ricardo's Theory of Distribution

The long-present controversies over the evaluation of Ricardo's contribution, approach and mode of theorizing have recently intensified. There have been concerted efforts, on the one hand, to revive and advance 'surplus-based' theories, investigating their origin and development in Smith, Ricardo and Marx and, on the other hand, to argue, as did Marshall for a doctrinal continuity from Smith to the modern neoclassicists. Samuel Hollander's *The Economics of David Ricardo* (1979)[1] underlines the continuity thesis, maintaining that both Smith and Ricardo shared a theory of resource allocation which rested upon a supply-and-demand analysis, akin to 'neoclassical procedures'. Thus Hollander argues against the idea of dual development in analytical history. His canvas is vast[2] and controversial as are his interpretations. Here we take up only one theme: Ricardo's theory of value and distribution with which Hollander is 'particularly concerned' as forming the 'analytical core' and which Ricardo himself regarded as his original contribution. After presenting some comments on the overall position of Hollander on this issue, we examine his interpretation of the genesis and development of Ricardo's theory of profits in three chronological parts: (1) the early period of the bullionist controversy; (2) the pre-*Essay*[3] correspondence of 1814, the *Essay*, and the post-*Essay* debates between Ricardo and Malthus; and, (3) the *Principles*.[4] In the last section we take up Hollander's view of Ricardo as a precursor of general equilibrium theory.

1 The Analytical Core of the Ricardian Theory: Counter-Positions on the Genesis and Development of Ricardo's Theory of Profit

Hollander's view that Ricardo's original contribution lay in the domain of value and distribution and that his value theory furnishes essentially 'a necessary preliminary' for the determination of the rate of profits is not disputed. However, Hollander sees 'the essence of the Ricardian contribution' and the development of Ricardo's theory of profit differently from Sraffa in his editorial introductions to Ricardo's *Works* and reconstructs the passage along a different – although apparently parallel – route. To Hollander 'the essence of the Ricardian contribution and the significance, indeed the primary objective, of Ricardo's analytical work' lay in his 'fundamental conception' that 'wage rate increases are non-inflationary and at most generate an alteration in relative prices within limited bounds' (p. 7). This position, Ricardo formulated as a direct challenge to Smith's proposition that all wages increases are passed on by capitalists in the form of higher prices of manufactures; in particular, that the price of corn regulates the prices of all other things. Hollander argues, more specifically, that the weakness of the Smithian position was recognized by Ricardo even during the bullionist controversy. Hence his inference that, from those early times onwards, Ricardo had cast his problem in terms of a relation between the (money) wage and the rate of profits; in fact that 'Ricardo was, throughout, preoccupied by the link between the money price of corn, the money wage, and the money price of manufacturers, and sought to demonstrate rigorously that an increase in the money-wage rate – assuming constancy in the 'value' of money – must entail a fall in the general profit rate' (pp. 11–12). Hollander regards his own view of the genesis of the theory of profit as having 'profound implications for any evaluation of the intended scope of Ricardo's model construction' (p. 7). In particular, the well-known reading of the *Essay* on profit, given by Sraffa, wherein Ricardo resorted to corn quantities to establish unambiguously a strict relation between wages and the rate of profits, is challenged (see below). Hollander's contention is that in the correspondence prior to the *Essay*, in the *Essay*, and after, as much as in the *Principles*, Ricardo was working in terms of a relation between changes in the *money* wage rate and the rate of profits, and further, that Ricardo utilized explicitly or implicitly principles of resource allocation, 'learned from the *Wealth of Nations*', relying on 'supply and demand mechanisms'.

This may be contrasted with the line of development of Ricardo's theory of profit traced by Sraffa in his editorial introduction to the *Principles* (I, pp. vii–lxii).[5] Up to March 1813, Ricardo was preoccupied with currency questions and by August 1813 the discussion between him and Malthus turns to the question of the effect of increase of capital on the rate of profits. While the issue of importing corn is not yet explicit, the essential elements of Ricardo's theory of profit appear to be already present: That, 'only improvements in agriculture, or new facilities for the production of food, that can prevent an increase of capital from lowering the rate of profits' (IV, p. 3). When, in February 1815, Malthus' (and others') pamphlets on rent appeared, Ricardo incorporated them easily into his already developed theory of profits, to be presented in the *Essay*. In the *Essay*, and in the letters of 1814, and early 1815, a basic principle is that the profits of the farmer regulate the profits of other trades. This principle disappears from the later *Principles* and is substituted there by the more general proposition that the productivity of labour on land which pays no rent is fundamental in determining general profits. Sraffa offers the by now well-known rational foundation for the principle of the determining role of the profits of agriculture, that 'in agriculture the same commodity, namely corn, forms both the capital (conceived as composed of the subsistence necessary for workers) and the product; so that the determination of profit by the difference between total product and capital advanced, and also the determination of the ratio of this profit to the capital, is done directly between quantities of corn without any question of valuation' (I, p. xxxi). If there is to be a uniform rate of profit in all trades, the exchange value of other products would have to adjust so as to yield the same rate of profit in them as in the growing of corn. While trying to expand this argument of the *Essay* and to generalize it, *in the face of the persistent criticism of Malthus*, Ricardo was bedevilled increasingly by the question of the relative values of commodities. Ricardo appears to have realized the unavoidable necessity of dealing with the subject of value when he wrote to Mill: 'I know I shall be soon stopped by the word Price' (VI, p. 348, letter dated 30 December, 1815).[6] In the *Essay*, at the cost of considerable simplification, he had been able to demonstrate how the rate of profit is determined without having to confront the problem of 'reducing to a common standard' a heterogenous collection of commodities. *It was only after he had adopted a general theory of value (labour theory) in the* Principles *that Ricardo was enabled firstly to demonstrate his principle of profit in a general setting and secondly 'he was enabled to abandon the simplification that wages consist only of corn'* (I, p. xxxii, italics added). The surplus approach to profit determination, transparently evident in the corn case, could then be vindicated in a more general setting: 'It was now labour, instead of corn, that appeared on both sides of the account ...' (I, p. xxxii). Ricardo realized that difficulties would be created by relative values changing with a change in wage, thanks to differential compositions of capital and labour and of capital itself – all reducible to one of 'time'.[7] The problem of value that engaged Ricardo until the last was one of finding a consistent measure which would be invariant with respect to changes in the division of product between wages and profits so that, adopting such a measure, the relation between changes in the wage-share and the rate of profits could be clearly and unambiguously perceived.

Sraffa comments that another theme is to be discerned developing *parallel to this* in Ricardo's thought. At first, Ricardo had not regarded the generally accepted view, derived from Smith, that a rise in corn prices, through its effect on wages, generates a rise in *all* other prices, as being contradictory to his own theory of profits. The contradiction did not emerge 'so long as the latter has been expressed in its primitive agricultural form', but appeared inevitably with his successive attempts towards a more general formulation of the theory 'since the supposed general rise of prices obscured the simple relation of the rise of wages to the fall of profits' (I, p. xxxiii). Already in the *Essay* the later developments were foreshadowed in certain passages (more on this, later). The hints present in the *Essay*, reflecting partially some elements in Ricardo's approach, were later taken up in the *Principles* 'with the addition of several new ones which were to be characteristic features of Ricardo's theory. The turning point in the transition from the *Essay* is suggested, according to Sraffa, when Ricardo realized, *encountering the criticism of Malthus in the post-*Essay *correspondence*, at the end of 1815,[8] the need for a systematic theory of value providing the basis for a general solution to the distribution problem. He saw the need to distinguish clearly between causes which affect the value of money and those affecting relative values, to discover the substantive principles for the invariance property of the value-standard and *to provide a rigorous basis for his opposition to Smith's view* (that the price of corn regulates all other prices). Further, Sraffa maintains that 'the importance which Ricardo came to attach to the principle that the value of a thing was regulated by the quantity of labour required for its production, and not by the remuneration of that labour, reflected his recognition that *what his new theory was opposed to was not merely the popular view of the effect of wages on prices but another and more general theory of Adam Smith (of which that effect came to appear as a particular case)* – what Ricardo referred to in writing to Mill as Adam Smith's 'original error respecting value'[9] (I, p. xxxv, italics added). This latter theory maintained that, with accumulation of stock and appropriation of land (that is emergence of profits and rents) the price of a commodity is arrived at by a process of *adding up* the wages, profits and rents.

The central theme in Sraffa's reading of Ricardo is the determination *of the rate of profits, applying the surplus principle. The manner in which Ricardo arrived at and viewed the successive difficulties in resolving the questions of the profit rate determination and the wage/profit relation as well as the approach he took in seeking the resolution of those problems reveal the peculiarities of the underlying surplus approach which continues through his successive formulations.*

While Sraffa's account thus turns on the elaboration and the extension of the surplus approach in Ricardo, Hollander spins his account around *a particular proposition* – the effect of corn prices, via the money wage, on all other prices. According to him, the weakness of the Smithian proposition is recognized by Ricardo as early as during the bullionist controversy; the *Essay's* 'corn-quantity calculations' are a *temporary reversion* to a grossly simple 'strong case', and the *Principles* is only a further extension and elaboration of the money wage/profit rate relation, under the assumption of fixed factor proportions whereby use of labour values is validated or under the explicit/implicit rules of 'resource allocation guided by the supply and demand mechanisms'. This interpretation leads, among others, to the following points of attack on the surplus-based interpretation of Ricardo, and with which we would be mainly concerned in the following:

(a) It seeks to refute Sraffa's view of the 'material rate' basis for the profit determination in the *Essay* and, at the same time, underplays the substantive importance of the determining role of the agricultural rate of profit in the early theory of profits. Hollander thereby negates the 'turning point' arguing that Ricardo was always, even in the pre-*Essay* period, preoccupied with the *money wage*/rate of profit relation.

(b) Hollander's exposition of the *Principles* is directed by a two-fold aim. He attacks, on the one hand, specific elements in the surplus explanations and, on the other hand, uses his own interpretations to forge links with 'the neoclassical procedures', adopting the by now familiar technique of attributing special assumptions to Ricardo, which, when relaxed, would, it is argued, establish compatibility with the neoclassical general equilibrium theory. To Ricardo, for whom money (or 'gold') was like any other commodity, the relation between *money* wage and the rate of profits posed an identical – and no other – requirement than the one that would arise in the case of a general relation between *real* wage, as a complex of commodities, and the rate of profits; namely, a consistent general theory of relative values and correspondingly defined 'invariant standard'. Hollander, however, reduces the labour theory of value and Ricardo's basis for defining an 'invariant standard' to 'an empirical principle'. Consequently, he negates any substantive role played by the more sophisticated standard proposed in the third edition of *Principles* while bypassing without comment the difficulties *seen by Ricardo* in measuring the 'quantity of capital'. He also rejects the generic similarity between Ricardo's attempts to deal with 'modifications' of the labour theory and Marx's transformation of values into prices. These specific elements and features of Ricardo which Hollander attempts to refute are indeed peculiarities characteristic of Ricardo's (surplus) approach.

2 The Pre-*Essay Period of the Bullionist Controversy*

Attempting to find the nature and timing of Ricardo's transition from the Smithian proposition on value stated above, Hollander finds the first clear indication of a theory of profit in early 1813, with roots extending back to 1811. The major significance[10] of thus carrying Ricardo's theory of profit backwards to the period of the monetary debates is that thereby Hollander bolsters up his thesis that, all through, Ricardo was concerned with establishing the relation between *money wage* and the rate of profits and that he explicitly considered the effect of changes in wages via the corn price on commodity prices, using relative values.

What supporting evidence and arguments does Hollander offer? First, Hollander refers to an early letter of Ricardo to Mill (dated 26 September 1811) where Ricardo 'shows an awareness' of the notions of relativity of value and, distinguishing between 'value' and 'price' mentions the 'invariable measure' (VI, p. 54). It is highly doubtful whether we can at all infer from this piece of evidence a clear perception of a theory of relative prices. At this juncture, the distinction between value and price remains purely definitional: value is expressed in terms of any other commodity, while price is expressed in terms of money. This involves no *theory* of relative prices. Again, while the invariance of the standard is mentioned in Ricardo's writings of this period, it is done incidentally, the context of the stability of prices being very different. As we shall see, the requirements of the 'invariant standard' in later Ricardo were intimately connected with his explanation of profit and the theory of exchange value developed in that context and, furthermore, these requirements changed along with his attempts at more rigorous formulations of the theory of exchange value. It is clear that, even at this early stage, Ricardo regards money as a commodity, so that its value varies when its conditions of production alter. However, no general analysis of these relations obtains and the notion of 'intrinsic value' is suggested to be dependent upon 'scarcity' which is described alternatively to mean the high quantity of labour bestowed in procuring the commodity (III, p. 52).[11]

By Hollander's own statement (pp. 105–6) Ricardo is a full-fledged Smithian during the bullionist debates, on all issues touching upon value and distribution. We find Ricardo denying any relation between money supply and the rate of interest and fully supporting the Smithian doctrine of the rate of profits in terms of 'competition of capitals'. *In particular, Ricardo holds the view that a rise in corn price is followed by a rise in all prices*.

Hollander offers a reconstruction of the transition from the Smithian phase to its refutation. He suggests that the constituent elements of Ricardo's theory of profit were available to him from a very early date (1811) and *'could logically have been brought together in 1813 to form a new (though incompletely formulated) theory of profit ...'* (p. 118, italics in original).[12] This suggestion is built upon a number of speculations. First, Hollander alleges Ricardo to be insistently holding the view that an increase in money supply is an essential condition for a (permanent) rise of general prices 'except where taxation is responsible for higher prices' (p. 108). This position would have been inconsistent with the Smithian proposition that money wage increases will be passed on to the consumers in higher prices. Indeed, Hollander stresses that Bentham (1954, p. 131 n) had already raised this difficulty of non-viability of a general rise in prices without an increased money supply. Thus Ricardo would appear to have grounds to dispute the Smithian proposition.

Hollander's interpretation faces two basic difficulties. It is questionable, first, whether Ricardo asserted the *essentiality* of an increased money supply in the stated context and, second, whether he himself perceived any such connection between the proposition and its incompatibility with the Smithian proposition. *On both*, Hollander's arguments are weak. The more extensive evidence that he offers on the first, in fact, concerns Ricardo's argument against Bosanquet,[13] that no additional money supply would be required for the same amount of commodities to be circulated when commodity prices increase due to taxation. Ricardo had argued that taxation brings about only a reallocation of purchasing power between government and private consumers.[14] From this Hollander derives an implication in the contrary case: 'if a higher general price level is to result from an increase in wages – the latter increase itself due to some cause *other than taxation* – a higher volume of currency would be required'. But this inference is not ascribable to Ricardo with any degree of confidence nor does it follow uniquely from Hollander's evidential support. In fact, Ricardo's discussions of the period point to various alternative possibilities. In the *Reply to Bosanquet*, Ricardo, alluding to the scarcity of corn and consequent increase in price, had argued that 'because its value is doubled, that double the value of money will be necessary to circulate it' is 'by no means obvious or necessary' (III, p. 244). Since Ricardo at that time accepted that a rise in corn price increases all other prices and Bosanquet was himself alluding to that result we may (as Hollander himself does) infer that the situation under consideration is of a general price-rise. In the *Notes on Bentham*, cited by Hollander (p. 110), Ricardo considers the rise in prices associated with reduced production and thus requiring no additional money supply for their circulation.[15] Ricardo in some places considers a rise in prices to imply a fall in the relative value of money, the latter being considered like any other commodity.[16] In the *High Price of Bullion*, he discusses the laws which regulate the value of money, its exports and imports, as being the same as for any other commodity, and traces the effects of 'successive bad harvests' on exports of money. Furthermore, Ricardo explicitly considered various distributive implications of the rise of prices, not only between the private consumer and the government when the price rise follows upon taxation, but among different social classes. Hollander himself discusses the former case.[17] Ricardo wrote about the differential impact of the change in the price of produce on farmers and landlords,[18] the creditor, the stockholder and the annuiant, etc. (III, pp. 137–8).[19] These redistributive effects are not dissimilar to the ones attributed to taxation. Hollander's inference, therefore, that Ricardo insisted upon an increased money supply as a precondition for a higher level of prices does not find adequate support. Further, Hollander himself appears uncertain as to whether Ricardo saw the difficulty that such a position would have posed for the Smithian proposition that a money wage increase will be passed on to the consumers in the form of higher prices.

The second building block in Hollander's reconstruction happens to be Trotter's formulation (Trotter, 1810) of the principle of diminishing returns – that, with increasing population poorer soils are taken under cultivation, 'and the produce therefore will be obtained and must be sold at an increased expence' (quoted, p. 112). This argument, however, was explicitly rejected by Ricardo, in favour of the Smithian position that increasing capitals, through their competition, lead to declining prices. Hollander has to concede that Ricardo himself was 'unaware of the potent mixture' which should have, in Hollander's view, yielded his theory of profit. Furthermore, not only does Ricardo reject Trotter but does so, *not on the basis of the monetary arguments, but on the basis of the Smithian 'competition of capitals'*. Hollander's 'attractive reconstruction' is confessedly weak (p. 118). In fact, the 'papers on profits' of 1813 were written by Ricardo while he continued allegiance to the Smithian result on the effect of a corn-price increase. And when he subsequently questioned the Smithian result it was not on monetary grounds. *Hollander himself finds this surprising* and has to maintain that 'Ricardo's attention was now [1814] upon the need for a real cost theory of money value, and accordingly reliance upon a form of quantity theory may not have been as attractive or as self-evident an expedient in 1814 as it has been a year earlier' (p. 123). A good reason for this unexplained shift of ground may be that Ricardo indeed, in the very first place, had not relied on such arguments as are used in Hollander's reconstruction. *Further, what is missed out in the reconstruction is that Ricardo, in order to link up effectively changes in corn price and the rate of profit via effects on money wage, would have required a systematic theory of relative values and not just variations in the 'general price level' permissible or otherwise on quantity theory grounds.*

*The Pre-*Essay *Correspondence: The Theory of Profits in 1814*
Hollander turns to the pre-*Essay* correspondence mainly to propose that Ricardo's theory of profit of 1814 developed as a sequel to that in 1813, taking into account the effect of corn-price increases upon the profit rate, manufacturing prices tending to rise in consequence of higher wages but in less proportion. Hollander's main concern here is to challenge, on the basis of the 1814 evidence, the view: 'that Ricardo in his *Essay* accorded agricultural profits the determining role on the basis of the assumption that only in agriculture does the same commodity constitute both input and output, and with the further notion that the *Essay* and *Principles* constitute two substantially different systems' (p. 123).[20] An explicit statement of the theory of profit, regarded by Sraffa as substantially the same as in the *Essay*, appears in Ricardo's letter to Trower dated 8 March 1814.[21] The letter contains the striking proposition that 'it is the profits of the farmer which regulates profits of all other trades', for which Sraffa provides the rational foundation (see above). Hollander introduces, in the course of his arguments, a distinction between the 'strong proposition': 'that the agricultural profit rate determines the profit rate elsewhere', or a more sophisticated variation thereof, 'that the state of agricultural productivity on the margin of cultivation is the *unique determinant* of the general profit rate, in so far as corn is the sole wage good'; and the 'weaker' proposition: 'that the state of agricultural productivity exerts an influence on the general profit rate although not to the exclusion of other forces' (p. 138, italics as in the original). Hollander's aim is to establish that Ricardo's position in the correspondence of 1814 as well as in the *Essay* implies the 'weak' formulation which is but a step from the *Principles*. To do this, he has first to explain (away) Ricardo's explicit statements on the determining role of agricultural profits,[22] and then, second, he has to challenge the evidence proferred by Sraffa in support of his position, providing alternative interpretations of the correspondence.

Furthermore, he has to explain how Ricardo could have established at this early stage a general relation between money wage and the rate of profits, requiring recourse to a scheme of 'relative prices'.

At the outset, certain general observations may be made regarding the pre-*Essay* 1814 correspondence between Ricardo and Malthus. *Both remain far from formulating a systematic theory of relative prices. Not only that, they appear not to have clearly grasped the source of their difficulties in the lack of such a formulation.* In fact, the question of relative prices emerges, and Ricardo decides to confront it, only after realizing the inadequacy of his earlier arguments resting basically on the material rates of produce (corn) and their analogous extensions to include other necessaries besides corn, in the course of the post-*Essay* debate with Malthus. We must also bear in mind an aspect of Ricardo's method brought out by Garegnani (1982). Ricardo, at this stage not yet possessing a theory of relative values, could not have obtained a general relation between money wages and the rate of profit. It appears that he asserted with confidence a theory of profit derived on the basis of corn quantities and extended it, relying on the strength of an analogy to other necessaries entering wages. The recurrent emphasis on 'corn', 'food', 'raw produce' which is a feature of the 1814 correspondence[23] (and of the *Essay*), the numerical illustrations therein (referred to by Hollander himself as a 'better' evidence of the corn argument) informs a style of reasoning by Ricardo wherein a general proposition linking wages to the rate of profits is closely followed by, or follows upon, a specific proposition referring to cheapening or otherwise of 'food', 'corn' or 'raw produce'. These illustrate the intuitive logical basis of Ricardo's derivation and insistent assertions and the method of analogy, referred to earlier. The corn (or material rate) argument appears, in unambiguous terms, when Malthus states Ricardo's position in order to controvert the determining role of agricultural rate of profit.[24] Garegnani (1982) has dealt intensively with these issues, including Hollander's handling of the evidence adduced by Sraffa in support of his interpretation. We shall focus on other supplementary issues.

A close look at the correspondence of 1814, keeping to the sequence in which arguments between Malthus and Ricardo develop, would be important in order to recognize the peculiarities of Ricardo's theory and, in that light, to view Hollander's interpretations. Even prior to the well-known letter to Trower, containing the farmer's profit principle, Ricardo, referring to his 'theory' maintains, in a letter to Malthus (dated 17 August 1813; VI, pp. 94–5) that 'increases in wealth and prosperity' need not necessarily be attended with increased profit; the latter is connected with 'facilities in the production of food'. Ricardo was to summarize his position to Trower (letter dated 8 March 1814, cited above).

> Nothing, I say, can increase the profit permanently on trade, with the same or an increased Capital, but a really cheaper mode of obtaining food. A cheaper mode of obtaining food will undoubtedly increase

profit says Mr Malthus but there are many other circumstances which may also increase profits with an increase of capital. The discovery of a new market where there will be a great demand for manufacturers is one. (VI, pp. 104–5)

Immediately following, Malthus must have raised the issue of a rise of corn price stimulating demand and hence profits. For, Ricardo, replying on 26 June, argues that corn-price-rise, without any augmentation of capital must necessarily diminish demand for other things. Ricardo, we note here, resorts to the Smithian proposition – all prices rising with corn – without recognizing the difficulties it would pose for his theory of profit. Further he maintains that with the same capital and higher prices there would be less production and hence less demand since 'demand has no other limits but the want of power of paying for the commodities demanded. Everything which tends to diminish production tends to diminish the power' (VI, p. 108).[25] We note that, while reacting to the issue of demand raised by Malthus, Ricardo presents his view on the determination of the rate of profit *as a separate issue*: 'The rate of profits and of interest must depend on the proportion of production to the consumption necessary to such production, – this again essentially depends upon the cheapness of provisions, which is after all, whatever intervals we may be willing to allow, the great regulator of the wages of labour' (VI, p. 108). Sraffa considers this as the nearest *explicit* statement by *Ricardo* now extant, indicating the use of material-rate-of-produce argument[26] and of which Malthus's refutation in the following words is an echo: 'In no case of production is the produce exactly of the same nature as the capital advanced. Consequently, we can never properly refer to a material rate of produce, independent of demand, and of the abundance or scarcity of capital' (letter dated 5 August; VI, p. 117). Hollander treating this remarkable phrasing of Malthus as casual stresses the contextual connection with the debate between Ricardo and Malthus on aggregate demand.[27] That Ricardo's determination of profit is independent of the issue of demand is evident from the same letter of 26 June where he draws implications from a restriction on imports of 'raw materials ... of which corn is the principal'; different from those following restrictions on other commodities. The former affects profits ('lowers the rate of interest') while the latter deprives the country of luxuries and abundance 'but the rate of interest would not fall' (VI, p. 109). Changes in 'demand' therefore affect the rate of profits only as mediated through changes in wage.

Malthus responds by letter dated 6 July, to argue that dearness of labour, following upon a rise in the corn price, would diminish, and necessarily so, he adds in a subsequent letter[28] – faster than revenue, so that there would be a smaller quantity of both corn, and of all other commodities, and 'every monied accumulation would command less labour and less produce'. The usual result of diminution of capital – a rise in the rate of profit – would follow. Malthus does not clarify whether the diminution of capital is only in terms of 'value commanded' or implies absolute reduction. Further, Malthus himself appears to recognize that Ricardo views his profit determination as a separate issue. For having controverted against the latter's position that anything which diminishes production tends to diminish effective demand, citing the case of wars when profits rise despite destruction of stocks, Malthus writes: 'But you must mean that it is the rate[29] of production, not the absolute quantity of produce which determines profits' (VI, p. 111). He proceeds to argue however, that 'even this rate of production ... seems to be determined by the quantity of accumulated capital, and not by the mere difficulty and expence of producing corn'. Not only does he thus cite the 'corn' case but goes on to illustrate using corn quantities.[30] He holds that 'the difficulty of procuring corn would result in a diminution of capital, less produce and a diminution in real wages or their price in corn, but not a diminution in profits' (VI, p. 111).

Ricardo view (cf. letter of 25 July to Malthus) the 'reduction of capital' and corn imports 'as separate causes with distinct effects on profits that may go together or entirely in opposite directions'. With reduction of capital, effective demand 'cannot augment or long continue stationary' but if capital diminishes faster than demand, profits could be augmented. 'This', he adds, 'is totally independent of the rate of production.' His meaning comes out clearer in a later letter of 16 September to Malthus. There he agrees that 'when capital is scanty compared with the means of employing it, from whatever cause arising, profits will be high (VI, p. 133). So stated, it is almost a truism. Hence, 'it is very important to ascertain what the causes are which make capital scanty compared with the means employing it – and how far when ascertained they may be considered temporary or permanent'. Ricardo was then to reaffirm that the state of cultivation of land is almost the only great permanent cause. Even the state of demand for capital, he was to contend, is regulated by 'the difficulty or expence of producing corn'. All these were Ricardo's attempts to retain the primacy of 'corn' in its profit-determining role even within the frame of Malthus's arguments relating to effective demand. That Ricardo himself must have continued to found his theory on the 'material rate of produce' proposition is evident when Malthus in his letter of 5 August protests: 'In no case of production, is the produce exactly of the same nature as the capital advanced. Consequently we can never properly refer to a material rate of produce, *independent of demand, and of the abundance of capital*' (italics added), which confirms that Ricardo maintained such an independence.[31] Ricardo, arguing within the context of Malthus, was attempting to show that ultimately 'the state of capital in relation to demand' would work through the 'state of cultivation': real diminution of capital would discourage the cultivation and raise the rate of profits while import restrictions on corn would encourage cultivation and lower the rate of profits. Further, he proposed a distinction between 'temporary' and 'permanent' influences. 'It will often happen that the scarcity of a commodity, or the increasing demand for it will for a time increase profits, but it is not therefore correct to say that where profits are high they are so because the demand for produce is great compared with the supply' (VI, p. 128). The state of cultivation was in fact the single permanent cause determining the rate of profits.

Parallel to this argument runs the controversy and mutual clarifications about what is demand and how it is determined. Ricardo rightly suspects that the term 'demand' is used in different senses by the two (VI, p. 129). For Ricardo, demand is increasing (decreasing) when actual quantity consumed increases (diminishes) and the power to purchase is represented by the 'produce of the country'. Malthus, distinguishing between 'the power' so represented and the 'will to purchase', believes that the latter 'will always be the greatest, the smaller is the produce compared with the population and the more scantily the wants of the society are supplied'. Malthus thus tended to recognize a situation as one of demand exceeding supply when all prices rise along with corn and associated a higher rate of profit with it. It is also in this context that Malthus holds that the power to purchase need not necessarily involve a proportionate will to purchase and challenges Mill's idea that supply can never exceed demand. Ricardo, however, holds that 'the will is seldom wanting where the power exists, for the desire for accumulation will occasion demand just as effectively as a desire to consume, it will only change the objects on which the demand will exercise itself' (VI, p. 133).[32] As Meek (1950) argues, the equality of savings and investment was accepted by both Ricardo and Malthus, and under that premise, Malthus's position was logically weak.

In the letter of 9 October, Malthus raised doubts about Ricardo's theory ('that the state of production from the land, compared with the means necessary to make it produce is almost the sole cause which regulates profits of stock') pointing out 'contemporaneous effects'.

> But unless it could be shewn that no improvements were ever to take place either in agriculture or manufacture, that upon a rise in the price of raw produce, new leases would be immediately granted, new taxes levied, and that the price of labour and of every other commodity both foreign and domestic would rise without delay exactly in proportion, the doctrine is evidently not correct in practice. (VI, p. 140)

Further, Malthus criticizes Ricardo for almost exclusively considering 'the expence of production without attending sufficiently to the price of produce'. He himself identifies a fall in the effective demand with a situation when 'the price of produce falls compared with expence of production and considers this as the only cause for fall of profits, and conversely, the case of a rise in effective demand.'[33]

Ricardo's reply of 23 October 1814 is extremely interesting because it brings out indirectly the structure of his early theory of profits. First, he clarifies that his theory of profit can easily accommodate the 'effects' Malthus talked about. Improvements of techniques or changes in wages of labour did not disprove this theory.[34] 'These points then are expressly allowed for in my proposition [that, the rate of profits is determined by the proportion of production to consumption necessary for that production] and are by no means at variance with it' (VI, p. 145). Furthermore, during temporary variations, the great cause, namely, the accumulation of capital, may be paving the way for permanently diminishing profits 'so that the state of cultivation' cannot long be ignored. He also notes, as a reminder to Malthus, that the causes occasioning a rise in the price of raw produce could be many, with diametrically opposite effects on profits (Malthus, we remember, associated high profits with high prices.) There may be temporary causes like a fall in the value of money or bad harvests that raise the price of corn. However, he considered a rise in the price of corn occasioned by gradual accumulation of capital, promoting cultivation of inferior lands, was the permanent cause of low rates of profits. In fact, he maintained 'a permanent rise in the rate of profits is never preceded by a rise but by a fall in the price of raw produce' (VI, pp. 146–7).

Of particular interest is the way Ricardo deals with Malthus's case of wages of labour not rising in proportion to the price of the produce.[35] Ricardo upholds the general validity of his principle on the same ground as in the case of improvements in agriculture above. He was to repeat the argument later (in a letter of 18 December to Malthus).

> A diminution of the proportion of produce, in consequence of the accumulation of capital, does not fall wholly on the owner of stock, but is shared with him by the labourers. The whole amount of wages paid will be greater, but the portion paid to each man, will in all probability, be somewhat diminished ... (VI, pp. 162–3)

What Ricardo was concerned with was that the 'whole value of wages paid as a proportion of produce will be greater compared with the whole value of the raw produce' in the case of extended cultivation. Hollander focuses on this point to challenge Sraffa's corn-profit-rate interpretation (pp. 128–9). Referring to a corn calculation of Ricardo,[36] taken on from an example of Malthus, where the capital employed estimated in money does not rise in proportion to the corn-price-rise, Hollander infers that the per capita corn wage declines in the given case,[37] having picked it out as an illustration of *wages consisting entirely of corn*. Hollander then concludes: 'The notion of a fixed corn wage per head was not part of the Ricardian scheme as the "corn profit" interpretation has it; a reduction in the ratio of corn profits to corn capital was the predicted pattern despite a fall in average corn wage' (p. 128). Thus a declining average corn wage is considered as casting doubt on the validity of the corn-profit interpretation (p. 129). Here we may note that what is required for the corn-profit interpretation is a '*given*' level of wages and not necessarily a 'fixed' wage; similarly, it takes a certain technique or the state of cultivation as 'given' (and not as 'invariant'). Ricardo could very well accommodate in his principle of obtaining the rate as 'proportion of production to consumption necessary for the production' both, changes in techniques as well as in wages.[38]

Ricardo's letter of 24 October to Malthus is also significant in shedding light on another aspect of the structure of his theory. He writes: 'I am not aware that I have under-rated the effect of the wants and tastes of mankind on profits, they frequently occasion large profits on particular commodities for short periods – but they do not I think often operate on general profits because they do not often influence the growth of raw produce.' (VI, pp. 147–8) Further, he elaborates the assumption behind Mill's (and his) theory:

> It does not attempt to say what the proportion will be to one another, of the commodities which will be produced in consequence of the accumulation of capital, *but presumes that those commodities only will be produced which will be suited to the wants and tastes of mankind, because none other will be demanded.* (VI, p. 148, italics added)

Thus Ricardo first of all distinguishes between the temporary profits and the (long run or natural) rate of profits that he is concerned with. Secondly, he clarifies the notion of effectual demand as a given position, similar to Adam Smith's notion, that underlies his theory of profits.[39]

As a counter to the corn-profit interpretation, Hollander ascribes to Ricardo a general reasoning in terms of a relation between money wage and the rate of profits. In support, he cites Ricardo's letter to Malthus, of August 1814, wherein he hints that rising money wages lead to a decline in profits in manufacturing goods: '... the rise of his [manufacturer's] goods will not be in the same proportion as the rise of labour'. (VI, p. 120) Does this argument substantiate the claim that Ricardo was already using a systematic reasoning in terms of relative prices? It is doubtful. First, it was in a letter, not much earlier, of 25 July 1814, to Malthus, that Ricardo had taken a clear Smithian position that prices of all commodities must increase if the price of corn increased, and the trace of that reasoning occurs also in the August letter.[40] Secondly, what strikes us in the Malthus–Ricardo correspondence of this period is precisely the absence of (or unpreparedness for) the confrontation with the theory of *relative* prices. Throughout the discussion, the recurrent, most-frequently-used phrases concern 'the rate of production' (used equivalently for 'the proportion between production and consumption necessary for it'), or the ratio of profits to capital or in terms of aggregates like 'the rise of wages of labour', 'the rise of commodities'. That Ricardo often argues from analogy, generalizing from the corn case, is evident from the fact that he reverts so characteristically to the 'case of food' while stating a general principle.[41] Further, he has no means of demonstrating why manufacturing prices should rise more slowly than money wages do (consequent upon a rise in the price of corn) except by intuitively presuming a lower rate of profit. The only logical basis he has to presume so, is the corn-profit argument. Malthus is equally remote from any general theory of relative prices. We have already seen how his arguments in terms of 'scantiness or abundance of capital' or high or deficient aggregate demand run the risk of circularity in definitions.[42] Also Malthus spoke of 'the increase in the value of the whole mass of commodities in the country, estimated either in money, or in corn and labour' (VI, p. 153) when Ricardo had to remind him about the relative value aspect, namely, 'If the mass of commodities be increased we diminish their exchangeable value as compared with those things whose quantity is not augmented' (VI, p. 163). It is clear, however, that no conception of a systematic theory of value and its relation to the theory of profit emerges.

Hollander himself notes that while the letter of August 1814 contains the assertion that the prices of manufactured goods rise less than proportionately to money wages, 'in the case of agricultural produce Ricardo did not allow for *any* price increase due to higher money wages' (p. 131) and considers it to be an oversight. However, this is not surprising. Ricardo, indeed, did not yet have any theory of relative prices resting on their detailed structure of production. In fact, an incidental suggestion of Malthus contained in his letter of 9 October 1814, that the principal difficulties in the debate 'arise from different effects of an increase, or diminution of capital on the land, and in manufactures and commerce; particularly with regard to price, occasioned by the different nature of the instruments employed' (VI, p. 142), is elaborated by neither Ricardo nor Malthus until well after the *Essay*. The lack of any clear perception and formulation of the relative value formation is evident in the tangled discussion between Ricardo and Malthus on the effect of a corn-price-rise on the value of capital engaged in agriculture.

Thus Hollander's construction of Ricardo's position, on the basis of the correspondence of 1814, that 'the rate of profit in agriculture does not strictly determine the profit rate elsewhere. Rather the general profit rate varies inversely with the movements in money wages' (p. 132), appears not to be substantiated. It has to ignore emphatic, explicit statements of Ricardo and Malthus concerning the determining role of the agricultural rate of profit. It is also striking that Ricardo upholds, in this period, his theory of profit simultaneously with the Smithian proposition regarding the effects of an increase in corn price. Moreover, not only is a systematic theory of relative prices not yet in hand but the issues are yet to be perceived with any clarity in terms of relative commodity pricing.

The Essay *on Profits (1815)*
Hollander's main contention is that, in the case of the *Essay*, as in the 1814 correspondence, Ricardo held the 'weak proposition' (see above). Hollander refers to a remark of Ricardo to argue that he did not imply that the general profit rate is 'literally governed' by the agricultural rate. The remark is: '... I am only desirous of proving that profits on agricultural capital cannot materially vary, without occasioning a similar variation in the profits on capital, employed on manufactures and commerce.' This is a footnote attached to a rather strong statement indicating a strict relation between agricultural and the general rate of profit.[43]

Here, however, Hollander neither gives the proper context nor indicates that he is quoting only a part of the footnote where the preceding part reads: 'It is not meant, that strictly the rate of profits on agriculture and manufactures will be the same, but that they will bear some proportion to each other' (IV, p. 12 n). Ricardo further elaborates to clarify that the 'uniformity of the rate of profits 'can still allow for a systematic proportional variations in profit rates due to such differences as in 'security, cleanliness', etc. of different employments (as in Adam Smith). Thus Ricardo here is not modifying or weakening the determining role of agricultural rate of profit, as Hollander suggests, but amplifying the content of 'uniformity' of profit rates.

Further, Hollander observes that Ricardo's proof[44] of the equalizing of profit rates does not preclude possibilities of variations induced by changes emanating from outside the agricultural sector. Indeed so, and this points to the need for providing a rational foundation to Ricardo's position. Hollander believes that Ricardo 'reverts' to the sophisticated 'weak' position of the 1814 correspondence in the latter part of the *Essay*, having adopted the 'strong' proposition in the opening part. If Hollander is correct in believing that Ricardo had reached a general relation between money wages and the rate of profits, it is not explained why Ricardo found it necessary to revert to the strong proposition and not only choose particular corn quantities but assert, in direct terms, the determining role of the agricultural profit rate (see, for instance, IV, pp. 12, 14, 18, 23, 26). While corn is used as a *numéraire* in the *Table* and in the text, Ricardo at times used corn quantities directly in arguments. Ricardo is explicit that expanded trade or technical progress in manufactures will have no influence upon the profit rate, 'because they do not augment the produce compared with the cost of production on the land, and it is impossible that all other profits should rise whilst the profits on land are either stationary, or retrograde' (IV, p.26).

We must note an important structural feature of the *Essay*: Ricardo's theory of profit was already formulated before the theory of rent appeared in the pamphlets of West, Torrens and Malthus and the first part of the *Essay* is probably a revised version of the text before the appearance of Malthus's two contributions (Malthus, 1815a and 1815b). The later part of the *Essay* is mainly addressed to issues raised by Malthus. The references to relative prices occur entirely in the later part of the *Essay*, while the determining role of the agricultural profit rate is expanded and illustrated with the *Table* in the first part.[45] The references – rather 'piecemeal' – to relative prices (of corn and manufactures) occur specifically when Ricardo contests opinions of Malthus concerning the consequences of the 'imports of a cheaper corn' on the 'real value' of rents, wages and profits in terms of their 'command over other commodities'. Ricardo is concerned with refuting Malthus's contention that cheapness of corn affects adversely the command over other commodities of rents and wages.[46] That the issue of relative prices is taken up in this specific context is clear from Ricardo's statement: 'This fact [concerning prices] is of more importance than at first sight appears, as it relates to the interest of the landlord, and the other parts of the community' (IV, p. 20). It is also in this context that a footnote, highlighted by Hollander, challenging the Smithian proposition on prices is attached.[47]

What is interesting is that the discussion involving relative prices appears after the inverse relation between rents and other incomes has already been worked out (in terms of corn) in the earlier part of the *Essay*. *Not only that: It is taken as already established and forms the basis of the arguments that follow in the second part.* In this later part of the *Essay*, Ricardo takes for granted a definite association, as analytically established, between the extension of cultivation, higher rents, lower rate of profits, on the one hand, and lower rents, lower price of corn and higher profits, on the other. The former situation is identified as effected by restraints on corn imports and a higher price of corn and the latter with free corn imports and cheaper corn. Following this, 'a rise in the price of corn' or a 'fall' become key phrases to represent typically the whole situation. Thus the relation between wage and the rate of profits does not seem to be analytically founded on the basis of a theory of exchangeable value. This also explains better the observation of Hollander on a peculiarity of Ricardo's arguments at this stage, quite distinct from the *Principles* (p. 140). Ricardo's argument in the *Essay* has two strands, notes Hollander: 'two (separable) causal influences on profits: the decline in agricultural productivity in the agricultural sector itself, and the rise in money wages (reflecting the higher corn price) in manufacturing', whereas, in *Principles*, the effect of a change in wage-rate is considered *simultaneously* on all prices without such a separation. Hollander also notes that Ricardo does not consider the effect of the corn price changes on the corn sector itself. The simplification in terms of corn wages ('capital' consisting of wages alone) and the lack of a systematic theory of relative prices would provide a consistent rationale for Ricardo's particular procedures noted by Hollander.

There are, no doubt, hints of a theory of value and a brief criticism of Smith's proposition, as noted above. The piecemeal applications, arising in a specific context, are what Sraffa probably has in mind when he speaks of passages in the *Essay* foreshadowing his theory of value to appear in *Principles*. Hollander's reading (that Ricardo had already obtained the *money* wage-rate of profit relation in the *Essay* and that there was no substantive 'turning point' in moving over to the *Principles*) faces the difficulty of having to explain the predominantly agricultural form of the theory of profits and why the principle of the determining role of agricultural rate of profit disappears in the *Principles*[48] (see Garegnani, 1982).

The Post-Essay Debate
The deficiency of a piecemeal treatment of value revealed itself progressively in the post-*Essay* debate between Ricardo and Malthus. In Ricardo's letter to Malthus, immediately following the publication of the *Essay* (9 March 1815, VI, p. 179), Ricardo realized that he had not made adequate

allowance for the altered value of raw materials in manufactured goods, which *would be an influence separate from wages on their price*. In the subsequent debate, the central question concerned the effects on the size of the surplus and 'the ratio of that surplus produce to the whole capital employed' following a relative cheapening of manufactured goods which formed a component of capital employed in cultivation.[49] Malthus argued that the surplus would be enlarged in such a case and Ricardo opposed the view, holding that a high price of corn is accompanied by (or even due to) increased expenses of cultivation, a rise in the corn price of labour and hence a fall in profits (VI, p. 189). Many of the confusions arise precisely because neither Ricardo nor Malthus appear to have possessed a rigorous perception of relative price formation and much of the debate is carried out in terms of aggregates like 'expenses of cultivation in terms of corn or labour'.[50] At this juncture, even the formulations and role of a labour theory of value in the explanation of the profit rate, appears not to have been clearly and rigorously perceived.[51]

The struggle to establish his case under alternative assumptions concerning the influence of the corn price on manufacturing prices (VI, pp. 212–14) was seen by Ricardo to be leading to 'a labyrinth of difficulties' in 'an endless succession'. He tended to return to the anchor of his 'simple theory', entreating Malthus 'to give my simple doctrine fair consideration' since it accounted for phenomena 'in an easy and natural manner' (VI, p. 214). However, the difficulties that emerged in the debate were far more serious than making allowances for commodities other than corn in wage goods. *They raised the question of the structure of production of different commodities and demanded a rigorous theory of relative price formation.* It is this realization that probably prompted Ricardo to write to James Mill, 'I know I shall soon be stopped by the word price', at the end of 1815 (VI, p. 348) and to give prominence to the value question in *Principles*.

3 The Theory of Profit in Principles

Following the protracted post-*Essay* debate with Malthus, Ricardo formulated, in his *Principles*, the theory of profit in most general terms, using the labour theory of value. Hollander proceeds first to give his interpretations of particular aspects of the labour theory of value and the notion of 'invariant standard' and, in the following chapter, attempts in a 'general overview', to establish continuity between Ricardo's theoretical framework and Marshall's 'allocation mechanisms'. Here, we take up some of his interpretations.

Hollander sees Ricardo's discussions on value to be mainly concerned with (a) countering Smith's rejection of the labour theory in a capitalist economy with private property in land, (b) explaining 'conditions under which a labour theory retains its validity', and (c) attempting 'to justify the use of a *labour measure of value*, in terms of which there will be no alterations in relative prices, and therefore in the value of output to be shared, in the face of changes in distributions[52] (p. 191). Hollander acknowledges that Ricardo's objection to Smith's confining the labour theory to the 'early and rude state' and to his proposing the labour-commanded measure in its place was theoretical and not purely definitional.[53] Ricardo argued that it was fallacious to regard the mere emergence of rents and profits among revenue shares as exerting an influence on relative prices *independently* of the conditions of production. Despite the modifications admitted to the doctrine that commodities exchange at labour values, arising from the differential composition of the means of production of different commodities, Ricardo did not consider them weighty enough to invalidate the doctrine.[54] He played down the effect of wage variations, Hollander observes, on the ground that, relevant to his theory were relative rather than absolute changes in values and that, the effects due to a rise (fall) in wages would be much less in extent as it would be necessarily accompanied by a fall (rise) in the rate of profits and profits themselves constitute 'but a small portion of price'. We note again that, despite the reference to the 'comparative extent' of effects, Ricardo's arguments rest primarily on a theoretical – and not empirical – basis. He presumes here the theoretical result of the inverse relation between wage and the rate of profits so that the net price is seen as composed of the two elements, wages and profits, moving in contrary directions. Hollander himself notes that Ricardo often adopts the 'not very elegant' procedure of presuming the inverse relation in the context of relative price movements. Not having the artillery of simultaneous equations, it would seem that Ricardo attempted to construct the device of the invariant measure to derive the inverse relation in situations where the simple labour value theory needed to be 'modified'.

Hollander's position that Ricardo's primary concern, in all his work, was to refute the Smithian proposition that all prices rise along with a rise in wages (which proved a 'stumbling block' in establishing the money-wage profit relation of Ricardo) has certain connotations for Hollander's evaluation of the 'invariant standard.' He argues that Ricardo had already achieved his objective in the first edition of *Principles* where he could show, on the basis of a standard suggested therein, that prices actually fall with a rise in wages. Hollander also points out that, despite the change in the standard in the third edition, the chapter on profits is not altered. He concludes therefore, that 'The more sophisticated medium of the third edition plays no substantive role in analysis; the issue of the effects upon the price structure due to a change in wages is set aside by resort to the assumption that commodities are produced by processes involving identical factor ratios' (p. 221).

Here, we need to give a closer look at the issue of the 'invariant standard.' As Sraffa puts it:

> ... the problem which mainly interested him [Ricardo] was not that of finding an actual commodity which would accurately measure the value of corn or silver at different times and places; but rather that of finding the conditions which a commodity would have to satisfy in

order to be invariable in value – and this came close to identifying the problem of a measure with that of the law of value. (I, pp. xl-xli)[55]

Sraffa also notes a peculiar consequence that, corresponding to the version of value theory Ricardo adopts, there would be an appropriate ideal invariant standard with definite properties. When he adhered to simple labour theory of value, the invariant measure was a commodity requiring a constant quantity of labour. However, 'in so far as there are exceptions to the theory, to the same extent the accuracy of the measure is affected' (I, p. xli, n. 1). In the first two editions of *Principles* the invariant standard was identified as 'requiring at all times and under all circumstances, precisely the same quantity of labour', while in the third edition, the standard adopted was gold 'produced with such proportions of the two kinds of capital as approach nearest to the average quantity employed in the production of most commodities' (I, p. 45). However, this standard adopted in the third edition turned out, for Ricardo, to be the same as in the first edition, that is 'a commodity produced by labour employed for a year', considered now as 'the mean proportion'. Hollander, therefore, should not be surprised to find the chapter on profits unaffected although a number of textual changes were introduced elsewhere (see p. 1, 28, n. 1, 29, n. 1). Hollander also suggests that Ricardo had cut the knot, despite his preoccupation with modifications of the labour-value principle, by the 'simple expedient of assuming identical factor proportions across the board'. While it is true that Ricardo considers some simple illustrations of the type, he nowhere adopts the assumption as a general case.

What is particularly notable is this: while Hollander refers repeatedly to the problem encountered by Ricardo in the derivation of the rate of profit in keeping the net output of constant value, in the face of variations in wage – and for which Hollander acknowledges the usefulness of the invariant standard – he bypasses entirely the parallel problem arising with the measurement of capital. In fact, while discussing Torrens's criticism of labour theory and his proposal for an alternative theory (that commodities are valuable according to the capital employed in their production and the time for which it is so employed), Hollander observes that Ricardo apparently missed the characteristic feature of Torrens's approach.[56] Surprisingly, however, Hollander makes no reference to the very significant objection Ricardo explicitly puts down against Torrens's theory, both in the 'Absolute Value and Exchangeable Value' and in the letter to McCulloch (IX, pp. 358–62) where Ricardo is perplexed by the problem of quantification of capital and asks pointedly: 'What means have you of ascertaining the equal value of these agents'[57] (IX, p. 357) Ricardo argued that 'the means of ascertaining their equality or variation of value is the very thing in dispute' (IX, p. 359 n). It is amply evident from Ricardo's references that he was seeking to strike at such a 'mean' commodity to be adopted as a standard that 'those commodities on one side of this medium, would rise in comparative value with it, with a rise in the price of labour, and a fall in the rate of profits; and those on the other side might fall from the same cause' (VIII, p. 193). Consequently, as Sraffa indicates,

'If measured in such a standard, the average price of all commodities, and their aggregate value, would remain unaffected by a rise or fall of wages' (I, pp. xliv–xv). Thus the 'sophisticated' invariant standard was suggested by Ricardo consistently in line with the 'modifications' that were attempted to be incorporated into the theory of value.

Hollander suggests emphatically that Ricardo's concern was with an empirical theory of exchange value: the labour theory and the choice of the invariant standard to be viewed in that light. His judgement is based on three characteristics of Ricardo's defence of his measure of value that he notes: first, that Ricardo was in pursuit of a *hypothetical* measure and admitted that the ideal measure may not exist. Second, Ricardo asserted that an adequate *approximation* to the ideal may be achieved in practice and, third, he was prepared to maintain the inverse relation between wages and profits even if such an approximation was unachievable. Indeed, Ricardo was seeking to define theoretical properties of an abstract standard consistent with his theory of value and which would measure suitably the heterogenous aggregates involved in profit determination. He was amply conscious that such a measure may not exist in practice. In fact, while with the measure of the first two editions, of constant labour value, the difficulty appeared to be a practical one, with the second, the difficulty was *theoretical*. Ricardo could not find an easy or consistent way of defining an average or mean *proportion* between fixed and circulating capital, with their differing durabilities.[58] Knowing full well the practical difficulties, Ricardo continued the pursuit of discovering the *properties* of the ideal standard. In this he did not succeed but he laid down the direction and the logical basis for the search which have been used in the latter-day 'transformation' procedures. The problem of deviations of natural prices from labour values took a particular form in Ricardo. It appeared in the form of a second cause of variation in relative values, apart from the changes in the labour requirements, namely a change in wage. The use of the invariant standard was a means of making manageable the deviations on that account. There is thus an intimate connection between the transformation problem and Ricardo's attempts at incorporating modifications of the labour theory in his theory of profit.[59] Further, even while Ricardo sought for an adequate approximation, failing to get the 'ideal' solution, his 'approximation' had a *theoretical* basis.[60] Confronted with the difficulty of finding any one 'unexceptionable' commodity to serve as a measure, he proposes a measure 'though confessedly an imperfect one' which will give some idea whether, when labour varies as compared with commodities, it is the value of labour which has undergone a change or whether it is the commodity which rises or falls. His argument against Malthus's measure in so far as it constitutes an extreme case of variation and not therefore suitable for the theory of profit, is a theoretical one. Despite failing to resolve the problem satisfactorily, Ricardo showed considerable confidence in the correctness of the direction of his search and pursued his efforts at defining accurately the theoretical properties of a standard, despite discouragements from James Mill and McCulloch.

Also of importance is the fact that Ricardo's opposition to the alternative measures suggested by Malthus, Torrens, McCulloch and James Mill *rested entirely on their theoretical inadequacy and not on their empirical unsuitability*. Furthermore, if the labour theory was merely an empirical proposition, as Hollander maintains, Ricardo should have been using wage costs rather than labour values. In that case, he would not have opened his *Principles* with the bold statement: 'The value of a commodity ... depends on the relative quantity of labour which is necessary for its production, and not on the greater or less compensation which is paid for that labour' (I, p. 11).

Hollander raises another important question: Did Ricardo or did he not assume commodity and factor substitution in relative price formation? He finds a rather conflicting situation. Ricardo's characterization of the invariant standard appears to Hollander to rule out substitution relations, for the standard would be unmanageable if the capital structure of the commodities alters with every wage variation. However, several instances appear not only in the third edition (with its celebrated discussion of machinery) but even in the first edition where substitution is discussed.[61] Hollander therefore concludes:

> The model was developed [by Ricardo] despite awareness of the phenomenon, on the grounds that the complications would not be ruinous to the basic structure – a theoretical model which illustrated the effect on the rate of profits of rising wage costs may be satisfactory although its assumptions are 'unrealistic' (p. 227).

A better interpretation could be that Ricardo, for the value-distribution question, adopted a framework of 'given' effectual demand, known methods of production in use and a given (but not a fixed) wage (see above). While changes in these elements and interactions among them were important, these would be dealt with in a broader socio-economic perspective. No rigid price-quantity relations bind these changes in functional forms and there would be no necessity to lay down a priori *the extent or direction* of the 'substitution effects'. It would seem, therefore, that while Ricardo did not shy away from discussing changes in methods of production, or in demand composition, etc. he did not have to posit for his theory the specific nature of the substitution effects. This is not a matter of 'unrealistic assumptions' but a characteristic of the structure of the underlying theory.

4 'Allocative Mechanisms' in Ricardo

In 'a general overview' Hollander suggests that Ricardo, explicitly or implicitly, relied upon 'demand and supply based allocation mechanisms', along Marshallian lines.[62] More specifically, he argues that Ricardo's formulation of the principle of profit rate equalization rests on allocation governed by supply-and-demand forces, as in the neoclassical theory. Further, that Ricardo extends these principles to factor-utilization.

In presenting Ricardo's principles of profit rate equalization, Hollander draws attention to two separate situations in Ricardo.[63] One generating 'an alteration in quantity, and consequent alteration in price' so as 'to ensure the (unchanged) general rates of wages and profits' and second, 'a disturbance affecting *all* sectors equally' and also bringing about a change in the general rate of profit (p. 271). The distinction between the two cases is highlighted by Hollander in the context of competitive process of profit rate equalization as well as of the consequences of a change in wages. He does not, however, provide a satisfactory rationale for this distinction within the logic of a general equilibrium framework, which he suggests is Ricardo's. A lame rationale is provided for the second case (where 'a disturbance' affects the general rate of profit), suggesting that much of Ricardo's analysis proceeded on the assumption of identical factor proportions (p. 242) – a suggestion hard to support by textual evidence.

In fact, these peculiarities of Ricardian procedure can be more consistently fitted into the surplus framework.[64] Ricardo assiduously maintains a significant distinction between 'market' and 'natural' prices, based on a characteristic separation of 'temporary' or 'accidental' from 'permanent' or 'stable' forces at work in the economy (I, pp. 90–2). The 'temporary variations' that would quite often arise when supplies do not match demand in single industries, would result in changes in prices and *temporary* differences in profits. This, in turn, would set into motion 'apportionment of capital' whereby the tendency towards profit rate equalization asserts itself.[65] Ricardo, however, added: 'It is perhaps very difficult to trace the steps by which this change is effected' (I, p. 89), implying that rigorous analysis of this process was tenuous. Even more interestingly, he envisages situations where the mere possibility of altering output is sufficient to reinforce the tendency towards profit rate equalization, without actual changes in quantities. These cases of single industries (with individual prices altering and temporary variations in individual, but not in the general rate of profit) occur mostly in the context of 'market prices'.

Changes in quantities affect the 'natural price'[66] *only* through either changes in the method of production or a change in wage. A change, not purely accidental, in any one of these two elements alters the 'natural rate of profit', but not every quantity variation does. Thus a tax or subsidy would have different consequences on the rate of profits for Ricardo, depending on whether the commodity taxed enters the wage basket or is a 'luxury' good. In the latter case, a change in quantity and/or price of the good is not followed by a variation in the general rate of profits. On the other hand, Ricardo attempts to show that, with methods of production unchanged, a change in wages would bring about an inverse variation in the rate of profits (relative prices remain unaffected only under the simple labour theory case).

Hollander, however, hopes to establish that the 'natural prices' are themselves an outcome of the process of supply-and-demand mechanism and to show that Ricardo's treatment of demand is closer to that in neoclassical theory than has thus far been recognized. We already have had occasion to observe, however, that Ricardo appears to have a notion of 'effectual demand' similar to that of Smith, as a position of average social demand around which temporary deviations could take place. Emergence of once-for-all changes, in the shape of new commodities, new uses, changes in habits, would call for a revision of effectual demand position. While for the discussion of value and distribution, the social demand would be taken as known, Ricardo (and Smith) allowed for changes in demand arising from the process of accumulation and from shifts in consumption habits, etc. The price-demand response was very rarely treated in isolation, and that, too, more in relation to 'temporary causes and effects'. Hollander himself has to admit that 'there is no evidence that Ricardo recognised the conception of response of demand to relative changes in price assuming unchanged purchasing power' (p. 276), and notes the absence of substitution effect in this sense. No doubt, the effect of a price variation on demand was discussed by Ricardo at specific places (more, in the context of 'market prices'). However, the price responses were neither systematic nor consistent complying with what a supply-and-demand-based theory would require. Hollander has to concede that 'he [Ricardo] insisted on ranges of inelasticity'. Individual vagaries, 'new uses' of commodities, stickiness of habits, 'income' rather than 'substitution' effects – as Hollander calls them – are so predominant in Ricardo's descriptive statements that Hollander has to read *specific* 'elasticity properties' into *individual* cases. When we recognize that an 'elasticity property' can be always read into a statement relating price to quantity and a surrogate demand function ascribed to each situation, the exercise loses much meaning particularly when we must note that a general and rigorous supply-and-demand theoretical explanation would have to insist on well-behaved demand (as well as supply) functions all round and the imputed price quantity relations may not obey the properties of such well-behavedness.

Hollander has further to concede that Ricardo 'failed to appreciate the conception of marginal utility'.[67] Hollander's counter-examples to show Ricardo's reliance on utility, indicate that he deemed it to be only a necessary attribute for commodities to possess value, and clearly separated the notion of riches from value.[68] Hollander, however, suggests that 'the absence of a conception of diminishing marginal utility should not be exaggerated. For Ricardo, like Smith before him, was thoroughly conscious of the fundamental role of scarcity in value formation' (p. 278). The examples cited by Hollander are again cases of temporary supply deficiencies, leading to a rise in (market) prices. 'Scarcity' itself has a different connotation, it would seem, in Ricardo. As is well known, Ricardo's preoccupation was with commodities that could be reproduced to an unlimited extent with human effort and on which the force of competition exerts itself. Scarcity would, as in the case of land, show itself in the fact that a superior method of production could not be extended to additional output and methods of unequal productivity would permanently coexist. There could also be 'scarcity' in the sense of deficient supply as a 'temporary' situation in the case of reproducible commodities. Scarcity, moreover, seen as 'difficulty in production' was used as synonymous with greater labour requirement.

Hollander also believes that 'allocation mechanisms' can be extended to include factor-pricing in Ricardo. He attributes to Ricardo 'an implicit assumption throughout much of the analysis' that consequent upon a variety of disturbances, factors are released (and absorbed) in proportion – the profit rate remaining unaltered consequently (p. 293). Hollander has in mind Ricardo's analysis of the effects of taxation and of free corn imports on effectual demand. Ricardo had reasoned that these would cause a redistribution of purchasing power among various parties (government, consumers) and among revenue classes, so that there would be no glut while there could be reallocation of labour and capital. Since, in some contexts, Ricardo presumed no variation in the general rate of profit, Hollander attributes to him the assumption of identical factor proportions in all sectors. Apart from the fact that Ricardo assumes no such thing, Hollander's interpretation here *presumes rather than proves* that Ricardo was employing a supply-and-demand-based allocation framework. The presumption goes against Ricardo's insistent opposition to Smith's explanation of profit in terms of 'competition of capitals'. Moreover, in the celebrated machinery problem where Ricardo considers displacement of labour by machinery, Hollander himself observes, 'he said little about the further consequences of excess labour on the original wage' (p. 299). Also Ricardo's recurrent and systematic practice of posing situations where 'changes affect factor returns in the particular industries involved but not the general rates', which Hollander sets aside 'as not involving a matter of principle', illustrates characteristically the method of Ricardo in separating temporary (market) prices from natural prices (see pp. 99–100 above). Further, Ricardo nowhere arrives at full employment of labour or of capital as a *logical consequence* of the 'allocative mechanisms' – a prominent result of the 'neoclassical procedures' of resource allocation.

5 Conclusion

Whether by 'scientific' or 'personal exegesis' – the criteria adopted by Hollander – Sraffa's reading of Ricardo stands. With respect to the first criterion Sraffa's interpretation of the development of Ricardo's theory of profit within the surplus approach helps us understand the peculiarities of Ricardo's theoretical propositions, the form they successively assumed in the development of the profit principle, the manner in which Ricardo envisaged the difficulties, the direction he took in resolving them and, more importantly, the stands he took *vis-à-vis* his contemporaries (Malthus, McCulloch, Torrens, Mill) on controversial issues. In terms of the personal exegesis, Sraffa's interpretation reveals, quite remarkably, the route Ricardo chose in his attempts at resolving his theoretical problems, particularly the question of simultaneous interdependency[69] between prices and the rate of profits by adopting analytical short-cuts. Hollander's interpretation leads him continually to resort to discovering a difference between 'Ricardo's formal statements' and 'intentions'. It leads to odd twists and turns in explanations, for example, when Ricardo is thought to be reverting midway to unrealistic and probably faulty constructions (like the corn simplification), or to 'strong cases' even while the more general and theoretically powerful results are supposedly in hand. It fails to explain the peculiarities like the disappearance of the determining role of the farmer's profit rate from the *Principles*, or the doggedly persistent search for a 'sophisticated standard'. On the other hand, Hollander has to attribute assumptions like identical factor proportions in all sectors, or specific 'elasticity properties' to bring Ricardo into the neoclassical fold. Hollander's attempted reconstruction fails to convince.

Notes: Chapter 4

This essay was first published in the *Cambridge Journal of Economics*, vol. 7, in March 1983 (pp. 11–36). I am grateful to Pierangelo Garegnani, Geoffrey Harcourt, Donald Harris and Alessandro Roncaglia for their suggestions and comments.

1 All page references in this chapter when the source is not indicated refer to this work.
2 Hollander's stated purpose in the work is to reduce 'the Ricardo Problem' to 'manageable proportions' (p. 5). He covers in this pursuit, a vast territory, confronting a number of commentaries on Ricardo. His main thrust is, however, two-pronged: one line of argument runs to refute the readings of Ricardo that place him as a major proponent of the surplus theory, viewed as having a distinctly separate structure from the marginalist theories. Hollander nowhere identifies the framework of that theory but contests particular assumptions and interpretations or formulation by different authors, clubbing together diverse constructions serving different purposes (see Appendix B of the book). Piero Sraffa, as the most prominent scholar whose commentaries on Ricardo have been important in the recent revival of classical approach, looms large, sometimes in the background but often in the forefront. The second strand seeks to develop the continuity thesis.
3 David Ricardo's *An Essay on the Influence of a Low Price of Corn on the Profits of Stock* (See *Works* IV, pp. 1–41) was published around 24 February 1815; hereafter referred to as the *Essay*. References to the *Works and Correspondence of David Ricardo* (1810–23 [1951–73]) are indicated by volume number in roman numerals followed by page number.
4 David Ricardo, *Principles of Political Economy and Taxation (Works*, I); hereafter *Principles*.
5 Here the more important aspects of Sraffa's reading which are explicitly or implicitly contested by Hollander and hence significant for our arguments

are recorded.

6   Ricardo also wrote to Malthus (as late as on 7 February 1816), 'If I could overcome the obstacles in the way of giving a clear insight into the origin and law of relative or exchangeable value I should have gained half the battle' (VII, p. 20).

7   The difficulty appeared in the form of a consistent measure of heterogenous aggregates: 'Even though nothing has occurred to change the magnitude of the aggregate, there may be *apparent* changes due solely to change in measurement, owing to the fact that measurement is in terms of value and relative values have been altered as a result of a change in the division between wages and profits' (I, p. xlviii). It also appeared in the case of the measurement of capital (see below).

8   Cf. Letter to James Mill where he writes, 'I know I shall soon be stopped by the word Price' (VI, p. 348).

9   Hollander, on the other hand, characterizes the 'original error' to be Smith's proposition that a rise in corn price raises all other prices (p. 5).

10 A more incidental use of the argument made by Hollander is to conclude that 'any stimulus provided by the corn law debates for Ricardo's new theory is not a self-evident one' (p. 122).

11 The condition for stability of the measure is seen by Hollander to be 'the stability of the conditions of supply of the monetary medium', although he believes Ricardo 'clouded the issue' in the *High Price of Bullion* by stating that 'gold and silver like other commodities have an intrinsic value which is not arbitary but is dependent on their scarcity, the quantity of labour bestowed in procuring them' (III, p. 52).

12 A first reference to the theory of profit occurs in Ricardo's letter to Malthus of 17 August 1813 (VI, pp. 94–5) and a clear statement in a letter to Trower of 8 March 1814 (VI, pp. 103–4).

13 Bosanquet (1810) and Ricardo's *Reply to Bosanquet* (III, pp. 155–279). Bosanquet had ascribed the rise in prices in the contemporary period to increased taxation.

14 'If the tax were laid upon bread, and in consequence, the wages of labour were raised, the tax would eventually fall on all those who consumed the produce of the labour of man. It would make no real difference to these consumers if they had at once paid the amount of such tax into the exchequer, or if it had gone through the circuitous channel which it would then take'. Further, 'nor would any additional sum be required. Government would be in the daily receipt of a portion of taxes, whether it was paid to the exciseman or to the tax-gatherer, and their expences in the one case would be precisely the same as in the other. Whatever the government expended would cause a diminished expenditure in the people to the same amount' (III, p. 243).

15 'If any rise in the price of commodities is caused in the way here supposed it must be by diminishing the amount of commodities, which will make the money which circulates them more relatively abundant' (III, p. 300).

16 'Commodities measure the value of money in the same manner as money measures the value of commodities' (III, p. 104).

17 Ricardo reasons: 'Whatever the government expended would cause a diminished expenditure in the people to the same amount: the same amount of commodities would be circulated, and the same money would be adequate to their circulation' (III, p.243). In *Notes on Trotter*, he writes 'Taxation does not require any addition of money, or if any so little as not to be worth

computing' (III, p. 385).

18. '... Whatever, therefore, lowers the price of produce is injurious to him [the farmer] ... The landlord will gain a great part of what the farmer loses' (III, p. 137).

19. A similar theme reappears in a later work, *Protection to Agriculture* (1822) (IV, pp. 229–30; also p. 257).

20. Evidently, Hollander has Piero Sraffa's explanation of the rational foundation of Ricardo's argument in mind (see pp. 78-9 above). His wording, however, is misleading: first, Sraffa does not attribute to Ricardo the 'assumption' in the strict sense of the term (see Garegnani, 1982). Also while Sraffa indicates a turning point when the *basis* of the argument shifts from quantities to values, the surplus principle underlying the profit rate determination is preserved.

21. cf. (VI, 103–4). 'I contend that the arena for the employment of new capital cannot increase in any country in the same or greater proportion than the capital itself, unless capital be withdrawn from the land – unless there be improvements in husbandry – or new facilities be offered for the introduction of food from foreign countries, that in short it is the profits of the farmer which regulate the profits of all other trades ...' In an earlier letter of 17 August 1813, to Malthus (VI, pp. 94–5), Ricardo refers to 'my theory' and Trower refers to 'your very interesting papers on the profits of capital' in his letter of 2 March 1814 (VI, p. 102). The 'papers' are not extant.

22. Hollander needs to justify attributing to Ricardo the 'sophisticated variation' of the farmer's profit principle while replacing his directly worded expression of the principle. A critique of Hollander on these issues is to be found in Garegnani (1982).

23. See, for example, VI, pp. 94, 104, 108–9, 113–15, 119, 133, 144, 162.

24. See VI, pp. 111, 118, 139–40, 152, 155.

25. Ricardo, we see later, tends to identify demand with 'quantity consumed' and production with 'power to purchase'.

26. 'Although this argument', Sraffa remarks, 'is never stated by Ricardo in any of his extant letters and papers, he must have formulated it either in his lost "papers on the profits of capital" of March 1814 or in conversation' (I, p. xxxi). Hollander suggests, thereby giving an erroneous impression, that this statement of Ricardo '*according to Piero Sraffa, implies a model* yielding the determining role of agricultural profits by *assuming* that agricultural capital and output both consist of the same physical commodity.' (p. 105, italics added). He suggests that Ricardo's definitional statement could hold also in value terms – which is true indeed. However, Hollander gives an entirely different twist to Piero Sraffa's cautious and well-chosen expressions by using phrases like 'implied', 'model', 'assuming', as if the statement of Ricardo being quoted is taken by Sraffa to correspond exactly to the 'rational foundation' he offers.

27. 'Ricardo's treatment of the rate of profit cannot be fully appreciated unless the position of his opponent regarding these issues is kept in mind'. Also, that 'Ricardo clearly believed that the success of his own theory of profits implied the corresponding failure of the entire Malthusian theory of effective demand, wherein the profit rate would be influenced by capital accumulation by way of a relative variation in aggregate demand' (pp. 125–26).

28. On Ricardo's pointing out that Malthus was raising a new and separate point, Malthus insists that the diminution of capital is a *necessary* consequence of import restrictions.

29 Malthus elaborates the phrase in the next sentence: as 'the proportion of production to the consumption necessary for that production' (VI, p. 111).
30 'If it [is] necessary to employ a hundred days labour instead of fifty, in order to produce a certain quantity of corn, there seems to be no reason whatever that the person who possesses an accumulation sufficient to make the necessary advances should have a less remuneration for his capital' (VI, p. 111). See p. 89 above for Ricardo's response to Malthus and Hollander's use of this illustration.
31 It is significant that Malthus adds: 'The more I reflect on the subject, the more firmly I feel convinced, that it is the state of capital, or the general profits of stock and interest of money, which determines the particular profit upon the land; and that it is not the particular profits or *rate of produce upon the land*, which determines the general profits of stock and the interest of money' (VI, pp. 117–18, italics added).
32 Further, he writes 'I consider the wants and tastes of mankind as unlimited. We all wish to add to our enjoyments or to our power. Consumption adds to our enjoyments, accumulation to our power, and they equally promote demand' (VI, pp. 134–135).
33 Malthus writes: '... Upon the supposition that a greater effective demand means a greater excess of the price of produce above the expence of production, you would surely allow that effective demand would always be greatest when the quantity of capital was comparatively the smallest, or the profits of stock highest' (VI, p. 142). *We note that this is hardly a theory of aggregate or effective demand; rather Malthus proposes only alternative vocabulary to describe a situation.* Ricardo was to remark in his *Notes on Malthus* 'What Mr Malthus calls a demand for capital I call high profits' (II, p. 331).
34 '... improvements in agriculture, or in machinery, which shall facilitate or augment production, will, according to my proposition, increase profits, because "it will augment production compared with the means necessary to that production" ...' (VI, p. 145).
35 Malthus had again asserted this in his letter of 23 November 1814. 'The diminution of wages is a more directly necessary consequence of a difficulty in obtaining food, than the diminution of profits' (VI, p. 155).
36 'The capitalist "who may find it necessary to employ a hundred days labour instead of fifty in order to produce a certain quantity of corn" cannot retain the same share for himself unless the labourers who are employed for a hundred days will be satisfied with the same quantity for their subsistence that the labourers employed for fifty had before. If you suppose the price of corn doubled, the capital to be employed estimated in money will probably also be nearly doubled – or at any rate will be greatly augmented ... how it is possible to conceive that the rate of his profits will not be diminished?' (VI, pp. 114–15). See Malthus's example in note 30 above.
37 Garegnani (1982), interprets the non-proportional rise in money value of capital to suggest the inclusion of non-corn elements in wage where capital is all wage-advances.
38 In fact, as Sraffa observes, Ricardo was often to use the phrase 'Value of wages' in the sense of 'proportion of total product going to wages' (I, p. lii).
39 Elsewhere defining 'natural price' Ricardo writes: 'By natural price I mean the usual price as is necessary to supply constantly a given demand' (II, p. 227).

40 The just-cited passage continues: 'Consequently his percentage of profit will be diminished if he values his capital, which he must do, in money at the increased value to which all goods would rise in consequence of the rise of the wages of labour' (VI, p. 120).

41 The following passage from Ricardo's letter of 18 December 1814, to Malthus is typical: 'I have been endeavouring to get you to admit that the profits on stock employed in Manufactures and Commerce are seldom permanently lowered or raised by any other cause than by the cheapness or dearness of necessaries, or of those objects on which the wages of labour are expended. Accumulation of capital has a tendency to lower profits. Why? because every accumulation is attended with increased difficulty in obtaining food, unless it is accompanied with improvements in agriculture ...' (VI, p. 162).

42 See note 36 above.

43 'In this state of society, when the profits on agricultural stock are fifty per cent, the profits on all other capital, employed either in the rude manufactures ... or in foreign commerce ... will be also, fifty per cent' (IV, p. 12).

44 'If the profits on capital employed in the trade were more than fifty per cent, capital would be withdrawn from the land to be employed in trade. If they were less, capital would be taken from trade to agriculture' (IV, p. 12).

45 Interestingly a clear watershed dividing the two parts can be identified when Ricardo, moving into the controversial arena, begins with a reference to the area of agreement between himself and Malthus (IV, p. 15 n).

46 Ricardo argues: 'Not only is the situation of landlord improved, (by the increasing difficulty of procuring food, in consequence of accumulation) by obtaining an increased quantity of the produce of the land, but also by the increased exchangeable value of that quantity' (IV, p. 20).

47 'It has been thought that the price of corn regulates the prices of all other things. This appears to me to be a mistake ... Commodities, I think, cannot materially rise or fall, whilst money and commodities continue in the same proportions, or rather whilst the cost of production of both estimated in corn continues the same' (IV, p. 21n).

48 Hollander's rather involved attempt to reconstruct an alternative explanation meets difficulties. He argues: 'if the agricultural margin is fixed, the productivity of labour (and capital) on land is unchanged and so accordingly is the price of corn. If, then, the money-wage rate is dependent upon the corn price alone, it is too constant, so that the agricultural profit rate remains unchanged. In this case the only way equality across the board can be achieved is if the profit rate elsewhere comes into line as a result of expansion of commerce and manufacturing' (p. 145). There are many ambiguities in the logical sequence of results. Evidently, wages consist of corn alone since the money wage depends upon corn price alone. Also capital here should consist of corn since he considers the corn price to be fixed with the fixity of the agricultural margin without reference to manufacturing prices. Would it not seem that Hollander is implicitly reaching out to a corn rate of profit?.

49 In an important letter to Horner (VI, pp. 186–8) Malthus had pinpointed that 'the fault of Mr Ricardo's table which is curious, is that the advances of the farmer instead of being calculated in corn, should be calculated either in the actual materials of which the capital consists, or in money which is the best representative of a variety of commodities'.

50 At one stage, while Ricardo concedes Malthus's argument to be ingenious, he continues: '... but I think you err in supposing it possible that the

proportion of the whole corn expenditure, to the produce obtained, can fall, with an increase of the price of corn. The two are incompatible – either the whole corn expences of production will be increased or not. If they be, the price of corn will rise – but if they be not I can see no reason for a rise in the price of corn' (VI, pp. 192–3). Here, Ricardo shows very little appreciation of the *relative* value question which is a hall mark of *Principles*.

51 For example, in an illustrative example (VI, p. 193) where Ricardo first supposes the price of corn to increase in proportion to the number of men employed, he adds: '... the price of corn would not I think rise in proportion to the greater number of men employed but to the greater amount of wages paid' (VI, p. 193). This stands in bold contrast to the very opening statement of Ricardo in *Principles* that the value of a commodity does not depend 'on the greater or less compensation which is paid for labour' (I, p. 11) (See Garegnani, 1982). Also when Ricardo discusses the applicability of his 'Table' with Malthus (letter dated 21 April 1815, VI, p. 220), it is striking that even after stating the labour theory of value in its incipient form, he harks back to the quantities of the *'Table'*.

52 It is interesting to compare this with Sraffa's reading of the role of labour theory. 'The surplus principle of profit determination is advanced from the corn case to a general one as, with the adoption of the labour theory, heterogenous aggregates like output, wages and capital entering that determination can be all reckoned in labour terms. Labour is the ideal standard sought corresponding to that of theory of value'. (see I, p. xxxii).

53 Hollander having maintained so, adds: 'In his [Ricardo's] view Smith went too far in modifying his original emphasis upon labour input as an explanation of exchange value' (p. 193), suggesting that Ricardo's objection is to the extent of modification. Such a suggestion is in line with Hollander's general view that adoption of labour theory is justified mainly on empirical grounds (see below).

54 Hollander supports the view of Piero Sraffa, in saying 'between the first and the third edition of *Principles, there was no retreat from the strict labour theory*' (p. 217, italics added), although on p. 209 he states that Ricardo 'has never formulated a strict labour theory'. It is interesting that Hollander goes on to argue that 'the quantitative significance' of modifications is actually increasingly played down in subsequent years', using Ricardo's arithmetical illustrations in support. A contrast between the basic arguments of Hollander and Sraffa against the 'weakening' is evident when we look closely at their interpretation of the change of wording in the third edition from the first which formed the ground for Cannan's suggestion about 'the weakening'. (In the third edition, 'almost exclusive determination' of relative values by labour replaced 'the sole determination' in the first.) While Sraffa explains that the change was necessitated by the properties of the different invariant standard adopted in the third edition – and hence by requirements of theoretical consistency – Hollander attributes it to Ricardo's 'need for greater care in avoiding excessively strong statements, which he had sometimes allowed to stand in the original edition' (p. 217, n. 77). This again links up with Hollander's interpretation of the choice of labour theory as primarily dictated by pragmatic, empiricist considerations.

55 Ricardo asks: 'Is it not clear then that as soon as we are in possession of the knowledge of the circumstances which determine the value of commodities, we are enabled to say what is necessary to give us an invariable measure of value?' (IX, p. 358).

56 '... Ricardo seems to have missed the characteristic feature of Torrens's approach to value which in effect amounts to an explanation of the structure of prices solely in terms of accumulated labour, current labour playing no part at all' (p. 211).
57 '... These capitals are not the same in kind ... and if they themselves are produced in unequal times they are subject to the same fluctuations as other commodities. Till you have fixed the criterion by which we are to ascertain value, you can say nothing of equal capitals' (IX, p. 360).
58 In the 'Absolute Value and Exchangeable Value', Ricardo attempted to reduce price to labour remaining dormant over various periods and sought to define the standard in terms of an average time duration over which advances are made. However, Ricardo recognized that 'the proportions in which immediate labour and accumulated labour enter into different commodities are exceedingly various and *will not admit of definite enumeration*' (IV, p. 379, italics added).
59 Hollander, however, is of the contrary opinion (p. 238).
60 'What we want is a standard measure of value which shall itself be invariable, and therefore shall accurately measure the variations of other things ... Whatever commodity any man selects as a measure of real value, has no other title for adoption, but with being a less variable commodity than any other' (II, pp. 29–30).
61 Hollander, therefore, opposes the view of Blaug (1958, p. 70) that the substitution effects of the third edition is an 'unintegrated afterthought' (p. 225).
62 Hollander equates the approach also with Walrasian general equilibrium.
63 'A disturbance limited to a *single* industry, such as a change in input coefficients or a tax or subsidy, will generate an alteration in quantity, and consequent alteration in price, to re-establish the original return on capital in that industry and assure that in the new long-run equilibrium price will again cover costs reckoned on the basis of the (unchanged) general rates of wages and profit. But a disturbance affecting *all* sectors equally (such as a change in wage rate) will have no *differential* effects on profitability at going prices and therefore will generate no changes in activity and will thus leave prices unchanged. The only effect will be on general profits; the unchanged prices will still cover costs but the make-up of costs will be altered' (p. 271).
64 For a discussion, see Eatwell (1975), Garegnani (1984), Bharadwaj (1978a) and Roncaglia (1978 and 1982).
65 'In the ordinary course of events, there is no commodity which continues for any length of time to be supplied precisely in that degree of abundance, which the wants and wishes of mankind require, and therefore there is none which is not subject to accidental and temporary variations of price'. Further, 'It is only in consequence of such variations, that capital is apportioned precisely, in the requisite abundance and no more, to the production of the different commodities which happen to be in demand' (I, p. 88, also p. 119).
66 The 'natural rate of profit' is defined when the effectual demand, the methods of production and wage are known. It is not necessary that the *natural* rate of profit prevails actually or that the *actual* rates of profit are uniform in all sectors. This is clear in all the classical writers, including Ricardo. If the methods of production remain unchanged, the movement in the rate of profit when wage changes, is along the same wage profit frontier; if the methods change, the frontier itself would shift.

67 Ricardo's unequivocal rejection of utility governing value in his comment on J. B. Say, is deemed by Hollander 'as hasty in his own terms' (p. 278 n. 22).
68 See Bharadwaj (1978b; Chapter 6 below) where the classical distinction between use value and exchange value is emphasized and Marshall's attempt to read the 'total/marginal' distinction in Ricardo is criticized.
69 The classical value and distribution system also involves simultaneous determination of prices, and the rate of profit in a different theoretical framework from that of Walras.

References: Chapter 4

Bentham, J. (1954), *Bentham's Economic Writings*, ed. W. Stark, Vol. III (London: George Allen & Unwin)

Bharadwaj, K. (1978a), *Classical Political Economy and the Rise to Dominance of Demand and Supply Theories* (Calcutta: Orient Longman); Revised edition, 1986

Bharadwaj, K. (1978b), 'The subversion of classical analysis: Alfred Marshall's early writing on value', *Cambridge Journal of Economics*, vol. 2, no. 3 (September), pp. 253–71; Chapter 6 in the present volume

Blaug, M. (1958), *Ricardian Economics: A Historical Study* (New Haven, Conn.: Yale University Press)

Bosanquet, C. (1810), *Practical Observations on the Report of the Bullion Committee* (London)

Dmitriev, V. K. (1974), *Economic Essay on Value, Competition and Utility*, ed. by D. M. Nuti (Cambridge: Cambridge University Press)

Dobb, M. H. (1973), *Theories of Value and Distribution since Adam Smith* (Cambridge: Cambridge University Press)

Eatwell, J. L. (1975), 'The interpretation of Ricardo's *Essay on Profits*', *Economica*, vol. 42, no. 166 (May), pp. 182–7

Garegnani, P. (1982), 'On Hollander's interpretation of Ricardo's early theory of profits', *Cambridge Journal of Economics* vol. 6, no. 1 (March)

Garegnani, P. (1984), 'Value and Distribution in the Classical Economists and Marx', *Oxford Economic Papers*, vol. 36, pp. 291–325

Hollander, S. (1973), 'Ricardo's analysis of the profit rate, 1813–15', *Economica*, XI (August), pp. 260–82

Hollander, S. (1975), 'Ricardo and the corn profit model: reply to Eatwell', *Economica*, XIII (May), pp. 188–202

Hollander, S. (1979), *The Economics of David Ricardo* (Toronto: Heinemann)

Hollander, S. (1982), 'A reply to Roncaglia', *Journal of Post-Keynesian Economics*, vol. 4, no. 3 (Spring), pp. 360–72

Malthus, T. R. (1815a), *The Grounds of an Opinion on the Policy of Restricting the Importation of Foreign Corn.* (London: Murray)

Malthus, T. R. (1815b), *An Inquiry into the Nature and Progress of Rent and the Principles by which it is Regulated* (London: Murray)

Malthus, T. R. (1836), *Principles of Political Economy*, 2nd edn, with additions and an original memoir (London: Murray)

Marshall, A. (1920), *Principles of Economics*, 8th edn (London: Macmillan)

Meek, R. L. (1950), 'The decline of Ricardian economics in England', reprinted in Meek, R. L., *Economics and Ideology and other Essays* (London), pp. 51–74

Mill, James (1821), *Elements of Political Economy*, 1st end (London: Bohn)

Pasinetti, L. L. (1974), *Growth and Income Distribution: Essays in Economic Theory* (Cambridge: Cambridge University Press)

Ricardo, D. (1810–23 [1951–73]), *Works and Correspondence of David Ricardo*, ed. by P. Sraffa, with the collaboration of M. H. Dobb, 10 vols and *Index* (Cambridge: Cambridge University Press)

Roncaglia, A. (1978), *Sraffa and the Theory of Prices* (New York: Wiley)

Roncaglia, A. (1982), 'Hollander's Ricardo', *Journal of Post-Keynesian Economics*, vol. 4, no. 3 (Spring), pp. 339–59 and 'Rejoinder', ibid., pp. 373–5

Schumpeter, J. (1954), *History of Economic Analysis* (London: Allen & Unwin)

Smith, A. (1776 [1937]), *An Inquiry into the Nature and Causes of the Wealth of Nations*, ed. by E. Cannan (New York: Modern Library)

Sraffa, P. (1951–73), Editorial introductions to *Works and Correspondence of David Ricardo*, Vols I–X, op. cit.

Trotter, C. (1810), *The Principles of Currency and Exchange* (London)

Walras, L. (1926), *Elements of Pure Economics*, ed. by W. Jaffe (London: George Allen & Unwin)

5

Sraffa's Ricardo

Sraffa's monumental edition, *The Works and Correspondence of David Ricardo* (1951–73)[1] in eleven volumes (with the collaboration of Maurice Dobb) is widely acknowledged in the profession for its rare and magnificent scholarship. Although the search for unpublished manuscripts for the edition commenced in 1930,[2] it was not until 1951 that the first volumes of the *Works* appeared in print. It is striking that Piero Sraffa, a remarkably original thinker and a nonconformist in many ways, immersed himself in editing the works of a single writer over such a protracted period of his youthful years. Stigler (1953) counts this as one among a number of 'fortunate' circumstances for Ricardo.[3] It, perhaps, reflects more Sraffa's own evaluation and perception of the crucial significance of Ricardo in the formation and development of economic theory, a deep concern engaging Sraffa from his earlier writings.[4] An understanding of Ricardo's theory is crucial in order to decipher the logical foundations of classical political economy in its formative beginnings, as well as to grasp the origins of the later marginalism which eventually submerged the classical approach. In his later work, *Production of Commodities by Means of Commodities* (1960), Sraffa was to seek a 'return' to the standpoint 'of the old classical economists from Adam Smith to Ricardo'. His work on Ricardo needs to be perceived in the light of this larger objective, although it does not contradict the fact that, in presenting Ricardo's works, he assiduously maintains the utmost objective neutrality in following Ricardo's own trail of inquiry.[5]

When the *Works* first appeared no reader or reviewer could but be impressed by the meticulous care and precision born of the indefatigable searches for information, in the minutest detail, which suffused the editorial commentaries. Sraffa's reputation until then rested on his razor-sharp logic as a critic, his introduction, particularly to English readers, being through his assaults on Marshallian orthodoxy and on Hayek (see Sraffa, 1925, 1926, 1930, 1932). The *Works* revealed another facet of his scholarship – as a patient explorer and constructive thinker. Reconstructing Ricardo from his own materials, Sraffa's commentary brought to light the analytical underpinnings of Ricardo's thought and the logical structure of his arguments. The brevity and severe self-abnegation reflected in these editorial notes, however, concealed, in the unobtrusive phrases and remarks, their powerful insights so that Stigler, who reviewed the first nine volumes and gave fulsome praise to their erudition, wrote that 'these nine volumes often amplify and sometimes modify our understanding of his [Ricardo's] doctrines, but they do not change it in essentials'. Further, 'Aside from the Introduction to Volume I, Sraffa's editorial prefaces and notes serve an informative rather than interpretative function. The editorial notes are superb; they are never obtrusive or pedantical; and they maintain unfailing neutrality' (1953, p. 304). As later events have proved, Sraffa's commentaries on Ricardo have had a far greater impact and influence than this appreciation recognized. We need to note, however, that Sraffa's originality in the interpretation of Ricardo is not that of an inventor, but of an explorer.

Sraffa's 'Introduction' to Volume 1 of Ricardo's *Principles*,[6] which Stigler, as quoted above, considers interpretative more than informative, attracted much attention; especially the single paragraph wherein Sraffa offered the 'rational foundation' for Ricardo's principle of the determining role of the profits of agriculture (expounded in the *Essay*).[7] He followed this argument up by indicating the instrumental role of the labour theory of value in the generalization of the theory of profits in *Principles* (I, pp. xxxi–xxxii). The attractive formal properties of the 'corn model' were to induce a number of theoretical exercises by authors with widely different perspectives (see Baumol, 1965; Kaldor, 1953–4; Pasinetti, 1974; Samuelson, 1959, among others). Many other perceptive remarks and passages in the widely – but not always deeply read – 'Introduction', containing insights into the logical structure of Ricardo's theory of value and distribution passed relatively unnoticed. Sraffa's *Production of Commodities*, reviving the classical standpoint, appears to have drawn out the fuller import of some of these perceptions and observations in the editorial commentaries, and has generated renewed controversy on the interpretation of Ricardo's theory and its position in classical political economy as well as its relation with marginalist theory. Ricardo once again arouses controversy, after more than a century and a half, as much as he did when he made his stormy entry into theoretical debates with his 1815 *Essay*.

In the following section we focus on the significance of the contribution that the Sraffa edition makes to our stock of knowledge on Ricardo, and the new light that his editorial commentaries throw upon a number of controversial issues. In Section 2, we note a theoretical standpoint that emerges in Sraffa's reading of Ricardo's theory of value and distribution in opposition to certain other viewpoints and interpretations that have had an important influence on the understanding of Ricardo. In the concluding section we refer briefly to certain prominent controversies that have emerged in more recent times, particularly after the publication of Sraffa's independent work, *Production of Commodities*.

1 Sraffa as Editor of Ricardo

In 1933 Keynes, who had entrusted the work of the Ricardo edition to Sraffa, had remarked that Piero Sraffa 'from whom nothing is hid' would bring out the works of Ricardo within that year (Keynes, 1933, p. 138). The long-delayed publication of the *Works* had its compensation in terms of the invaluable finds that rewarded the relentless investigations of Sraffa, who pursued every minute clue for tracing missing papers and collecting relevant evidence. Among these new materials were the discovery of both sides of the extensive correspondence between Ricardo and James Mill, and Malthus's letters to Ricardo, as well as other miscellaneous letters published in the volumes of letters (*Works*, VI–IX). Among the several papers and notes, previously unpublished, was found the paper on 'Absolute Value and Exchangeable Value', left unfinished by Ricardo at the time of his sudden death. The story of the discoveries is narrated by Sraffa in the general preface in his characteristic style: all the relevant information and concrete details are densely packed into brief observations which, nevertheless, are alive with a sense of drama and the thrill of discovery. While 'providence' and 'accident' played their part, it is probably the diligent and relentless pursuit, tracking down persons and materials with an investigator's ingenuity and armed with a familiarity of historical events and records, that allowed Sraffa to achieve the comprehensiveness of the *Works* and to suffuse the editorial notes with the vast fund of information on the events and personages, as well as the economics, of the period. Illustrative of this is the Appendix, 'Mr.— of the Bullion Report' (*Works*, III, pp. 425–34), wherein Sraffa builds up a conjecture as to the identity of 'Mr.—' in the Bullion Report, an 'anonymous continental merchant'. As in many other cases, Sraffa's conjecture was later confirmed by independent evidence. (For example, Stigler [1953] reports how Sraffa's conjecture as to how two chapter eights appeared in the first edition [*Works*, I, p. xxviii] was verified by the discovery of a copy in the Columbia Library.)

Sraffa's primary role is not merely that of an intellectual sleuth: the analytical order that he brought to the entire material is evident even in the forms of presentation that he carefully adopted. For example, in annotating changes in the successive editions of Ricardo's *Principles*, he provided a useful table of concordance. The arrangement was used profitably by Sraffa in his own 'Introduction' to adduce important evidence for his analytical interpretations of the changes in the text which had earlier provided fertile ground for speculation on Ricardo's ideas, their logical content and his 'intentions'. Ricardo's *Notes on Malthus* are also presented in a form (*Works*, II) which immediately brings to the readers the textual context of Ricardo's notes and the exact points of controversy between Ricardo and Malthus. The historical material is presented with a concrete sense of events and persons. In presenting the correspondence, for example, Sraffa so arranges and annotates the letters that 'the reader is thus placed as it were behind Ricardo's desk at Gatcomb Park and reads the letters as Ricardo writes them or receives them' (*Works*, VI, p. xiv). Volume XI, the *Index* for the *Works*, is a masterpiece by itself, where the meticulously phrased entries capture their analytical essence in precise terms. We know that the final version of the *Index* was published after several earlier efforts had been discarded by

Sraffa as unsatisfactory. The *Index*, too, as other parts of the *Works*, exudes brevity but not at the cost of precision.

Thanks to his Herculean efforts, Sraffa offers a complete picture of Ricardo's intellectual activities and associations during his short but active career. Further, as Sraffa himself remarks:

> It is perhaps unique in economic literature for the writings, letters and speeches of one thinker to have such unity of subject matter ... that although his works and correspondence are extant almost complete, they admit of publication virtually in their entirety as being all of them of interest to the economist. (I, p. vii)

It is this unity of the subject-matter and comprehensiveness which Sraffa uses profitably to present Ricardo's intellectual itinerary.

The filling in of the major gaps in the Ricardo papers thus gives a unity and historical continuity to the development of Ricardo's ideas. This is all the more important because Ricardo, carving out his own theoretical framework and attempting to achieve consistency within the same, discussed his 'peculiar' theories and ideas in the correspondence which, along with the published works, presents a continuous flow and exchange of ideas. With their help, Sraffa helps us to perceive the manner in which Ricardo posed certain central questions (particularly on the explanation of the rate of profits on which he appears to have been continuously engaged), the form which theoretical difficulties successively assumed in his frame of thinking – and were perceived, as such, by him and his contemporaries – as well as the means which he sought to resolve the difficulties.

Speculations about Ricardo's theoretical positions and changes in them, and also about the grounds of differences with his contemporaries, have arisen on the basis of the diverse interpretations by scholars who often could not have access to Ricardo's correspondence and notes – at least, not in their entirety. Some of these instances are examined by Sraffa in his 'Introduction', utilizing the new exegetical and other evidence. An important example is that of assessing the exact content and nature of James Mill's contribution to Ricardo's theoretical writings. While the correspondence bears out Mill's influence in stimulating and encouraging Ricardo, Sraffa shows that 'it was less than might have been expected from the promises and encouragement', and certainly does not support a view that was first voiced by Professor Dunbar (1887, p. 471) that 'Ricardo's book was written, not for the public eye but as a statement of opinions made for his own purposes, and that its publication was an afterthought of his friends'. This comment was not confined to incidental observations on Ricardo's personal character, but had a much deeper impact when Marshall used the same ground to suggest that this explained Ricardo's proclivity to omit 'many things' which were necessary to the logical completeness of his arguments but which would have been regarded by him as obvious to the 'statesmen and businessmen' to whom he primarily addressed his researches.[8]

Marshall then attempted to provide the logical complements to Ricardo's theory, and thence to suggest that Ricardo shared the same theoretical perspective and approach as his own. What is even more important is that certain misunderstandings of Ricardo's position on value appear to have crept into the 'Index' to his *Principles* (*Works*, I) which was probably compiled by James Mill. Critics pointing out inconsistencies between the text and the 'Index' interpreted these inconsistencies as reflecting Ricardo's ambivalencies and contradictions, particularly on the labour theory of value (see pp. xxi–xxii).[9] It may seem that the influence of James Mill on Ricardo's theoretical writings or Ricardo's writing habits are rather trivial matters to deserve the elaborate attention they receive in Sraffa's 'Introduction', but this is not so. Indeed, it is remarkable how the related misunderstandings on these matters provided a basis for bold and significant inferences regarding the logical status and structure of Ricardo's theory, persuading generous interpreters to impose their own system and logical order – and hostile critics to discard Ricardo's theory altogether.

Similarly important are Sraffa's detailed discussions of what may seem purely technical and formalistic matters regarding 'arrangements and subdivisions' of chapters in Ricardo's *Principles*. Ricardo's critics commented on the lack of system and the defective structure of the *Principles*, not only attributing these to a lack of orderly design, but also interpreting them as reflecting impromptu and incomplete theoretical reasoning, with the resultant vacillations. Sraffa retraces the history of the publication of the *Principles* in order to bring out convincingly the analytical considerations which Ricardo would have had in altering the arrangements of his subject-matter. In another instance, too, using a comparison between Ricardo's *Principles* and Smith's *Wealth of Nations* with respect to their chapter sequences and subject orderings, Sraffa throws light on the analytical content of Ricardo's critique of Smith. Thus what may appear in these commentaries as the preoccupation of a fastidious perfectionist with purely technical points bears a significance for the understanding of Ricardo's theory.

2 Sraffa's Interpretation of Ricardo

It is mainly Sraffa's 'Introduction' to the *Principles* that suggested a fresh reading of Ricardo on the basis of the comprehensive material. Ricardo's theory has roused incessant controversy almost from its inception. There is hardly any opinion on any aspect of Ricardo that has passed unquestioned. Controversies have ranged over a wide range of issues, such as

(1) The *content* of the Ricardian system: What are the central tenets or what forms the central core of his theory?[10]
(2) The *structure of his value and distribution theory*: is he to be considered as one of the pillars of the classical approach which has a

distinctive structure and standpoint, or is he one of the progenitors who provided building blocks for the supply-and-demand-based equilibrium theory?[11]

(3) The *inception* of Ricardo's theory: did he make any original contributions, or did he essentially borrow theories from others to use them for the pragmatic purposes of supporting certain policy conclusions? (see Patten, 1893; Gordon, 1976; Hutchison, 1952).

(4) The *reception* of Ricardian theory (see, among others, S. Hollander, 1979; Fetter, 1969; Stigler, 1958). Did Ricardo's doctrines dominate the theoretical scene or did they meet with stiff resistance during and after his lifetime?

(5) The 'decline' of Ricardian economics: did the decline occur at all, and if so, when?

(6) Ricardo's *method*: was he an abstract thinker with a love for paradoxes who took delight in theoretical speculation on the basis of 'strong cases', or was he a man of practical affairs, caring little for theoretical neatness and completeness? (See, among others, Dunbar, 1887; Marshall, 1920; J. H. Hollander, 1876; Patten, 1893).

(7) The *evaluation* of Ricardo's contribution has been equally diverse. To mention only a few, Schumpeter (1954) considered his theory an 'unnecessary detour'; Jevons (1871) argued vehemently that he had shunted the car of theory onto a wrong line; Marshall (1920) believed that his exposition was as confused as his thought was profound; Marx (1862–3) thought that 'scientific political economy' attained its acme in Ricardo.

The picture of Ricardo that emerges from the *Works* is of an original thinker engaged in a constant struggle to formulate a consistent theory of value and distribution within the framework of analysis handed down from the Physiocrats and Adam Smith. While Ricardo was conscious of the fact that he was not trained in the art of literary expression and expressed his modesty and hesitation on that account several times, he had a penetrating mind which could grasp the essentials of a logical argument (as becomes clear from the many exchanges with Malthus) and he was confident of the correct direction and the meaningfulness of his questions. More important, he appears often to be sufficiently aware that he did not possess adequate answers, as in the case of the 'modifications' of the labour values needed to accommodate variations in relative values caused by a variation in the division of produce between wages and profits, or the connected issue of the properties required of an 'invariant standard' corresponding to the theory of value proposed. His genuine modesty and diffidence in the matter of the literary execution of his ideas does not inhibit him from stating his case boldly and persistently. This confidence in his own propositions does not appear to be born of unyielding doggedness, for he did borrow theories from others when he found that they fitted suitably into his framework, and he did modify his opinions when confronted with what he regarded as superior arguments. The controversy with Malthus was particularly productive, as often Malthus's objections stimulated Ricardo's ideas towards greater cogency. We shall take up what appears to be Ricardo's theoretical system for detailed consideration in Section 3. Here we shall confine ourselves to the important analytical issues which Sraffa takes up directly in his 'Introduction' to the *Principles* which provide insights into the rational basis of Ricardo's particular statements, especially those that have been the subject of controversy.

While many of the evaluations of Ricardo have been prompted by the not-uncommon proclivity of theorists to discover in his work happy anticipations of their own viewpoints and perceptions, there remained also an inherent difficulty in the task of interpreting him. For his theoretical efforts in their formative stage involved new concepts or the novel use or interpretation of old concepts. Ricardo was himself conscious of his 'peculiar' opinions and doctrines, the elucidation and modification of which occurred in his correspondence and unpublished notes, as well as his published works. The unique feature of this correspondence has already been remarked upon above. Ricardo's short career in political economy, and his premature death when he was struggling with the problem of value (as testified in the unfinished manuscript on 'Absolute Value and Exchangeable Value') had left many loose ends and abortive attempts at reconciliation of his theory. Difficulty or absence of access to these papers – which now, thanks to Sraffa, are made available – had left room for speculation. Some instances of the misunderstandings about Ricardo's theory originating from this are noted by Sraffa in his 'Introduction'.

It was from the vantage point of a close and careful knowledge of the comprehensive materials on Ricardo that Sraffa reconstructed, in his 'Introduction', the process through which Ricardo's ideas developed. It is by following closely in Ricardo's tracks (the way in which he formulates and approaches the problem of distribution and, through it, of value and the form in which difficulties successively arise and are perceived by Ricardo, and the rationale of the procedures he adopts to resolve the difficulties) that Sraffa seeks to delineate the theoretical structure underlying Ricardo's various propositions and theoretical stances.

3   The Development of Ricardo's Theory of Profits

Sraffa focuses upon the theory of profits as the central and continuing concern of Ricardo and shows that he arrives at the value problem, in the peculiar form it takes in his theory, in the course of his attempts to provide a consistent explanation of the rate of profits and of a definite relation between the share of wages in net product and the rate of profits. This accent on the profits theory and the derivative significance of the value problem are an important reflection of the classical structure of value- and distribution-determination which Ricardo appears to follow. (More on this, in Section 4 below.) This view stands somewhat in contrast to the one that is more commonly held, particularly among the marginalists, that the significant elements in Ricardo are the theory of rent (or the principle of diminishing returns), and the population doctrine (or the notion of a fixed, subsistence 'equilibrium' wage). Jevons, for example, was to maintain that, among all the Ricardian tenets, the theories of rent and of population were 'scientific in form and consonant with facts', and he saw the theory of rent as giving 'a clue to the correct mode of treating a whole science' (Jevons, 1871 [1971], p. 43). Stigler, writing on the Ricardian theory of value and distribution in an article which was submitted for publication prior to the arrival of the Ricardo volumes (see Stigler, 1952, fn 1) considered these two principles as the 'two main strands' and 'pillars' of the Ricardian system. Baumol (1965) saw the 'magnificent dynamics' of the Ricardian system in the tendency to stationary state envisaged by Ricardo, following the tendency to a declining rate of profit with progressive cultivation. Blaug (1958, p. 5) saw the Ricardian approach to economic development, 'broadly conceived in terms of a conflict between tendencies towards increasing or diminishing returns' survive down to the present. Sraffa's account of the history of Ricardo's theory of profits establishes that the explanation of profit, which was first published in the *Essay on Profits* around 24 February 1815, had been formulated by Ricardo prior to the appearance of the theory of rent in publications by Malthus, West and Torrens.

> In February 1814 Ricardo had written some 'papers on the profits of capital' which he had shown to Malthus, Trower and Mill. These papers have not survived, but a summary of their contents, contained in a letter to Trower of 8th March 1814 shows that the theory of profits, which was to appear in the pamphlet of the following year, was already fully developed. (*Works*, IV, p. 3)

In February 1815, Malthus's pamphlet on rent appeared and Ricardo was able 'to write [his essay] within a few days by using his already developed theory of profits', incorporating Malthus's theory of rent. Ricardo's theory of profits was also formed independently of West's pamphlet on rent, as Ricardo had already mentioned his theory in his letters of 1813 to Malthus and Torrens. Sraffa concludes:

> Although Ricardo opens his Introduction with the statement that in treating the subject of profits it is necessary to consider the principle of rent, the fact is that for the previous two years in his letters he had been working out his theory of profits without ever finding it necessary explicitly to mention rent. Indeed, the theory of profits presented in the pamphlet adds little to what was already contained in his letters of 1813 and 1814, before his attention had been directed to the connection between rent and profits. (*Works*, IV, pp. 7–8)

As Patten (1893, p. 329) observed: 'The law of rent came into Ricardo's system, not as a basis, but as a better proof of a theory already developed.'

In the history of economic thought, the debate on the Ricardian origins of the theory of rent has been treated primarily as an issue concerning the priority or originality of Ricardo. Sraffa's concern, however, is to lay bare the logical basis of Ricardo's theory of profits and its relation to the theory of rent.

The importance attached to rent as explained by the diminishing returns (extensive and intensive) in agriculture in the 'Ricardian system', particularly by marginalist interpreters, has had some important consequences for the interpretation of the basis of Ricardo's explanation of profits, and of the structure of Ricardo's theory of value and distribution, in general. Sraffa points out that a consequence of the mistaken popular belief that Ricardo actually invented the theory of rent, is 'that of regarding Ricardo as the originator of the whole marginal theory' (*Works*, IV, p. 6). In later marginalist theory, the principle of diminishing marginal returns in agriculture was generalized into the law of variable proportions to yield monotonic functional relations between factor-intensity and factor-prices – whereby the 'marginal principle' seen as underlying rent theory was extended to explain all factor-returns. Sraffa (*Works*, IV, p. 6, fn 1) quotes Clark (1931) as testifying to this development: 'The Ricardian law of rents ... is the first great example of the marginal method, later to become the keystone of the entire Austrian system of economic theory.'

Ricardo was indeed aware of the phenomenon of diminishing returns on land, as observed by Sraffa (*Works*, IV, p. 5), but in his letters of 1813 and 1814 he had applied the principle only to his theory of profits. In fact, in these letters he discusses how only improvements in agriculture or new facilities for the production of food can prevent an increase of capital from lowering the rate of profits. The theory of rent allowed Ricardo to get rid of rents from the net produce so as to isolate the relation between wages and profits. His discussion suggested a particular relation between the produce and unit costs in the case of agriculture where land was a non-reproducible asset fixed in supply for the economy. This was not generalized by Ricardo to all cases of production, as was done in later theory. Furthermore, Ricardo insisted that rents did not enter price and he did not rely on the phenomenon of 'diminishing returns' to explain the formation of price. Indeed, when Ricardo does attempt to generalize his theory of profits, he turns to the labour theory of value as an explanation of value consistent with his theory of profits, as we shall see below.

A basic principle that Ricardo adheres to in his letters of 1814 and early 1815 is that 'it is the profits of the farmer that regulate the profits of all the other trades'. This principle met strong opposition in Malthus, who argues that the profits of the farmer no more regulate those of the other trades than vice versa. Sraffa points out that 'After the *Essay* this principle disappears from view, and is not to be found in the *Principles*' (I, p. xxxi). In *Principles*, the more general proposition that the productivity on land which pays no rent is fundamental in determining general profits continues to occupy a central position.

Thus the determining principle of the rate of profits appears to have been worked out by Ricardo prior to, and independently of, the theory of rent. The contribution of the explanation of rent appears to have been to allow Ricardo to isolate the part of net product going to wages and profits by eliminating rents. In thus arriving at a determination of the rate of profits, Ricardo appears to have followed the method, known to classical economists from the Physiocrats, of determining the part of produce available for distribution among the revenue-sharers as gross produce minus 'productive consumption', the latter constituting the material means of production and the sustenance of labour required for producing that gross output. Profits were the difference between total product (after eliminating rents) and 'capital advanced' (constituting material means of production and the sustenance of labour), and the rate of profits is the ratio of profits to capital advanced.

Sraffa suggests a 'rational foundation' for the principle of the determining role of the profits of agriculture (clarifying, however, that it is never explicitly stated by Ricardo): namely, that in agriculture the same commodity, corn, forms both the capital and the product, so that the rate of profits emerges directly as a ratio between quantities of corn without any question of valuation. If the other trades then have to yield a uniform rate of profit, under competition, it is the value of other trades that must adjust. Thus in the *Essay*, at the cost of considerable simplification, Ricardo had been able to demonstrate clearly the relation between profits and wages. Once the wage and the methods of production are 'given' ('given', meaning that the given 'effectual' or social demand for corn fixes the limit to the cultivation (extensive/intensive) and hence determines the method of production which pays no rent),[12] profits are seen as the 'surplus produce' of corn, that is, the residual output after payment of corn wages and corn capital. This rate of profits could also be shown to be 'dependent upon wages' since the rate of profit and wages were clearly inversely related.

Malthus opposed the determining role of agricultural profits by attacking the notion that wages consist of corn alone. Ricardo's attempt to generalize the profits determination brought him to the realization that his theory would need a consistent theory of relative values. Sraffa identifies 'a turning point' in the transition from the *Essay* to the *Principles* when, at the end of 1815, having set to work on the *Principles*, he wrote to Mill: 'I know I shall soon be stopped by the word price.' (*Works*, VI, p. 348; letter dated 30 December 1815). It is also pointed out by Sraffa (*Works*, I, p. xiv) that, even in the letters of October and November 1815, when Ricardo was discussing the main headings of the proposed work with Mill, there is no reference to 'value'. This is mentioned for the first time in the letter of 30 December 1815 above. It would seem that Ricardo realized the inadequacy of dealing piecemeal with the question of relative values in particular contexts, as he had done in his previous writings (see Bharadwaj, 1983a).

Several pieces of evidence are offered by Sraffa to show how Ricardo became aware of the need for a theory of relative values for the purpose of determining profits. Both 'net produce' and 'capital advanced', in the general case, would constitute heterogeneous aggregates. In the post-*Essay* correspondence, it is clear that while Ricardo quickly acceded to the reasonableness of Malthus's criticism he also attempted to carry forward the argument in terms of the aggregates, on the analogy of corn (Garegnani, 1982). During the post-*Essay* debate with Malthus, Ricardo realized that he had not made adequate allowance for the altered value of raw-manufacture costs which would be an influence separate from wages on their price. In the debate, questions were persistently raised as to the effects of the increasing difficulty of agricultural production and the consequent rise in corn price and wage on the size of the net product and the ratio of that surplus produce to the whole capital employed. From the terms of this discussion, it is obvious that neither Ricardo nor Malthus had, at this stage, a rigorous perception of the formation of relative prices. The struggle to establish his theory of profits under alternative assumptions concerning the influence of the corn price on manufacturing prices was seen by Ricardo to be leading to a 'labyrinth' of difficulties in 'an endless succession' (*Works*, VI, pp. 212–14).

The significance of the labour theory of value in this context is seen by Sraffa thus:

> In the *Principles* ... with the adoption of a general theory of value, it became possible for Ricardo to demonstrate the determination of the rate of profit in society as a whole instead of through the microcosm of one special branch of production ... It was now labour, instead of corn, that appeared on both sides of the account – in modern terms, both as input and output: as a result, the rate of profits was no longer determined by the ratio of corn produced to the corn used up in production, but, instead, by the ratio of the total labour of the country to the labour required to produce the necessaries for that labour (*Works*, I, p. xxxii).

It was inevitable that the question of relative values would emerge demanding explicit consideration, once Ricardo attempted to move away from the early explanation of profits in its primitive, agricultural form. In this early, pre-*Essay* phase, Ricardo continues to adhere to the Smithian position that a rise in the price of corn leads to a rise in all prices. He did not recognize the contradiction between his theory of profits and the Smithian proposition, since in the case of the primitive agricultural form of the theory, the problem of valuation did not surface. In the *Essay* some elements in the *Principles* are foreshadowed, when he states the proposition that no other prices need change as a consequence of the rise in value of corn and measures 'the difficulty of production' by the amount of labour required for production. He does not, however, at this stage, either elaborate or consistently formulate his own theory of value in opposition to Smith. These elements in the *Essay* are carried forward and, with new additional arguments, developed into a more systematic theory of value in the *Principles*.

Investigating the influence of a change in wage on relative values, Ricardo was to realize that differences in the composition of the means of production of commodities would create another cause for changes in their relative values. A change in wage would not cause a change in the relative value of commodities unless their conditions of production differed. His attention was particularly drawn to the 'curious effect' which the rise of wage produced on the prices of those commodities 'chiefly obtained by the aid of machinery and fixed capital'.

This theme of the effect of a rise in corn price ran parallel to Ricardo's theory of profits which, however, as we saw earlier, developed initially in a context where Ricardo did not see valuation as an integral problem.[13] As Sraffa remarks:

> The importance which Ricardo came to attach to the principle that the value of a thing was regulated by the quantity of labour required for its production, and not by the remuneration of that labour, reflected his recognition that what his new theory was opposed to was not merely the popular view of the effect of wages on prices but another and more general theory of Adam Smith (of which that effect came to appear as a particular case) – what Ricardo referred to in writing to Mill as Adam Smith's 'original error respecting value'. (*Works*, I, p. xxxv)

The adding-up view of Smith prompted him to maintain that, 'as soon as stock is accumulated in the hands of particular persons' and 'as soon as land of any country has become private property', commodities no longer exchange according to the labour entering their production, but their price is arrived at by adding up the wages, profits and rents, and that all three are component parts of price, and hence sources of exchange value. Smith had proceeded from there to give an independent explanation of rents, profits and wages; in particular, the rate of profit was determined by 'competitions of capitals'. With the adding-up view, it was also easy to fall into the error of supposing all prices to rise or fall with a rise or fall in wage. Ricardo, on the other hand, maintains that 'profits depend upon wages', that is, for given methods of production, the rate of profits and the share of wages in net product vary inversely. Ricardo saw, therefore, that Smith's position on prices contradicted his theory of profits.

Ricardo's opposition to Smith was thus not confined to challenging his proposition on the effect of wage variation on prices. A number of critical readers of the *Principles* discovered an inconsistency in Ricardo's assertion against Smith in the opening chapter, that 'the value of a commodity ... depends on the relative quantity of labour which is necessary for its production, and not on the greater or less compensation which is paid for that labour' (I, p. 11), and his statement in Section IV, in seeming contradiction of above, that the same principle is 'considerably modified' by the employment of machinery and other fixed and durable capital. In that section he agreed that, 'besides the greater or less quantity of labour necessary to produce commodities', the rise or fall in the value of labour could also be the second cause of variation in relative values.

It is the discovery of Ricardo's letter to James Mill (28 December 1818, now available in the *Works* VII, p. 377), that reveals the full import and gives an accurate statement by Ricardo of his position. In the letter, answering a misinterpretation of Torrens, he explains that his opposition to Smith is to his theory that [and] 'after stock was accumulated a part (of produce of labour) went to profits, that accumulation, necessarily, without any regard to the different degrees of durability of capital, or any other circumstance whatever, raised the prices of exchangeable values of commodities'. Ricardo, in contrast, maintains that it is not because of the division into profits and wages, but because of two causes alone that exchange values vary: one, the greater or less quantity of labour required and, two, the greater or less durability of capital. He added that 'the former is never superseded by the latter, but is only modified by it'. The influence that variations in wages have on relative prices cannot be independent of the quantity of labour required in their production. This would seem particularly strengthened by the fact that Ricardo attempted to reduce capital to dated labour (or, to labour invested over time); that is, he saw the influence of wage as mediating through the structure of the means of production. Indeed, Ricardo also saw that a change in wage would have no influence on relative prices if the proportion of the means of production to labour was uniform for all commodities. Although this implied that Ricardo would allow for a modification of the principle that the quantity of labour bestowed on the commodity determines its relative value, he would not abandon that principle altogether. In fact, he attempted to redefine the properties of the required 'invariant standard' to accommodate modifications arising because of the 'durability' factor.

Sraffa, in a detailed scrutiny and comparison of successive texts of the *Principles*, examines a widely accepted hypothesis, disseminated by J. H. Hollander (1904, pp. 455–91) and extended further by Cannan (1929, p. 185) – that Ricardo, over the successive editions, weakened over the labour theory of value. Sraffa shows that all the evidence in support of this hypothesis arises because of certain misunderstandings of changes in the text and that, although no essential change was made in successive editions about the rule which determines values, some important changes occurred in connection with the choice of an invariable measure of value.

The role that labour values played in Ricardo's theory of profits and Ricardo's notion of an 'invariant standard' is better comprehended when we follow the logical trail in Ricardo, as delineated by Sraffa. In the determination of the rate of profits, Ricardo appears to have operated in terms of the aggregates of net output, wages and capital. In the corn case, these aggregates were conceived in homogeneous terms. If the relative values were proportional to labour embodied (i.e., the labour theory of value applies), labour could replace corn as a measure independent of the division of produce between wages and profits. Ricardo realized that the differences in the structure and composition of the means of production of different commodities imply that variations in relative values will be occasioned by a change in wage, even when methods of production remain the same. As Sraffa observes:

> Even though nothing has occurred to change the magnitude of the aggregate, there may be *apparent* changes due solely to change in measurement, owing to the fact that measurement is in terms of values and relative values have been altered as a result of a change in the division between wages and profits. (*Works*, I, p. xlviii)

Relative values thus could change for two reasons: one, because of a change in the method of production and, second, as a result of a change in wage. The first cause of variation could be handled by the labour theory, if the second cause did not operate or was held in abeyance. It was the presence of the second cause which called for a 'modification'. Further, the influence of a variation in wage also worked through the relative conditions of production, and hence the problem which interested Ricardo was to find a commodity as a measure of value which would be invariant in value with respect to changes in distribution of the produce, since, if a rise or fall of wages by itself brought about a change in the magnitude of the social product, it would be hard to determine accurately the effect on profits (*Works*, I, p. xlviii). A similar problem also appeared in the case of the measurement of capital, the other heterogeneous aggregate entering the determining equation of the rate of profits (*Works*, I, p. xlix).

The preoccupation with the effect of a change in wages, the simultaneous adherence to labour theory of value and the search for the 'invariant standard' in Ricardo have thus to be understood in the light of his theory of profits. The notion of the invariant measure is also peculiar to Ricardo's theory of value. The problem of discovering an 'invariant standard' was not primarily an empirical one, of finding an actual commodity as a measure. The problem occurred to Ricardo as mainly a theoretical question, namely, defining the conditions a commodity must satisfy in order to be construed as 'invariable' in its value with respect to a change in distribution. The search for such properties that ensure invariance was identical therefore with the discovery of the causes of variations in value. Ricardo recognizes this explicitly in his unfinished manuscript, 'Absolute Value and Exchangeable Value', one of Sraffa's important finds.[14] The problem of the cause and measure of value appeared to have been identified in this case. Further, as a result, the properties of invariance also relied upon the particular explanation of value. Thus, in Ricardo, there was an appropriate invariant measure corresponding to the particular theory of value he proposes: when he adhered to the simple labour theory of value, the 'invariant standard' was defined as a commodity requiring constant quantity of labour at all times and all circumstances. This was the standard adopted in the first two editions. In the third, making allowance for the 'modifications' introduced in the labour-value principle, the standard adopted was one 'produced with such proportions of the two kinds of capital [i.e., fixed and circulating capital] as nearest to the average quantity employed in the production of most commodities' (I, p. 45). The close connection between the theory of profits and the theory of value, which Ricardo sought to handle analytically, is evident from the above.[15]

Another element in Ricardo's theory that has caused puzzlement and misunderstanding is the 'curious phrase', 'price of wages' which Ricardo removed in several cases from the second edition of *Principles*, and eliminated further in the third edition (*Works*, I, p. li). The expression is in places treated as interchangeable with 'price of labour', or simply 'wages'. Sraffa explains:

> ... it must originally have been related to the expression 'real value of wages', which he uses in explaining the peculiar sense in which he is to be understood when he speaks of the rise or fall of wages: namely as referring to the *proportion* of the total product going to labour, and not to the absolute quantity of commodities received by the labourers. (I, p. lii; italics in original)

This peculiar usage was criticized both by Malthus (see *Works*, I, p. 19) and Marshall (1920, p. 350). It also led to misinterpretations of Ricardo's theory of profit when the theory was charged with being only tautologous – the share remaining for profit inversely varying with the share of wages. Ricardo, in fact, sought to relate the rate of profits with the share of wages in net product. This form of representing wages is also characteristic of the surplus-based determination of the rate of profit of the classical theorists, noted earlier (see p. 120 above).

What we learn from Sraffa's insightful commentaries is that Ricardo had a theoretical system within which he was seeking to achieve consistency between his theories of profit and of relative values. Sraffa's interpretation of the development of Ricardo's ideas appears to be consistent with the available evidence; it portrays Ricardo's own struggles to devise conceptual tools suitable for the problem formulated by him.[16] Sraffa provides a rational basis – an analytical context and meaning – to Ricardo's concepts which were often deplored as 'new and unusual', and to Ricardo's seeming inconsistencies, contradictions and swift changes in his opinions. Many saw these as simply errors, a lack of systematic thinking, or attributed them to Ricardo's wrong-headedness and confused thought, although recognizing him as 'able' or 'profound'. What emerges from Sraffa's reading of Ricardo is that, untutored and technically ill-equipped as Ricardo was, he was persistently striving to attain consistency within a theoretical system. This system is distinct from the one that became dominant after the 1870s with the rise of the supply-and-demand-based equilibrium theories and, often, inconsistencies attributed to Ricardo arise because of interpreters imposing their different theoretical system on his theory.

4 Some controversies

Sraffa's interpretation of Ricardo has stimulated controversy over wider theoretical issues concerning the development of economic theory, particularly after the publication of *Production of Commodities*, in which Sraffa seeks to revive the classical standpoint. Minor differences notwithstanding, one broad view (found, among others, in Dobb, 1973; Roncaglia, 1974; Harcourt, 1975; Meek, 1977; Bharadwaj, 1978a; Garegnani, 1984) is that the classical political economy has a distinct theoretical structure and approach which originated with the Physiocrats, was elaborated and refined by English political economists from Smith to Ricardo, and was critically extended in many different directions by Marx. The central notion characteristic of these theories is of 'social surplus' or 'net product' which is defined as the total produce of the economy minus the requirements of productive consumption (i.e., the material requirements of production and for the sustenance of labour). The economy is described as in a 'natural' state (as an average, observed position), that is, a state in which the economic activities (of production, distribution and exchange) could be reproduced. The determination of the size of the surplus, its distribution among the revenue-classes and the accumulation of this surplus are the central concerns of the theory. The social surplus, in a particular natural position of the economy, is derived by taking as 'given' the following data: (a) the social product (i.e., the gross product); (b) the methods of production; and (c) the wage with its constituent quantities of commodities. The produce going to shares other than wages (i.e., 'surplus') was treated as a residual by deducting the productive consumption from social product. As Garegnani (1984, p. 294) points out:

> The peculiar feature of these theories – the determination of the shares of the product other than wages as a residuum or 'surplus' – thus has its logical basis in the consideration of the real wage and social product as being determinable prior to these shares.

The determination of the wage from 'outside' is crucial to this surplus-based theory of value and distribution.

This way of determining the rate of profits and prices does not rule out considering, at a different stage of analysis, the interactions among wage, methods of production and social product. The determination of these 'quantities' is germane to the determination of the 'surplus', whose 'distribution' is then analysed, at a separate stage, given the 'quantities'. Such an approach does not imply that the *value* of social product or of surplus is considered independent of prices. As is clear from the discussions in Ricardo, an important problem that he faced was precisely in the simultaneous determination of the rate of profits and relative values which he misidentified as a problem of circularity.[17] Ricardo's successive attempts to formulate his theory of profit in a simple agricultural form and then to generalize it by using the labour theory of value, and modifying it further, using the 'invariant standard' reflect successive elaborations of such an approach (see Garegnani, 1984).

An interpretation of Ricardo which differs from the above, namely, that Ricardo as well as Smith were among the progenitors of the supply-and-demand-based theory, was advanced by Marshall (1920). His position and interpretations continue to be influential. Marshall, unlike Jevons and Bohm Bawerk who believed that the Ricardian system should be discarded, claimed a continuity with Ricardo and Mill. In the famous Appendix I of *Principles of Economics*, Marshall offered a generous interpretation: ' ... his [Ricardo's] doctrines though very far from complete, are free from many of the errors that are commonly attributed to them'. Proceeding to complete Ricardo's 'profound but incomplete' reasoning, Marshall suggested that in the discussion of 'Value and Riches' Ricardo was 'feeling his way towards the distinction between marginal utility and total utility'. 'Ricardo was aware', he claimed, 'that commodities fall into three classes according as they obey the law of diminishing, of constant, or of increasing returns', but justified himself in assuming provisionally that they all obeyed the law of constant return (1920, p. 814).

Marshall attributed to Ricardo a 'cost of production theory',[18] arguing, however, that:

> he knew that demand played an essential part in governing value, but that he regarded its action as less obscure than that of cost of production, and therefore passed it lightly over in the notes which he made for the use of his friends, and himself; for he never essayed to write a formal treatise; also that he regarded cost of production as dependent – not as Marx asserted him to have done on the mere quantity of labour used up in production, but – on the quality as well as quantity of that labour; together with the amount of stored up capital needed to aid labour, and the length of time during which such aid was invoked. (1920, p. 503)

Ricardo's emphasis on the cost (supply) blade of the scissors was due, in Marshall's view, to the implicit assumption of constant returns (which is also constant costs, in Marshall's partial equilibrium frame).[19]

Marshall in fact ignored altogether the role which labour theory played in Ricardo. Stigler (1958) denies that any analytical role is played by the labour theory and sees it more as an empirical principle, emphasizing the predominant role which wage costs play in the costs of production. Stigler, too, holds that Ricardo had a cost-of-production theory. Cassels (1935) similarly argues that Ricardo's concern was much more with the *variations* in relative prices occasioned by *variations* in wages, and Ricardo's argument was to hold that these variations are proportional to the labour embodied. In Cassels' view the labour-value principle was an empirical one concerned with the 'variations', and Ricardo held not a labour theory but a cost-of-production theory of prices. These interpretations of labour values as a purely empirical principle go against the evidence, because Ricardo emphatically asserts that commodities exchange according to the relative quantity of labour which is necessary for their production, *and not on the greater or less compensation which is paid for that labour*, and the hypothesis that this position of Ricardo 'weakened' over successive sections and editions is convincingly refuted by Sraffa (see above). Further, Ricardo discussed the influence of variations in wages on relative values as a 'second cause' which necessitated modification in the labour-value principle. His concern regarding the influence of wage *variations* on prices was derived, as we have seen, from his particular theory of profits.

Samuel Hollander's voluminous book on *The Economics of David Ricardo* (1979) has renewed the older controversies, challenging Sraffa's interpretation, particularly of what is called 'the corn model'. Hollander sees 'the essence of the Ricardian contribution and the significance, indeed the primary objective, of Ricardo's analytical work' in his 'fundamental conception' that 'wage rate increases are non-inflationary and at most generate an alteration in relative prices within limited bounds' (1979, p. 7). This leads Ricardo to challenge the Smithian position that the price of corn regulates the price of all other things. Given that this is the central theme of Ricardo, Hollander argues that Ricardo had worked out his theory of profits in terms of a relation between the (money) wage and the rate of profit from early on (pre-*Essay*), and hence the 'rational foundation' provided by Sraffa to the *Essay* (and hence, the later development) has no exegetical or analytical basis. We may not pursue here the extensive controversy that has followed (see S. Hollander, 1973; Eatwell, 1975; O'Brien, 1981; Garegnani, 1982; Roncaglia, 1982; Bharadwaj, 1983a; and replies by S. Hollander, 1975, 1982, 1983; and Caravale 1985). Hollander also argues that Ricardo's concern was only with an empirical theory of value and sees no substantive role for the 'sophisticated invariant standard' of the third edition, since the 'invariant standard' of the first two editions had already accomplished its analytical purpose of refuting the Smithian proposition. Hollander fails to show how Ricardo could have established the relationship between the money wage and relative prices for his theory of profit. He also fails to explain why, having established that general relation prior to the *Essay*, Ricardo needed to revert to the strong case of the 'corn model' where the profits of the farmer determine the general rate of profits, or how Ricardo could have held to the determining role of the farmer's profit while accepting the Smithian proposition, and why this farmer's profit principle disappears in the *Principles*. Hollander's interpretation leads him, like Marshall, to resort to discovering a difference between 'Ricardo's formal statements' and 'intentions'. It fails to explain the 'peculiarities' of Ricardo's analytical constructions. By contrast, Sraffa's reading of Ricardo is consistent with the Ricardo papers available to us.

Notes: Chapter 5

This essay was first published in the *Cambridge Journal of Economics*, vol. no. 12 (1988), pp. 67–84. My thanks are due to Jayati Ghosh, Geoffrey Harcourt, Michael Landesmann and Roberto Scazzieri for their comments on the earlier version of this paper.

1. Hereafter referred to as *Works*. References to the *Works* are indicated by volume number in roman numerals followed by page number.
2. E. A. G. Robinson (1951, p. 848) notes in his review of *Works*, Vols I and II: 'It was in 1925 that the Council of the Royal Economic Society first agreed in principle to a proposal to produce a definitive edition of Ricardo and in 1930 that it was agreed, on Keynes's suggestion, to ask Mr Sraffa to take on the responsibilities of editorship.'
3. 'Ricardo was a fortunate man. He lived in a period – then drawing to a close – when an untutored genius could still make economic science. He lived in a nation where two great problems, inflation and free trade gave direction and significance to economics. And now 130 years after his death, he is as fortunate as ever; he has been befriended by Sraffa – who has been befriended by Dobb' (Stigler, 1953, p. 302).
4. Hutchison (1952), reviewing Sraffa (1951, *Works*, I), acknowledged that 'there can be no edition in English of the complete works of any economist which remotely begins to compare with this edition of Ricardo' but raised a certain 'querulous and insidious' question: 'How far does the actual content and influence of these works measure up to this unique position' which Ricardo acquires in the history of economics. Hutchison's own evaluation, contrary to our own, suggests that Ricardo's significance has been overrated.
5. E. A. G. Robinson (1951) writes: 'Mr Sraffa's preface which runs to a little over sixty pages, is a model of what such a preface should be. He is concerned wholly and exclusively with Ricardo, with Ricardo's own controversies with his contemporaries, and with anything in Ricardo's own letters and writings which can contribute to our ability to understand what Ricardo was trying to say. He is not concerned to provide us with ready-made judgements as to whether it was Ricardo, or Jevons, or neither, who "shunted the car of economic science on to a wrong line". He does not provide us with "Ricardo in modern dress", with Ricardo's ideas translated into the terminology which most of us can more readily think today. But just so far as he can help Ricardo to speak to us for himself, and in his own language, he gives us every possible assistance ...' (p. 850).
6. David Ricardo, *On the Principles of Political Economy and Taxation* (*Works*, I; hereafter, *Principles*).
7. David Ricardo (1815), *Essay on the Influence of a Low Price of Corn on the Profits of Stock* (*Works*, IV, pp. 1–42; hereafter, the *Essay*).
8. Marshall thus sought to interpret Ricardo 'generously': 'When his words are ambiguous, we must give them that interpretation which other passages in his writings indicate that he would have wished to give them' (1920, p. 813). Consequently, Marshall saw, in Ricardo, anticipations of his own theory (see p. 127 below).
9. The reception of Ricardo's theory through the hands of James Mill appears to have also had other consequences. As Ashley (1909 [1965]) observes: 'For good or for ill ... John Mill's economics remained those of his father down

to the end of his life ... it was through James Mill, and, as shaped by James Mill that it [the 'deposits' of doctrines of Ricardo, Malthus, Adam Smith and the French Physiocrats] chiefly reached his son' (pp. vii–ix). Marshall, in turn, claimed to have brought rigour and consistency to Mill's ideas, affording them a 'mathematical form'. It was precisely the beginnings in Mill of deviations from Ricardo's theory of value and distribution that received extensions and refinements in Marshall's hands (see Bharadwaj, 1978b; chapter 6 below).

10 One or other feature of the 'Ricardian system', namely, the law of diminishing returns, the population principle, the fixed subsistence wage, Say's Law, the 'stationary state', is identified as a main characteristic of Ricardian theory.

11 While Sraffa, Dobb and some Marxist writers have recognized a divide in theory, with the supply-and-demand-based theory emerging after 1870 as an alternative, with a distinctly different structure of theory to explain value and distribution, Marshall maintained that there was a continuity in the development of economic theory and that Ricardo did not have any systematic, separate theoretical standpoint.

12 This, fixation of the limit to the cultivation by demand, has often been interpreted as 'demand' entering into the determination of value in Ricardo (see, e.g., Samuelson, 1959). However, what Ricardo needs is a 'given effectual demand', not fixed or invariable demand. Changes in effectual demand occur due to variations of social and economic forces and, unlike the demand schedule in marginalist theory, do not rely solely upon relative quantity changes brought about through 'substitution' in response to changes in relative prices.

13 Referring to Ricardo's oft-quoted passage from his letter to McCulloch of 13 June 1820 (quoted also by Sraffa, *Works*, I, p. xxxiii): 'After all, the great questions of Rent, Wages and Profits must be explained by the proportions in which the whole produce is divided between landlords, capitalists and labourers, and which are not essentially connected with the doctrine of value', Hutchison (1952, p. 420) maintains that 'in his whole original approach his problem of value was, for Ricardo, quite separate from his problem of distribution' and this, Hutchison maintains, is 'unMarxian'. Also, the sequence in which Ricardo proceeds from the distribution to the value problem, Hutchison holds, differentiates him from both the Marxian and the neoclassical way of treating value and distribution. However, when one follows Sraffa on the trail of Ricardo, the form which the value problem takes in Ricardo's surplus-based explanation of profits and its origin becomes clear. It also allows us to see how Marx essentially adopts the same approach for his theory of distribution, but attempts to resolve, in a different way, the same difficulty caused by deviations of labour values from prices: Marx sets up the 'transformation problem', while Ricardo proceeds in pursuit of his invariant standard (see Garegnani, 1984).

14 This unfinished manuscript is of great value for clearing up certain misunderstandings about Ricardo's position on value. It outlines more clearly the differences among Ricardo's, James Mill's, McCulloch's and Torrens's attempts to deal with 'capital', and indicates the difficulty, as seen by Ricardo, in separating labour and time as independent causes of value. While Ricardo did not succeed in discovering the 'invariant standard' in this last work, he provided clues to the analysis of the problem of variations in prices effected by variation in wages which have been explored by later scholars working on the 'transformation' problem.

15 See note 13 above.
16 It is to the credit of his ingenuity that Ricardo recognized, in principle, the interdependence between distribution and exchange values but, not having a clear conception and formulation of a simultaneous system of price relations, he looked upon the problem as one of circularity. His peculiar procedure – criticized by Marx – of deriving changes in relative values consequent upon a change in wage (by first presuming an inverse relation between wages and the rate of profits and then using the rate of profits corresponding to the altered wage to deduce changes in exchange values) reflected Ricardo's difficulty in handling simultaneity. His proposal to construct the 'invariant standard', even if unsuccessful, was an attempt to provide an ingenious device to overcome the same difficulty.
17 cf. note 16 above.
18 Ricardo's remarks in the *Notes on Malthus* (*Works*, II, p. 42), 'By cost of production, I invariably mean wages and profits' and, in *Principles* [*Works*, I, p. 47], 'Mr Malthus appears to think that it is a part of my doctrine, that the cost and value of a thing should be the same; – it is, if he means by cost, "cost of production including profits"' are quoted to support that he had a cost-of-production theory. Our discussion on Ricardo's opposition to the 'adding-up' view of Adam Smith clarifies that, while Ricardo would agree to a definition of 'natural price' or 'value' as cost of production including profits, he would not consider profits as determined independently of wages and constituting an independently determined component of value.
19 Sraffa (1926) was to show that, within the premises of Marshall's partial equilibrium theory, the only assumption consistent with Marshall's supply schedule (which was conceived of as independent of demand) was that of constant returns. Marshall deemed the case of constant costs as purely accidental arising out of the balancing of the tendencies to increasing and decreasing returns.

References: Chapter 5

Ashley, W. J. (1891), 'The rehabilitation of Ricardo', *Economic Journal* (September), pp. 474–89

Ashley, W. J. (1909 [1965]), Editorial introduction to J. S. Mill's *Principles of Political Economy* (New York: A. M. Kelley reprint)

Baumol, W. (1965), *Economic Dynamics* (Princeton, NJ: Princeton University Press)

Bharadwaj, K. (1978a), *Classical Political Economy and the Rise to Dominance of Supply and Demand Theories* (Calcutta: Orient Longman); Revised edition, 1986

Bharadwaj, K. (1978b), 'The subversion of classical analysis: Alfred Marshall's early writing on value', *Cambridge Journal of Economics*, vol. 2, no. 3 (September), pp. 253–71; Chapter 6 in the present volume

Bharadwaj, K. (1983a), 'On a controversy over Ricardo's theory of distribution', *Cambridge Journal of Economics*, vol. 7, no. 1, (March), pp. 11–36; Chapter 4 in the present volume

Bharadwaj, K. (1983b), 'Ricardian theory and Ricardianism', *Contributions to Political Economy*, vol. 2; Chapter 3 in the present volume

Blaug, M. (1958), *Ricardian Economics: A Historical Study* (New Haven, Conn.: Yale University Press)

Cannan, E. (1929), *A Review of Economic Theory* (London: P. S. King)

Caravale, G. A. (ed.) (1985), *The Legacy of Ricardo* (Oxford: Blackwell)
Cassels, J. M. (1935), 'A reinterpretation of Ricardo on value', *Quarterly Journal of Economics*, vol. XLIX (May), pp. 518–32
Clark, J. M. (1931), 'Distribution', in *Encyclopaedia of the Social Sciences* (New York)
Dobb, M. H. (1973), *Theories of Value and Distribution since Adam Smith* (Cambridge: Cambridge University Press)
Dunbar, C. F. (1886), 'The reaction to political economy', *Quarterly Journal of Economics*, vol. 1 (October)
Dunbar, C. F. (1887), 'Ricardo's use of facts', *Quarterly Journal of Economics*, vol 1 (July).
Eatwell, J. L. (1975), 'The interpretation of Ricardo's Essay on Profits', *Economica*, vol. 42, no. 166 (May), pp. 182–7
Fetter, F. W. (1969), 'The rise and decline of Ricardian economics', *History of Political Economy*, 1 (Spring), pp. 67–84
Garegnani, P. (1982), 'On Hollander's interpretation of Ricardo's early theory of profits', *Cambridge Journal of Economics*, vol. 6, no. 1 (March), pp. 65–77
Garegnani, P. (1983), 'Ricardo's early theory of profits and its 'rational foundation': a reply to Professor Hollander', *Cambridge Journal of Economics*, vol. 7, no. 2 (June), pp. 175–8
Garegnani, P. (1984), 'Value and distribution in the classical economists and Marx', *Oxford Economic Papers*, vol. 36, pp. 291–325
Gordon, B. (1969), 'Criticism of Ricardian views on value and distribution in the British periodicals, 1820–1850', *History of Political Economy*, I, Fall
Harcourt, G. C. (1982), *The Social Science Imperialists* (London: Routledge & Kegan Paul)
Hollander, J. H. (1876), *David Ricardo, Studies in Historical and Political Science* (Baltimore, Md: Johns Hopkins University Press)
Hollander, J. H. (1904), 'The development of Ricardo's theory of value', *Quarterly Journal of Economics*, XVIII (August), pp. 455–91
Hollander, S. (1973), 'Ricardo's analysis of the profit rate, 1813–1815', *Economica*, vol. 40, pp. 260–82
Hollander, S. (1975), 'Ricardo and the corn profit model: reply to Eatwell', *Economica*, XLII (May), pp. 188–202
Hollander, S. (1977), 'The reception of Ricardian economics', *Oxford Economics Papers*, vol. XX (July), pp. 221–57
Hollander, S. (1979), *The Economics of David Ricardo* (Toronto: Heinemann)
Hollander, S. (1981), 'The economics of David Ricardo: a response to Professor O'Brien', *Oxford Economic Papers*, vol. 33, no. 3, pp. 224–46
Hollander, S. (1982), 'A reply to Roncaglia', *Journal of Post-Keynesian Economics*, vol. 4, no. 3 (spring), pp. 360–72
Hollander, S. (1983), 'Professor Garegnani's defence of Sraffa on the material rate of profit', *Cambridge Journal of Economics*, vol. 7, no. 2 (June), pp. 167–74
Hutchison, T. W. (1952), 'Some questions about Ricardo', *Economica*, xix (November), pp. 415–32
Jevons, W. S. (1871 [1971]), *The Theory of Political Economy* (Harmondsworth: Penguin)
Kaldor, N. (1955–6), 'Alternative theories of distribution', *Review of Economic Studies*, vol. xxii, no. 2, pp. 83–100
Keynes, J. M. (1933), *Essays in Biography* (London: Macmillan)
Marshall, A. (1920), *Principles of Economics*, 8th edn (London: Macmillan)

Marx, Karl (1862–3 [1963–71]), *Theories of Surplus Value*, 3 parts (Moscow: Progress Publishers)
Meek, R. L. (1950), 'The decline of Ricardian economics in England', *Economica*, vol. 17, no. 1 (February), pp. 43–62
Meek, R. L. (1977), *Smith, Marx and After* (London: Chapman & Hall)
Mill, James (1821), *Elements of Political Economy*, 1st edn (London: Bohn)
O'Brien, D. P. (1981), 'Ricardian economics and the economics of David Ricardo', *Oxford Economic Papers*, vol. 33, no. 3 (November), pp. 352–86
Pasinetti, L. L. (1974), *Growth and Income Distribution: Essays in Economic Theory* (Cambridge: Cambridge University Press)
Patten, S. (1893), 'The interpretation of Ricardo', *Quarterly Journal of Economics*, vol. vii (April), pp. 322–52
Ricardo, D. (1810–23 [1951–73]), *Works and Correspondence of David Ricardo*, ed. by P. Sraffa, with the collaboration of M. H. Dobb, 10 vols and Index (Cambridge: Cambridge University Press)
Robinson, E. A. G. (1951), 'The works and correspondence of David Ricardo': Vols I and II', *Economic Journal*, vol. 61 (December), pp. 848–51
Roncaglia, A. (1974), *Sraffa and the Theory of Prices* (New York: Wiley)
Roncaglia, A. (1982), 'Hollander's Ricardo', *Journal of Post-Keynesian Economics*, vol. 4, no. 3 (spring) pp. 339–59
Samuelson, P. A. (1959), 'A modern treatment of the Ricardian economy', *Quarterly Journal of Economics*, vol. 73 (February and May), pp. 1–35 and 217–31
Schumpeter, J. A. (1954), *History of Economic Analysis* (London: Allen & Unwin)
Sraffa, P. (1925), 'Sulle relazioni fra costo e quantità prodotta', *Annali di Economia*, vol. 2, no. 1, pp. 277–328
Sraffa, P. (1926), 'The laws of returns under competitive conditions', *Economic Journal*, vol. 36 (December), pp. 535–50
Sraffa, P. (1930), 'A "criticism" and a "rejoinder" in the "Symposium of increasing returns and the representative firm" ', *Economic Journal*, vol. 11 (March), pp. 89–93
Sraffa, P. (1932), 'Dr Hayek on money and capital', *Economic Journal*, vol. xlii, pp. 42–53 and 'Rejoinder', ibid., pp. 249–51
Sraffa, P. (1951–73), Editorial introductions to *Works and Correspondence of David Ricardo*, vols i–x, op. cit.
Sraffa, P. (1960), *Production of Commodities by Means of Commodities: Prelude to a Critique of Economic Theory* (Cambridge: Cambridge University Press)
Stigler, George J. (1952), 'The Ricardian theory of value and distribution', *Journal of Political Economy* (June), reprinted in Stigler (1965), op. cit.
Stigler, George J. (1953), 'Sraffa's Ricardo', *American Economic Review* (September), reprinted in Stigler (1965), op. cit.
Stigler, George J. (1958), 'Ricardo and the 93% labour theory of value', *American Economic Review*, vol. xlviii (June), reprinted in Stigler (1965), pp. 326–42
Stigler, George J. (1965), *Essays in the History of Economics* (Chicago: Chicago University Press)

6
The Subversion of Classical Analysis: Alfred Marshall's Early Writing on Value

With the publication of Alfred Marshall's *Early Writings (1867-90)* (1975)[1] it is now possible, with greater confidence, to place his ideas in the historical perspective of the development of economic doctrines; in particular, the *Early Writings* shed further light on the vexed and debated question as to whether Marshall should be counted amongst the progenitors of the marginalist school. The enigma surrounding this question had been magnified by his own elusiveness and reticence – his constant attempts to suppress overt manifestations of his originality, dressing up his ideas in traditional garb and stressing continuity with the Smith–Ricardo–Mill tradition, on the one hand; while, on the other, giving numerous hints in private correspondence[2] as well as in print[3] that many 'Jevonian' ideas which were claimed as a revolutionary break with the past were but 'familiar truths' to him, already propounded in his lectures and early unpublished work.

Marshall's friends and disciples[4] claimed with confidence that he had already advanced considerably towards the new marginalist theory in the 1870s, concurrently with Jevons and Walras. But there appears to be a sharp division of opinion, even among his followers,[5] as to whether his ideas are essentially a continuation and advancement of the Ricardo–Mill tradition or whether he was an eclectic, compromising between classical ideas and those of the new utilitarian school; Marshall himself protested against the latter view.[6] The *Early Writings* provide some firmer evidence on which to assess and reinterpret these issues. Our purpose here, however, is not to probe into the question of priority of ideas or into a comparison of Marshall and Jevons or Walras in regard to their ideas on price theory, although these may enter incidentally into our discussion. We are interested mainly in tracing Marshall's ideas to the more immediate source in Mill; we shall indicate how a silent revolution in the direction of the marginalist supply-and-demand theory was brought about in the course of adopting, extending and transforming some ideas in Mill. As Mill himself had departed considerably from Ricardo,

Marshall was thus moving even farther away from the Ricardian source. While the *Early Writings* cover a wide ground (value, distribution, money, international trade, etc.), our focus here will be on the piece on value (hereafter the 'Essay'; the text occurring on pp. 125–64 of Marshall, 1975, Vol. I). The 'Essay' is important in so far as Marshall himself claims that it was his first systematic account of value and that it continued to provide the basic core of his later ideas on the subject.

In Section I the theoretical background will be presented, as well as the elements in the Mill–Thornton controversy which appear to have stimulated Marshall's formulations. In Section II, we focus on the seminal ideas contained in the 'Essay', with some comments about their later developments in Marshall's mature writings. The concluding Section III will briefly discuss Marshall's contradictory posture, as a follower of the classical tradition as well as the progenitor of the new marginalist school. While his roots in Mill are clearly discernible, the departures from Ricardo are radical and entirely systematic, so that however much he himself disliked such a role, Marshall effectively joins those who 'shunted the car of economic science' away from Ricardian lines.

I

1 The Background

Explaining his initiation into political economy, Marshall wrote to Colson (in 1908 or 1909);

> Briefly – I read Mill's Political Economy in 1866 or 67 while I was teaching advanced mathematics; and as I thought much more easily in mathematics at that time than in English, I tried to translate him into mathematics before forming an opinion as to the validity of his work. I found much amiss in his analysis, and especially in two matters. He did not seem to have assimilated the notion of gradual growth by imperceptible increments; and he did not seem to have a sufficient responsibility...for keeping the number of his equations equal to the number of his variables, neither more nor less. (Marshall, 1933, p. 221)

In a letter to J. B. Clark at around the same time, he wrote:

> ...my main position as to the theory of value and distribution was practically completed in the years 1867–70, when I translated *Mill's version of Ricardo's or Smith's doctrines* into mathematics; [so] that, when Jevons' book appeared, I knew at once how far I agreed with him and how far I did not. (Pigou, 1925, p. 416, italics added).

In an account of himself contributed to a German compilation on leading economists, Marshall wrote: 'While still giving private lessons in mathematics [in 1867] he translated as many as possible of *Ricardo's reasonings* into mathematics; and he endeavoured to make them more general' (Pigou, 1925, p. 20, italics added).

What the *Early Writings* on value bring out clearly is the link with Mill and, at most, with Mill's version of Ricardo, but hardly any Ricardian ideas appear to have a directly dominant influence. In particular, the deviationist beginnings in Mill, paving the way towards the acceptance and proliferation of the supply-and-demand approach, act as the thin end of the wedge. Thornton's attack (Thornton, 1870) on Mill's rather ambivalent formulation of that approach in fact exposed the weak links in Mill – although Thornton's own arguments were confused and not weighty. The debate appears to have helped Marshall to spot the weaknesses clearly and from them to reconstruct, extend and reinforce the supply-and-demand argument into a more comprehensive statement. We shall, in the following, note those elements in Mill's exposition of value and those aspects of the debate with Thornton that appear to have provided the basis for Marshall's virtual transformation of the classical ideas.

2 Mill on Value in Principles of Political Economy

While apparently adhering to the Smith–Ricardo distinction between 'natural price' and 'market price' (the former explained in terms of the conditions of production as the 'ultimate regulator of value' and the latter viewed as arising out of deviations around natural prices brought about by temporary and accidental fluctuations in conditions of demand and supply), Mill introduced a number of novelties – some explicitly, but some imperceptibly – that were to amount to fundamental deviations from Ricardian ideas. He himself appears to have been unaware of the extent to which his inroads had weakened the classical structure when he pronounced (1871, [1929] p. 436): 'Happily, there is nothing in the laws of value which remains, for the present or any future writer to clear up', a statement for which Jevons (1911, p. v) was rightly to reprimand him.

Those deviationist ideas in Mill which are directly relevant to Marshall's 'Essay' are discussed in the following paragraphs.

Mill began his discussion on value, in the classical tradition, by referring to the celebrated paradox between use-value and exchange value (1871 [1929], pp. 436–7). He accepted De Quincey's criticism (De Quincey, 1844 [1863], pp. 266–7) of Adam Smith's statement of the paradox and, in so doing, paved the way for an altogether different notion of value-in-use which, as we shall see, Marshall adopted in the 'Essay' and was fundamental to his notion of consumer's rent. De Quincey, while accepting Smith's observation that things with a high value-in-use often have little or no value-in-exchange (since that which can be obtained without labour will command no price, although useful), refuted the possibility that things which have high exchange value may have little use-value. His argument was that 'political economy had nothing to do with the comparative estimates of different uses in the judgement of a philosopher or moralist'. De Quincey in fact redefined use-value ('teleologic value') to mean 'the capacity of a thing to satisfy a desire or serve a purpose' and argued that value-in-use was the 'extreme limit' of value-in-exchange, in the sense that the latter might fall short of, but could not exceed, the former. Were it to do so, he argued, it would presuppose that persons will give, to possess a thing, more than the utmost value which they themselves put upon it as a means of gratifying their inclinations.

This was a different notion of use-value than that accepted by Smith and Ricardo, for whom use-value was a necessary condition for a commodity to possess in order to be an object of exchange, but referred to the physical properties socially known to belong to a commodity, and not dependent upon the *individual's estimation* of its capacity to gratify subjective inclinations, measured in quantitative terms. In fact, use-value and exchange value were incomparable in so far as the former covered the qualitative aspect and the latter was a quantitative notion. In De Quincey and Mill, the two notions had become quantitatively comparable (one acting as an extreme limit upon another) and this was only a step towards the later resolution of the paradox in terms of 'total' and 'marginal' utility.

De Quincey, in fact, indirectly proposed the measure of use-value in terms of the price an individual would be prepared to pay ('Let the thing (measured by its uses) be, for your purposes, worth ten guineas, so that you would rather give ten guineas than lose it'); Mill approved of this notion of use-value as 'the intrinsic worth of an article in your individual estimate for your individual purposes' and its measure. As we shall see, this notion and its measure were fundamental to Marshall's demand side of price determination.

3 Mill's Three 'Classes' of Commodities

In his endeavour to systematize the law of value, Mill had proposed three distinct classes of commodities, *with their own respective laws of value*. The first were scarce commodities, meaning those which faced absolute limitations on supply (scarce paintings, etc. Ricardo had excluded such exceptional cases.) The second included commodities which were reproducible without limit (with which Ricardo's discussion of natural prices was concerned). The third class, defined as 'intermediate between the two preceding and rather more complex' and 'the importance of which in political economy is extremely great', referred to those 'commodities which can be multiplied to an indefinite extent by labour and expenditure, *but not by a fixed amount of labour and expenditure. Only a limited quantity can be produced at a given cost: if more is wanted, it must be produced at a greater cost*' (Mill, 1871 [1929], p. 445, italics added). This *class* was typified by agricultural commodities and raw produce. It must be emphasized that the 'increasing difficulty in production' in Ricardo had been focused on in the context of the explanation of rent and not as a special class of commodities with a distinctly separate law of value of its own.

Mill had not only classified commodities into distinct classes, but had also attributed to them distinct laws of value. The law of value for the first class of scarce commodities was based on the equalization of supply and demand. He was to introduce firmer notions of price-dependent changes in demand and supply: while supply was defined as the *quantity* offered for sale at a given time and place, demand was symmetrically defined as *quantity* demanded and Mill had added further:

> the quantity demanded is not a fixed quantity, even at the same time and place; it varies according to the value;... The demand, therefore, partly depends on the value ... the idea of a *ratio*, as between demand and supply, is out of place ... The proper mathematical analogy is that of an equation. Demand and supply ... will be made equal. If unequal, at any moment, competition equalises them, and the manner in which this is done is by an adjustment of the value. (ibid. pp. 446–8)

In explaining this adjustment as a law of value, Mill was conscious that he was breaking new ground, for he wrote that he could not recall anyone, except possibly 'the eminently clear thinker and skilful expositor, J. B. Say', having resolved the question similarly.

Ricardo's response and opposition to Say's and Malthus's reliance on supply-and-demand determination were extensively recorded in his comments (Ricardo, 1951a, pp. 382–5, 119–20, 164–5; 1951b, pp. 224–5), so that one can safely reject the interpretation that Mill was merely stating an accepted position. (Incidentally, in the course of this discussion, Mill defined 'effectual demand' as the 'wish to possess combined with purchasing power', clarifying only in a footnote that the Smithian concept referred to the demand of those who are willing and able to give for the commodity its 'natural price'. Mill apparently did not realize that he had altered the sense of the term in the process of generalizing it, by dropping the reference to 'natural price'.)

Although the first class of commodities was called 'exceptional' (following Ricardo), Mill had stretched the principle of exception over a large group of cases, to cover most commodities which required time for supply to accommodate demand. In addition, there was one specific case to which the law of equalization of supply and demand was deemed to apply invariably – 'the commodity labour' (Mill, 1871 [1929], p. 450). He had adopted the rigid form of the wages-fund doctrine, and it was this view that was to come under fire from Thornton (see below).

Value for the second, much larger, class of commodities which admit of indefinite multiplication was governed by the cost of production. The 'necessary price' included the cost of production together with 'the ordinary profit'. In the 'ultimate analysis of cost of production' Mill had included, not only the remuneration for all the labour required, but also, following Senior,[7] 'the abstinences of all the persons who had advanced the wages'. Mill argued that profits were not made up exclusively of the surplus remaining to the capitalist after the deductions for his outlay, but formed a part of the outlay itself; the basis for such an argument being that the capitalist advanced wages *and* materials and that the latter already incorporated the profits due to their producers. Profits *as well as* wages, therefore, were not only constituent elements of the cost of production but also *determinants* of value. The latter position was a significant departure from Ricardo. True, Ricardo, too, included profits in the cost of production; but, so defined, he considered cost of production as 'synonymous' with value or 'only another name for value' (see Ricardo, 1951a, p. 47 n and 1951b, pp. 34–5, 101). In other words, Ricardo saw in it a definition, not a *theory* of the determination of value.

Marshall, in his Appendix I (Marshall, 1961, pp. 813–21), was to interpret Ricardo's definition of the cost of production, to include profits, as a cost-of-production *explanation* of value.[8] (See also below.) Ricardo's repeated emphasis on profits depending solely on wages can easily be understood when it is recognized that, in the simultaneous schema of value determination, once the methods of production (in terms of labour embodied and its time-pattern) and the wage were given, the rate of profits and prices would be simultaneously determined. The wage and the rate of profits could not both be *determinants* of value. Marshall was to use Mill's concept of labour *and* abstinence to define the 'real costs' of production and to render them quantitatively into 'expenses of production', as the 'supply price' (see Pigou, 1925, p. 127; Marshall, 1961, p. 339).

It is the third class of commodities, marked by the coexistence of 'several costs of production' and by costs which vary with changes in supply, that provided the basis for the later marginalist conception of a supply function. The law of value in their case was stated by Mill thus: The value is determined by the cost of that portion of the supply which is produced and brought to market at the greatest expense. (Mill, 1871 [1929], p. 471). The so-called 'law of diminishing returns' was to interest Jevons[9] and Marshall and to play a significant role in the analytical development of marginalism, through its generalization to situations other than that of explaining rent; 'The law of diminishing marginal utility' was to be its counterpart in the theory of consumption, while it led to a more general notion of diminishing returns to a variable factor in the theory of production (see Bharadwaj, 1978). The *Early Writings* of Marshall reveal his great interest in the rent doctrine; as he himself remarked, 'improvements in cultivation decided me to adopt curves as an engine' (Marshall, 1975, I, pp. 40–1, p. 41, n. 12). In this third law of value, the functional link between costs and scale of output was clearly evident and provided the ground for a generalized 'supply function'.

It is interesting to note that Mill extended this class of commodities to include a number of situations in industry where extra profits analogous to rents could occur, due to the possession of superior skills and talents, patents, etc. This idea developed in Marshall into 'quasi-rents' and 'producer's surplus'. Rent became 'not a thing by itself, but ... the leading species of a large genus'(Marshall, 1961, p. viii).

4 Thornton's Attack on Supply-and-Demand Determination of Price

Thornton, in his book *On Labour*, was provoked to take issue with the wages-fund doctrine and with the more general idea 'that [the] price of all things, labour included, depends upon the proportion between supply and demand' (1870, p. 43). Under the wages-fund doctrine, argued Thornton, at any given instant a sum of wealth is available as a fixed quantity for the payment of wages and the only means for increasing wages is by restricting the supply of labour, leading to 'a millhorse circle':

> Labour can be rendered connubially discrete only by having their standard of living raised. But their standard of living cannot be raised without a permanent rise in the price of labour, and the price of labour cannot be permanently raised, unless the multiplication of labourers be checked.(p. 43)

The supply-and-demand theory underlying the doctrine, Thornton contested, was not only imperfect, but intrinsically unsound; he intended to establish this by logic and by examples.

Thornton's first complaint was that no consistent and satisfactory definitions of demand, supply, or price had been offered. He himself suggested 'for the first time' that demand, like supply, had to be represented as a function of price. Further, he defined prices as 'selling price'. In attacking the supply-and-demand explanation, Thornton was not reverting to the classical explanation of 'natural price'. In fact, he questioned the conceptual soundness of differentiating between 'market price', temporarily regulated by supply and demand, and 'natural price', 'ultimately regulated by cost of production'; his argument being that 'for an individual sale there can be no separable first and last' (1870, p. 45). He completely failed here to comprehend the role of a theoretical abstraction, but his emphatic assertion that 'the selling price cannot depend upon supply and demand at one time and upon cost of production subsequently' appears to have suggested to Marshall the need to develop an integrated framework.

Thornton's criticism of the supply-and demand explanation of price was based mainly on the fact that most commodities on sale have a 'reserve price', so that the price appears to be inflexible in relation to changes in demand and supply. When goods are offered unreservedly for sale, he further argued that, while prices may tend to be lowered whenever supply exceeds demand, they are not usually raised when the converse situation holds. The resulting price, in either situation, need not be one equating demand and supply. Thornton illustrated his arguments with rather restrictive examples, such as fish of a certain quantity fetching different prices in the same market, depending on whether it was sold in a Dutch auction or a British auction; or of markets where, at the seller's quoted price, there could be more buyers willing to buy but not prepared to pay a higher price. While Thornton's examples were somewhat artificially constructed, they presented certain situations occasioned by restrictions on supply or by inflexibility of demand, thus suggesting to Marshall the possibility of generalizing these cases within the framework of supply-and-demand theory, as he appears to have done in the 'Essay'.

Thornton's own suggestions for an alternative approach were confessedly inconclusive and vague. According to him the price settles down between two limits: the upper limit is the utility, real or supposed, of the commodity to the consumer; the lower its utility to the dealer. The price is so settled by the dealer's calculation of the possibilities, the object of every dealer being to obtain the highest aggregate price 'within the period during which it will suit him to keep part of his stock unsold'. (p.76). Each dealer estimates his 'reserve price' by assessing the actual state and future prospects of the market (the important data being the quantities in hand, the additional quantities that may be brought in, the rival's strategy, the state of present and future demand). In particular, the seller allows for the possible cost of tying up finance in unsold stocks in terms of interest earnings thereby forgone. Competition among sellers implies that the lowest reserve price will prevail. It is interesting to observe that in the 'Essay' Marshall started off with a situation of 'barter', where, as in Thornton, the exchange value is supposed to be within the limits set by value-in-use for the two transacting parties. He also referred to the seller's calculations of the prospective prices, as did Thornton, but then went on to describe the varying market situations that influence the estimated prospective prices.

Thornton's critique of the wages-fund, however, was far more successful. He argued that the wages-fund was itself an indeterminate quantity. The argument was built up by considering each individual employer's allocation to the wages-fund, which emerged as a residual after deducting (a) family and personal expenses, and (b) expenditure on maintenance and investment in fixed assets, from the aggregate funds at his disposal. Since both these deductions were variable, so, too, was the residual. Moreover, the residual funds might not all be dispensed as wage payments. If the individual employer's allocation to wage payments was thus 'indeterminate', the aggregate wage fund would be similarly 'indeterminate'.

The alternative explanation of wage determination which Thornton offered rested on two particular features of labour: namely, that it will not 'keep' (i.e., the sale cannot be indefinitely postponed) and that labour is habitually 'united with poverty'.

> Whereas what determines the price of tangible commodities is almost always the competition of dealers, the price of labour may be determined by the competition of customers. This is owing to the

fact that labour is almost always offered for sale without reservation of price. (1870, p. 93)

The labour of uncombined labourers is thus sold at a disadvantage. Here he echoed Adam Smith's picturesque phrases concerning the uneven struggle between 'masters' and 'workers', the former forearmed not only with economic power but with judicial and political support.

Thornton's attack on the wages-fund elicited from Mill a full recantation (Mill, 1869). While he viewed Thornton's discussions on supply and demand as 'additions' rather than 'corrections' of the received doctrine, he considered his examples to be only restrictive special cases, allowing for multiple equilibrium prices or their absence. Thornton's own arguments were rather confusing and weak, but in that crucial period of transition in theories he appears to have acted, as Whitaker puts it (Marshall, 1975, I p. 121), as a gadfly. His criticisms pointed out the necessity for accurate characterization of supply-and-demand relations and their properties. In the 'Essay' as well as in his later article, 'Mr Mill's theory of value' (Pigou, 1925, pp. 119–34), Marshall's references to Thornton were highly complimentary. In the early writing on wages (not considered in detail here: Marshall, 1975, pp. 178–204), he adopted Thornton's treatment of the individual employer's wage fund and sought a simultaneous-equation solution to wage determination by treating the individual capitalist's consumption expenditure, as well as expenditure on fixed assets, as functions of the rate of profit. (Marshall did not as yet have a principle of substitution.) It is interesting to note, however, that once Marshall had worked out his comprehensive theory of supply and demand in *Principles*, his estimation of Thornton was severely diminished. He wrote in the first edition of *Principles* (1961, II, pp. 818–9), commenting on Mill's wages-fund doctrine,

> But it was the treatise *On Labour* by Thornton ... that impressed Mill most, and indeed it seems to have so over-weighted his judgement that when publishing his recantation of his old doctrine he took to himself blame for confusions of thought, of which it is not certain that he had been guilty ...

Having reconstructed and transformed Mill's thought, Marshall, as Whitaker remarks (Marshall, 1975, I, p. 48, n. 38), was probably reading his own ideas retrospectively into Mill.

II

The 'Essay on value' appears to have been written around 1870,[10] probably before Jevons's *Principles of Political Economy* appeared in 1871. The immediate stimulus appears to have been provided by the ongoing debate on the adequacy of the supply-and-demand-based determination of value. That this remarkable, compact

'Essay' provided a fulcrum for Marshall's more mature writings is evident from his letter to J. N. Keynes[11] in 1888, written while he was preparing the *Principles* for publication. The letter was evidently sent along with the manuscript of the 'Essay':

> The inclosed was part of the first systematic account of my views on value... In them I have divided markets according to lengths of periods A, B, C, D ... and make the supply curve a horizontal straight line for A, necessarily inclined positively for B and C, and of all sorts of shapes for D ... Substantially I believe the account given in these papers to be right ...

Marshall went on to explain in the letter that, for fear of overcomplexity, he had not used the curves in his later writings and wondered whether he ought not to introduce the substance of them in *Principles* (which he did; see below).

5 Seminal Ideas in the *Essay*

On Use-value and Exchange Value

The 'Essay' opens with a discussion of the Smithian paradox between value-in-use and value-in-exchange. Marshall writes: 'Adam Smith regarded the "value in use" of any particular object as depending upon its utility. He thereby makes himself the judge of what is useful to other people and introduces unnecessary confusion' (Marshall, 1975, I, p. 125). This objection reminds us of De Quincey's standpoint on use-value (see above). At this stage of the development of his ideas, Marshall appeared somewhat averse to the use of 'utility'; he instead proceeded to define the value-in-use of a thing *to a person* as 'the value of the things which must be given him in order that he may be induced to give it up, or which he will give rather than not obtain it' (1975, I, p. 125). By so defining it, Marshall was already moving on to a *measure* of use-value in terms of the price that the individual is willing to pay for a certain unit of a commodity rather than forgo its possession.

Marshall built up the connection between use-value and exchange value by using the case of simple barter, when the exchange ratio settles somewhere between the limits of the use-values (as defined above) of the articles to the parties desiring exchange. In a more general case, a buyer (a seller) is defined as one who wishes to obtain (part with) a certain commodity in exchange for money or a command over commodities in general; demand and supply are then defined in relational terms as continuous functions of the price, and the equilibrium price is defined at the intersection of these curves, where demand and supply are equated. The treatment is purely formal and graphical at this point. Marshall went on to derive the stability conditions on equilibrium, namely, that the supply curve should lie below the demand curve to the left of the point of intersection.

As to what lies behind the seller's willingness to supply the amount at a particular price, Marshall argued on somewhat similar lines as Thornton: 'In general terms he will accept an offer if he thinks that if he refuses this he will not be able to get a better one' (Marshall, 1975, I, p. 133). The cost of waiting, that is, of tying up finances in holding on to stocks, was calculated at the interest payable on an equivalent cash loan. The seller would also adjust the future or prospective price for the probability of its occurrence, since it was uncertain.

Types of Market Situations: Periodization

Where Marshall departed from Thornton was in his probing further into the following question: 'What are the data which buyers and sellers have to ascertain in order to decide on the probability of their obtaining better offers by waiting?' (p. 133). Or, in other words, what determines the general conditions of demand and supply in the market? As they depend on 'the circumstances of the particular market at a particular time', Marshall introduced different types of market situations, called A, B, C and D. 'The circumstances which determine the supply and demand of a commodity are widely different for different cases, the differences depending mainly on the length of the period of time to which the investigation applies' (p. 134).

In A, the time period is very short; the whole amount purchased is a very small proportion of the amount on sale and the commodity is offered at a price fixed exogenously in some larger market. In this situation, familiar in retail trade (and characteristic of some of Thornton's examples), the supply curve is taken to be almost horizontal at a fixed price. Marshall considered class A as unimportant.

In class B, the dealers take into account only the amount already in existence during the time period, which is not long enough for fresh supplies to be produced. The price varies from time to time as buyers and sellers become aware of fresh circumstances affecting the supply-and-demand situation. Although supply price (Marshall does not use this term, but calls it, the 'value-in-use to the seller') is not necessarily calculated with reference to cost of production, it does generally cover costs, including profits. Thus both A and B are short-period situations, where supplies do not adjust completely to alterations in demand.

In contrast, situations C and D are characterized as those corresponding to 'natural prices', referring to 'periods sufficiently long for any additional amount required to be produced as the demand alters and for all casual variations to be neglected' (p. 139, n. 11). In class C

> no change in the modes of production is contemplated but the periods are sufficiently long to enable the supply to be regulated so as to meet the demand. Thus taking average results, the value in use to the sellers, the price at which they are willing to sell when any given amount of the commodity is sold in a given time, is the cost of production, including profits, at which this amount can be permanently sold. (pp. 137–8)

Importantly, Marshall states, as a general hypothesis, that an increase in the amount produced can only be effected at an increase in price, so that the supply curve rises towards the right.

Class D is characterized by changes in 'the modes of production'. The phrase has a limited connotation here, for Marshall was careful to exclude all major social changes in 'habits and skills of the people and in their command over mechanical resources'. What is noteworthy is that the rather vague phrases hold the concrete analytical consequence that *only such changes in the methods of production as could be associated with a change in the scale of output were to be considered*; class D being essentially distinguished from class C by the possibility of a downward-sloping supply curve in the former and consequently of the existence of multiple equilibria. The analytical classification of supply conditions according to 'returns to scale', with its tripartite division of 'increasing', 'constant' and 'diminishing', is heralded by this linking up of variations in costs to those in the scale of output.

Marshall then proceeded to question whether there was any limit on the analytically permissible forms of these curves. The propositions he suggested in the 'Essay' were repeated in his *Pure Theory of Domestic Values* (1879 [1930]): namely, that the supply curve cannot cut the same vertical line more than once but can do so on a horizontal line, implying that, for each quantum of supply (plotted along the abscissa), there is only one supply price and that the demand curve cannot cut the vertical or the horizontal line more than once, so that, at each price, there is a uniquely determined demand (indicated along the abscissa). A number of graphical exercises illustrating various types of equilibrium situations (stable, unstable, neutral) and their implications in terms of equilibrium price were discussed. What held Marshall's interest was the case of D markets, where, with the downward-sloping supply curve, multiple equilibria are suggested as possible. He posed the problem concerning the interpretation of the existence of such multiple equilibria and of the transition from one stable equilibrium to another (at a lower price and larger output) – a problem that was to recur repeatedly in his later writings. (We shall return to this later.) The graphical apparatus was also extended by Marshall to apply to cases of joint demand and composite supply.

Striking Features of the 'Essay'
What are the striking features of the 'Essay'? We comment on them in the following:

(1) As Shove speculated,[12] Marshall appears 'to have begun with the objective demand and supply schedules, the phenomena of the market place and worked back from them to their psychological basis, not (as was the case with Jevons) the other way about'. Marshall's major concern was the graphical or mathematical properties of these functions and their simultaneous determination of price. His letter to Colson, quoted at the beginning of Section I, in which he found fault with Mill for not realizing the importance of the principle of continuity and the

conditions for solvability of his system, reveals his formal preoccupation with these. In the 'Essay', in fact, Marshall showed very little concern about working out what lies behind the demand schedules. The basis of the demand curve in utility or 'satisfaction' was not developed. In this, possibly Cournot's influence on the 'form' of his thought, to which he himself testified (see Pigou, 1925, p. 100), is discernible. Although much more concern is revealed in his building up of the supply side of the argument, here too, the real cost basis is not explicitly elaborated upon. (However, in the early writings on distribution, the analysis of cost of production did develop in that direction.) The concern in the 'Essay' is primarily to construe a functional relation between the scale of output and the 'supply price'. (The latter is referred to in the 'Essay' as 'value in use to the producer'.) Throughout Marshall's work, even in his mature writings, we find a relatively greater concern about the validity of the supply relation, while the demand relation, in its algebraic form, was taken more as a matter of fact.[13]

(2) Marshall implicitly assumed in the 'Essay' that each consumer buys a certain fixed quantity of the commodity, so that variations in demand are associated with those in the number of buyers. (See Marshall, 1975, I, p. 122.) It was assumed that at least as many buyers would be willing to purchase the commodity at a lower price as at a slightly higher one. The notion of marginal utility or marginal cost did not appear in that form but was hinted at when Marshall spoke of the 'value in use to those buyers who are the last induced to buy the commodity' and the 'value-in-use' to the last of those who produce for sale, or 'the cost of production of that portion which is produced under greatest difficulty'. It is interesting to see that while the demand curve was invariably shown as downward sloping, in some diagrams (ibid., p. 138, fig. 6), it was drawn concave to the origin. The properties of an individual demand curve required for consistency with marginalist theory were yet to be fully developed.

(3) Marshall spoke of the 'supply price' as value-in-use to the producer of that portion of supply. The notion of quasi-rents was hinted at when he referred to some producers obtaining extra profits due to natural or artificial advantages, analogous to rents. As noted above, Mill had already developed this notion, in an incipient form.

(4) In classifying *markets*, Marshall took a major step ahead of Mill who, as we have seen, had categorized commodities into classes according to the law of value applicable to each. In Marshall the classification was now in terms of *market situations*, the law of value based on the balancing of supply-and-demand forces being generalized, gaining universality. (In the *Early Writings* the law was yet to be comprehensively developed to incorporate distribution or the explanation of 'factor prices'.) The market situations were differentiated on the basis of the time taken for the forces of supply and demand to adjust themselves. In the 'Essay', Marshall's emphasis still remained on the adjustment of supply *to* demand, the latter element not having been sufficiently analysed and the full symmetry between the two (supply and demand)

yet to be constructed, as it was to be in *Principles*, with the provision of diminishing marginal utility on the demand side to match up with the laws of returns on the supply side and the principle of substitution playing its all-pervasive role in consumption as well as production.

While the basis of classification of markets was altered (see Marshall, 1975, pp. 72–3), and rendered analytically more consistent with the generalized application of the supply-and-demand view in the mature writings of Marshall, the principle of classification – the 'time element' – persisted throughout. In *Principles*, class B was characterized as 'temporary equilibrium of demand and supply', while the short-period and long-period normal supply curves (comparable to class C and class D markets, respectively) were based on a different distinction from that between C and D markets. In the former (the short-period normal supply curve), the short period implied the fixity of 'stocks of productive appliances and skilled labour', etc., while the long period involved full adjustment of stocks of all kinds, sustained by a steady flow of replacements; in the 'Essay', D markets were distinguished from C markets mainly on the basis of the downward-sloping supply curve in the former. The prominence given to the D market situation (later described as the 'increasing returns' situation) was to be progressively diluted in later works, as the logical difficulties in fitting them into the equilibrium analysis became evident (see below).

The various market situations were brought into analytical 'continuity', the philosophical principle Marshall staunchly advocated in the *Preface* in the *Principles*. Marshall did not accept the sharp line of division between 'normal values' and 'current', 'market' or 'occasional' values.

> ... there is no impassable gulf between these two; they shade into one another by continuous gradations... For the element of Time, which is the centre of the chief difficulty of almost every economic problem, is itself absolutely continuous: Nature knows no absolute partition of time into long periods and short. (Marshall, 1961, p. vii)

This analytical continuity was afforded by the device of impounding 'diverse causes' into a *ceteris paribus* clause, from which they would be released, step by step, as the investigation proceeded.

> The general drift of the term normal supply price is always the same whether the period to which it refers is short or long;...In every case reference is made to a certain given rate of aggregate production...In every case the price is that the expectation of which is sufficient and only just sufficient to make it worthwhile for people to set themselves to produce that aggregate amount; in every case the cost of production is marginal;...But the causes which determine this margin vary with the length of the period under consideration. (ibid., p. 373–4)

According to this principle, four classes of situations were identified:

In each, price is governed by the relations between demand and supply. As regards *market* prices, Supply is taken to mean the stock of the commodity in question which is on hand, or at all events 'in sight'. As regards *normal* prices, when the term Normal is taken to relate to *short* periods of a few months or a year, Supply means broadly what can be produced for the price in question with the existing stock of plant, personal and impersonal, in the given time. As regards *normal* prices when the term *Normal* is to refer to *long* periods of several years, Supply means what can be produced by plant, which itself can be remuneratively produced and applied within the given time; while lastly, there are very gradual or *secular* movements of normal price, caused by the gradual growth of knowledge, of population and of capital, and the changing conditions of demand and supply from one generation to another. (ibid. p. 378–9)

In so applying the principle of continuity to a generalization of the supply-and-demand determination of prices, Marshall had moved on to a different *theory* of prices; while retaining the distinction between 'market prices' and 'normal prices', he altered their explanatory basis. His distinction rested merely on periodization of the adjustment process. He had reached this formalization by stages: in *Economics of Industry* written with Mary Marshall (1881; later withdrawn as evidently Marshall was not satisfied with his formative and still not cohesive ideas), the distinction between normal values and market values is different, and closer to the classical notion. It is made on the basis of the qualitatively different character of the forces acting on the two:

> Normal results are those which competition would bring about *in the long run*. The periods to which they relate must be sufficiently long to give time for the active forces of competition to overcome the passive resistance of ignorance, prejudice, custom, etc. They must be sufficiently long to enable us to neglect temporary fluctuations of supply and demand ... (Marshall and Marshall, 1881, p. vii)

Market prices were considered applicable in cases where there were combinations of buyers and sellers, a prevalence of ignorance, inertia, etc., but 'the Normal action of economic forces is hindered, or even overriden, but never destroyed by friction, by combination or by the passing events which exercise a restless influence on Market values' (ibid, p.vi). Market prices thus were not systematically analysable, affected as they were by diverse, transient factors. In the *Principles*, however, the distinction appeared as a matter of gradation.

It must, however, be emphasized that, even while proposing the same theoretical apparatus to explain market and normal values, Marshall considered long-period normal values to be the relevant ones on which to rest the general theoretical propositions. In 1902, in a letter to Edgeworth, he wrote: 'You know I never apply curves or mathematics to market values. For I don't think they help much, and market values are, I think, either absolutely abstract or terribly concrete and full of ever-varying (though individually vital) side-issues' (Pigou, 1925, p. 435). It was possibly because of the same hesitation, voiced in the letter to Keynes quoted above, that the explicit and detailed discussion of A, B, C and D markets was not pursued in later writings, although the major results were introduced, particularly in the *Pure Theory* (Marshall, 1879 [1930]).

(5) In the 'Essay', the notion of returns to scale was not yet formalized, although its rudiments were present. It is interesting to note that Marshall was already concerned with the problem of the downward-sloping supply curve. He saw it here mainly as a problem of multiple equilibria. This was to receive much more prominence in *Pure Theory*. Elsewhere (Bharadwaj, 1972 and 1984; Chapters 7 and 13 in the present volume), we have discussed the nature of the challenge to Marshall's theory posed by increasing returns and his not-so-successful attempts to give logically consistent answers within his framework.

Some hints regarding the basis for future discussion and the proposed solutions by which attempts were to be made to reconcile the downward-sloping supply curve (or 'the increasing returns' situation) with the equilibrium framework were present in the 'Essay'. In an attempt to explain how such multiple equilibria could occur and how a transition from one stable equilibrium situation to another (with larger output and lower unit costs) was possible, Marshall pointed to sudden changes in circumstances of demand (luxuries becoming part of ordinary demand); accidental disturbances having pushed the market into the new equilibrium situation, it stabilizes at the new level of price. Such reasoning also appeared in the *Pure Theory* and *Principles* (Appendix H). However, Marshall realized in these later works that this might introduce the notion of irreversibilities, so that the economies once created could not be withdrawn when output was reduced and the supply curve would have to be redrawn in its backward movement. This (discussed in Bharadwaj, Chapter 7 below) would have jeopardized the theoretical foundation of the supply curve (based on an *ex ante* notion of supplies forthcoming at hypothetical, alternative prices) relevant to the determination of equilibrium; the 'redrawing' of the supply curve which Marshall suggested would turn it into a 'historical', descriptive one.

In the 'Essay', irreversibilities were not referred to. However, Marshall did envisage the Cournot-type situation, in which competition itself would be endangered by a single producer monopolizing the market.

> If capital moved perfectly freely and there were no practical limit to the proportion of the whole trade connection which a firm can obtain this result [transition to a new stable equilibrium at lower unit costs] might often be brought about through the displacement of small manufactures by one or a few large ones. (Marshall, 1975, I, p. 151)

It is well known that Marshall was not very happy with this implication, arrived at logically by Cournot, and objected to it for being too 'mechanical' a deduction. In the 'Essay' he visualized practical difficulties in such a formation of large-scale manufactures, which however may be *occasionally* overcome...'in those trades in which the final manufacture is not dependent for some of its stages on subsidiary trades in which increased economy of labour is not readily induced without an increase of the total amount demanded' (ibid., p. 151). Here, one can see, in embryo, the notion of 'external economies', made possible by the development of subsidiary trades and skills, which was developed in *Pure Theory* as a generic cause for increasing returns. Sraffa (1925 and 1926) was to point out later that such an explanation would logically contradict Marshall's framework of partial equilibrium, in which the supply curve was a relation between the supply price and the scale of output *within* the individual industry.

Marshall also hinted in the 'Essay' that the answer to the problem of multiple equilibria might be found in the case of patented articles or articles 'from a particular firm of established reputation', where the price might settle between the two equilibria. The idea was not developed, but could have been the precursor of Marshall's later suggestion that competition may still survive in the face of increasing returns in the form of monopolistic competition.

(6) The utilitarian basis of the demand side was not worked out in the 'Essay'. The word 'utility' itself was used only once in relation to Adam Smith, and not approvingly. In *Pure Theory*, too, Marshall was to rely on 'satisfaction'. The initial reluctance to use 'utility' appears to be due to its narrow Benthamite, ethical connotation, which Marshall resisted. As Shove (1942, p. 306) pointed out: 'From the first he insisted that to say that the strength of motives at work in the business world is measurable does not imply any assumption as to their character or "quality", still less to their ethical value.' Marshall elaborated his position in 'The Present Position of Economics': the motives could be manifold (altruism, desire for distinction, for wealth) and need not always spring from 'the desire for pleasure or the avoidance of pain' (Pigou, 1925, pp. 152–73). Motives became relevant to and entered into economics through their 'measurability', making quantitative analysis possible:

> The outward form of economic theory has been shaped by its connection with material wealth. But it is becoming clear that the true philosophic raison d'être of the theory is that it supplies a machinery to aid us in reasoning about those motives of human action which are measurable. (ibid., p. 158)

In Marshall, 'the play of measurable motives for and against one another, balancing one another and being substituted for one another' became the engine of economic analysis. This measurability of motives in terms of the price which individuals are prepared to pay, rather than forgo a certain satisfaction, provided the basis for the notion of consumer's surplus. On the same principle of measurability, Marshall translated the 'real costs' (the efforts and sacrifices incurred by labour and by capitalists 'in waiting') into 'expenses of production', and by doing so hoped to resolve all the difficulties involved in aggregating/comparing heterogeneous kinds of subjectively incurred efforts and sacrifices.

In 'Mr Mill's theory of value' (1876), Marshall attributed the idea of 'measurable motives' to Adam Smith, stating that 'A point of view was conquered for us by Adam Smith, from which a commodity is regarded as the embodiment of measurable efforts and sacrifices' (Pigou, 1925, p. 126). Evidently the reference is to the 'toil and trouble' which Adam Smith spoke of. No doubt Mill had advanced further towards 'real costs', acquiescing in Senior's idea of abstinence. However far-stretched this attribution to Smith, the 'real costs' idea was, as Shove put it, quite definitely 'un-Ricardian'. To quote Shove (1942, p. 306):

> For Ricardo, labour is not a 'disutility' but the productive force available to the commodity, the stuff, so to speak, by means of which commodities are made and the cost of a thing is the quantity of this force or stuff, together with the quantity of capital, absorbed on its production, not the effort and sacrifice entailed in providing it. And though in his view the minimum rate of profit was the necessary compensation for the 'trouble and risk' ...undertaken by the investor, both he and Mill habitually conceive of the second element in cost also (the capital employed) in objective terms – as the quantity or value of the wages advanced and the length of time for which advance is made, not as a subjective discommodity or sacrifice. (See, for a further discussion, p. 152 below)

The idea of 'measurable motives' does not appear to be central to classical theory, as suggested by Marshall. Here his departure was definitive and it was only in the *Principles* that he would express himself more openly regarding the utilitarian foundation; directly, on the demand side, but indirectly, through 'expenses of production as measuring real costs', on the supply side.

III

6 Marshall's Claim of Continuity with Ricardo-Mill

From the 'Essay on value' and other early writings (not all covered by our discussion) it appears likely that when Jevons's book appeared Marshall had already developed substantive ideas on the supply-and-demand approach, although the demand side (and especially its basis in utility) had not been worked out comprehensively or clearly; and the 'marginal' principle was not stated as explicitly as in Jevons.

Starting with propositions from Mill's *Principles* and impelled by the Mill–Thornton controversy, Marshall had attempted to systematize the supply-and-demand approach by moving towards an analytical symmetry between the two equilibrating forces. His strong reaction to Jevons's *Theory*, reflected in his review of that work (Pigou, 1925, pp. 93-9), appears to have been provoked (apart probably from feelings of incipient rivalry) by the latter's emphasis on the utilitarian motivational basis and the one-sided over emphasis on utility as an explanation of value. Marshall expressed his position in a letter to Pierson (in 1891), maintaining that his own *Principles*

> was written to express one idea; & one only. That idea is that whereas Ricardo and company maintain that value is determined by cost of production, & Malthus, McLeod, Jevons & (in a measure) the Austrians that it is determined by utility, each was right in what he affirmed but wrong in what he denied. They none of them, paid, I think, sufficient attention to the element of *time*. That I believe holds the key of all the paradoxes which this long controversy has raised. When Ricardo spoke of Cost of production as determining value he had in mind periods as to which cost of production is the dominant force: when Jevons emphasised utility, he had in mind shorter periods. The attempt to work all existing knowledge on the subject of value into one continuous & harmonious whole, by means of a complex study of the element of Time, permeates every Book, almost every page of my volume. It is the backbone of all that, from a scientific point of view, I care to say. (Marshall, 1975, pp. 97–8)

Yet Marshall expressed irritation at being thought of as one who 'compromised between' or 'reconciled' divergent schools of thought (see his letter to J. B. Clark in Pigou, 1925, p. 418). Indeed, Shove staunchly upheld the view that 'so far as its strictly analytical content is concerned the *Principles* is in direct line of descent through Mill from Ricardo and through Ricardo from Adam Smith. It is of the true Ricardian stock, neither a cross-bred nor sport' (Shove, 1942, p. 295). While refuting the idea that the analytical backbone of the *Principles* is either a conflation of Ricardian notions with the use of the 'marginal utility' school or an 'attempt to substitute for Ricardian doctrine a new system of ideas arrived by a different line of approach', Shove conceded that the process of completion and generalization involved a transformation more thoroughgoing than Marshall himself was disposed to admit (p. 295).

On the basis of the 'Essay on value' (as well as those on wages, profits and rent), the links with Mill are amply evident. Marshall was himself to comment in 'Mr Mill's theory of value' that 'Readers...may find in Mill's economic doctrines much exposition that requires to be supplemented, and many abrupt lines of thought which require to be continued' (Pigou, 1925, p. 121). This, indeed, is what he appears to have done – to have brought rigour and consistency to Mill's ideas, affording them a 'mathematical form'. However, it was precisely the beginnings in Mill of considerable deviations from Ricardo's theory of value and distribution (See Chapter 3 in the present volume) that called for and received at Marshall's hands such extension and refinement; so that Marshall's deliberations on value and distribution departed systematically from the questions Ricardo posed and the framework of analysis he employed.[14] Apart from the fragment on rent, Marshall appears to have shared little common ground with Ricardo in these *Early Writings*. In the theory of distribution, which concerned Ricardo most, there were hardly any traces of Ricardian reasoning.

In fact, Marshall's early pronouncements regarding the origin of his ideas stressed his allegiance to Mill. It appears as though it was almost as a reaction to Jevons's strongly worded, virulent attack on Ricardo ('the able but wrong headed man, David Ricardo ... who shunted the car of economic science on to a wrong line', 1911, p. li) that Marshall linked himself more firmly with Ricardo ('my youthful loyalty to him [Ricardo] boiled over when I read Jevons' *Theory*', Pigou, 1925, p. 100). Indeed, he regarded Ricardo's genius and ability as far above those of Mill (ibid., pp. 99–100, 162; also Marshall, 1975, I, p. 50, n. 48).

However, what Shove regarded as extensions and generalizations of Ricardo in *Principles* (the introduction of the demand side, the functional relation between costs and output, the supply-and-demand determination of wages and profits) are radical departures from the Ricardian standpoint. A careful reading of Ricardo's *Notes on Malthus* (Ricardo, 1951b) clearly shows that he had forcefully rejected similar propositions (much less rigorously stated) emanating from Malthus. It is also now possible for us to see, after Piero Sraffa's masterly commentaries on Ricardo's *Works* and his subsequent reconstruction and extension of the classical schema (Sraffa, 1960), how, for Ricardo's theory of value and distribution, the so-called 'law of diminishing returns' and the Malthusian theory of population were more of a fifth wheel. Shove's position can no longer be validated when one remembers that these were indeed the basis for discovering 'marginalism' in Ricardo and provided fertile ground for later extensions into neoclassical theory (arguing, for example, as Marshall did, that demand *functions* had to be introduced in the classical theory for logical completeness).

Marshall's Reading of Ricardo and Mill
Marshall himself conveyed the impression that his task was mainly one of clarification, explanation and generalization: he frequently maintained that Smith, Ricardo and Mill were often 'not conscious of the full drift of their reasoning'; and that Ricardo's unclear exposition was particularly conducive to much interpretation and mischief ('His expression is as confused as his thought is profound', Marshall, 1961, p. 813). In Appendix I of his *Principles*, on Ricardo's theory of value, Marshall transferred his own views onto Ricardo by undertaking to interpret him generously: he read Ricardo's difference between riches and value as corresponding to that between total and marginal utility, and suggested that, although Ricardo was aware that commodities fell into three classes according to how they obeyed the law of diminishing,

constant or increasing returns, he ignored the distinction, concentrating on the limited case of constant returns. However, as Sraffa (1925 and 1926) has argued, there is no presumption in classical theory regarding any sort of functional relation between outputs and costs essential for the theory and hence the notion of returns to scale is essentially irrelevant to the Ricardian theory.

Marshall interpreted Ricardo's proposition, that relative values are dependent on the relative time distribution of labour embodied, as supporting his own inclusion of 'waiting' as an independent element in the determination of value. As the quotation from Shove cited above clearly brings out, Ricardo's dated labour was a concept far removed from Marshall's subjective real costs in terms of efforts and sacrifices. Ricardo no doubt admitted that the determination of relative values on the basis of relative quantities of labour embodied was modified, in that they were also influenced by 'the element of time' – the latter used by Ricardo as a summary expression to connote differences among commodities in their conditions of production (i.e., in the proportions between fixed and circulating capital, in the durability of fixed capital and in the time elapsing before the commodities were brought to the market). While referring to these differing proportions of the constituent elements of capital, Ricardo did not, however, consider *quantity* of capital as an independent 'cause' of value.

It would seem that Ricardo was aware of the difference in approach between an explanation in terms of 'dated' labour and one treating labour and time as two independent causes of value. In his letter to McCulloch, dated 13 June 1820 (Ricardo, 1952b, p. 194), much quoted, as Sraffa observes (Ricardo, 1951a, p.xxxix), as illustrative of Ricardo's weakening over the labour theory of value, he wrote:

> I sometimes think that if I were to write the chapter on value again which is in my book, I should acknowledge that the relative value of commodities was regulated by two causes instead of by one, namely, by the relative quantity of labour necessary to produce the commodities in question, and by the rate of profit for the time that the capital remained dormant, and until the commodities were brought to market. Perhaps I should find the difficulties nearly as great in this view of the subject as in that which I have adopted.

As Sraffa shows, providing further evidence (Ricardo, 1951a, pp. xxxix–xl), this weakening was 'no more than a passing mood'; Ricardo certainly did not veer round in the direction which he momentarily regarded as an alternative, possibly because the difficulties in that course, as he surmised, were no less. His views on value evidently remained substantially unaltered in the third edition of *Principles*, published in 1821.

Marshall also criticized Ricardo's carelessness with regard to the element of time, referring to his own distinction between short-period and long-period normal values. We have already seen above, how, in the process of introducing continuity in terms of different market situations, he had moved on to a different theoretical explanation of price and hence a different basis for the distinction.

Crossing the Divide
While Marshall was initially averse to accepting the Jevonian utility-based approach, his attitude towards the new theories softened over time and in the *Principles* he incorporated a number of such ideas, especially on the demand side of his value explanation. In extending and generalizing Mill's propositions, he entered a new theoretical domain. When he claimed that the new theories of Jevons and Walras were familiar truths, he was conscious of the novelty of his own ideas and the basic similarities he shared with these other, self-conscious innovators in developing a new framework, depending on a theory of equilibrium between demand and supply. On the other hand, his stubborn emphasis on the continuity of doctrines goaded him to preface his *Principles* with the remark

> Some of the best work of the present generation has indeed appeared at first sight to be antagonistic to that of earlier writers; but when it has had time to settle down into its proper place, and its rough edges have been worn away, it has been found to involve no real breach of continuity in the development of the science. The new doctrines have supplemented the older, have extended, developed and sometimes corrected them and often have given them a different tone by a new distribution of emphasis; but very seldom have subverted them. (1961, preface to 1st edition, p. V)

However the old doctrines were indeed subverted and Marshall's theorizing played a major role in abandoning the old and in heralding and establishing the new. The phenomenon of exchange, cast in the generalized theoretical schema of supply and demand, was extended to cover the entire range of problems – of production, consumption and distribution – and subjective valuations of individuals, regarded as optimizing agents, permeated economic theory, with the 'measurable motives' providing the organon of analysis. This, indeed, was a total change of regime.

Notes: Chapter 6

This essay was first published in the *Cambridge Journal of Economics*, vol. 2, no. 3 (September 1978), pp. 253–71. I came across the manuscript on value in the Marshall Papers at the Marshall Library, Cambridge, in early 1969 and recognized it as being the one referred to by Marshall in his letter to J. M. Keynes (quoted on p. 143 above) and reported 'not extant' by C. W. Guillebaud in his comment on that letter in the Variorium edition of Marshall's *Principles* (1960, Vol. II, p. 365). I postponed the publication of comments on the manuscript on being informed by Professor E. A. G. Robinson that the Whitaker edition of the early writings of Marshall was in progress. I should like to thank the referees of the Journal, Pierangelo Garegnani, the late Ronald L. Meek and Ian Steedman for helpful comments.

1. The text of the MSS 'Essay on value' appears on pp. 119–64 of Vol. I. The editor prefaces the *Writings* with a helpful and extensive commentary on the development of Marshall's thought (Vol. I, pp 1–113).
2. Among others, see: letter to Walras in Walras (1965), p. 794; letter to J. B. Clark in Pigou (1925), p. 416, also pp. 412–13; letter to L. C. Colson in Marshall (1933), pp. 221–2.
3. Marshall hinted in his review of Jevons's *Theory of Political Economy* (Pigou, 1925, pp. 93–100) that many of his ideas were 'familiar truths' and stated, in *Principles of Economics*, that he had borrowed the term 'marginal' from von Thünen before he adopted Jevons's term 'final', only to revert to the original term (Preface, 1st edition). Marshall maintained that he was mainly influenced by von Thünen as to his ideas and Cournot as to the form of thought (see Pigou, 1925, pp. 99–100).
4. Panteleoni asserted that Marshall had been teaching marginal utility at Cambridge before he had read Jevons's *Theory*. Foxwell, Marshall's student during 1869–71, claimed priority for Marshall in his letters to Jevons; J. M. Keynes's famous memoir in Pigou (1925) attributed the rather ungenerous review of Jevons's *Theory* by Marshall to the latter's possible annoyance and disappointment at Jevons's work taking the novelty from his own ideas. For a detailed coverage, see Howey (1960), pp. 76–92.
5. See, for contending views, Shove (1942) and L. L. Price's review article on Marshall's *Principles*, quoted in Howey (1960), pp. 89–90.
6. Writing to J. B. Clark (Pigou, 1925, p. 418), Marshall protested: 'One thing alone in American criticism irritates me, though it be not unkindly meant. It is the suggestion that I try to "compromise between" or "reconcile" divergent schools of thought.'
7. 'As the wages of the labourer are the remuneration of labour, so the profits of the capitalist are properly, according to Mr Senior's well-chosen expression, the remuneration of abstinence. They are what he gains by forbearing to consume his capital for his own uses, and allowing it to be consumed by productive labourers for their uses. For this forbearance he requires a recompense' (Mill, 1871 [1929], p. 405).
8. For a criticism of Marshall's interpretation, see Ashley (1891).
9. Jevons wrote in the Preface to the first edition of his *Theory of Political Economy* (included in the fourth edition): 'There are many portions of Economical doctrine which appear to me as scientific in form as they are consonant with facts. I would especially mention the Theories of Population and Rent, the latter a theory of distinctly mathematical character, *which seems to give a clue to the correct mode of treating the whole science*' (Jevons, 1911, p. vi, italics added).
10. See, for a discussion on the question of the dating of the MSS, Marshall (1975), pp. 117–18.
11. See, for the full text, Marshall (1961), II, p. 365; also Marshall (1975), I, pp. 119–20.
12. Shove begins this remark 'Though one cannot speak with confidence, one may hazard the guess ...' (Shove, 1942, p. 307).

13 Marshall considered 'the conditions of normal supply' as 'less definite' than of demand (1961, p. 342). He was aware of the difficulties created particularly by the possibility of increasing returns (see Bharadwaj, 1972, Chapter 7 in the present volume). Pigou (1953, pp. 22–4) found puzzling a similar position, namely, Marshall's reluctance to extend the notion of elasticity of supply except as regards very short periods, and regarded it as 'an unnecessary scruple'. Pigou wondered why Marshall, who was aware of similar difficulties arising on the demand side, due to the difficulty of keeping conditions constant within the *ceteris paribus* clause in the long period, should have felt particular scruples about extending the elasticity concept to the long-period supply curve. He noted, however, that 'Marshall has not been followed by later writers. On the contrary, the notion of elasticity has spread itself, not merely to supply, but in a number of other directions also' (p. 24). Marshall had expressed reservations concerning Pigou's use of the long-period supply curve in the latter's *Wealth and Welfare*. His doubts, if pursued in depth, would have called into question the logical basis of the supply-and-demand theory (see Bharadwaj, 1972, Chapter 7 in the present volume).

14 Schumpeter emphatically refused to include J. S. Mill in 'Ricardo's school'. He observed that 'the economics of the *Principles* are no longer Ricardian. This is obscured by filial respect and also, independently of this, by J. S. Mill's own belief that he was only qualifying Ricardian doctrine. But this belief was erroneous. His qualifications affect essentials of theory and, still more, of course, of social outlook. Ricardianism meant no doubt more to him than it did to Marshall. But Mill's and Marshall's cases are similar in that, for reasons of their own, commendable or not, they stressed Ricardian influences unduly at the expense of others. From Marshall's *Principles*, Ricardianism can be removed without being missed at all. From Mill's *Principles*, it could be dropped without being missed very greatly' (1961, p. 529). On Mill's deviations from Ricardo, see also Dobb (1973), pp. 121–36. See also Meek (1950), p. 62.

References: Chapter 6

Ashley, W. J. (1891), 'The rehabilitation of Ricardo', *Economic Journal*, Vol. I (September), pp. 474-89.

Bharadwaj, K. (1972), 'Marshall on Pigou's *Wealth and Welfare*', *Economica*, vol. xxxix, no. 153 (February), pp. 32–46; Chapter 7 in the present volume.

Bharadwaj, K. (1978), *Classical Political Economy and the Rise to Dominance of the Supply and Demand Theories* (Calcutta: Orient Longman); Revised edition, 1986

De Quincey, T. (1844 [1863]), *The Logic of Political Economy*, in *Collected Works*, Vol. XIII (Edinburgh: A. & C. Black).

Dobb, M. H. (1973), *Theories of Value and Distribution since Adam Smith* (Cambridge: Cambridge University Press).

Howey, R. S. (1960), *The Rise of the Marginal Utility School 1870–89* (Lawrence: University of Kansas Press).

Jevons, W. S. (1911), *Theory of Political Economy*, 4th edn., ed. H. Stanley Jevons (London: Macmillan).

Keynes, J. M. (1924), 'Alfred Marshall, 1842–1924', *Economic Journal*, vol.34, September, reprinted in Pigou, A.C. (ed.), *Memorials*, op. cit.

Marshall, A. (1879 [1930]), *Pure Theory of Foreign Trade. The Pure Theory of Domestic Values*. Series of Reprints of Scarce Tracts in Economic and Political Science, no. 1 (London: London School of Economics and Political Science).
Marshall, A. (1933), 'Alfred Marshall the mathematician as seen by himself', *Econometrica* (April).
Marshall, A. (1961), *Principles of Economics*, 9th Variorum edn, ed. by C. W. Guillebaud, 2 vols (London: Macmillan).
Marshall, A. (1975), *Early Writings (1867–1890)*, 2 vols, ed. by J. K. Whitaker (London: Macmillan).
Marshall, A., and Marshall, M. P. (1881), *The Economics of Industry*, 2nd edn (London: Macmillan).
Meek, R. L. (1950), 'The decline of Ricardian economics in England', *Economica*, vol. 17, no. 1 (February), pp. 43–62.
Mill, J. S. (1871 [1929]), *Principles of Political Economy*, ed. W. J. Ashley (London: Longman).
Mill, J. S. (1869 [1968]), 'Thornton on labour and its claims', *Fortnightly Review* (May/June), reprinted in *Collected Works*, Vol. V, ed. by J. M. Robson (Toronto: Toronto University Press).
Pigou, A. C. (ed.) (1925), *Memorials of Alfred Marshall* (London: Macmillan).
Pigou, A.C. (1953), *Alfred Marshall and Current Thought* (London: Macmillan).
Ricardo, D. (1951a), *Principles of Political Economy*, Vol. I of *Works and Correspondence of David Ricardo*, ed. P. Sraffa with the collaboration of M. H. Dobb (Cambridge: Cambridge University Press).
Ricardo, D. (1951b), *Notes on Malthus*, Vol. II of *Works and Correspondence of David Ricardo*, ed. by P. Sraffa with the collaboration of M. H. Dobb (Cambridge: Cambridge University Press).
Ricardo, D. (1951c), The Works and Correspondence of David Ricardo, vol. VIII, Letters 1819–June 1821, ed. p. Sraffa with the collaboration of M. H. Dobb (Cambridge: Cambridge University Press).
Schumpeter, J. A. (1961), *History of Economic Analysis* (London: Allen & Unwin).
Senior, N. (1836 [1965]), *An Outline of the Science of Political Economy* (New York: Augustus M. Kelley).
Shove, G. F. (1942), 'The place of Marshall's *Principles* in the development of economic theory', *Economic Journal*, vol. 52 (December), pp. 294–329.
Smith, A. (1776[1930]), *An Inquiry into the Nature and Causes of the Wealth of Nations*, ed. by E. Cannan, 5th edn (London: Methuen).
Sraffa, P. (1925), 'Sulle relazioni fra costo e quantità prodotta', *Annali di Economia*, vol. 2, no. 1, pp. 277–328
Sraffa, P. (1926), 'The laws of returns under competitive conditions', *Economic Journal*, vol. 36 (December), pp. 535–50.
Sraffa, P. (1960), *Production of Commodities by Means of Commodities: Prelude to a Critique of Economic Theory* (Cambridge: Cambridge University Press).
Thornton, W. T. (1870), *On Labour: Its Wrongful Claims and Rightful Duties*, 2nd edn (London: Macmillan).
Walras, L. (1965), *Correspondence and Related Papers*, ed. by W. Jaffe, Vol. I (Amsterdam: North Holland).

7
Marshall on Pigou's *Wealth and Welfare*

As Marshall's favourite pupil and successor, Pigou is considered to have confirmed and extended Marshall's conclusions on the question of maximum satisfaction under free competition. In the words of Keynes (1924): 'Marshall's proof that *laissez faire* breaks down in certain conditions, *theoretically* and not merely practically, regarded as a principle of maximum social advantage, was of great philosophical importance (Pigou, 1925, p. 44) But, as Keynes adds, Marshall did not pursue this argument in all its ramifications, and it was Pigou who worked out fully its consequences for social policy.

While Pigou (1910, p. 366) looked upon his early work as being 'merely supplementary' to that of Marshall, there has been no direct evidence as to how Marshall viewed the extension of his method by Pigou. Marshall's manuscript notes in his own copy of Pigou's *Wealth and Welfare* (1912), reveal that Marshall had strong reservations concerning Pigou's conclusions in that book which, however, he did not intend to disclose 'for the present', even to Pigou himself.[1]

It is notable that Marshall's comments, dated 10 October 1914, were made more than two years after the publication of Pigou's book. It is probable that the comments were occasioned by the attack on marginalism made by J. A. Hobson in his *Work and Wealth: A Human Valuation*, published in 1914. Hobson noted that Pigou, by showing that the supply price and the 'marginal supply price' of an industry diverge excepting under constant returns, had virtually admitted the failure of marginalism to establish that competition ensures *maximum satisfaction*.[2] Marshall refers twice to this passage of Hobson in his comments (see §§1 and 11 below). He agrees with Hobson if only to the extent that he himself considers Pigou as overrating 'the possibilities of the statical method'.

Marshall's manuscript notes are presented in Section I in the form of sixteen numbered comments.[3] Where appropriate, the relevant passage from *Wealth and Welfare* or a summary of the relevant portion of the text is presented in smaller print before the comment itself. Abbreviations used by Marshall are expanded in square brackets. Asterisks are reproduced as placed in the text by Marshall. Underscorings by Marshall are discussed in the Notes provided at the end of this Chapter. The page reference at the beginning of each comment is to the appropriate page in *Wealth and Welfare*.

In Section II of the article we discuss differences between Marshall and Pigou in the light of the Comments in Section I; we have also drawn upon other unpublished supporting evidence in the Marshall Papers.

1 Marshall's Comments on Pigou

§1

On the front end-paper of *Wealth and Welfare*, Marshall makes the following general comment.

10.10.1914

I incline to think that the marginal supply curve Part II Ch. VIII has no reality; I think he overrates the possibilities of the statical method, and so far I agree with Hobson's criticism of marginalism, *Work and Wealth* p. 174,[4] though most of what J. A. H[obson] says on the subject seems to me invalid.

In this I may be wrong. For I can't follow all that A. C. P[igou] says: and it is possible that he has some recondite meaning. Anyhow I incline not to controvert him, even under 4 eyes, for the present. When he translates his W[ealth] & W[elfare] into realism, then I may perhaps raise a question, if I still cannot follow him. But on the whole I incline to keep my[self] close to Pr[inciples] (especially in regard to the limitations of the statical method) in [Book] IV.[5]

§2

(p.17)
Pigou contrasts Marshall's definition of national dividend, as comprising the whole of the gross dividend minus such part as would suffice to maintain the country's capital intact, with that of Irving Fisher. 'Professor Fisher, on the other hand, placing in the forefront of his argument the proposition that the savings are in no circumstance income, claims unequivocally to identify the national dividend with those services, and those only, that enter directly into consumption.'

This is a definite unit; but I do not think 'income' is the right name for it.

§3

(p. 18)
'When...we are concerned, not with an imaginary stationary state, but with the condition of affairs that actually exists, the mere maintenance of the physical efficiency of our plant is no longer obviously equivalent to the maintenance of our capital intact. Machinery that has become obsolete because of the development of improved forms is not really left intact, however excellent its physical condition; and the same thing is true of machinery for whose products popular taste has declined. If, however, in deference to these considerations, we decide to make an allowance for cases of obsolescence, we are exposed to the retort that this concession logically implies the recognition of the value, and not the physical efficiency, of instrumental goods as the object which is to be maintained intact.'*

* I do not follow this. I regard an obsolescent machine as I do a horse that is 'ageing' perhaps prematurely. On the other hand, in so far as invention etc. cause the efficiency of plants to increase relatively to its cost I take the addition to be included in my main statement. I am however aware that I have made no attempts to supply suggestions for avoiding double entry in so far as (i) an improved machine and (ii) its (improved) product are both entered. I do not think such subtleties are appropriate in a broad statement.

§4

(p. 149)
'By the "social net product"[6] is meant the aggregate contribution made to the national dividend; by the "private net product"* the contribution made to the earnings of those responsible for the industry under review.'

* i.e. private net product is the 'remuneration' of the worker whether it comes in the form of wages or in the price of the product or service wh[ich] he makes and markets on his own account.

§5

(pp. 172–3)
'In respect of any industry, construct a demand curve DD ... Construct, secondly, a supply curve SS^1 of the ordinary type, a curve namely, such that, if a perpendicular PM be drawn from any point P upon it to cut the base line in M, PM represents the price which, in the long run, tends to maintain an annual output OM. Finally, construct a curve of marginal supply prices SS^2 such that, if a perpendicular QM be drawn from any point

Q upon it to cut the base line in M, QM represents the difference made to the aggregate expenses of the industry*[7] concerned by the production of the OMth unit of output. Let the curve of marginal supply prices cut the demand curve in Q. Then in order that equality may be established between the marginal net product of resources in our selected industry and in other industries, it is necessary that the output of our industry be OM units.'

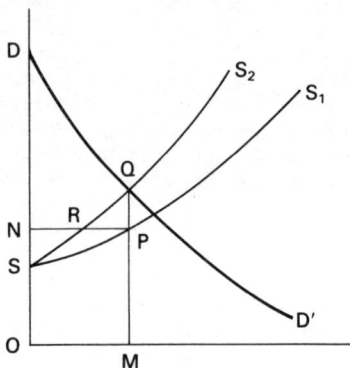

Fig. 1.

I rather think that QP is (neglecting influences on the technical economies of farming caused by increased production) not a real expense but an extra charge wh[ich] landlords will be able to put on producers, in consequence of the increased value of land. I understand this to be implied by F. Y. E[dgeworth]'s statement, Ec[onomic] J[ournal] 1913,p. 210[8] (mag[azine]s[9] Transport 1914, No. 10) that area OMQS = OMPN, i.e. SPQ = SPN.

* I do not understand 'the aggregate expenses of the industry'. If all economies appertaining to an increased scale of prod[uctio]n were 'internal' to particular firms, then I think one sh[ould] look to the expenses of an increased production (not hurried) of a 'representative' firm. But as in fact increased economies in shipbuilding depend in part on correlated economies in the manufacture of plates there seems to me to be no one point at which the 'aggregate expenses' act as a specific motive force.

§6

(p.173, footnote)
'It must be carefully observed that "the difference made to aggregate expenses" by the production of the OMth unit of output, means the difference between the aggregate expenses of an industry when it is producing and is fully adjusted to producing x units and when it is producing and is *fully adjusted to* producing $(x + \triangle x)$ units ... This...may be illustrated from the facts of railway transportation ... The loading of all

trucks will be different according to the total quantity to be carried. The next step after 40 overloaded trucks would not be 40 overloaded trucks *plus* one truck containing one parcel but 41 lightly loaded trucks.'[10]

I think he means that if the demand for such trainloads had been anticipated as permanent the trucks w[oul]d have been made a little smaller so that 41 c[oul]d have just been filled.

§7

(p. 176)
'It is objected that, since, under diminishing returns, our argument makes the supply price of any quantity of output less than the marginal supply price, it implies that the marginal unit is continuously produced at a loss to the producer of it; and that this is impossible and absurd. This reasoning derives its plausibility from an implicit assumption that the *curve of marginal supply prices* employed here is equivalent to Dr Marshall's *particular expenses curve*. That assumption, however, under conditions of simple competition is not correct.'

Certainly the two seem to have nothing in common.

§8

(p. 176)
'When x units are being produced...the particular expenses to the representative producer of producing any one unit, *all costs, including the hire of the necessary land being reckoned in*, is equal to the particular expense of producing any other unit. That is to say, if p is the average full cost per unit of producing x units, the particular expenses curve, corresponding to the production of x units, is a horizontal line drawn parallel to the base line at a height representative of p.'

No, my curve represents avowedly *no* actual conditions.

§9

(p. 176)
'The general result is that, in industries of constant returns, the supply price and the marginal supply price of all quantities of output are equal; in industries of increasing returns the supply price is greater than the marginal supply price.'

This, I think is better treated in my App[endix] H of Pr[inciples].

§10

(p. 176)
'In industries of diminishing returns the supply price is less than the marginal price...'

This seems invalid if rent be taken as a charge.

§11

(Top margin of p. 176)

Hobson, Work and Wealth, p. 174 says[11] that this page is 'a virtual confession of the futility' of the doctrine of marginalism. Is it not the fact that the contrast between the supply price and marginal supply price is inconsistent with A. C. P[igou]'s own definition at top of §3 (p. 174);[12] and that the important facts on which he insists can be set out without suggesting any such contradiction[?].

§12

(p.216)
Pigou argues against the proposition that the transport of copper and that of coal are joint products on the ground that 'a very large fixed plant *for varied* purposes is essential to the operation of joint costs ...A sufficient answer...is to observe that the carriage of tons of different things from A to B *is*[13] a single homogeneous commodity, on precisely the same footing as plain cotton cloth.'

No, it is not. The whole doctrine of costs of manufacturing in the higher technical, as well as academic developments, turns largely on the difficulty of assigning to different products their several shares of the common costs of such things as powerful shears, hand saws, turret lathes, etc; which spend part of their time idly, but when at work perform almost identical operations for these various products. Like the supply of transport by the locomotive, the supply of every such machine of similar operations for different things is an instance of common supply (not 'joint' in the sense in which sirloin and shin of beef are joint, but joint in the ordinary use of the term). Similarly the cost of an expensive frontage for selling a hundred different products has to be shared out among them, and raises difficulties of joint supply of the same service to different things on all fours with the railway problem. This is not inconsistent with the position that monopoly plays an exceptionally large part in the vagaries of monopoly charges.

§13

(top margin of chapter on the 'Variability of Errors in Business Forecasts', p. 453)

This chapter puts many points in new settings; but on the whole it seems to repeat the old explanation of crises, without taking account of the new causes chiefly since 1857 (1866 was exceptional) which have checked the rise, mitigated the fall and blunted the sharpness of the apex.

§14

(p. 457, referring to Hull's *Industrial Depression*)
'Mr Hull has rightly observed that the effect of forward buying, in expanding the range of variability of business expectations, would be mitigated, if the state were to publish monthly "all pertinent information in relation to the existing volume of construction under contract for further months".'

But it is already done by trade journals better than it could be by government.

§15

(p. 464, footnote)
'It is, thus, a true saying which Mr Burton quotes from John Mills: "As a rule, panics do not destroy capital;* they merely reveal the extent to which it has been previously destroyed by its betrayal into hopelessly unproductive works..."'

* This use of 'capital' is unsatisfactory. In effect it refers mainly to material capital, to the exclusion of business reputation, adjustment of means to ends. The collapse of a part of a printing press may destroy much capital invested in type tho' the lead can all be recovered.

§16

(p. 485, footnote, referring to the Minority Report in the Report of the Royal Commission on the Poor Laws, p. 1196.)
'The Minority's argument...is associated with the suggestion that an addition of £10,000,000 to the wage fund of the worst year would suffice to reduce unemployment in that year to the normal amount. This result, which is based upon statistical evidence by Mr Bowley, assumes that the whole of the extra ten millions would go in employing new hands, and none of it in raising wages... To...equate the total wage fund of bad years to that of good would require a sum nearer to 100 millions than to 10 millions.'

Both of these arithmetics seem hazardous. £m.10+ adjustment *might* do all. The question is w[oul]d adjustment improve much? If it did employment w[oul]d make employment .

2 Discussion

In his *Principles* Marshall suggested that a community's satisfaction could be increased by levying a tax on an industry subject to decreasing returns to finance a bounty to an industry in which the law of increasing returns 'acts sharply'. This 'tentative' conclusion was arrived at by considering the effects, mainly on consumers' surplus, of a tax or a bounty. Marshall found the effects of a tax to be the least injurious to consumers when levied on an industry under decreasing returns, and that a bounty to an industry subject to increasing returns would add to the community's satisfaction.[14]

In *Wealth and Welfare* (1912), Pigou, adopting the national dividend as a measure of a community's welfare, stipulated the equality of marginal net product of resources in all uses as the condition for maximum welfare. To show that, under certain conditions, the competitive output fails to satisfy this criterion, he introduced the notion of 'the marginal supply price' of an industry, defined as 'the difference made to aggregate expenses of production (in terms of money) of all producers by an increase in total production from x to $(x+\triangle x)$ units'.[15] He argued that, while in the case of increasing returns, the marginal supply price curve lies *below* the supply curve, in the case of decreasing returns it lies *above* it, so that the 'ideal output', given by the intersection of the marginal supply price curve and the demand curve, exceeds competitive output under increasing returns and falls short of it under decreasing returns. Only under constant returns do the 'ideal' and the competitive outputs coincide. These results led Pigou to advocate a tax on *every* industry subject to decreasing returns *and* a bounty to *every* industry subject to increasing returns (1912, pp. 178-9).

This unconventional result, that competition, in general, failed to achieve maximum satisfaction, provided the ground for Hobson to observe that Pigou's findings amounted to an admission of the futility of marginalism. And it was Hobson's remark which stimulated Marshall to criticize Pigou's method. Marshall's criticism is mainly directed against the notion of the 'marginal supply price' which, he says, 'has no reality' (§1). He objects to its use in the case of decreasing returns as well as that of increasing returns, but for different reasons. In the former case, he finds the contrast between marginal supply price and the supply price to be inconsistent with Pigou's own definition of the supply price (§11). More important and interesting is the objection Marshall raises with regard to increasing returns: that, in applying the marginal method in a cut-and-dried fashion Pigou 'overrates the possibilities of the statical method'. Marshall had written in his *Principles* (already in the fourth edition of 1898, p. 516):

> The statical theory of equilibrium...is barely even an introduction to the study of the progress and development of industries which show a tendency to increasing return. Its limitations are so constantly overlooked, especially by those who approach it from an abstract point of view, that there is a danger in throwing it into definite form at all.

It may be noted at the outset that Pigou's use of the term marginal supply price is misleading, and indeed he himself appears initially to have been misled by it. In constructing the curve of marginal supply prices, Pigou appears to have assumed that the average cost curve of the industry is its supply curve under *both* decreasing and increasing returns. However, it is so only under increasing returns, and can hold for decreasing returns only if such returns are wholly due to external diseconomies. When decreasing returns are due to a fixed factor, as is generally supposed, the supply curve is itself the marginal cost curve, and the curve of marginal supply prices is then merely a derivative curve of this marginal cost curve.[16]

Marshall's comment that the marginal supply price has no reality can be understood, with regard to decreasing returns, from the preceding: a derivative curve of a marginal cost curve can be said to have no 'real' significance. Marshall's §5 brings this out explicitly. He observes that 'neglecting the influence of technical economies' the difference between the marginal supply price and the supply price 'is not a real expense but an extra charge which landlords will be able to put on producers, in consequence of the increased value of land'. It can be seen that the ordinate on the marginal supply curve at a given output measures the cost of producing the marginal unit which pays no rent (indicated on the supply curve) *plus* the additional rent payments on all the rest of the units, due to the marginal increase in output. These additional payments are not for the use of additional real resources but are increased costs of a fixed factor already in use. (This argument underlies §10 also.)

We may recall here that Allyn Young (1913) in his review of *Wealth and Welfare* published in August 1913 had already pointed out that the difference between the marginal supply price and the supply price in the case of decreasing returns was to be interpreted as 'transferences of purchasing power' to owners of the fixed factor rather than as additional cost in terms of real resources. Although this criticism of Young was thus before Marshall's (dated October 1914), there is nothing to suggest that Marshall was aware of it at the time of writing his own comment. Pigou, in response to Young's criticism, corrected this anomaly with regard to the case of decreasing returns in the second edition of *Economics of Welfare* (1924). In the third edition of that book (1928) he replaced the marginal supply price by 'the supply price from the standpoint of the community' and defined it in such a way as to eliminate transfer elements (p. 222).

The more interesting comments of Marshall relate to the case of increasing returns.[17] He displays strong misgivings about Pigou's unqualified use of the statical method in relation to increasing returns. He himself had, in the *Principles*, appended cautionary remarks to the results arrived at in this case, drawing the readers' attention to Appendix H where he discussed at some length 'the limitation of the statical method', (see §9 ;as also §§1 and 11).

Before considering Marshall's own treatment of increasing returns in Appendix H, we adduce here an additional piece of evidence which helps one to formulate a little more pointedly Marshall's objection to Pigou's use of the long-period supply curve. This evidence is a pencilled comment by Marshall on Pigou's article 'Producers' and consumers' surplus',[18] where Pigou gives the following definition: 'Let the supply price, in any market, be defined as the price which is able, and any lesser price than which is not able, to evoke in the market the production of exactly $(x+\Delta x)$ units.' Marshall adds to this: 'in a given period of time'; and objects to Pigou's phraseology ('a price is *able* to evoke'):

> Nor does the change of phrase obviate the necessity for the conditioning clause as to time. He excludes short periods but treats all long periods, say 10 to 50 years, as having the same effect. *That is, he commits, in silence, violence similar to and greater than that which I confess to in regard to consumption.* (Italics added)

The implication of this becomes clear when we note that Marshall was greatly perturbed by the problem of ensuring the stability of demand-and-supply curves in the face of difficulties arising from what he called 'the element of time'. The comment reveals that, while he was more troubled over the hypothesis of the stability of the long-period supply curve, he was far from happy even about his long-period demand curve. Even the possibility that the conditions impounded in the *ceteris paribus* clause used in defining the demand curve would alter over time had led him to state that 'our list of demand prices is highly conjectural except in the neighbourhood of the customary price' see (*Principles* 1910, pp. 109–13 and 129–35). However, Marshall relied upon the stability of the demand curve as, for example, in the present problem, when calculating changes in consumers' surplus. As for the supply curve, he appears to have had stronger doubts whether the theory coped satisfactorily with 'the elements of time', especially in the presence of increasing returns. For he saw the difficulties as arising mainly from the irreversibility of changes in production conditions;[19] and it was to these that he mainly devoted Appendix H.[20]

In Appendix H Marshall focuses on the fact that increasing returns are due to 'extensive improvements in organization, creation of skills' etc., which bring about changes through time that are not reversible: economies once created can scarcely be withdrawn. He also recognizes that irreversibilities violate the assumption, central to the equilibrium approach, that 'if the normal production of a commodity increases and afterwards diminishes to its old amount, the demand and supply price will return to their old positions' (p. 807). He argues that, if the supply is diminished, once having been expanded, 'the supply price would not move back by the course by which it had come', and suggests that a method of handling irreversibilities would be to show the backward movement by a separate curve. This treatment means, however, that there would be no uniquely defined 'supply price' for a given output. This can be illustrated with the aid of Marshall's diagram (on p. 806). The supply price of the output OM could be MP, MP_1 or MP_2, depending upon whether output expands continuously to OM, or whether it decreases to OM after once having reached OM_1, or does so after having reached OM_2. In fact, since along SS there are economies operating continuously, there would be a separate curve for backward movement at each point and the supply price of OM would be indeterminate, in the sense that it would vary with every change in the *sequence* of output levels by which it is approached. Or, to put it differently, with every change in output, the supply curve needs to be redrawn. Such an ever-shifting supply curve cannot be used to determine equilibrium price and output, as it is essential for that purpose that the supply curve should remain stable for hypothetical movements along it. Here, *given a sequence of output levels*, we may depict the supply price at each output level in that sequence, taking into account irreversibilities. But such a curve would be in the nature of an 'historical curve', and not the one required by the theory of equilibrium price.

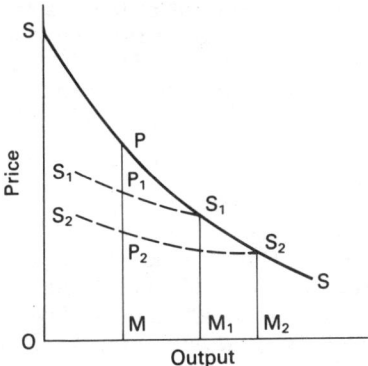

Fig. 2.

In the same Appendix H, Marshall suggests a way of obtaining a 'true long period normal supply curve' in the case of increasing returns, by treating 'time' as a third dimension (pp. 809–10, n. 2):

> We might take a series of curves, of which the first allowed for economies to be introduced as a result of each increase in the scale of production during one year, a second curve doing the same for two years...and so on. Cutting them out of cardboard and standing them up side by side, we should obtain a *surface*, of which the three dimensions represented amount, price, and time respectively. If we had marked on each curve the point corresponding to that amount for which, so far as can be foreseen, seems likely to be the normal amount for the year to which that curve related, then these points would form a curve on the surface, and that curve would be a fairly true long period normal supply curve.

There are two points to be noted about this suggestion. First, the matter dealt with here is not one of irreversibilities but a different one, namely, that 'a suitable time to allow for the introduction of economies appertaining to one increase in the scale of production is not long enough for another and larger increase – which is a matter of the time lags in reaping economies of scale. However, the *long-period* supply curve is obtained under the hypothesis that sufficient time is allowed for forces to work out their full effects.[21] Second, the supply curve is needed to *determine*, in conjunction with the demand curve, the equilibrium price and output, whereas what is required here are the foreseeable 'likely' normal outputs, in order to obtain the supply curve. There are any number of such curves, each corresponding to a sequence of likely outputs. Indeed, the exercise becomes meaningless for the theory of equilibrium price when we see that, since the forecasts are forecasts of equilibrium outputs, they could also be considered as forecasts of normal quantities demanded; and the curve connecting them could be said to represent the long-period normal demand curve. We are left then with only one blade of the well-known pair of scissors.

Marshall, while he was acutely aware of the difficulties posed by irreversibilities and 'the element of time' in the case of increasing returns, nevertheless tried to present them only as 'limitations' which qualified the results.[22] His criticism of Pigou is directed against Pigou's application of the statical method to the case of increasing returns without the qualifications that he himself had laid down. Pigou had thereby cast in a rigid form the results which he himself had put forward in tentative and flexible terms.

These differences in approach are reflected in policy implications as well. A tax on an industry subject to decreasing returns is favoured by Marshall only as the least harmful among the commodity taxes from the standpoint of the consumers. He showed that the tax receipts would exceed the loss of consumers' surplus if the supply curve were sufficiently steeply inclined relatively to the demand curve. However, the decrease in output would also bring about a loss of producers' surplus and the combined reductions of consumers' and producers surplus would exceed the tax receipts.[23] Marshall's recommendation for a bounty to an increasing-returns industry rested on a positive argument – that it would increase the community's satisfaction. Here, too, he recommended the bounty only where increasing returns acted sharply. This qualification follows upon his treating the entire amount of the bounty as a cost to society which needed to be off-set by the gain in consumers' surplus arising from the bounty. However, the question whether the entire expense of the bounty is to be reckoned as a cost to society depends upon how the bounty is raised, and it cannot be answered without considering effects on the rest of the economy of raising the required revenue.

Pigou, as we have seen in *Wealth and Welfare* (1912), treated decreasing returns and increasing returns symmetrically, the implication being that both are due to externalities. He favoured a tax on an industry subject to decreasing returns for the same reason as he favoured a bounty to an industry subject to increasing returns, namely, in order to correct deviations from 'ideal output'. Pigou appears to have treated the cost of the bounty as a transfer. This becomes explicit only in his *Economics of Welfare*, in which he added the following qualification for the grant of a bounty: 'provided that the funds for the bounty can be raised by a mere transfer that does not inflict any indirect injury on production' (4th edn, p. 224). The treatment of the amount of the bounty as a transfer had the consequence that *any* degree of increasing returns qualified the industry for the bounty.

Although Pigou continued to speak in terms of taxation, he had cast the net of tax policy very widely indeed, with a tax on *every* industry under decreasing returns *and* a bounty to *every* industry under increasing returns. Such complicated and comprehensive taxation would have brought the state into the economy on a grand scale. The boldness of this policy was in sharp contrast with Marshall's own position. Apart from the fact that his suggestions were limited in scope, he had further tempered them by the recognition of considerations 'other than economic'. He warned against the 'administrative side of state interference' (pp. 712–13) and against evils such as the opportunities for the corruption of public officials opened up by a scheme of bounties; and he feared that bounties could 'sap the springs of free initiative and strength of character' (p. 714).[24]

What appeared in Marshall as aberrations in the working of the competitive system were transformed by Pigou (in generalizing and extending Marshall's results) into the failure of the competitive system to achieve maximum welfare. When Hobson emphasized this failure of the system, Marshall was impelled to record – if only for posterity – his criticism of Pigou's conclusions. In the case of decreasing returns, he notices an error in the argument of Pigou. In the case of increasing returns, however, his criticism raises questions which are not confined to Pigou's application of the statical method to the problem of welfare, but relate more generally to the validity of the statical approach to the theory of equilibrium itself.

Marshall, while bringing out the difficulties confronting that approach, nevertheless had characterized them as being no more than 'limitations' of the method which qualified the results. They were locked up in that Pandora's box – Appendix H of Marshall's *Principles*.

Notes: Chapter 7

This essay was first published in *Economica* (February 1972). I was then in Cambridge and the late Piero Sraffa suggested this topic to me. I gained invaluably from discussions with him during the course of its preparation and learnt from his insights. M. H. Dobb and Joan Robinson – both, no more with us now – showed keen interest in the subject. I am grateful also to Pierangelo Garegnani and Austin Robinson for their helpful advice and comments.

1. Marshall's library (including the Pigou volume) was given to the University of Cambridge after his death. The volume was withdrawn by Mrs Marshall when the Librarian of the Marshall Library, Mr P. Sraffa (incautiously, as he realized too late) drew her attention to the notes. After her death the volume was returned to the Library, but was kept in reserve during Pigou's lifetime.
2. 'Professor Pigou (*Wealth and Welfare*, p. 176) though adopting the general position of marginalism, makes a concession, as to its applicability, which is a virtual admission of its futility. For, by showing that only in "industries of constant returns" are "supply price" and "marginal supply price" equal, and that in industries of "decreasing" or of "increasing returns" there exists a tendency to exceed or fall short of the "marginal net product yielded in industries in general" he virtually endorses the criticism that "marginalism" assumes a statical condition of industry. For only in a statical condition would all industries be found conforming to constant returns: the operation of increasing or diminishing returns means nothing else than that changes in volume or methods of production are raising or lowering productivity and remuneration above or below the equal level which "marginalism" desiderates' (Hobson, 1914, p. 175, n.)

    In Marshall's copy of Hobson's *Work and Wealth*, which is now in the Marshall Library, the passage quoted here is marked with an asterisk. He writes in the margin: 'See my pencil note on this passage', which presumably refers to the pencil annotation on Pigou's *Wealth and Welfare* (§11 below; see also §1).
3. Some incidental comments of Marshall on transportation, economies of large scale and joint costs, etc. have been omitted on the suggestion of the Editors.
4. See note 2, above.
5. The sixth edition of Marshall's *Principles* (1910) was the latest in print when Marshall wrote this comment. Chapter 13 of Book IV of that edition included the section. 'Correlation of the tendencies to increasing and to diminishing return'.
6. The word 'net' is underscored and the words 'i.e. Net product' written in the margin by Marshall.
7. Marshall underscores 'aggregate expenses of the industry'.

8 In 'Contribution to Theory of Railway Rates - IV'. The statement is: 'If the ordinate of any point of the abscissa, M, intersects SS_1 at P and SS_2 at Q, the area OMQS is equal to the area OMPN. But the area OMPN represents the total expenses incident to the production of quantity OM; inclusive of rent (the area PSN) and of entrepreneur's remuneration...'
9 'Magazines' are volumes of articles from periodicals bound together, for Marshall, according to subjects. These are now in the Marshall Library.
10 The last two sentences in this passage are sidescored by Marshall and the words "lightly loaded" underscored.
11 See note 2 above.
12 Pigou's definition of the supply price of any quantity of output is: 'the price which tends to call out the production of that quantity annually'. The 'marginal supply price' was defined by him as 'the difference made to aggregate expenses of production of all producers, by an increase in production from x to $(x+\Delta x)$ units' (1910, p. 363).
13 This is underscored by Marshall as well.
14 *Principles*, pp. 462–76. Unless otherwise stated, all references are to the sixth edition, 1910 (see note 5 above); and those to Pigou are to his *Wealth and Welfare*.
15 This notion was first defined by Pigou in his article, 'Producers' and consumers' surplus' (1910) p. 363.
16 In fact, Pigou himself wrote in his earlier article, 'Producers' and consumers' surplus': 'The supply curve for all values in respect of which it is inclined positively coincides with the curve of collective marginal supply prices and for all values in respect of which it is inclined negatively, with the curve of average full expenses of production.' In *Wealth and Welfare* (1912), however, he takes the supply curve to be *below* the curve of marginal supply prices for decreasing returns, while it continues to be *above* for increasing returns.
17 Marshall raises here an objection against Pigou's use of the *aggregate expenses of the industry* (see §5). His objection that it lacks 'specific motive force' could be interpreted to mean that, unlike the 'supply price' which is defined in relation to producers' motivation (a price at which producers would be willing to supply the specified output), the marginal supply price in terms of *aggregate expenses of the industry* has no such motivational basis. It is somewhat puzzling, however, to find that Marshall rests a part of his objection on the ground that economies in one industry (say, shipbuilding) depend upon correlated economies in another (say, manufacture of plates). This recoils on the method of partial equilibrium itself since it challenges the notion that economies would be *internal to the industry* even if they are external to the firm, required to validate Pigou's partial equilibrium method. Moreover, Marshall's criticism strengthens further Pigou's argument that the welfare-maximizing output and the competitive output diverge under increasing returns.
18 This copy of the *Economic Journal* (1910) is in the Marshall Library, Cambridge.
19 It is of interest to find that in his early work, *Pure Theory of Foreign Trade and Domestic Value* (1879 [1930]) Marshall stressed the difficulties that custom and habits raised for the demand curve by introducing irreversibilities in consumption. He recognized that 'consequently, every movement of the exchange index entails some alteration in the shape of the curves and therefore the forces which determine succeeding movements'

(p. 32). In *Principles*, irreversibilities in consumption are not given the same importance, although they are alluded to in Appendix H.

20 Marshall was so concerned about the difficulties created for his theory by irreversibilities that he appears to have devoted much thought as to where he should place their discussion in the text. The following manuscript note was found in the Marshall papers, written by him on a sheet of paper in which were enclosed some printed pages taken from a copy of his *Pure Theory*:

> General suggestions: 31: VIII: 96.
> Postpone case II altogether and treat it on different footing.
> Decide early what to do about elasticity.
> Make much shorter all attempts to bring the curves into reality.

Case II, in *Pure Theory*, it will be recalled, is that of the supply curve under increasing returns. It was as an attempt to bring the curves closer to reality that Marshall discussed irreversibilities at some length. Indeed, he treated irreversibilities on a different footing from the fourth edition of *Principles* (1898) onwards, when they were shifted from the central chapter to a 'Note on Pure Theory of Stable and Unstable Equilibria'; and from the fifth edition onwards (1902) they were transferred to Appendix H, where irreversibilities were introduced in an argument against the possibility of multiple equilibrium positions under increasing returns. Hence the attention was now shifted to the 'stability' and 'uniqueness' of equilibrium from the issue of existence.

21 On p. 497 Marshall explains that the long-period normal price relates to periods '...in which those economies that normally result from an increase in the scale of production...have time to develop themselves'.

22 For example, in the context of the problem of *maximum satisfaction*, when discussing the shift of the supply curve following a tax, he warns us that the new supply curve in the case of increasing returns 'ought properly not to have the same shape as the old one' (p. 469, n. 1). The argument he offers is that, even when the industry shrinks following the tax, it would at least in part preserve the economies already gained. This brings in the question of irreversibilities which jeopardizes the very notion of the supply curve and not only its shift as Marshall suggests.

23 Marshall treated the effects on producers' surplus on a different footing and concerned himself mainly with those on consumers' surplus. He argues, for example, that the tax on an industry subject to decreasing returns is desirable as consumers would be discouraged thereby from incurring expenditure on a commodity which reduces the real purchasing power of income. No mention is made of increases in landlords' incomes (p. 474). Also, when discussing the effects of taxes and bounties in terms of diagrams (pp. 464–9), he is concerned with changes in consumers' surplus alone. Only in one case, where he discusses a tax on agricultural produce, does he take explicit account of producers' surplus (p. 473). But even here he adds that the question of the effects on landlords differs 'so much as not to be fitly discussed here'. Marshall realized that the concept of producers' surplus which had a clear interpretation in agriculture could not be extended to industry. He suggested a parallel in terms of the particular expenses curve in Appendix H, but realized that this curve is not a normal supply curve. (In §§7 and 8, Marshall disclaims any association between the particular expenses curve and the supply curve.) Producers' surplus calculated from such a curve cannot be treated conceptually as a counterpart of consumers' surplus calculated from a demand curve.

24 Marshall's general reluctance to bring in the state is reflected in §§14 and 16, where he differs from Pigou on specific points of practical policies. In §14, Pigou having agreed that the variability of business expectations would be mitigated if the state published monthly statistics of the existing volume of construction, Marshall comments that the trade journals have done it already, better than it could be done by government, §16 relates to Pigou's questioning of the Minority's argument in the *Report on Poor Laws* that an addition of £10 million to the wage fund of the worst year would suffice to reduce unemployment in that year to its normal amount. Pigou argues that a sum nearer to £100 million would be required, since an allowance has to be made for a possible rise in wages. Marshall comments: 'Both these arithmetics seem hazardous'. He thinks a small adjustment should suffice, and that if it improves the situation, employment would then create further employment. In the *Principles* he had argued that the chief cause of unemployment was a want of confidence, and that 'the greater part of it could be removed almost in an instant if confidence could return, touch all industries with her magic wand, and make them continue their production and their demand for the wares of others' (p. 711). While arguing that increased production itself creates increased demand, Marshall sees the way to the cumulative increases in employment through revival of confidence rather than large-scale public expenditure.

References: Chapter 7

Hobson, J. A. (1914), *Work and Wealth: A Human Valuation* (London: Macmillan).

Keynes, J. M. (1924), 'Alfred Marshall, 1842–1924', *Economic Journal*, vol. 34 (September), reprinted in A.C. Pigou (ed.) *Memorials of Alfred Marshall* (London: Macmillan).

Marshall, A. (1879 [1930]), *The Pure Theory of Foreign Trade. The Pure Theory of Domestic Values*. Series of Reprints of Scarce Tracts in Economic and Political Science, no. 1 (London: London School of Economics and Political Science).

Marshall, A. (1898), *Principles of Economics*, 4th edn (London: Macmillan).

Marshall, A. (1902), *Principles of Economics*, 5th edn (London: Macmillan).

Marshall, A. (1910), *Principles of Economics*, 6th edn (London: Macmillan).

Pigou, A. C. (1910), 'Producers' and consumers' surplus', *Economic Journal*, vol. 20. pp. 358–70

Pigou, A. C. (1912), *Wealth and Welfare* (London: Macmillan).

Pigou, A. C. (1924), *Economics of Welfare*, 2nd edn 1924, 3rd edn 1929, 4th edn, (London: Macmillan)

Pigou, A. C. (ed.) (1925), *Memorials of Alfred Marshall* (London: Macmillan),

Young, Allyn (1913), 'review of *Wealth and Welfare*', *Quarterly Journal of Economics*, vol. 27 (August), pp. 672–86.

8
Maurice Dobb's Critique of Theories of Value and Distribution

I

The economic writings of Maurice Dobb cover a remarkably wide range, cutting across the narrow boundaries that professional specialization has evolved. This essay addresses itself to a segment of his work, namely, the critique of economic theory that Dobb presents through his review of economic thought. The task is by no means easy, because Dobb was engaged continuously in such a review over a long period of creative writing. Unavoidably, we have to concentrate here on only a few central issues; we have chosen those concerning the alternative theories of value and distribution. The main sources drawn up for our purposes are his *Wages* (first published in 1927), *Political Economy and Capitalism* (first published in 1937, hereafter *PEC*), *On Economic Theory and Socialism* (first published in 1955, being a collection of earlier articles, hereafter *ETS*), and his last major work, *Theories of Value and Distribution* (1973, hereafter *Theories*).

1 Historical Conditioning of Theory

An outstanding feature that marks Dobb's critique, giving it an integral character and unity of approach, is his attempt to bring to bear upon theory a historical interpretation; to stress its historically relativist character in the choice of problems and of modes of formalization. Dobb prefaced his *PEC* with the remark:

> The selection of themes...has been guided by the opinion that Political Economy and the controversies which beset it have meaning as answers to certain questions of an essentially practical kind – questions concerning the nature and behaviour of the economic system which we know as capitalism ... (1937 [1972], p. vii).

The original questions may become submerged and forgotten in the course of the development of theory, but Dobb believed that economic thought, if it is to be of realistic worth, must critically expose the notions 'encumbering its roots'. Dobb was to emphasize in his last major work, *Theories*, another aspect, probably of greater import. There he maintained that to inquire into the historical contingency of particular doctrines is important only as a starting point towards a historical inquiry into the process through which old concepts are modified or new concepts and theorems formulated, within a logical structure. The latter inquiry into theories must critically assess their formal consistency as well as adequacy to answer questions to which they arise as a response (see particularly 1973, pp. 35–6). This elaboration and extension of the historical approach, of assessing critically the formal structure of theories, was directly implied by the position Dobb held in *Theories*: that is, economic theories as formal frameworks are no more divorced from historical judgement, social perspective and 'vision', than are the problems they choose; thus challenging 'the box of tools' view of theories as pure techniques, neutral with respect to social preconceptions. The formal framework contains, often implicitly, a social 'vision' structured in terms of the causalities and the nature of interdependencies they suggest or build upon.

Dobb's critique in its earlier phase was much more concerned with the former aspect of historical interpretation – the origin and progress of ideas in relation to contingent historical problems and the social philosophy underlying them. A critical scrutiny of alternative conceptualizations and, more particularly, of the logical structure of theories appears to have acquired a greater emphasis in the later work, especially *Theories*.

The significance of such a historical approach to a critique of economic theory could not have been better illustrated than in terms of the variegated and epochal experiences that Dobb's generation lived through and the responses which they aroused in terms of theorizing. Broadly four phases in theoretical developments can be sketched.

When Dobb began writing as an economist (in the 1920s), the sanguine orthodoxy of competitive capitalism was already drifting into troubled waters. The mood, however, was set by the benign liberal reformism of Marshall and Pigou, with a faith in the market mechanism, whose occasional aberrations needed to be corrected by benevolent but cautious state interference. It was the heyday of Marshallianism, whose influence was proving longer lasting than warranted by the growing awareness of actual historical reality.

The emergence of excess capacities, persistent unemployment and depression were demonstrating that the maladies were not of an order or nature that could be considered merely 'frictional' or 'cyclical' phenomena. Already the Marshallian system had come under severe logical attack from Piero Sraffa (1925, 1926). In this second phase, the theory of the firm moved in the direction of non-competitive structures, and the 'Keynesian revolution' challenged the orthodoxy concerning the spontaneous tendency of the market system to guarantee full utilization of resources; it thereby paved the way for the acceptance of fiscal policy as a necessary instrument, to be operative on a more or less permanent basis in a capitalist economy in order to manipulate effective demand.

The 'revolution', however, appears to have been reabsorbed in the form of a 'neoclassical synthesis', whereby active state policy was incorporated as a premise for assuming full employment and the traditional theories of supply and demand came into their own, with that proviso. In this third phase of the post-war era, new problems emerged – the concern for steady growth of capitalist economies, and the problems of planning and development of both the newly independent Third World countries and the now advanced socialist economies. A boom in the neoclassical and neo-Keynesian theories of growth followed, to be somewhat dampened by the complexities of historical experience – of inflation, accompanied by continuing unemployment, excess capacity, increasing income inequalities, balance-of-payments problems, the instability of the international monetary order and increasing internationalization of monopoly capital. The ongoing fourth phase is characterized, on the one hand, by deepening doubts about the adequacy of the neoclassical synthesis and, on the other hand, by a revival of classical and Marxian political economy, affording a theoretical basis on which to rebuild alternative systems of theorizing.

Dobb's review of theory runs through all these phases and, not surprisingly, his own emphasis on different aspects of his critique is influenced by the dominant theme of the day. What persists throughout is his Marxian point of view: his remarkable attempt to view theoretical formations as arising out of the historical specificities of development, and to judge their adequacy and theoretical role in providing a solution to (or sometimes in obfuscating) such issues. In such a venture Dobb was, as Hobsbawm (1969) narrates, somewhat isolated from the mainstream of the dominant concerns of his academic colleagues. No doubt the struggle to grapple with these problems in isolation, in an atmosphere at best non-responsive, left its mark on his work.

On an analytical plane, a major theme that runs through Dobb's review is his recognition that the development of economic theory has been characterized by two main contending frameworks, despite the many variations within each: the first, offered by classical political economy reached its apex in Marx. It was prematurely replaced, on theoretically insufficient, while ideologically identifiable, grounds by the second, the 'Jevonian revolution' of the 1870s, leading to the dominance to date of the supply-and-demand-based neoclassical theories. According to Dobb, the rupture in fact occurred earlier, in the 1830s, as a conscious attempt to overcome the disturbing conclusions of Ricardian theory about the inevitability of conflicts of class interests. These conflicts emanated from the diverse status of the different distributive classes, in terms of their positioning in production and the character of their revenues. However, a theoretical structure, posing a rigorously argued alternative, emerged clearly in the 1870s. Dobb considered the 'Jevonian revolution' as of far greater significance than the Keynesian (see below). In what follows we shall focus upon this part of Dobb's critique, although his review of theory spanned a much wider range (growth, planning, socialist theories of planning and resource allocation, etc.).

The recent revival of interest in classical political economy – to which the works of Sraffa and Dobb have contributed much – has led to a clearer theoretical appreciation, bringing into sharp focus the grounds of debate between the two contending streams of theory. Since the main theoretical divide happens to be our concern, in Section II we present the salient features of the classical theory of value and distribution and those of the alternative, supply-and-demand-based systems. In Section III Dobb's critique is discussed. It is inevitable that, over the many years the critique has continued, the emphasis on particular elements and interpretations has changed, reflecting the specific concerns of the time as well as the theoretical understanding reached at the stage. It is suggested that Dobb's critique, in earlier work, is occasionally weakened by misleading interpretations of certain elements in classical theory. A number of these appear to be traceable to Marshall's peculiar presentation of the classicals, especially Smith and Ricardo. Dobb's use of the Marshallian idiom, if not ideas, in these works, while understandable, considering the dominance that Marshall's ideas then held, could continue to be a source of misinterpretations. While these are mostly amended in later writings, not all are confronted directly in later discussions. A somewhat debatable attribution of the supply-and-demand approach to Adam Smith in *Theories* (along lines suggested by Schumpeter) appears to reflect a vestigial continuance of such reasoning. Secondly, a related difficulty arises: the lack of a clear-cut, even if somewhat stylized, view of the logical structure of the classical, as well as the supply-and-demand-based, theories appears to have rendered the critique less sharp, while allowing some ambiguities to creep in. These are minor deficiencies in the otherwise impressive achievement of Dobb; 'minor' in Dobb, particularly since he himself rectified a number of them in *Theories*. If they are brought out here, it is only in dispute with those continuing to misuse such doubtful interpretations to undermine the strength of the classical theory.

II

Here, at the risk of stark simplification, we present certain salient features of the two contending theories of value and distribution (many of these issues are discussed in greater detail in Bharadwaj, 1978; see also Eatwell, 1977). This is done partly to focus our discussion on the theme that concerned Dobb most and also to provide a frame of reference to discuss his critique. While it is not suggested that there are no differences among individual authors contributing to either of the contending schools, there appear to be sufficiently significant unifying elements within each, despite the variations, for the two streams of analysis to be clearly demarcated from each other. The classical theory of value is presented here from the vantage point of interpretations reached currently and it is not implied that each individual author in that tradition adhered strictly to the framework, consistently or overtly; the outline is discernible more clearly in Marx than in others. Further, we concern ourselves here with long-run positions of value (or, prices of production), not entering into questions such as those of 'realization', to the analysis of which the former are a logical prelude.

2 The Structure of the Classical Theory of Value and Distribution

The classical theory of value draws an important distinction between 'market prices' and 'natural prices' by making a qualitative differentiation between the forces that determine them: the former are susceptible to the influences of temporary or accidental causes and are mainly seen as deviating from 'natural prices', which constitute the 'centres of gravitation' around which these fluctuations occur.[1] The factors responsible for these deviations may be many: temporary monopoly advantages, changes in fashion, political events, etc. Hence, in studying problems of distribution and accumulation, natural prices (or 'prices of production'), as long-run positions, are considered relevant. (For Ricardo's argument for the adoption of 'natural prices' in the analysis of distribution see Ricardo, 1951, pp. 91–2.)

3 Data for the Value Problem

The classical analysis of value is carried out in terms of certain conditions provisionally adopted as data. It is assumed, though not always explicitly, that social output (level and composition) and methods of production for those output levels are given. A tendency towards a uniformity of the wage and the rate of profit is stipulated as a characteristic of competition. The real wage is taken as given, determined variously, as we shall see, according to different authors. The exchange values (or prices of production) are then such as to be consistent with the postulated uniformity of the rate of profit under these conditions. Thus the rate of profit and prices are determined uniquely once the real wage is specified. The point to note is that, because the wage is taken as given, the determination of distribution, whilst linked with the determination of prices, is not identified with it as constituting one and the same process, as happens in the supply-and-demand theories.

In taking output, methods of production and wage as given for the value problem, it may appear that the classical theorists operated within a very narrow, restricted domain. In fact, later theorists (e.g., Marshall) attempted to present the classical prices of production as a particular case of supply-and-demand determined prices, when the forces of demand are kept in abeyance by some special assumptions.[2]

It was alleged that the classical theories had played down the 'demand' side, and their assumption of a 'given' wage was often misconstrued as a rigidly fixed wage (see below).

These misinterpretations possibly arise because an important fact is overlooked: that the value-and-distribution problem in classical theory is worked out in a framework of economic interdependencies among production, consumption, distribution and exchange altogether different from that envisaged in the supply-and-demand-based theories. The problem of value-determination, though essentially linked with those of distribution, consumption and accumulation, is not solved within the *same* scheme of abstraction. The scheme chosen for the value analysis is an open one, with certain elements (wages, social output) 'given', i.e., determined by a number of factors outside the immediate frame of reference. In fact, while the classical economists, including Marx, shared the price-determination scheme, they differed in their emphasis on the problems of distribution, accumulation, etc. Adam Smith was mainly interested in accumulation and Ricardo primarily in distribution, while Marx's interest ranged comprehensively over the functioning of the capitalist mode of production in all its aspects. In Marx's introduction to his critique of political economy (Marx (1857–8) [1973], pp. 83–111), we find a fuller discussion of the interdependencies among production, distribution, consumption and exchange that characterize the approach.

4 The Assumption of a 'Given' Wage

A 'given' wage does not imply an invariable or fixed wage, although Malthus's theory of population reduced it to a physiological minimum for survival. The determining factors vary from author to author: Adam Smith placed much stress on the relative bargaining strength of masters and workers: 'What are the common wages of labour depends everywhere upon the contract usually made between these two parties, whose interests are by no means the same.' Given the unequal social and political power, 'It is not difficult, however, to foresee which of the two parties must, upon all ordinary occasions, have the advantage in the dispute, and force the other into a compliance with their terms' (Smith, 1776 [1930], pp. 68–9). Wages would therefore usually tend to settle at subsistence level, although they could rise in times of progressive accumulation. Ricardo, while resorting to the Malthusian theory of population, took prominent account of the conventional elements of customs and habits (Ricardo, 1951a, p. 93). For Marx, a historical element always entered the determination of wages, which varied also with the size of the reserve army of the unemployed; the latter was partly dependent upon the capitalists' responses to potential or actual wage rises, preventing sustained increases in wages (Marx, 1867 [1971], p. 171).

5 'Given' Methods of Production

Of the known methods of production, the least-cost method, at the going wage, would be the one relevant to the calculation of 'natural prices'. 'Given' methods do not therefore imply an absence of choice among alternative methods. The classical economists did not, however, envisage a functional connection between output and costs, operating through substitution of methods, as presumed by the laws of returns under the supply-and-demand theories. No doubt in the case of land, a relation between output and increasing costs did appear to emerge (later to be christened 'the law of diminishing returns'). The context however was that of explaining the increase in rents, following upon advancing population, with land being a non-reproducible resource, limited in availability for the whole economy (see Sraffa, 1925). This special case (subsequently interpreted as an instance of marginalism) was not generalized to all cases of commodity production, as it was to be by later marginalists. At any given wage and level of output, one (or more, as at a switchpoint) method(s) of production will come to be in use. With a change in the wage or the level of output some other method may be adopted as more profitable in the changed situation. There was, however, no presumption *essential* to this value-and-distribution theory that methods of production so adopted should preserve a ranking order in terms of, say, capital intensity, with the change in the wage so as to generate a well-behaved factor-demand curve; or that the change in unit costs ought to vary (or not vary) functionally depending upon variations in output levels. It is in this latter sense that propositions were advanced irrespective of whether 'constant' or 'variable' returns prevail. In fact the notion of returns has been only retrospectively superimposed upon the classical theory, possibly due to the later habitual mode of reasoning in terms of the 'laws of returns'.

The introduction of new, not previously known, methods of production is, on the other hand, connected with a whole set of historical factors; to name only a few, expansion of markets affording new discoveries and extended division of labour, as in Smith; the share going to wages, as in Ricardo; the advance of scientific knowledge at the frontiers of discovery as well as in adoption, shaped by social relations, as in Marx. All these are part and parcel of the historical development of productive forces and the accompanying changes in social relations.

6 'Given' Social Output

For the value problem, social output was similarly 'given' only in the sense that the determinants of its level and composition required a much more general analytical scheme than was immediately relevant for the value question. Social output was composed of the requirements of production and accumulation (sometimes called 'productive consumption') and social consumption. The classical theory did not have a 'demand theory', in the sense of 'demand functions' relating hypothetical individual/collective demands to hypothetical prices, just as it did not use a notion of supply functions relating hypothetical quantities supplied to hypothetical prices. One may not, however, conclude that classical economists were not interested in problems of consumption. As Marshall remarks (1920, pp. 84–5), they were indeed keenly engaged in the analysis of particular problems, such as the effects of taxes and bounties on consumption. In fact, in contrast to later theory, where the individual's scale of preferences were 'atomistically' determined, and the theory required to assume that the individual's preferences were independent of actual prices on the market and of the decisions made by other individuals as producers or as consumers, the classical theory – and Marx, in particular – envisaged a number of factors directly influencing the very formation of these preferences. In Smith and Ricardo, 'customs and habits' were seen to play an important role in determining landlords' and workers' consumption; Smith placed considerable emphasis on the development of division of labour, expansion of markets, introduction of new commodities in opening up new consumption possibilities; Marx stressed the interconnection between the level and mode of consumption and the development of productive forces, the availability of commodities and the distinctive pattern of distributive relations that accompanied such a development.

In short, classical political economy acknowledged the determinants of distribution, consumption and accumulation to be more complex, and to require a more comprehensive analytical scheme than the one constructed for the value problem. To calculate values these could be postulated as data. An analysis of value was required as a foundation for arriving at the more complex theoretical propositions concerning distribution and accumulation.

7 The Problem of Distribution

The central notion for classical distribution theory is that of surplus,[3] the size of which is determined by the methods of production and distribution. Under competitive capitalist relations, the surplus accruing as non-wage revenue is determined, given the social output, methods of production and the wage. For an analysis of the problems of distribution and accumulation, a proper formulation of value relations becomes a prerequisite. For Adam Smith, whose central concern was comparing unambiguously surpluses over time and between places, in a situation where the surplus was a heterogeneous mass of commodities, the problem of obtaining or constructing a suitable 'measure' of value, itself 'invariant', became pressing. Smith's approach to the explanation of value is motivated primarily by this, and his accent on labour commanded as a 'measure' and on the 'components' of price, after a hurried retreat from 'labour embodied', has to be understood in that light. For Ricardo, the question of how the rate of profit is determined became a crucial inquiry for establishing that the limit to profits is set by the conditions of production and that there is an inevitable inverse relation between the share of wages and the profit rate. In trying to settle these questions, in continued controversy with Malthus, he was to put his energies into a search for an 'invariant standard'. The problem appeared to him thus: the rate of profit is the ratio between what remains of social net product after paying for wages, and social capital (granting that the rate of profit is determined on the no-rent land). Thus the determination of the rate of profit involved heterogeneous value aggregates (social output, wages and capital), each susceptible to variations consequent upon a change in the rate of profit itself. This seemingly brought in a circularity, which not only made the rate of profit seem indeterminate, but obfuscated the underlying relations between it and wages. The necessity for the inverse relation between the rate of profit and wages had been challenged by Malthus, arguing that a rise in wages could as well be compensated (or more than compensated) by a rise in prices and hence would not necessarily be followed by a decline in the rate of profit. Ricardo had found his propositions easily and clearly demonstrable in the single commodity ('corn') case, which suggested to him a possible solution: that of reducing the heterogeneous value aggregates in terms of an 'invariant standard' (i.e., a value standard not itself varying in value consequent upon a change in distribution). This could eliminate the circularity and the relations between the distributive shares could be made transparent, without the obfuscating variations arising from a variable standard of value. If the labour theory of value held strictly, or could be suitably modified, it would have afforded such a standard in labour embodied. Marx also found in the labour theory a powerful analytical device to answer another related question; namely how a surplus could arise in a situation where all commodities, including labour power, exchanged against equivalents, according to the rules of competitive capitalism. Marx was to explain the source of surplus in terms of the surplus value created in production by labour.[4] Both Ricardo and Marx were fully aware of the deviation of labour values from the competitive prices of production (i.e. 'exchange values'). One reason for using labour values appears to have been, for Ricardo, that it clarified certain analytical relations relevant to distribution theory, establishing them directly within the sphere of production; whilst for Marx it not only clarified these relations, but also offered transparency to the process of generation and appropriation of surplus. Marx believed that these propositions could be sustained even when prices of production replaced labour values. The search for solutions to the 'transformation problem' was indeed actuated by this analytical purpose. The non-equivalence of labour values and prices of production (or the 'non-transformability') at this juncture, in the last century, provided the critics with grounds for jettisoning the classical theory, along with its entire approach, and offering the supply-and-demand theories as an alternative.

8 The Shift to Supply-and-Demand Theories

The important change that was brought about by these alternative theories was to interpret relative prices as being formed at the equilibrium between the opposite and symmetric forces of demand and supply. The notion of the long-run position was retained, but the classical 'market prices' were replaced by 'short-period prices' and 'natural prices' by 'long-run equilibrium or normal prices', both being explained in terms of the equilibrating forces of demand and supply operative in the competitive exchange processes (see below). Furthermore, land, labour and capital were viewed as primary resources or 'factors of production', with their own markets in which the factor prices (rents, wages, profits per respective unit) were similarly determined by the operation of supply-and-demand forces, as in the case of individual commodities. Thus a perfect symmetry was established in the determination of their revenues and in their positioning in the productive process.

9 The Derivation of Supply-and-Demand Schedules and the Data of the System

The forces of demand and supply are generated by the optimizing behaviour of individuals entering markets as producers and consumers (i.e., as buyers and sellers of commodities and resources). A certain symmetry characterizes the behaviour of both; each individual producer, given the technology transforming inputs into outputs, chooses the profit-maximizing bundle of products at the going prices; similarly, each consumer, given his budget constraint and scale of preferences, maximizes his satisfaction at the going prices. Thus the data of the system are the initial endowment of resources, together with their distribution among individuals, the technology transforming resources into goods and the system of preferences. The initial resource position is variously formulated by different authors: while Wicksell considered land and labour (being primary resources) along with capital (expressed as land and labour invested over time) as given aggregates, Walras postulated each heterogeneous resource (different kinds of personal and land capitals and of machines) as available in stipulated quantities of its respective physical unit. Jevons and Marshall favoured taking the supply of resources as variable quantities, determined by the balancing of disutilities involved in efforts and sacrifices against the utility of the incomes paid as a recompense.

The 'given' technology is also variously characterized: in terms of the aggregate production function relating commodity outputs to 'primary' factors in their aggregative form; or, as detailed bills of inputs and outputs in the form of 'activities'; with continuous substitutability among 'factors'; or, as 'fixed coefficient' activities, with substitution occurring through various linear combinations of such activities.

The consumer's feasible choices are also variously depicted, the notion of preference ordering having replaced the earlier cardinal notion of utility. These 'preferences' are autonomously given for each individual, independent of the prevailing prices or the actions of producers or other consumers. In fact all 'externalities', in the sense of the direct influence (that is not transmitted through price signals) of any one individual's choice of action (as either a producer or a consumer) on any other individual are eliminated by assumption.

Given availabilities of factors and their distribution, preferences and technology, under certain conditions imposed upon the system of preferences and the set of feasible technological choices, the existence of an equilibrium yielding a vector of equilibrium market-clearing prices (one for each commodity and factor) is established. Thus the formation of these prices explains distribution, along with commodity prices, within the same mechanisms of exchange.

10 The Principle of Substitution

A notion central to this framework is the 'principle of substitution', which gives the system the resilience required by the processes which bring about and maintain equilibrium. For example, a relative cheapening of a factor A in relation to factor B induces substitution, given its possibilities; the commodities using relatively more of the cheapened factor experience a decline in price relative to those commodities using relatively less of it, thus inducing a substitution in products via changes in consumption prompted by these price variations. Secondly, a comparable process of substitution occurs in production: technical processes utilizing relatively more of the cheapened factor are substituted for those utilizing relatively less of it. The combined consequence of these substitutions is expected to yield an inverse relation between the factor intensity (the ratio of A to B) and the relative factor prices (the price of A relative to that of B). The substitution principle, in general, is relied upon to yield appropriate forms of price-dependent demand-and-supply relations.

III

In this section we take a close look at Dobb's critique of economic theory, in particular at his views on, and assessment of, the 'Jevonian revolution'. His early writings on the subject concentrate on certain conceptual shifts introduced by the supply-and-demand theories and on the wider philosophical implications of the general theoretical setting within which the problems were cast. The logical structure and internal consistency of the alternative theories are not central to his discussions. In fact, because these are not sufficiently clearly investigated, his critique, while strong in general arguments, reveals weaknesses on specific analytical points and loses in sharpness. It also appears that, particularly in the earlier phase of the critique, a subtle but noticeable Marshallian influence creeps in. It is in the later work, in *Theories*, that Dobb raises more pointedly certain questions about the logical structure of the theories and their internal consistency. We shall note specific instances of these in what follows. First, however, we shall briefly sketch the main points of Dobb's critique.

11 Basic Elements in Dobb's Critique

Dobb recognizes a fundamental shift in the replacement of the objective basis of the classical theory of value and distribution, with its search for real relations in production, by the subjective foundation of the supply-and-demand theories in utility, focusing primarily upon relations in exchange. The shift was spurred on, Dobb argues in his 'The trend of modern economics' (included in *PEC*, 1937 [1972]), by the need to provide apologetics for profits. Within the classical theory, profits emerged as part of the surplus, while wages were a constituent element of costs of production on a par with other material requisites; as *physical* sustenance of labour, they become an objective precondition for production to take place at all. Thus the two distributive categories have a distinctly different origin and status in terms of the production process. The supply-and-demand theories attempted to introduce a symmetry between profits and wages, reducing both to rewards paid out of the product, either on the basis of their net contribution to the product or to utility (as in the productivity/Austrian theories), or by making them constituents of costs on an equal basis, both involving 'real costs'. As illustrative of the former, Dobb details the Austrian concept of a hierarchical ordering of goods, whereby all commodities, including primary commodities or factors, derive their value from the utilities they directly or indirectly produce. As illustrative of the latter, he discusses Marshall's extension of 'real costs' to include not only the 'toil and trouble' of labour, but also the 'waiting' of capitalists.

In the sphere of exchange, since all factors are paid according to the rules of the competitive game, no obvious distinction can be made in the explanations of the several forms of revenue. Thus in shifting the focus from production to exchange, the notion of surplus, as well as the distinctiveness of the distributive shares in terms of their origin and determination, is lost:

> ... only in terms of the latter [the cost principle] can the concept of surplus acquire a meaning; while without it (or something akin to it) no criterion of differentiation between class incomes seems able to exist. The reason for this is that a cost-principle essentially makes some statement concerning the nature of productive activities – of the relation between men in the activity of production – whereas a demand-theory is a generalisation about consumption and exchange – about the relations between men *qua* consumers and the commodities

which result from production...A principle which interprets value purely in terms of demand can define the productive 'contribution' of a person or a class only according to the value of what *eventuates*; it cannot define this contribution according to the activity or process in which the contribution *originates*, since it includes no statement about any productive relationship of this kind. Hence any participant in production which acquires a price – any agent which figures on the market at all – must *ipso facto* have made a 'contribution', this being synonymous with the value which consumers have directly or indirectly placed upon his services. (ibid., pp. 30–1, italics as in original)

And, since the sum total of values thus contributed must equal the value of the results, the inquiry concerning 'surplus' was rendered meaningless.

A criticism that runs through Dobb's works is that the supply-and-demand theories 'sought to derive an explanation of exchange-values from the attitudes of individual consumers towards commodities as use values catering for the satisfaction of individual wants' (*Theories*, 1973, p. 33). In so doing, the theory treated the individual's structure of wants as autonomous. Dobb attacked this assumption of the independence of the scale of preferences in 'The trend of modern economics'. Apart from pointing out that a misleading identification between 'utility' and 'satisfaction' was involved, he emphatically criticized the failure of the theory to concern itself with the social conditioning of the individual's desires or behaviour reactions. The concept of the individual making free choices on the basis of an autonomously given scale of preferences conflicted directly with reality, when consumers' preferences were directly moulded by the availability of consumables and by the individual's social environment and class position. Dobb also raised an additional logical difficulty: namely, that the structure of market demands being dependent upon the initial income distribution, the whole pricing process was relative to the postulated initial distribution (see ibid., p. 34). This had serious consequences for the tenability of welfare propositions based on money measures.

A criticism of neoclassical theory that acquires emphasis and sharpness in Dobb's last major work, *Theories*, is aimed at the logical tenability of its theory of distribution in terms of 'factor prices' determined by the equilibrium of demand and supply in factor and commodity markets. The critique draws heavily upon the recent debates in capital theory which highlighted certain logical difficulties faced by the theory, especially in the determination of the rate of profit. The difficulty arose primarily in the form of a failure to ensure a well-behaved demand function for capital, mainly because a theoretically adequate measure of capital, independent of distribution, could not be constructed. The logical inconsistency was shown to appear in the various formulations of the supply-and-demand theories, the difficulty manifesting itself in different forms (see, for a comprehensive treatment, Garegnani, 1960). Furthermore, Dobb emphasized certain implications of the different ways in which distribution was explained in the classical and the rival supply-and-demand theories. In the former, income distribution is treated as being the result of social institutions and social relations, while in the latter it is determined by conditions of exchange. This shift to exchange 'tilted back again – back to a portrayal of the economic problem in its essentials as shaped and moulded by universal and supra-historical conditions of any exchange society, whatever its particular social relations, class structure and property institutions might be' (*Theories*, 1973, p. 27).

These, in brief, are the basic and the more significant elements in Dobb's critique of neoclassical theory. The critique, as already observed, moved through various phases: while Dobb persistently and vigorously criticized the 'new theories' for seeking explanations of value and distribution in exchange, focusing on the fetishist character of market relations which obscured the real relations of production and thus divested the theory of a specific historico-social context, his logical critique did not emerge as forcefully. In the initial stages, the then-prevalent Marshallian orthodoxy (to the social philosophy of which he was definitely opposed) appears to have surreptitiously influenced Dobb's interpretations of certain elements in classical theory and inclined him to accept uncritically some of Marshall's own viewpoints and theoretical constructions.[5] Although some of these were rectified in Dobb's own later writings, it is particularly necessary to confront these interpretations which have a continuing influence and are frequently used by critics of classical theory.

12 Marshallian Bias in Interpretation of Classical Theories

'Given' or 'Fixed' Wage?
It is in *Wages* (1927 [1959]) – a little volume remarkable for discussing a number of socio-institutional issues usually ignored in theoretical works – that one finds a striking use of the Marshallian idiom and interpretations in the chapter on 'Theories of wages'. Dobb, in a characteristically Marshallian fashion, classifies the theories into two main types, according to the type of determining factor on which their emphasis has rested.

> On the one hand are those theories which have explained wages predominantly in terms of factors which influence the *supply* of labour-power ... On the other hand are those theories which have treated wages as being determined primarily by certain factors which influence employers' *demand* for labour,... Some economists (most notably, Marshall) have tried to erect a synthesis of the two types of explanation and to hold a balance between the two sets of determining influence; and so have produced a theory of a hybrid type. (p. 91)

This characterization of the classical theory as primarily a 'one-sided' supply theory is very much in line with the view that Marshall tried to popularize, namely, that the classical writers (more particularly Ricardo) tended to overemphasize the cost-of-production side, ignoring or paying insufficient attention to the demand side (Marshall, 1920, p. 503 and Appendix I). Marshall saw himself as continuing and supplementing their line of reasoning, giving it much needed balance by providing the demand half of the picture.

Furthermore, what is striking is that Dobb attributes to the classical notion of a 'given' wage an inflexibility mostly derived from the Malthusian law of population. While it is true that Malthus did argue that wages would be kept at the physiological miminum for survival (by the inexorable law of increasing fecundity catching up with every betterment of living conditions), and Smith and Ricardo did envisage the possibility of better wage conditions stimulating population, the attribution of an iron law of wages to the classical theory is overstretching the point. As already noted, Smith talked specifically and explicitly about the relative bargaining position of masters and workers; of Ricardo, Dobb himself writes later (in *Theories*) that, although Ricardo did use the Malthusian population argument to explain the stability of wage, 'he did not give it a crudely physical-subsistence interpretation as some have imagined and as such have lightly dismissed it. "Habits and customs" entered into what was conventionally "necessary" at any period or place' (1973, p. 91). In Marx, Dobb himself notes that there is an explicit refutation of the Malthusian dogma, the concept of the reserve army of the unemployed playing a crucial role instead. The stage of capitalist development was then such that the 'given' wage was likely to be near 'subsistence'. However, in *Wages*, Dobb does not appear to recognize that it was the 'given' rather than the 'fixed' wage that was required by the theory. Nor does he stress the significance of the fact that such a wage determination allows for specific socio-institutional factors – a point which he was to highlight later.

In fact, Dobb's interpretation of the 'given' wage as the 'fixed' wage leads him to argue incorrectly that

> the exponents of this Subsistence Theory themselves made one admission which really undermined their theory as a complete explanation of wages...To admit a variable quantity such as habit as being important was to make an appreciable hole in the completeness of the theory. (Dobb, 1927 [1959], p. 97)

For, according to him, the wage could no longer be fixed if new habits and conventional necessities were formed along with changing wages. Dobb then thought that Marshall had rescued the theory by allowing for a flexible supply price of labour, making the labour supply schedule dependent on wages. In *Wages*, the 'Marshallian synthesis', the supply-and-demand determination of wages, is presented without critical scrutiny, if not with approval. In Marshall's scheme, the demand for labour is governed by the aggregate 'investment fund' (itself resulting from individuals' decisions on the allocation of income between savings and consumption, dependent upon the rate of interest) and technical conditions, allowing for alternative ways of combining labour and capital in production; while the supply of labour is determined, at the margin, by equating the labourer's disutility of effort and utility of income. (It is surprising that Dobb retained all the above arguments in later revised versions of *Wages*, even as late as in 1959.)

It is in a later article written in 1929, 'A sceptical view of the theory of wages' (in *ETS*, 1955), that Dobb criticizes the Marshallian explanation. The ground for the attack is provided, as Dobb acknowledges, by Piero Sraffa's onslaught on the Marshallian derivation of the long-run normal supply curve on the basis of the laws of returns (Sraffa, 1926); particularly regarding the logical tenability of the mutual independence of the supply-and-demand functions in the Marshallian partial equilibrium scheme. Extending Sraffa's argument regarding commodity markets to labour, Dobb argues that, since the sale of labour constitutes the worker's entire income, the wage is the principal determinant of his subjective valuations and hence a change in the wage-rate would itself stimulate a change in the supply price of labour. If further note is taken of customs and habits formed by income, neither 'the will to save' nor 'the will to work' can be deemed to be independent of distribution. This, Dobb contended, would render the equilibrium in the labour market indeterminate. It must, however, be noted that this criticism is particularly damaging for the partial equilibrium setting of Marshall where the independence of the demand and supply forces is presumed.

Influence of Demand on Value Determination

The continuity of reasoning with the classicals, particularly Ricardo, claimed by Marshall, has shrouded later interpretations of classical theory by British economists, and Dobb did not entirely escape that influence in his earlier writings. Marshall maintained that Ricardo had inadvertently and incautiously underestimated the influence of demand and that 'the cost-of-production view of prices' could be deemed valid under certain special conditions – namely, when constant returns to scale (implying constant costs in his scheme) prevailed. However, such a possibility was rare and could come about only by an accidental balancing of the forces leading to increasing and diminishing returns. This view that the classical theory is either a 'partial' theory or a special case has survived to this day.

In his early work, *PEC* (1937 [1972]), Dobb remarks, 'Given conditions of "constant returns" it [labour-embodied values] was independent also of demand' (p. 14), and refers later in the same volume (p. 45) to the

> familiar classical doctrine that the configuration of demand was irrelevant to the distribution of the product between profit and wages (except in so far as it might accelerate the tendency to diminishing returns on land and hence raise the cost of subsistence). Like so much of Ricardian reasoning, it rested on a particular assumption: namely, that the proportions between capital and labour were equal

in all industries. Without this assumption, the statement would no longer be valid.

It is true that if methods of production do not change (with or without a change in demand), labour embodied in a commodity will not change, and that if the means of production/labour ratio is the same for all industries the exchange values will not change with a change in distribution. However, as observed in Section II, Ricardian theory did not envisage any functional link between distribution and output nor a functional relation between output and unit costs in the form of laws of returns. As far as the effect of changing distribution on exchange values is concerned, Ricardo, far from assuming away the problem, made it an issue central to his inquiry. However, the problem arose independently, whether or not there were changes in demand. (The parenthetical reference to the diminishing returns on land is also misleading. Ricardo specifically 'eliminated' rents by arguing that the rate of profit was determined on the no-rent land; the no-rent land itself was specified once the output levels were given. The determinants of the latter were diverse and not all changes in demand would therefore shift the boundary of no-rent land.)

Interpretation of Adam Smith
Another disputable interpretation occurs in a number of writers reading into the classical theory, particularly Adam Smith, the concepts of supply-and-demand relations of later theories. Confusion is caused mainly because of the continuance of the same phraseology in different theoretical structures. As was mentioned in Section II, 'natural prices' in classical theory were derivable from the methods of production in use at specified output levels, given the wage; while 'market prices' were viewed as deviations from natural prices caused by accidental factors affecting conditions of supply and demand. Marshall introduced what he regarded only as a 'conceptual continuity' (which, in effect, was an analytical jump) by interpreting 'market prices' as 'short-period prices' and natural prices as 'long-period normal prices', both determined by the equilibrating forces of demand and supply, 'the element of time' alone being the differentiating factor (see, Bharadwaj, 1978b; Chapter 6 in this volume). The influence of time was seen mainly as yielding different shapes and hence 'elasticities' of the demand and supply curves, due to differences in the conditions impounded in *ceteris paribus*. When the classical writers talked of temporary changes in 'conditions of demand and supply', the latter phrase was not used in the 'schedule' sense, showing quantities demanded (supplied) against hypothetical prices; each 'market price' was only a single *observed* position.

The temptation to attribute retrospectively a supply and demand approach appears strongest in the case of Adam Smith, thanks partly to his own ambiguities. Schumpeter regarded Adam Smith as the progenitor of the Mill–Marshall genealogy. Dobb suggests a similar continuity in Smith's frequent allusions to 'demand' and 'supply' and his discussion of the 'components of price'. Dobb holds this view in his *Theories*, not denying, however, that Smith's writing also suggests an incipient surplus approach. While it is true that Smith's analysis of value is neither wholly consistent nor altogether lucid, so that it permits a number of conflicting interpretations, a distinction needs to be made between his specific use of 'supply' and 'demand' in his particular context and the later *supply-and-demand theories*. Dobb writes in *Theories*:

> Whereas by Quesnay this [the 'natural laws' of self-regulating economic order] had been conceived of in terms of a flow or exchange-circuit fertilising the realm, by Smith it was viewed in terms of market forces establishing certain 'natural values' by dint of the operation of competition upon supplies and upon demand...'Market price', on the other hand, dependent on particular and *ad hoc* configuration of supply and demand at any given time and place ('regulated by the quantity which is actually brought to market and the demand of those...who may be called the effectual demanders') tended, when conditions of freedom allowed, towards the 'natural' level in the course of time. (1973, p, 43)

This may give the misleading impression that Smith had a supply-and-demand explanation of both natural and market prices, differentiated only by the time element. This impression is further strengthened when Dobb goes on to say:

> When it came to more precise definition of this natural value and its determination, Adam Smith had remarkably little to say beyond the statement that this was the equilibrium price that competition would in due course yield through the operations of supply and demand – towards which 'the prices of all commodities are continually gravitating'. A commodity's 'natural price' is defined as being equal to the sum of the 'natural rates of wages, profit and rent', which are in turn defined as the 'ordinary or average rate' of wages, profit or rent prevailing in 'the general circumstances of the society' at the time: in other words, as determined by the general conditions of supply and demand for labour, stock and land...It is then shown how when 'the quantity brought to market should at any time fall short of the effectual demand', or conversely, 'some of the component parts of its price must rise above their natural rate', or alternatively fall below it, and how this will influence the supply forthcoming in the ensuing period in such a way as to adapt it to the level of demand. (ibid., p. 44)

Here, the sense in which Smith uses the terms 'supply', 'effectual demand' and 'natural rates' must be carefully looked into. First, he defines the natural rates of wages and profit as the ordinary or average rates that prevail at the time and place, 'naturally regulated by the general circumstances of society, their riches, poverty, advancing or stationary or declining situation and partly by the nature of employment'. Smith brings in a large number of historical, sociological and even political factors, including law, custom, conventions, the state and level of economic and social organizations, etc., to explain the general level of wages and the differences in emoluments in different employments. He, in fact, considers the wage differentials to remain more or less stable even while the general level of wages rises. His discussion of the natural rate of profits and differences in profits between different avenues similarly brings in a rich complexity of different factors, and suggests a similar stability in profit differentials.[6] The multiplicity of different factors and the stability of differentials suggests that Smith's analysis would suffer drastic oversimplification and inconsistencies if forced into the framework of the later supply-and-demand theories, with their dependence on functional relations between quantities and prices, bearing definite, specified properties.

Secondly, the notion of 'effectual demand' is in no sense analogous to a demand schedule. Smith states clearly that the

> ...market price of every particular commodity is regulated by the proportion between the quantity which is actually brought to market and the demand of those who are willing to pay the natural price of the commodity, or the whole value of the rent, labour and profit, which must be paid in order to bring it thither. Such people may be called the effectual demanders, and their demand the effectual demand ... (Smith, 1776 [1930], p. 58)

It is clear from this that, for Smith, 'effectual demand' is not a schedule but a single position. Smith does not conceive of hypothetical demands at hypothetical prices. Further, it is in relation to this 'effectual demand' that the quantities brought into the market at particular times are compared. When the two are equal, 'natural prices' rule. The circumstances that regulate the deviations are not systematic and 'obstacles which hinder them from settling in this centre of repose and continuance' could be accidental. If market prices deviate from natural prices this implies that some revenue-recipients are securing less than their average or 'natural' rate of payment, a situation which under competition cannot long persist, but may otherwise.

Dobb's approving citation of Ricardo in the Malthus–Ricardo debate elsewhere in the text (*Theories*, 1973, p. 120), however, contradicts his own interpretation of Smithian natural value as depending upon the operations of demand and supply. Malthus had asserted his belief 'that the great principle of demand and supply is called into action to determine what Adam Smith calls natural price as well as market price'. Not only that, he had argued also that the 'natural' rates of wages and profits were determined by the same principle (Malthus, 1820, pp. 73-5). To this Ricardo replies:

> The author forgets Adam Smith's definition of natural price, or he would not say that demand and supply could determine natural price.

Natural price is only another name for cost of production. When any commodity sells for that price which will repay the wages for labour expended on it, will also afford rent, and profit at their then current rate, Adam Smith would say that commodity was at its natural price. Now these charges would remain the same whether commodities were much or little demanded, whether they sold at a high or low market price. (Ricardo, 1951b, p. 46)

There is no doubt that Adam Smith's discussion of value and distribution is ambivalent, allowing conflicting interpretations (Bharadwaj, 1976). His interest in value had been primarily invoked by the need for a 'real measure' so as to give a quantitative meaning to 'surplus' and variations in it. Labour, he argued, was such a measure. This led him to explain relative values in terms of 'labour embodied', which, however, he found valid only at the early and rude stage of society before the accumulation of capital and private appropriation of land. The 'labour-commanded' notion which he suggested as an alternative (prompted by the strict proportionality between prices and labour commanded) was scarcely a 'theory' of value and, as a measure, suffered from all the disadvantages of 'corn' or 'silver', as Ricardo was quick to point out. Smith's analysis of 'component parts of prices' was essentially no more than a definition of price, decomposed into the revenues paid out to landlords, capitalists and labourers. He had erroneously inferred on the basis of such 'adding-up' that a rise in wages leads to a rise in price, generally. He had also treated these separate forms of revenue as 'original sources of value', thus making possible the interpretation that he originated the idea of including 'profits' as a constituent part of costs, on a basis symmetrical with wages. It must be remembered, however, that Smith explicitly maintained that there were qualitative differences between rents, profits and wages as forms of revenue, and offered different determinants in each case. As to wages, while he did talk of the 'toil and trouble' of labour, he considered wages specifically as constituting 'necessary maintenance'. He even considers one of the important determinants of differentials in wage payments to be the cost incurred in training skilled labour. Likewise, although he talks occasionally of profits as inducements towards investment, Dobb himself points out that Smith offered a theory of exploitation, in embryo, in so far as he looked upon profits (and rents) as 'deductions' from the produce of labour. Marx, commenting upon Smith's vacillations and confusions, notes that, in many substantive propositions involving the nature and origin of surplus and its distribution, Smith kept firmly to the relations in production (Marx, 1862-3 [1963], I, pp. 69–103). This is not surprising, since Smith's constant battle was against the mercantilist fallacies, resting on fetishist conceptions based on relations in circulation. One should be wary, therefore, of identifying Smith's 'adding-up' or 'component parts of price' analysis with later efforts to reduce profits, wages and rents to symmetrical components of costs by the neoclassical theory.

13 The Interpretation of the Logical Structure of the Classical and Supply-and-Demand Theories

On a more general plane, some weaknesses in Dobb's critique can also be traced to a failure to bring out clearly the logical structure of the classical as well as the supply-and-demand theories. Some specific instances of this are discussed below.

Dobb specifically raises some problems of logic concerning value theory in 'The requirements of a theory of value' (1937). The specific way in which the theories of value and distribution are linked together in classical theory does not emerge clearly in his discussion, and the exposition consequently lacks both clarity and accuracy. He writes:

> an essential condition of a theory of value is that it must solve the problem of distribution (i.e. determine the price of labour-power, of capital and of land) as well as the problem of commodity values; and it must do so not only because the former is an essential, indeed major, part of the practical inquiry with which Political Economy is concerned, but because the one cannot be determined without the other. In other words, neither Distribution nor Commodity-Exchange can be properly treated as 'isolated systems'. (*PEC* 1937 [1972], p. 9)

This interconnectedness of the two problems is no doubt a fact. However, the framework within which the interdependency is worked out is radically different in the classical and the supply-and-demand theories. In the former, prices and the rate of profit are simultaneously determined once the wage is known. The determination of wages and of the surplus remains outside the prices schema and hence in a sense prior to the pricing problem. In the latter theory, however, distribution and pricing problems are identically solved within the same process of price determination. This difference Dobb identified and emphasized in his later work, *Theories*. There (Dobb, 1970), the position was more clearly spelt out:

> ... did not Marx say that the existence of profit as surplus value has to be explained in terms of the law of value or it cannot be explained at all; and did this not mean that he determined distribution within the framework of a theory of value, just as much as did Jevons and the Austrians? There are, I think, two answers to this: Firstly, his value theory was itself written in terms of (and prices derived from) conditions of production and not from conditions of demand and individual consumption. Secondly, what he meant was that existence of surplus value must be explained *consistently* with the rules and requirements of a competitive market: he did *not* mean that the determination of surplus value and the rules of the exchange process must be *identified*; or the former derived esoterically from the latter. (p. 358)

However, in 'The requirements of a theory of value', the different structure of the two theories in this respect not being clearly explicated, it is difficult to understand Dobb's assertion that 'a principle of value is not adequate which merely expresses value in terms of some one or other particular value: *the determining constants must express a relationship with some quantity which is not itself a value*' (1937 [1972], pp. 9-10). In the classical theory of value and distribution (emphasizing relations in production) there arose an analytical need for an 'invariant standard', especially in the determination of a consistent explanation of the rate of profit. ('Invariance' did not, it may be noted, necessarily require a standard 'not itself a value', although it was often expressed in such terms. This, however, is a stricter condition than required.) However, no such requirement arises in the context of the supply-and-demand theories. The difficulty for a consistent theory of distribution here arises in a very different form, which, in turn, rests on the construction of a suitable measure of capital, independent of distribution. Neither in 'The requirements of a theory of value', nor in 'The trend of modern economics' where he extensively discusses the Austrian theory and its shifts to utility-based explanations, does Dobb confront the different nature of the logical difficulties peculiar to the structure of the respective theories.

The lack of a clear exposition of the distribution problem in classical theory and the rationale of the invariant standard also meant that Dobb's defence of labour values (in 'The requirements of a theory of value') had to rest on very weak arguments.

> This principle of the identity of value-ratios with labour-ratios rested on conditions which defined the nature of the dominant tendencies in an exchange-society. In an exchange-society characterised by the division of labour, by competition and the mobility of resources, competition would ensure that labour was distributed between the various lines of production in such a way that these ratios were equal. (ibid, p. 14)

Dobb adds that the equality implied the 'important simplifying assumption' that the ratio of capital to labour employed in different lines of production was the same, but considers the assumption to be only an abstract approximation to concrete exchange values. It would seem that Dobb here implies that there was an actual tendency towards an identity of labour ratios and prices. He goes on to say that the analytical assumption, being only an abstraction, could be criticized only if 'its implied assumptions preclude the generalisation from sustaining the corollaries which it is employed to sustain'. This shifts the defence of labour values to a logical plane, but Dobb does not elaborate as to what specific corollaries the labour values helped to sustain as to which of these could be sustained if the simplifying was relaxed. As later discussions, especially of th problem, have shown, the use of labour val analytical role in giving transparency to locating surplus in production and unambiguously relating wages to profit). To the extent that these propositions could also be generalized to the scheme of prices, labour values were a useful 'abstraction', especially in bringing out certain central issues which otherwise could not possibly have been posed. Considering the fact that it was precisely hostility to the conclusions of that theory that propelled a search for an alternative framework, such an obfuscation of issues would not have been unlikely.

In 'The requirements of a theory of value', Dobb resorts to a logically weaker argument to justify labour values, namely, that Ricardo considered the restrictive assumption (of equality of the ratio of means of production to labour in all branches of production) as not of importance for the purpose of the main inquiry in hand, which concerned the 'macroscopic' problems of society. Ricardo, preoccupied as he was with the relative movements of the three great revenues (rents, profits and wages), was more concerned with broad classes of commodities than with particular commodities and, according to Dobb, must have considered labour values as a good-enough approximation to deal with aggregates. This argument is not convincing. Ricardo was far from complacent on this question and it was precisely because of the heterogeneous composition of the aggregates (social output, wages and capital), susceptible to fluctuations in value due to a change in distribution, that he had to search for an 'invariant standard'. It is not, however, on formal grounds, but because of the 'realistic worth', that Dobb defends the labour principle in this essay (PEC, 1937 [1972], 20–1). He refers in justification of labour values to an *extremely important but separate* issue: the exclusive importance attached to labour, as a quantitative expression of 'the struggle of man with nature to wrest a livelihood for himself under various forms of production at various stages of history': in comprehending the process, through history, of the generation and appropriation of surplus.

Dobb's critique of the supply-and-demand theories appears at times to have been similarly clouded because he did not confront the totality of the structure, but concentrated instead on isolated elements. For example, the assumption of an *independently given* scale of preferences for individuals is not by itself damaging. We have seen that classical theory did consider the determinants of social consumption and output as lying outside the immediate scope of value determination. What does create a logical problem for the supply-and-demand theories is that they seek an explanation of consumption choices within the scheme of price determination and therefore have to postulate that the scale of preferences is independent of prevailing prices or of the direct influence (not channelled through price movements) exerted by producers or other consumers. In short, the structure of theory is such as to require certain types of influence on the formation of preferences and on the behaviour of consumers to be *ex hypothesi* ruled out.

Similarly, the assumption in these theories that quantities of resources and their distribution between individuals are given does not by itself appear objectionable. After all, it may be argued that even within a historical continuity one may choose some cut-off point at which to begin. And, as some proponents of that theory may argue, the postulate of an initial distribution of endowments may permit us to take account of specific capitalist relations, with some individuals endowed with labour alone and others with capital or land. The difficulty, however, arises because the supply-and-demand theories seek to explain distribution within their price-determination schema and the assumption of initially given resources leads to certain logical inconsistencies within that framework: when capital is considered as a given value-sum, independent of distribution, the problem appears to be that of generating a 'normally' shaped demand function for capital; when, on the other hand, it is considered as a list of quantities of heterogeneous assets, the problem is to ensure the uniformity of the rate of profit in the long-run equilibrium. It is only in *Theories* that these logical problems are raised. In the earlier discussions, Dobb concentrated on individual assumptions and concepts. In 'The trend of modern economies', for example, he devotes considerable space to a discussion of the Austrian theory, with its shift to the utility basis. However, no logical arguments are there offered against such a utility-based framework. Even in *Theories* Dobb refers to the more flexible concept of the 'wages-fund' as the 'subsistence fund' in the Austrian theory, where it represents the availability of 'capital'. However, he ends the discussion abruptly without any comment about the logical tenability of such a conception of capital within that theory (1973, p. 134). The comparative neglect of the logical critique in earlier writings also manifests itself in the fact that Dobb paid remarkably little attention to the principle of substitution, central to the supply-and-demand framework: it is that principle which, by eliciting the appropriate price-responsive changes in quantities, generates the right sort of demand-and-supply relations.

We may conclude this discussion with some incidental observations. Dobb consistently held the view that the 'Keynesian revolution' could scarcely be put on a level with the 'Jevonian'; for 'its effect upon the general conceptual framework of economic theory went less deep, whatever the significance of its policy-implication for the conduct of a modern capitalist economy may have been' (ibid., p. 214). One may agree with Dobb that Keynes's own formulation 'may be said to have moved within the general framework of the existing theory of value and distribution'. The later 'neoclassical synthesis' may have been aided by Keynes's own view that, while the traditional theory had erred in its determination of the level of aggregate output and employment, it retained its validity as a theory of resource allocation. A critical examination of Keynesian theory, however, reveals that the questions it raised, particularly concerning the traditional determination of the rate of interest through a savings/investment balance, raise deeper doubts abo⁻ the supply-and-demand framework in general. While Dobb is ⸺ right, as far as the initial impact of the theory goes, in ⸺ Keynesian ideas 'challenged traditional doctrine ⸺ namely, its assumption of a unique position ⸺

full employment of all available productive resources as a necessary condition' (ibid., p. 215), they have initiated a questioning of the internal consistency of the value and distribution framework going beyond the immediate context (see Garegnani, 1964 and 1965). So perhaps more attention was due to Keynes than Dobb gives him in his critique. Among the other notable absences in Dobb's detailed critique are Wicksell and, paradoxically, Marshall. While Wicksell receives occasional passing mention as one among the Austrians, Marshall is often quoted with approval for his caution and 'realism'. However, Dobb does not discuss their theoretical systems in any detail.

14 Conclusion

There can be no doubt that Dobb's critique of economic theory has played a major role in the revival of interest in classical and Marxian political economy; not merely as a subject for the historian's curiosity about primitive efforts at theorizing, but as offering a powerful theoretical system on whose foundations further analyses of economic problems can be attempted. In the pages above, we have raised certain points requiring clarification where Dobb's interpretations seemed doubtful. Many of these, as the text indicates at relevant places, Dobb himself clarified in *Theories*; when he, like all of us, had the opportunity to look back from the vantage point of the present state of theoretical understanding. Nevertheless, if these points are raised here, it is on the ground that, although constituting only minor deficiencies in Dobb, they could yet afford a basis for continuing misinterpretations, undermining the force of the classical theory.

A major thrust of Dobb's work was to show that the theoretical framework of classical political economy, and of Marx in particular, made it possible to analyse meaningfully problems of distribution, accumulation and economic change in the context of specific historical conditions. In fact, Dobb's major works in economic history, addressed to such problems, reveal a rare and masterly competence (see, e.g., Dobb, 1946). The constructive aspect of the on-going critique of economic theory lies in clarifying the logical basis and the social philosophy of the approach as an essential preliminary to such tasks ahead. Dobb, in this task, has led the way.

Notes: Chapter 8

This essay was first published in the *Cambridge Journal of Economics*, vol. 2 (1978), pp. 153–74. My thanks are due to the editors of the Journal, John Eatwell and Geoffrey Harcourt for their helpful suggestions. Written while at Manchester, I received careful comments from Barbara MacLennan and Ian Steadman. It was through discussions of this paper that I had the opportunity to start a correspondence with Ronald Meek, unfortunately terminated abruptly by his demise.

1. 'The natural price, therefore, is, as it were, the central price, to which the prices of all commodities are continually gravitating. Different accidents may sometimes keep them suspended a good deal above it, and sometimes force them down even somewhat below it. But whatever may be the obstacles which hinder them from settling in this centre of repose and continuance, they are constantly tending towards it' (Smith, 1776 [1930] p. 60).
2. See Section III of this chapter for a fuller discussion of Marshall. A similar attempt was made by Samuelson (1951, 1961) by proposing the 'Non-substitution theorems', according to which, under the assumptions of no joint production, constant returns to scale and a single primary factor, the methods of production and relative prices remain invariant with changes in demand and/or factor availabilities. Samuelson (1959, 1971) has also argued that the 'Walrasian conditions' on the demand side are necessary to locate the marginal no-rent land, and hence the Ricardian system is incomplete. For a similar argument see Shove (1942). Such arguments arise from a basic misconception regarding the structure of classical theory.
3. The notion of surplus or 'net product' was first introduced by the Physiocrats, who used it in the sense of material surplus product in agriculture. It was defined as that part of the gross produce remaining after deducting wages and material input requirements. The concept was generalized by Adam Smith to apply to all production. 'Net product' or surplus is usually netted for wages (along with material inputs) where wages are paid in advance. In some cases (as in Smith and later in Sraffa, 1960), it is netted out for material costs but includes wages. The former conception, of wages advanced, is more commonly used in classical political economy.
4. As Bortkiewicz (1952) demonstrates, using the department schemes in Marx, the rate of profit is determined within the wage goods sector, once the real wage is specified. This has the important implication that: 'If it is indeed true that the level of the rate of profit in no way depends on the conditions of production of those goods which do not enter into real wages, then the origin of profit must clearly be sought in wage-relationship and not in that ability of capital to increase production' (p.33).
5. For example, in his early work, Dobb, even while perceptively recognizing and opposing the social philosophy of the Cambridge neoclassicists, was persuaded by the view that Marshall had continued the Ricardo-Mill tradition, rendering their doctrines rigorous and divesting them of some of their 'obvious oddities' (see 'The entrepreneur myth' in ETS, 1955, and Dobb, 1931b). He also used the Marshallian subjective utility calculus while simultaneously adopting a Marxian historical approach, so that a curious mixture of Marx and Marshall emerged. The influence of Marshallian ideas and idiom was much reduced, if not absent in the subsequent work.
6. 'Though pecuniary wages and profit are very different in the different employments of labour and stock; yet a certain proportion seems commonly to take place between both the pecuniary wages in all the different employments of labour, and the pecuniary profits in all the different employments of stock. This proportion, it will appear hereafter, depends partly upon the nature of the different employments, and partly upon the different laws and policy of the society in which they are carried on. But though in many respects dependent upon the laws and policy, this proportion seems to be little affected by the

riches or poverty of that society; by its advancing, stationary or declining condition; but to remain the same or very nearly the same in all those different states' (Smith, 1776 [1930], p. 65).

References: Chapter 8

Bharadwaj, K. (1976), 'On some conflicting views of Adam Smith', paper presented to seminar at the bicentennial celebration of *The Wealth of Nations*, mimeo (Madras).
Bharadwaj, K.(1978a), *Classical Political Economy and the Rise to Dominance of Supply and Demand Theories* (Calcutta: Orient Longman); Revised edition, 1986
Bharadwaj, K. (1978b), 'The subversion of classical analysis: Alfred Marshall's early writing on value', *Cambridge Journal of Economics*, vol. 2, no. 3 (September), pp. 253–71; Chapter 6 in the present volume.
Bortkiewicz, L. von (1952), 'Value and Price in the Marxian system', *International Economic Papers*, no. 2.
Dobb, M. H. (1927 [1959]), *Wages*, 6th edn (Cambridge: Cambridge University Press).
Dobb, M. H. (1931a), 'An introduction to economics', in W. Rose (ed.), *An Outline of Modern Knowledge* (London: Gollancz).
Dobb, M. H. (1931b), 'The Cambridge School', in *Encyclopaedia of the Social Sciences*, Vols V–VI (New York: Macmillan).
Dobb, M. H. (1937 [1972]), *Political Economy and Capitalism*, 2nd edn (London: Routledge)
Dobb, M. H. (1946), *Studies in the Development of Capitalism* (London: Routledge)
Dobb, M. H. (1955), *On Economic Theory and Socialism* (London: Routledge).
Dobb, M. H. (1970), 'The Sraffa system and critique of the neoclassical theory', *De Economist*, vol. 118, reprinted in E. K. Hunt and Jesse Schwartz (ed.) (1972) *A Critique of Economic Theory* (London: Penguin)
Dobb, M. H. (1973), *Theories of Value and Distribution since Adam Smith* (Cambridge: Cambridge University Press).
Eatwell, J. L. (1977), 'The irrelevance of returns to scale in Sraffa's analysis', *Journal of Economic Literature* (March).
Garegnani, P. (1960), *Il capitale nelle teorie della distribuzione* (Milan: Giuffre).
Garegnani, P. (1978 and 1979), 'Notes on Consumption, Investment and Effective Demand', in two parts, Part I, *Cambridge Journal of Economics*, 2 (December), pp. 335–53 and Part II, ibid. (March 1979), pp. 63–82.
Garegnani, P. (1970), 'Heterogeneous capital, the production function and the theory of distribution', *Review of Economic Studies* vol. xxxvii, no. 3 (July), pp. 407–36.
Hobsbawm, E. G. (1969), 'Maurice Dobb', in C. H. Feinstein (ed.), *Capitalism, Socialism and Economic Growth* (Cambridge: Cambridge University Press).
Keynes, J. M. (1936), *The General Theory of Employment, Interest and Money* (London: Macmillan).
Malthus, T. R. (1820), *Principles of Political Economy*, 1st edn (London: Murray).
Marshall, A. (1920), *Principles of Economics*, 8th edn (London: Macmillan).
Marx, K. (1862–3 [1963]), *Theories of Surplus Value*, Part I (Moscow: Progress Publishers).

Marx, K. (1867 [1971]), *Capital: A Critique of Political Economy*, 3 vols (London: Lawrence & Wishart).
Marx, K. (1857–8 [1973]), *Grundrisse. Foundations of the Critique of Political Economy* (Harmondsworth: Penguin in association with New Left Review).
Ricardo, D. (1951a), *Principles of Political Economy*, Vol. I of *Works and Correspondence of David Ricardo*, ed. by P. Sraffa with the collaboration of M. H. Dobb (Cambridge: Cambridge University Press).
Ricardo, D. (1951b), *Notes on Malthus*, Vol II of *Works and Correspondence of David Ricardo*, ed. by P. Sraffa (Cambridge: Cambridge University Press).
Samuelson, P. A. (1951), 'Abstract of a theorem concerning substitutability in open Leontief models', in T. C. Koopmans (ed.), *Activity Analysis of Production and Allocation* (New York: Wiley).
Samuelson, P. A. (1959), 'A modern treatment of the Ricardian economy', *Quarterly Journal of Economics* (February and May), pp. 1–35 and 217–31.
Samuelson, P. A. (1961), 'A new theorem on non-substitution', in H. Hegeland (ed.), *Money Growth and Methodology and Other Essays in Economics* (Lund: Gleerup)
Samuelson, P. A. (1971), 'Understanding the Marxian notion of exploitation: a summary of the so-called transformation problem between Marxian values and competitive prices', *Journal of Economic Literature* vol. 9, no. 2 (June), pp. 399–432.
Shove, G. F. (1942), 'The place of Marshall's *Principles* in the development of economic theory', *Economic Journal*, vol. 52 (December), pp. 294–329.
Smith, A. (1776[1930]), *An Inquiry into the Nature and Causes of the Wealth of Nations*, 5th edn, ed. by E. Cannan (London: Methuen).
Sraffa, P. (1925), 'Sulle relazione fra costo e quantità prodotta', *Annali di Economia*, vol. 2, n. 1, pp. 277–328.
Sraffa, P. (1926), 'The laws of returns under competitive conditions', *Economic Journal*, vol. 36 (December), pp. 535–50.
Sraffa, P. (1960), *Production of Commodities by Means of Commodities: Prelude to a Critique of Economic Theory* (Cambridge: Cambridge University Press).

9

On Certain Theoretical Issues in Classical Political Economy

The book under review, *Smith, Marx and After* (1977) – the last to be published by Professor Ronald Meek – is a collection of ten essays on an important tradition in economic thought which had its beginning in the Physiocrats and Smith, found continued development in the hands, particularly, of David Ricardo. It was critically extended in many original directions and was integrated into a comprehensive theoretical system of political economy by Marx. The essays are divided into three parts. Part I, on Smith, opens with a discussion of the relation which some of Smith's ideas bear to those of Marx, followed by a presentation of the four-stages theory of stadial development originating, as the author shows, in Smith. The next two essays present some highly interesting original materials now available in the form of a student's notes on Smith's lectures delivered at Glasgow and extracts from the notebooks of Anderson, a colleague of Smith. The three essays in Part II are devoted to a single theme in Marx's theory of value, the much-debated 'transformation problem'. Part III tries to link up some of the on-going debates to the past and reviews the interpretations that have been handed down to us by authorities in the history of economic analysis, such as Schumpeter. Meek's themes thus touch upon many questions at the centre of current controversy and, while the present reviewer has felt strongly drawn to comment upon Meek's interpretations, the remarks necessarily have had to be suggestive so as to remain within the bounds of a review article. In the following, we shall discuss the three parts of the book sequentially in three sections (Page references when not indicated otherwise are to the book under review.)

I

Meek opens his essay on 'Smith and Marx' with a genial proprietary claim made by George Stigler at Glasgow University during the bicentennial celebration of the *Wealth of Nations* in 1976: 'I bring you greetings from Adam Smith, who is alive and well and living in Chicago' (p. 3).

As Meek remarks, 'the picture ... the claim was meant to conjure up, of course, was of the Adam Smith who stood out as the great pioneering advocate of competitive capitalism, free trade, and the price mechanism and whose *Wealth of Nations* was destined to become the Bible of the liberal bourgeoisie' (p. 3). Smith's spirited defence of *laissez-faire*, for which ample quotations may be found in his work, no doubt, may be cited in support of this view. However, the phrase 'living in Chicago' which Stigler adds has implications which go much beyond. First, the historical context of Smith's advocacy of *laissez-faire* is totally ignored. Smith wrote at a time when the forces of emerging capitalism were striving against the fetters of the artificial system of restraints under feudal-mercantile dominance. The advocacy of the freedom of enterprise at such a time meant voicing the needs of an advancing, progressive system of production based on generalized exchange. The optimism of Smith in the progressiveness of competitive capitalism was based on the potentialities of a system yet to be historically operative and which the growing forces of production required for their advancement. Within less than a century, however, the other side of the coin – the internal contradictions within the system – were to show up prominently. Smith was not unaware of these but tended to attribute them to artificial monopolizing tendencies and hence to an interference with competition. The difference between Smith's advocacy of *laissez-faire* and the present-day Chicago school defence of competitive capitalism would be clear to most who do not shut their eyes to history. And Meek, with his sense of history, does not miss this.

More important and relevant for us today, however, is the second implication of Stigler's claim which has a much wider and deeper currency: that Adam Smith is the theoretical progenitor of the later equilibrium theory based on the supply-and-demand market mechanism. Meek does not sufficiently debate this view. In the current history of economic thought a notion that prevails rather widely is that Smith is the precursor of two very divergent streams of thought, the surplus theories developed by Ricardo and Marx, on the one hand, and the supply-and-demand theories which are characteristic of the neoclassical schools, on the other, with the balance perhaps tilting in favour of the latter. No doubt as would be expected in one of the earliest pioneering expositors of a general interdependent system of the economy, Smith has his share of inadequate analysis, inconsistencies and ambiguities. However, it is possible to argue, that Smith's links with surplus analysis are much more systematic whereas, despite a common terminology and suggestive phrases which favour casting him into the supply-and-demand mould, the later supply-and-demand-based theories are vastly different, in spirit, in construction and in their analytical role from what Smith purported. (See Chapter 2 above.)

Meek's discussion of the relation between Smith and Marx is important from this point of view. It was Marx who saw through the ambiguities in Smith and recognized the underlying framework providing the basic rudiments of the surplus approach. Meek follows Marx's discussion rather closely although differing slightly in interpretation. The fundamentally approving and sanguinely optimistic view of capitalism which Smith holds contrasts, no doubt markedly, with Marx's picture of capitalism as riddled with internal contradictions: 'Two very different worlds, it would seem, and two very different men' (p. 4).

Nevertheless Marx saw in Smith one of the best representatives of scientific political economy who had launched into the investigation of the real relations of production. Smith, unlike the mercantilists, recognized the fundamental importance of analysing the process of production, the importance of the notion of surplus, of the component parts of the requisites of production, of the expanding course of generalized commodity exchange through the division of labour and, above all, of the division of the society into distributive classes with their specific relations in production. He was the first to set out clearly the tripartite division into classes: receivers of rents, profits and wages. However, Smith, as Marx puts it, presented both the 'exoteric' and 'esoteric' elements side by side, without working out the connection between them so that his analysis remained often inconsistent and ambiguous. On the one hand, as Marx writes,

> [Smith] traces the intrinsic connection existing between economic categories or the obscure structure of the bourgeois economic system. On the other, he simultaneously sets forth the connection as it appears in the phenomena of competition and thus as it presents itself to the unscientific observer just as to him who is actually involved and interested in the process of bourgeois production. One of these conceptions fathoms the inner connection, the physiology so to speak, of the bourgeois system, whereas the other takes the external phenomena of life, as they seem and appear and merely describes, catalogues, recounts and arranges them under formal definitions. (1969–72, II, p. 165)

An important addition to this, which Meek quotes only in the footnote, goes on to say that with Smith this dualism was justifiable

> ... since his task was indeed a two fold one. On the one hand he attempted to penetrate the inner physiology of bourgeois society but on the other, he partly tried to describe its externally apparent forms of life for the first time, to show its relations as they appear outwardly and partly he had even to find a nomenclature and corresponding mental concepts for these phenomena. (ibid., p. 165)

These 'exoteric' elements, Marx argues, to which recourse was taken by the later 'vulgar' opponents of Ricardo, provided the basis for fathering upon Smith the latter-day supply-and-demand theories. Smith, as observed above, had laid down the basic rudiments of the surplus approach to be developed by Ricardo and Marx. Although he rejected the labour-embodied explanation of exchange value in a capitalist (as opposed to pre-capitalist) economy, he did, as Marx argues, use labour values implicitly in some substantive propositions concerning the generations and distribution of surplus, in contradiction to his own rejection, and he suggested that profits and rents be considered as deductions from the produce of labour, hence providing an incipient 'exploitation' theory.

Meek, however, does not examine the 'exoteric' side of Smith in this essay and leaves the issue somewhat ambiguous by suggesting that 'Smith can also, perhaps, be regarded as the founder of the other main tradition in value and distribution theory – the tradition which takes as its starting point the *conditions of exchange* rather than the conditions of production' (p. 17). He does take up the question, rather cursorily, in another essay in the volume (pp. 156–8) contesting Schumpeter's view of Smith's ideas as pointing towards Walras's general equilibrium. Systematic attempts have been made in the history of economic thought (written by authors sympathetic to the neoclassical school) to depict Smith and Ricardo as either groping, although inconsistently, towards a coherent scheme which was to culminate into the general interdependent supply-and-demand framework (such was the attempt of Marshall 'generously' to interpret Ricardo as profound but confused, 'not quite understanding the full drift of his own arguments') or as wrongheaded deviationists who shunted 'the car of economic analysis' into a wrong track – the latter applied particularly to Ricardo. The attempts to so absorb and synthesize Smith and Ricardo within the stream of 'equilibrium' theories serve, it would seem, two objects. First, to refuse to recognize that there was a distinctive theoretical approach emerging in political economy. Its disturbing conclusions, rendered ominous by an equally explosive political historical situation in the 1830s, propelled a strong political reaction against it and provided an impetus to the formation and acceptance of an alternative theoretical system. (Meek's essay on 'The decline of Ricardian economics in England' (1950) provides much evidence of this.) Secondly, Marx's political economy, thus isolated as an idiosyncratic creation of an idealogue, could be left to itself without historical roots. (Schumpeter, (1954), however, clearly saw the links between Smith, Ricardo and Marx. Marshall set the tradition of ignoring Marx altogether.) While this review would not be the place to argue in detail against the close allegiance that has been built up between Smith and the supply-and-demand theories, we may refer to it briefly.

As Marx remarks, many of the 'exoteric' elements in Smith arose out of describing external appearances, 'finding a nomenclature and corresponding mental concepts, (1862–3 [1963–71]), II, p. 165. True, Smith, because he recognized that the labour that a commodity can purchase deviated from the labour embodied in it in a situation where profits were paid out of the receipts, rejected the labour-embodied theory of prices as inconsistent. This, as Meek points out, posed the question in a form which gave a direction to future efforts in evolving a labour theory of value, bringing out the logical difficulty as well as its historical root. Smith abandoned the theory in favour of a 'labour-commanded' explanation. The latter was no theory at all but afforded only a measure which, however, did not possess the property of 'invariance' which Smith sought. That Smith often enough lapsed into a labour-embodied approach is therefore not surprising. It is also not surprising that the latter-day neoclassical theorists, except when they wish to present Smith's model of accumulation à la Hicks where the 'measure' is used, rarely refer to 'labour-commanded theory'. It is the 'adding-up' view of Smith which led him to describe price as decomposable into the trinity of wages, profits and rents, that is alluded to by the later theorists and was in later versions made into the 'supply price' or cost of production. The definitive turn came with Mill introducing abstinence in the form of profits in the cost of production and Marshall carrying it over into the 'real costs' approach (see Bharadwaj, 1978). Schumpeter, as Meek points out, singled out Smith's discussion on components of price for special praise as it pointed 'towards Say, and through the latter's work, to Walras'. However, Smith's exercise of the decomposition appears to be more a classificatory one, with the status of a definition rather than a theory. Where he used it to derive a theoretical proposition, as Ricardo and Marx pointed out, he was inconsistent. For example, the then commonly believed Smithian proposition that a rise in wages gives rise to an increase in all prices, which was derived presumably from such an 'adding-up', was, as Ricardo was to argue, logically insupportable. So also the idea that prices are reducible ultimately to these three components without a 'commodity residual' was challenged by Marx. Even more basically, the 'adding-up' was no theory and has no relation to the later 'adding-up' problem under the marginal productivity theory. Smith specifically argued that the determinants of rents, profits and wages were diverse and they were explained in different terms. Interests were paid out of profits, rents were payments to the landlord after deducting wages and profits at a 'normal' rate. True, Smith brought into the explanation of 'natural' rates of profits, wages and rents an interplay of competitive forces in the form of supply and demand. But the nature of these supply-and-demand forces is vastly different from those conceived in the Walras-like theories. Reference is made by Smith in connection with these forces to 'the general circumstances of society, their riches or poverty, their advancing, stationary or declining condition; and partly by particular nature of employment' (Smith, 1776 [1930], I, p. 72). Smith refers to legal and institutional conditions, geophysical and social factors. 'Supply' and 'demand' are convenient catch-all phrases and are not used in any strict functional or schedule sense. It was not until much later, around the time of Mill, that price-dependent supply-and-demand schedules were being hypothesized; but then, a new theoretical structure was already emerging.

The conflicting viewpoints in Smith can also be interpreted, following Marx, as arising from the contrast between the real relations as they are, and as they manifest themselves to the participants. To the individual capitalist, profits are a payment, an inducement to carry on investment. Smith recognized it as such and this has been adduced as an evidence of his support for the 'real cost theory' (see Marshall in Pigou, 1925, p. 126). However, Smith, looking at the production system as a whole, also recognized profits as a part of the surplus and therefore as originating within, and limited by, production. The phrase 'toil and trouble' of labour was picked up by later theorists to attribute to Smith the subjective cost approach. However, he was possibly one of the first economists to discuss the reduction of skilled labour to general labour by considering the costs of acquiring skills and to look upon wages, following Cantillon, as the costs of rearing the labourer and his family. Instances can be multiplied. It appears that while certainly Adam Smith was quoted later on by Say, Malthus and the anti-Ricardians for support of their theories, vaguely couched in terms of supply and demand, Smith's more substantive contribution was as one of the founder members of the surplus school.

Meek's assessment that many of Smith's critical and extremely perspicuous statements about the motives and behaviour of capitalists, merchants and landlords do not amount to a serious indictment against capitalism is well taken. A keen observer of his times, Smith did not fail to take notice of the conflict of interests among the workers and masters, the landlords and the tenants. His view of rents and profits as deductions from wages could not but suggest to him an opposition of interests. Times were such that frank comments on the existing inequalities and the differences in the social and economic status of different classes were accepted more as scientific observations about an order that existed and not necessarily with the pejorative connotations that they acquired as the conflicts sharpened. Moreover, the 'monopolizing spirit', the 'interested sophistry' of the 'merchants and manufacturers' as well as the 'greed' of the landlords to reap where they did not sow, the legislative biases favouring combinations of masters but condemning those of the workers, etc, appeared to Smith more as imperfections in the natural system of liberty. Not having a clear theory of distribution, Smith did not foresee the long-term consequences, nor the real basis of these conflicts, as Ricardo and Marx were to do later.

The key to the 'inconsistencies' they led to is possibly to be found, as the present reviewer has argued elsewhere (Bharadwaj, 1979), in Smith's dual basis in 'social moralism' and the materialistic view of the development of society. Smith was one among the first of the eighteenth-century philosophers who presented a stadial view of the development of society, occurring through successive stages, characterized by a certain mode of subsistence. Each such social formation was associated with the development of its own social stratification and a political, moral, legal structure. This essentially materialistic interpretation, which Meek discusses in an essay in this volume and in more detail in a book published earlier (Meek, 1967), is combined in Smith with a related but not well-integrated view, inspired by a system of morality. The latter concerns a theory propounding the existence of certain propensities in human nature that incline an individual to a social existence, that is, the view advocates that man, at each stage of his social existence, is endowed by nature with certain faculties and propensities that befit him to maintain his social state. This stream of his reasoning (reflected in his *The Theory of Moral Sentiments*, 1793) seems to have prompted him to refer so often to the 'nature' of the individual (for example, Smith attributes division of labour to the innate human propensity to barter and to exchange and views the pursuit of self-interest as ultimately making a competitive society viable). It must, however, be immediately clarified that Smith's individual was located in society and was not an autonomous atomistic entity. This connotes, therefore, philosophically, a very different viewpoint from that of the later methodological individualism. Smith lent philosophical support to the demands for freedom for individual initiative and enterprise by conceptualizing the 'nature' of the individual in terms of certain faculties and propensities that incline him to a social betterment even without his conscious design, and make society viable as a collectivity. Thus the pursuit of self-interest is divested of its ill-effects by the faculty of empathy and the desire for social approbation; balancing 'selfish' against 'social'. In the economic sphere, individual actions in pursuance of self-interest would be reconciled with the social requirements through the competition on the market, its punitive checks and encouraging rewards. No doubt, individual actions violating such restraints need to be countered. Hence Smith's ringing denunciation cf monopoly privileges and artificial checks on, and violations of, the free operations of the system. It would seem that the optimism of Smith concerning the capitalist system may have been prompted by his view that a compatible social morality which would make such a system viable would indeed develop.

Side by side with this 'social moralism' is also the historical materialist view that looked into the 'physiology of the bourgeois system'. In the essay 'Smith, Turgot and the four stages theory', Meek provides interesting material with which to trace this viewpoint which was popularized in Scotland and in France. Meek seeks to establish Adam Smith as the early progenitor, together with Turgot, the former having expounded it in his lectures at Edinburgh as early as in 1750–1 (pp. 18–32). In brief, the elements that comprised the four-stages theory, as summarized from Meek, are the following:

(1) It is possible to reason about historical and social developments in terms of rational causes and their effects.
(2) Society develops blindly, but not arbitrarily. While changes occur as a result of human action, they are not merely the execution of autonomous human design (here the Newtonian influence seems predominant). Social changes occur and in the process of change certain uniformities and regularities are observable. The task is to discover such laws of social development.
(3) The key factor in the process is the mode of subsistence. According to how that varies, laws and policies also vary.
(4) Emphasis is placed on the reciprocal interconnection between property and the form of government.

(5) The emergence and growth of social surplus is seen as the main stimulus to the rise of towns, the arts and manufactures, and a new social order (i.e., classes).

(6) Development is regarded as proceeding through four consecutive socio-economic stages, each based on a particular mode of subsistence: namely, hunting, pasturage, agriculture and commerce. To each stage correspond ideas and institutions, relating to property and government and, in relation to each, general statements can be made with regard to the accrual and distribution of the social surplus, the moral and legal system, the form of division of labour and so on.

It was this viewpoint of social development that led Smith to concentrate upon the division into classes, the magnitude of surplus and the factors affecting its growth. Meek points out that, in a sense, this viewpoint is a precursor of the later materialistic interpretation of history which found a fuller development in Marx, while recognizing that Marx's 'mode of production' was by no means the same as Smith's 'mode of subsistence'; Marx's sociology was completely emancipated from theology, whereas Smith's was not; and Marx's 'laws of motion of capitalism' acted maleficently, whereas Smith's 'by and large acted beneficently' (p. 15). However, we may note that Smith's materialistic view failed to be integrated with his 'moral system', leading to some ambivalencies in his analytical positions. While the materialist viewpoint led him to recognize the presence of contending classes, his moral system led him to stress the innate propensities of human nature working towards a viable social existence and harmony. This dual basis possibly prevented Smith from pursuing the logical outcome of the contending interests of the different classes, and from seeing the inevitable contradictions that the system would dialectically develop with its advancement (See Chapter 2 above).

The two subsequent essays on Smith (as is the one on the four-stages theory) are of primary interest to the historians of economic thought, as they pertain to some very interesting new material recently discovered: namely, a set of student's notes of the Glasgow lectures, which is attributed by Meek to the 1762–3 academic session, and notes by a professional colleague of Smith – John Anderson. Meek goes into a detailed and painstaking analysis of the documents, relating them to the set of notes published already by Cannan (1896). In view of their rather specialist interest, we shall refrain here from any detailed comments.

II

In Part II, the three essays address themselves to the so-called 'transformation problem' in Marx. The first offers a short non-technical account of the terms of the problem, followed by a survey of Marx's own attempt to transform values into prices and the rather more elaborate algebraic formulations addressed to the same question in the more recent writings of Bortkiewicz, Winternitz, Seton, Morishima and Meek. The second essay addresses itself to the controversial question of 'why Marx started with values' and whether the route was necessary for his basic propositions. The third, to the problem of whether the analysis does or does not possess a meaningful historical dimension.

That labour values deviate from competitive exchange values (under the uniformity of the rate of profit) was certainly not a discovery of Marx's critics. Adam Smith himself had rejected the labour-embodied values since prices were no more proportional to them under capitalist exchange, while he was unable to give any other consistent theory of prices. Ricardo, while criticizing the reason that Smith offered for abandoning the labour-embodied theory (namely, that the division of surplus into profits, rents, and wages, *by itself* was a sufficient cause for the divergence) went on to analyse the effects of a change in wage on exchange values arising from the differences within industries in their 'time' pattern of embodied labour (signified also by the ratio of means of production to labour and the different constituents of capitals). Ricardo's main concern was to show that the rate of profit was determined, once the wage-rate and the methods of production were given and hence the limits to profits were set by the conditions of production. Also that the rate of profits could only vary inversely with the wage. If the labour theory of value had worked accurately, he could demonstrate the propositions without any analytical difficulty, as the rate of profit would then emerge as a pure number with social net output, wages and social capital all reckoned in terms of labour values. With a change in the wage affecting the exchange values of these aggregates non-uniformly, the results could no more be demonstrated in that simple fashion. Therefore, the problem of deviation of prices from values appeared in Ricardo in a different form, and he sought its solution in the direction of a search for an 'invariant standard': he sought to express those aggregates in terms of a standard which would itself not vary in price with a change in the wage. Marx who, in addition to the above propositions of Ricardo, also sought to explain the origin of profit in surplus value, that is, in the exploitation of labour within the production process, formulated the transformation problem as one of 'transforming values into prices', separately defining values and prices.

The latter problem (namely, the source of surplus value) was analysed by Marx in terms of values; the distinction between labour and labour power permitted Marx to attribute the generation of surplus within the productive process through the exploitation of labour even under conditions of equivalent exchange where commodities exchanged according to values. The question as posed by Marx was: How can a surplus arise within a system where commodities exchange equivalently? He found the answer in the labour-power becoming historically a commodity paid according to its value, but which contributed a surplus to the value of the product. Knowing very well that prices deviated from values, if Ricardo and Marx carried out their analysis in terms of labour values, it was because they believed that the logical propositions they were interested in demonstrating, and which were transparently demonstrable in terms of labour values, would hold even when conducted in terms of prices. Marx openly posed the problem of transformation and attempted to demonstrate that it was soluble, although his solution was not satisfactory.

Hence one could say that the transformation problem can be discussed at two levels: the first and the rather less significant one, the algebraic problem of translating magnitudes of values into those of prices; and another, analytically more interesting one, namely demonstrating the validity of logical propositions, arrived at in the value framework, as well as within the prices framework as well. It was essentially the latter purpose that Ricardo and Marx (and we) should be interested in, although it is the first form - the algebraic conversion - that has dominated the discussions. Marx's own procedure which was based on an arithmetical transformation and contained errors (of some of which Marx was aware) has been responsible for a certain misleading emphasis on purely algebraic conditions. Meek gives Marx's procedure step by step; the incompleteness of Marx's procedure and its errors have by now been so extensively commented upon as not to warrant any detailed mention here. The later solutions, which are also widely known, offered by Bortkiewicz (1949 and 1952), Winternitz (1948), and Seton (1956–7) have revealed that the conditions which Marx postulated (total value = total price and total profits = total surplus value) cannot all be simultaneously satisfied in a general case. In fact, as Seton (1956–7) remarks, the selection of a definite aggregate (or other characteristic) of the value system which is to remain invariant to the transformation into prices remains open to the arbitrary choice of the analyst. If, however, one agrees with Meek that 'Marx's real concern was that profit is not determined by 'competition' or 'demand and supply' but the conditions of production, independently of and in a sense prior to prices' and that competition was a means of redistribution of the surplus according to the uniform rate of profits, then, as Bortkiewicz (1952) argues, the arithmetical equalities of total price to total value and total surplus value to total profit are not essential to the demonstration. Had such equalities also been regularly demonstrated to exist, no doubt, Marx's result would have had a perspicuity and simplicity. However, it is in the transformation of the logical results from the value to prices schema that one is more interested rather than in such 'invariances'.

In fact, it is this concern of transferring the logical results from values to prices schema that has inspired recent efforts. Attempts at solving the 'transformation' problem have revealed two alternative routes (see Garegnani, 1984). The works of Dmitriev (1974), Bortkiewicz (1952), and Garegnani (1984) have made use of some form of dated labour values to depict methods of production, and a given bundle of real wages constituting the 'wage sector'. Arguing on the basis of such a schema, the authors have drawn out fundamental results concerning the determination of profit within production, and the relations between wages and the rate of profits forming 'the inner connections of bourgeois relations' that Marx was so interested in exposing. Garegnani (1984) shows that Sraffa (1960) offers some implicit solutions to the transformation problem in alternative forms. He starts from the price-equations scheme, the simultaneous solution of prices and the rate of profit which contains an implicit transformation. Sraffa also employs the notion of the 'standard commodity' which allows him to determine the rate of profit and the inverse wage-profit relation without the intervention of prices. (See Garegnani, 1984 and Pasinetti, 1977.)

The question which naturally follows is posed by Meek in the following essay: 'Was Marx's journey really necessary?' As Meek observes, such issues have acquired a dimension out of all proportion since 'the particular attitude one takes towards them is widely supposed to be indicative of one's position on a whole number of other apparently quite unrelated questions' (p. 120). Meek disposes of, and rightly so, the rather less convincing arguments, such as that Marx was not really interested in prices and his theory of values was not intended to explain the level of prices (If so, why did Marx pursue the problem of transformation at all?) Or that, in Volume I of *Capital*, Marx uses values as approximations, implicitly assuming equal organic composition of capital (Meek offers textual evidence contrary to such a presumption). Meek's explanation is that Marx was anxious not to let the competitive processes (of 'equivalent exchange') disguise the origin of profits in exploitation.

> This process of the creation of surplus value was conceived by Marx as operating independently of, and in a sense prior to, the process of competition between capitalists in different industries which resulted in the formation of the final equilibrium prices of commodities ... It was vitally necessary, then, Marx believed, if the illusions created by competition were to be fully dispelled, to postulate the existence of a prior concrete magnitude – i.e. roughly, a magnitude which was independent of market [sic] prices – which could possibly be regarded as constituting the ultimate source of profit and rent and as limiting the aggregate level of these revenues. (pp. 126–7).

Meek, however, recognizes that this result could have been achieved, as recent approaches to the problem by Dmitriev, Bortkiewicz and Sraffa have demonstrated, by directly proceeding to what he calls commodity-production models (with methods of production specified in terms of physical means of production and labour, and a stipulated wage). Trying to answer the question of whether Marx's task could not have have been achieved by a suitable adaptation of the commodity-production models, Meek offers an interesting interpretation of what he calls 'Marxian-Sraffian commodity models' depicting institutional variants from simple commodity production to more complex ones and concludes, 'With the specification where necessary of the appropriate institutional Datum, then, and with remarkably little modification and elaboration, a sequence of Sraffian models can be made to do essentially the same job which Marx's labour theory of value was employed to do' (p. 133). He points out that there is scope to introduce the social and institutional factors in the distribution of income. The job is done even better as it is logically neat (see also Steedman, 1977). Does this imply that the value-based analysis has to be looked upon as having been unnecessarily diversionary and misleading?

Meek considers that the main reason why Marx thought that starting with values made good sense has to be sought in certain features of his economic methodology. Marx regarded, according to Meek, 'this transformation not simply as something which one worked out in one's mind, in the form of a chain of logical propositions, but also as something which, in a certain sense, had happened in history' (p. 129). Looking at capitalism from the perspective of a stadial scheme of development, Marx visualized capitalist production as a particular form of the system of commodity production, the logical starting point for which was the analysis of simple commodity production and circulation; values were thus not only theoretically but historically prior to prices of production. Meek is aware that this interpretation treads on the rather treacherous ground concerning the proper relation between history and logic and, in fact, in the next essay on the 'historical' transformation problem, he attempts to clarify and defend the notion of the 'logical-historical method' as applied to the transformation problem against the criticism of Morishima and Catephores (1975). The latter have challenged the historical existence of a value-regime (as an empirical historical reality). The discussion in Meek's last essay remains somewhat obscure and ambivalent. Meek concedes that to characterize the general method of Marx as logical-historical (that every logical stage in analysis corresponds sequentially to an actual historical stage in development) may be too much of a simplification. Meek notes that Marx himself pointed out that some categories in the logical analysis must be determined by 'their relation to one another in modern bourgeois society' rather than by the sequence 'in which they were historically decisive' which may precisely be the opposite. But, by and large, especially in his analysis of commodities, money and the transformation of values into prices, Meek believes that Marx can be interpreted as essentially following the logical-historical method. Hoewever, the interpretation of the latter method as applied to the transformation problem cannot be taken to mean that there in fact existed, in natural empirical history, a period when commodities exchanged according to values, and the rate of surplus value equalized under generalized exchange. Meek sees it as a process, the gradual transformation from a historical state of affairs where the majority of producers operated as simple commodity producers to another where capitalist commodity production was generalized.

While the present reviewer would be inclined to agree that the analytical significance and the interpretation of the labour theory of value has to be appreciated in a historical perspective, the interpretation that the transformation of values into prices of production is itself a historical process appears rather dubious. We may suggest here a way of looking at the problem. If one interprets the labour process as a general depiction of production, irrespective of the particular institutional form (capitalist or otherwise) in which it is instituted, then labour values may be looked upon as measuring the expenditure of human energies in the struggle with nature. Here, it must be noted that the term 'value' is used in a loose sense as a 'labour-embodied' measure and does not connote the prevalence of a value-regime with equalization of the rate of surplus value in all production. Each specific mode of production has its own form of exchange value determined by the mode of appropriation and distribution of the surplus. Through history, the labour process continues, but the form in which it is instituted changes, together with production relations. Within each abstracted category of the mode of production, there is the logical problem of establishing the relation between 'values' (in this general sense) and the particular *form* of exchange values (e.g., prices of production under capitalist production). The problem of transformation is entirely logical, although with each historical identification of the mode of production there would be a different specification of the problem depending upon the form of exchange value characterizing that mode.

Coming back to the question as to why it may have been or could be significant to work with labour values, we note that not only must the answer have logical validity, but also that one must not turn a blind eye to the analytical history. As to the first, it must be recognized that the surplus approach reformulated to rest on a modified value scheme (see Gareganani, 1984) yet survives, although Marx's own particular method of solving the transformation problem and some of the erroneous propositions following upon the faulty procedure have to be abandoned. It is the surplus approach which is fundamental to Marx's theory. Turning to the analytical history we must also recognize that the analytical results as to the origin of surplus value, its mode of appropriation and distribution were given an immediate transparency in terms of the value analysis. The surplus approach continues to have this advantage over the price-equations approach. As Marx was never tired of emphasizing, one had to enter into the realm of production, and the capital/labour relations therein, to understand how historically the possibility of the exploitation of labour within the bounds of competitive exchange had emerged. If one had started from the sphere of circulation, many of the propositions, that now, with hindsight, can be established using prices of production directly could not have been suggested, let alone sought to be established. The fact that the clamour to abandon the labour theory of value arose even before an alternative theory was cogently formulated, when class struggle became acute in the 1830s and the efforts of the opposition all went in the direction of trying to explain prices in terms of the interplay of supply-and-demand forces in circulation, shows that such obfuscation or total avoidance of the questions that interested Ricardo and Marx was not at all improbable.

More importantly, there is, in a sense, also a historical validation of theory in terms of interpreting actual experience and predicting future possibilities. Under competitive exchange, where each individual capitalist is subjected to the 'anarchy' of a competitive market, the capitalist's strategy is, in fact, concentrated in extending as far as possible the difference between the use-value of labour he has purchased and the value of labour power. Marx's masterly and detailed investigation of the means adopted by the capitalists to extend the working day in the phase of manufacture, and to increase the intensive exploitation through adoption of new technology in the phase of 'machinery' gives us a graphic analytico-historical description of capitalism at work. There appears a cogent explanation as to how successive strategies were actually adopted and why they had to be changed (e.g., why the Factory Laws limiting the working day became imminent when extracting 'absolute surplus value' became counter-productive and could be, in a regime of competing capitalists, controlled only collectively through legislation). The theory presented a scheme which afforded an analytical understanding of the historical experiences, so that they could be interpreted and future possibilities predicted on their basis.

III

In Part III Meek looks back on the Ricardian-Marxian stream of thought from the vantage point of the present. His contention is that in our own time this stream has reached a new point in Sraffa's work and, as a result, a great deal of history of value theory has now to be rewritten. It is certainly true that Sraffa's excellent edition of Ricardo's works and his subsequent *Production of Commodities by Means of Commodities* (which he subtitled 'prelude to a critique of economic theory') (1960) have thrown new light on classical theory. In particular, he has culled out a coherent body of theoretical propositions (specially in his commentaries on Ricardo) and, contrary to the opinions popularized in established history of thought, has advanced the view that the classical writers (Smith, Ricardo and Marx, in particular) indeed had developed a theoretical framework to discuss value and distribution to which a 'return' is worthwhile and which can be fruitfully reconstructed. Sraffa has thus shown that their efforts were not all chaotic, inconsistent and fragmentary to be seen, as Schumpeter (1954) did, as deviations from a more logically sustained development of theories based on 'utility and scarcity'.

Meek begins his critical review with Schumpeter's *History of Economic Analysis* (1954) which by its mass of scholarship has dominated the field. Meek's account here is somewhat autobiographical. Schumpeter had impressed upon his readers that Smith and Ricardo, in deviating from the traditional analysis of utility and scarcity, had introduced baneful influences. Ricardo, in particular, received trenchant criticism for having been blind to the nature and the logical place of supply-and-demand apparatus, to have ignored the rudiments of the equilibrium approach leading to Say and Walras, and for casting his analysis in terms of social classes rather than 'categories of economic types'. It is by now clear to us through Sraffa's work that the opposition to the then prevalent supply-and-demand apparatus in terms of classes were the necessary features of his logical approach, and Ricardo's analysis of profits involved explicit consideration of general interdependence, however, in an alternative economic framework.

Meek's discussion of the comparison of theoretical approaches is not quite satisfactory. He points out that all economic theories, whether Walrasian or Ricardian-Marxian, are based on some idea of general interdependence; the difference arises from an explanatory principle which underlines the causal directions. He identifies three principles underlying explanation of prices; the first explains prices in terms of man's activities and relations as a producer; the second explains prices on the basis of various demand and supply interactions, presenting price as an adding-up of different component parts of expenses or costs which, in turn, are explained in terms of demand and supply; the third explains prices in terms of man's activities and relations as a 'consumer'. The Ricardian-Marxian theory accepts the first, while the opponents of this school adopt the second and the third. This classification of theories is based upon the differences in relative emphasis on some component or the other of theories rather than according to the differences in their structure. The distinction between the theories resting on the second and the third 'explanatory' principles is, in fact, not so fundamental in the last analysis, although apparently so. Take, for example, the alleged differences in the Marshallian and the Austrian theories. Marshall himself and a number of Marshallians attached, no doubt, some significance to them. However, despite differences in emphasis and many a detail, it is obvious by now that both these approaches ultimately rely on the supply-and-demand explanations and face similar basic difficulties (e.g. in explaining distribution) within their framework. On the other hand, despite the 'adding up view' of Smith, he cannot be dubbed with the 'opponents' of the Ricardian-Marxian theory.

Such a presentation of 'alternative approaches' appears also to leave the matter rather undecided. It would seem almost as if one can choose one approach or the other according to one's personal taste or 'vision'. Meek does not raise the issue – which, however, is an important one – on what criteria does one adopt to accept/reject a theory in social sciences? Surprisingly, in this 'After Marx' section, Meek does not refer to the criticisms of the logical consistency of the supply-and-demand theories that have gradually come up, starting with Keynes. While logical consistency is one powerful mode of settling theoretical debates, for social theories, there must also be some criterion of historical vindication in terms of interpretation of experience. The return to political economy is to be favoured on both these grounds.

The short essay on 'Marginalism and Marxism' covers familiar ground, the rise of marginalism with its emphasis on market relations and abstraction from socio-economic relations between men as producers. Meek observes that the rise of the marginalism up to a point was a purely analytical affair, while no doubt it was also a reaction to the dominance of the labour theory and its inferences concerning class relations.

Thereafter, Meek treads on slippery ground, however. Relying on Lange (1963), Meek acknowledges the principle of economic rationality (that optimality consists in either the use of given means with maximum efficiency or given ends to be attained with minimum outlay of means) as the dominating and comprehensive principle contributed by marginal analysis. As a branch of praxiology, he sees its use in socialist economies where the principle can be applied and where Marxian political economy, with its concentration on capitalist relations, has much less to offer: 'it is precisely here that we have to bring in welfare economics, programming, operations research, cybernetics etc. – i.e., the whole panoply of praxiological principles which, as we have seen, is the end-product not of the Marxian but of the marginalist trend' (p. 174). This view is not entirely novel; it had its beginnings in the Lange–Lerner economics of control. We may remind ourselves of Maurice Dobb's critical reaction to the latter:

> Those who dream of marrying collectivism to economic anarchy must, at any rate, not pretend that the progeny of this strange match will inherit only the virtues of its ill-mated parents ... By an economic law one must mean a generalized description of how things actually behave in the real world. If this is our meaning, then it should be immediately clear that the alleged identity of the economic laws which rule a capitalist and a socialist economy is based on an abstract analogy...' (Dobb, 1972, p. 276)

There are two questions, furthermore. If it is purely mathematical techniques of optimization and cybernetics that are found to be practically useful, why call them 'marginalist', which has a definite economic-theoretic connotation?

Secondly, when these tools are borrowed as applied, say, in the current welfare economics, is there not an unavoidable danger that more would be acquiesced in, due to the very structure and framework in which the problem is cast, than is essential for the facility of using the techniques? Are we not already familiar with such muddles as in talking of the 'social rate of return' surreptitiously to explain capitalist rate of profit because, in some sense, it is believed that 'perfect competitive markets' and 'socialist planning' converge? The definitions of 'efficiency', 'optimality', 'rationality' would have specific theoretic connotations which may creep in if one is not only applying the techniques (which surely are not the monopoly of any particular economic theory), but also model their usage on the basis of their current applications in marginalist theory.

Professor Meek has raised many significant and controversial questions in this book which should continue to stimulate further debate. With the resurgence of classical and Marxian theory emerging as a powerful theoretical alternative, Professor Meek's endeavours to present systematically the important landmarks in the classics – the works of the Physiocrats, Turgot, the precursors of Smith and now Smith – will prove invaluable. As Professor Meek indicates in this last work, much of the analytical history of economic thought as recorded hitherto calls for a new interpretation, and he himself will stand out as one of the early pioneers in that attempt.

Notes: Chapter 9

This review article of Ronald Meek's last essays, *Smith, Marx and After* (1977) was published, as a tribute to a great scholar and a much-loved teacher and colleague, in *Australian Economic Papers* (December 1980), pp. 349–63. An earlier version of the article was published in *Economic and Political Weekly*, vol. 13 (1978), pp. 839–46. I had the privilege of discussing an earlier draft of this article with Professor Ronald Meek barely a month before his sudden demise.

References: Chapter 9

Bharadwaj, K. (1979), 'The historical conditioning of theory: a study of Adam Smith's political economy', *Studies in History*, Vol 1, no. 1 (January-June), pp. 45–72 (Chapter 2 in the present volume).

Bharadwaj, K. (1978), 'The subversion of classical analysis: Alfred Marshall's early writing on value', *Cambridge Journal of Economics*, vol. 2, no. 3 (September), pp. 253–71; Chapter 6 in the present volume.

Bortkiewicz, L. von (1907 [1949]), 'On the correction of Marx's fundamental theoretical construction in the third volume of *Capital*', in Paul Sweezy (ed.), *Karl Marx and the Close of His System* (New York: A. M. Kelley).

Bortkiewicz, L. von (1952), 'Value and price in the Marxian system', *Economic Papers*, no. 2. pp. 5–60.

Cannan, E. (ed.), (1896) *Lectures on Justice, Police, Revenue and Arms* (Oxford: Oxford University Press).

Dobb, M. H. (1972), *Political Economy and Capitalism*, 2nd edn (London: Routledge).

Dobb, M. H. (1973), *Theories of Value and Distribution since Adam Smith* (Cambridge: Cambridge University Press).

Dmitriev, V. K. (1974), *Economic Essays on Value, Competition and Utility*, ed. by D. M. Nuti (Cambridge: Cambridge University Press).

Garegnani, P. (1960), *Il capitale nelle teorie della distribuzione* (Milan: Giuffre).

Garegnani, P. (1984), 'Value and distribution in the Classical Economists and Marx', *Oxford Economic Papers*, vol. 36, pp. 291–325.

Marshall, A. (1920), *Principles of Economics*, 8th edn (London: Macmillan).

Marx, Karl (1971), *Capital*, 3 vols (London: Lawrence & Wishart).

Marx, Karl (1862–3 [1963–71]), *Theories of Surplus Value, 3 Parts* (Moscow: Progress Publishers).

Meek, R. L. (1950), 'The decline of Ricardian economics in England', *Economica*, vol. 17, no. 1 (February) pp. 43–62.

Meek, R. L. (1967), *Economics and Ideology and Other Essays* (London: Chapman & Hall).

Meek, R. L. (1976), *Social Science and the Ignoble Savage* (Cambridge: Cambridge University Press).

Meek, R. L. (1977), *Smith, Marx and After* (London: Chapman & Hall).

Morishima, M., and Catephores, G. (1975), 'Is there an "historical transformation problem"?' *Economic Journal*, vol. 85, no. 85 (June) pp. 309–27.

Lange, Oscar, (1963) *Political Economy*, Vol I, translated by A. H. Walker (New York: Pergamon Press).

Morishima, M. (1973), *Marx's Economics: A Dual Theory of Value and Growth* (Cambridge: Cambridge University Press).

Pasinetti, L. L. (1977), *Lectures on the Theory of Production* (London: Macmillan).

Pigou, A. C. (ed.) (1925), *Memorials of Alfred Marshall* (London: Macmillan).

Ricardo, D. (1951) *Principles of Political Economy*, Vol. I of *Works and Correspondence of David Ricardo*, ed. by P. Sraffa (Cambridge: Cambridge University Press). Also Vol. IV of the same *Works*.

Samuelson, P. A. (1971), 'Understanding the Marxian notion of exploitation: a summary of the so-called transformation problem between Marxian values and competitive prices', *Journal of Economic Literature*, vol. 9, no. 2 (June), pp. 399–432.

Schumpeter, J. A. (1954), *History of Economic Analysis* (London: Allen & Unwin).

Seton, F. (1956–7), 'The transformation problem', *Review of Economic Studies*, vol. 24, no. 64, pp. 149–60.

Smith, Adam (1776 [1930]), *An Inquiry into the Nature and Causes of the Wealth of Nations*, 5th edn, ed. by E. Cannan (London: Methuen).

Smith, Adam (1793), *The Theory of Moral Sentiments* in Dugald Stewart (ed.), *Essays on Philosophical Subjects by the late Adam Smith* (Edinburgh: A & C Black).

Smith, Adam (1896), *Lectures on Justice, Police, Revenue and Arms*, ed. by E. Cannan (Oxford: Clarendon Press).

Sraffa, P. (1951), Editorial Introduction to *Works and Correspondence of David Ricardo*, Vol. I (Cambridge: Cambridge University Press).

Sraffa, P. (1960), *Production of Commodities by Means of Commodities; Prelude to a Critique of Economic Theory* (Cambridge: Cambridge University Press).

Steedman, I. (1977), *Marx after Sraffa* (London: New Left Books).

Walras, Leon (1874) [1954] *Elements of Pure Economics*, translated by William Jaffe (London: Allen & Unwin).

Winternitz, J. (1948), 'Value and prices: a solution of so-called transformation problem', *Economic Journal*, vol. 58 (June) pp. 276–80.

10
Sraffa's Return to Classical Theory

In the preface to his *Production of Commodities* (1960), Sraffa revealed the dual objectives pursued by him in that work (subtitled, 'Prelude to a critique of economic theory'): one was a return to the approach of the old classical economists from Adam Smith to Ricardo and the other, to provide the basis for a critique of the marginalist theory. A unique and impressive feature of the book is that a set of basic propositions are developed designed to serve both these tasks and they effectively reveal the contrasting structures and standpoints of the two theoretical – 'classical' and 'marginal' – approaches.

Sraffa himself identifies his 'return to the classical ways of thought' thus:

> The investigation is concerned exclusively with such properties of an economic system as do not depend on the changes in the scale of production or in the proportions of 'factors' (p.v);

or, that it examines 'the conditions of production in a given situation irrespective of whether constant or variable returns prevail'.

Sraffa adds:

> This standpoint, which is that of the old classical economists from Adam Smith to Ricardo has been submerged and forgotten since the advent of the 'marginal' method ... the marginal approach required attention to be focused on change, for without change either in the scale of an industry or in the 'proportions of the factors of production' there can be neither marginal product nor marginal cost. (ibid, p. V)

The second feature of the 'return' to the classical standpoint is 'to regard production as a circular process in which the same kind of commodities appear both among the means of production and among the products – rather than as a process beginning with "factors of production" and ending with consumption goods, a "one way avenue" of the "modern" theory.' (See Appendix D, p. 93.)

The particular standpoint adopted by Sraffa in this 'investigation of properties of an economic system that do not depend upon change', has often been misinterpreted, prompted by the habitual modes of marginalist thought, as connoting an avowed admission of the assumption of 'stationarity' which rules out a priori changes in the system, or else as presuming 'invariance' in the face of exogenous changes. The latter is evident in the reading of the Sraffa system as a particular case of general equilibrium under conditions when the 'non-substitution theorem' is applicable.) It has also prompted a number of authors to look upon Sraffa's theory as an abstract 'intellectual experiment'. At the same time, the marginalist theory, with its focus on 'changes', apparently bestows generality and flexibility on the conditions defining the system. Notwithstanding this, paradoxically as it may seem, there have been a growing unease, ambivalent admissions and sometimes protests against the sterility of the neoclassical (demand-and-supply-based-equilibrium) theory even among its practitioners; in particular, against its incapacity to handle effectively even descriptive interpretations of historical experience, let alone predictions based thereupon. This state of affairs points to the need for a clear comprehension of the implications of Sraffa's distinction between the 'classical' and the 'marginal' methods and the distinctiveness of his critique.

Criticisms of the mainstream theory have arisen from various quarters and viewpoints.[1] Our attempt, in this essay, will be to argue that the analytical inadequacies, as well as the ahistoricity that appears to plague the mainstream theory, arise from the *specific structure* of the theory of value and distribution based on demand and supply. We also note that writers of very different persuasions have acknowledged that Smith, Ricardo and Marx incorporated elements of historical change into their theoretical schemes, particularly in their analysis of accumulation, technical change and distributive relations. We attempt here to trace these differences in perspectives to differences in the *structures* of the surplus-based classical theory and of the supply-and-demand-based equilibrium theory, following certain suggestive hints and ideas from Sraffa's constructive and critical writings.[2]

Our discussion on the distinctiveness of the *structures* of theories concentrates on the theory of value and distribution which also appears to be the central theme in Sraffa's critical and constructive writings. The theory of value, for very different reasons, acquired analytical importance in the two theories: the particular *structure* of neoclassical theory wherein all *prices* (including 'factor prices') *and quantities* were simultaneously determined, led to the 'value theory taking the centre of the stage'. In the classical theory an explanation of value that was consistent with the surplus-based explanation of the rate of profit acquired critical importance for the theory.[3] The contrasting structures of the two theoretical approaches are best revealed in their theories of value and distribution which are at the foundation of the theory of accumulation. We also note the crucial significance of the theory of distribution in the history of economic theories, acting as a prime mover that propelled them in new directions, leading to the acceptance of some, and the abandonment of other, frameworks – sometimes so even prematurely.[4]

In the following we explore the differences in the structures of the two theories. In Section 1, we discuss briefly some developments in the formation of neoclassical theory which, in fact, constituted radical departures from the earlier classical theory, although they often appeared covertly as modifications or extensions. While not attempting to offer here a comprehensive account of all the changes in theory during the transitional stage, we focus particularly on those that seemingly maintained a semblance of 'continuity' in theory, creating thereby a false appearance of gains in generality and rigour. These radical departures rather than 'modifications' rendered the theory increasingly rigid and incapable of dealing with the complexity and diversity of the nature and causes of changes in economic activities.

A continuity in theoretical developments was vehemently asserted by Marshall.[5] It is in Marshall that we see attempts at reconciling elements drawn from the two theories, leading to contradictions. In him we also note conscious awareness of the alternative theoretical positions which he attempted to forge together and an occasional recognition – even if garbed and cautious – of the theoretical troubles so concealed. The reason for Sraffa's critical attacks on Marshall's theory appears mainly due to the latter's strategic position in the theoretical transition.[6] For this reason, we too would have frequent references to Marshall in the following when we attempt to trace how the domain of the demand-and-supply-based theoretical model got progressively extended to cover all economic spheres and, consequently, led to the dictatorship of the relative-price-based, scarce-resources-allocational scheme. In particular, we shall attempt to trace how the 'reductionist' approach (i.e. reducing all collective or 'market' phenomena to individuals' choices) and the quantity-price-response mechanisms presumed in the demand-and-supply based equilibrium theory got progressively extended to cover all spheres of economic decisions and all phenomena of economic change.

In Section 2 we shall outline some consequences of such analytical extensions and of attempts at constructing symmetries on theoretical notions such as 'change', 'competition' and 'equilibrium'. In Section 3 we shall briefly consider the relatively more open character of the classical structure which renders it more flexible to deal with a wider range of historical changes, and shall indicate some of the misinterpretations that have crept in because of an insufficient appreciation of the distinctive character of the classical structure.

1   The Two Structures and the Transition

The classical approach to which Sraffa seeks a return is centred on the process of generation, appropriation and distribution of surplus and its accumulation, mainly in the context of a competitive capitalist economy, where competition is characterized by the active tendency towards a uniform rate of profit and wages.[7] The theory of prices emerged in this approach as an important prerequisite for a consistent explanation of the rate of profit.[8] Proceeding to make an important distinction between 'temporary' or 'accidental', and 'persistent' or 'stable' economic forces influencing prices, the classical writers distinguished between the 'market prices' (or, the actually observed prices), and the 'natural prices' (or the central prices around which 'market prices' oscillate). The 'natural prices' (or the 'prices of production', the form in which they occur in Sraffa's *Production of Commodities*) are those prices compatible with the condition of a uniform rate of profit and wage, under given 'effectual demand', the observed methods of production in use and given wage. Without repeating the rather well-known ground,[9] we shall only point out some features of the theory relevant to our purpose. First, it is the material and social conditions of production (as reflected in the observed methods of production), along with the level of wages, (determined by social and historical conditions) that determine prices. This is consistent with the rule of surplus distribution (here, the rule of uniformity of the rate of profit) among the surplus sharers (here, the capitalists). The level and composition of social output, as well as methods of production, are determined prior to prices, in the sense that it is acknowledged that factors determining output levels and composition, methods of production in use and the pace of accumulation, are not entirely subsumed within the domain of price determination. This is not to deny or even undermine the interdependence and interaction between levels of output (and changes therein), distribution and technology, but to recognize that such interrelations are considered diverse and complex enough to require deeper analysis outside the core of the price theory.[10] This implies, in the first instance, a sequential separation of the analysis of quantities from that of prices. In contrast, the currently dominant supply-and-demand equilibrium theory simultaneously explains prices of commodities, as well as distribution ('factor prices'), along with the quantities (output and factor utilizations which, in equilibrium, are fully utilized). It does so within the theoretical structure of given supplies of 'factors of production', given technological transformation possibilities, and given the structure of preferences. Under certain assumptions, the required kinds of price-quantity relations are expected to be generated through a choice behaviour resting on the relative-prices-guided principle of substitution. First, all economic magnitudes are thus determined through the interplay of the forces of demand and supply presumably leading to an equilibrium. Secondly, economic forces operating to determine these are taken to be reducible, comprehensively and consistently, to domains of individual choices.

Many proponents of the general equilibrium theory would consider their theoretical scheme to be the most general and rigorous one, and the classical scheme to be a sub-system, thus proposing a common theoretical structure. It will be interesting, therefore, to turn to the evolution of the present theory and its radical departures from the older framework.

Generalization of the Rent Principle

The classical theory of rent (Malthusian in origin and adopted by Ricardo)[11] became the fountainhead for most basic marginalist ideas. The idea of differential rents, cast into the mould of 'the principle of diminishing marginal returns' (accruing to the 'doses of capital and labour' applied to a fixed 'factor', i.e., land) was extended into directions and put to theoretical purposes different from those envisaged by the classical originators of the theory. As Sraffa points out (1925, 1926), in the classical approach, the theory of rent appeared under distribution, where land, a non-reproducible social asset was taken as fixed in supply to the whole community, in the sense that land of uniform quality was limited.[12] Further, 'it had always been perfectly obvious that its operation (i.e. of diminishing returns) affected not merely rent but also the cost of the product: but this was not emphasized as a cause of variation in the relative price of the individual commodities produced' (1926, p. 182). To the extent that diminishing returns was reflected in the difficulty of production, requiring higher labour input per unit of output, the value increased. But no general and functional association between output and cost was derived therefrom which was applicable to all commodities.[13]

The general notion of the law of decreasing returns appeared to have been derived in two steps. First, was the near-elimination of the distinction between the 'extensive' and the 'intensive' case and the eventual dominance of the latter as a generalized principle. The classical theory, directed to the explanation of rents rather than the prices of individual commodities, rested more predominantly on the extensive case of the simultaneous cultivation of lands of different fertilities or qualities. No doubt, the intensive case was also referred to, but only with some hesitation (see, Sraffa, *Works*, IV, p. 14). While the differential productivities of lands of different qualities were directly observable in a single situation, the 'marginal product' of the marginal dose referred to an incremental output attributable to a potential additional 'dose', requiring hypothetical 'change' in the situation. The marginal dose, no different from any other, was identified as such due to its ordered position in successive application, involving thus a change in the situation.[14]

Secondly, this subtle shift towards intensive margins implied an important change in the method of analysis – a shift from 'observable' to 'potential' or hypothetical changes. This facilitated the illegitimate generalization and construction of symmetry between land and other factors, and an analysis in terms of potential changes and variable proportions of factors. The generalization proceeding from the case of land as a fixed 'factor' led to the general assumption of given factor endowments, thus extinguishing a distinction, crucial to the classical writers, between non-reproducible and reproducible resources. 'The Ricardian law of rent ... is the first great example of the marginal method, later to become the key-stone of the entire Austrian system of economic theory', remarks J. M. Clark (1931, quoted by Sraffa, *Works*, IV, p. 6, n. 3). Jevons, who was critical of Ricardo's system and announced its closure, conceded:

There are many portions in economical doctrines which appear to me as scientific in form as they are consonant with facts. I would especially mention the themes of population and rent, the latter a theory of a distinctly mathematical character which seems to give a clue to the correct mode of treating the whole science. (Jevons, 1871 [1971], p. 43)

The Laws of Returns and the Supply Schedule

Another instance of altering an inherited notion so as to force it into the strait-jacket of a supply schedule, functionally linking unit costs and output, was Marshall's attempt to co-opt and co-ordinate the laws of increasing returns along with that of decreasing returns. This process of co-opting the idea into a different theory led to a drastic change in the content and scope of the law of increasing returns itself. As Sraffa (1926, p. 182) comments: 'The position occupied in classical economics by the law of increasing returns was much less prominent as it was regarded merely as an important aspect of the division of labour and thus rather as a result of general economic progress than of an increase in the scale of production.' For Adam Smith, division of labour was an important source, as much as a consequence, of technical changes and of extensions of the market (or, of accumulation, putting it more generally). This meant that the notion of increasing returns could no longer be confined to the scale of an individual industry, but would be connected with a whole group of interrelated industries; and the unit cost of output in an industry could not be linked to changes in its output alone. Marshall himself devoted much attention to this aspect of the problem in his early work, *Pure Theory* (1879 [1930]), where he saw the more significant economies arising from the localization and geographical conglomeration of industries, but put increasing returns on a different footing in his later work (see Bharadwaj, 1972, Chapter 7 in the present volume). Marshall introduced the notion of externalities; Sraffa (1926) demonstrated how logic would then confine increasing returns to the implausible case where there were 'external economies', external to the firm and internal to the industry. The tortuous course of these attempts did not lead to a satisfactory resolution, and Sraffa's trenchant critique of Marshall's supply curve demonstrated the contradictions they ran into (see, Sraffa, 1925, 1926 and 1930). Furthermore, there was the problem of irreversibilities. Economies once achieved through such general economic progress (or even expansion of the industry) could hardly recede, even if the output of the individual industry were to decline. This implied, as Marshall himself realized, the impossibility of moving backwards and forwards on the same supply curve and suggested a redrawing of the curve whenever 'great additional economies are introduced' (Marshall, 1879 [1930], p. 30). If such advice was to be followed, however, the supply schedule could be only a 'historical curve', describing events *ex post facto* (see, Bharadwaj, 1972, Chapter 7 in the present volume) and could not remain a predictive theoretical supply curve as required for the determination of equilibrium. Thus the phenomenon of increasing returns created a number of logical hurdles, jeopardizing the assumption of competition, challenging the meaningfulness of the supply curve for the industry, and endangering the mechanistic postulate of reversible movements along the supply curve. Marshall, aware of the problems, remained more cautious about his supply curve than about his demand curve, on which he also had certain reservations (see, Bharadwaj, ibid.).

In the theory of the firm, the notion of monopolistic competition attempted to meet only a part of the difficulty – namely, that created by the irreconcilability of increasing returns with competition. But, as is well known, the easier way adopted was to exclude, through an assumption, increasing returns and postulate convexity conditions, which Koopmans (1957) concedes:

> Such assumptions can lay no general claim to realism ... the principal reason for making a convexity assumption lies not in its degree of realism but in the present state of our knowledge ... [it] enables us to state minimum assumptions for the validity of important parts of existing economic theory thus helping to reduce this part of our knowledge to its logical and mathematical essentials (p. 25).

We must note here, however, that Sraffa's critique is directed not so much against the lack of realism of the theory, but to its logical consistency (see Sraffa, 1930, p. 93 quoted below).

Symmetrical Theory of Demand

The notion of a demand schedule – wherein, given the preferences of the consumer and his budget constraint, quantities of a good demanded are obtained as a function of prices – did not exist in classical theory. Adam Smith's 'effectual demand' was a 'central' position depicting the average state of social demand in the economy. The first deviant but uncertain steps towards a functional relation between price and quantity demanded were taken by J. S. Mill when he tried to relate quantitatively use-values and exchange values, following the suggestion of De Quincey (see Bharadwaj, 1978b). The demand and supply schedules so constructed as symmetric but opposite forces provided the foundation for a new theory of equilibrium. While the principle of diminishing marginal utility appears to have been prompted by a recourse to the individual's psychology, its use as one blade of a pair of scissors appears to have been strengthened, as by Marshall (see *Principles*, 1920, pp. 356–7), on the analogy of diminishing returns on land. For example, while Marshall held that the demand function rested on the 'self evident', 'fundamental and universal' principle of diminishing marginal utility, he wrote:

> This law [of satiable wants or of diminishing utility] holds a priority of position to the law of *diminishing returns* from land which however has the priority in time; since it was the first to be subjected to a rigid analysis of semi-mathematical character. And if, by anticipation we borrow some of its terms, we may say that the

return of pleasure which a person gets from each additional *dose* of a commodity diminishes till at last a margin is reached at which it is no longer worth his while to acquire any more of it (ibid., p. 93, fn. 1)

Marshall, however, also claimed that the tendency of diminishing utility had its roots in the qualities of human nature, while that of diminishing returns had roots in the technical conditions of industry (ibid., p.70). Sraffa (1925) questions the apparent dichotomy. Is it not strange, he asks, that two such heterogeneous elements as human nature and industrial technology should bring about results so similar and, even more improbable, that the tendency towards diminishing returns reflecting technical conditions should operate alike in a large number of very different industries and even in the 'production of utility'! The resemblance arises from the common premise about the behaviour of individuals and the presumed operation of the 'substitution' principle. Diminishing returns and diminishing utility both presuppose the operation of the principle of substitution when the individual (producer or consumer), optimizing his returns (profits or utility), ranks the alternatives open to him according to returns and allocates his limited, given resources. This ranking of alternatives does not arise due to material/technical necessity for which the uses must follow a particular sequence. They call into question difficult problems of a priori ranking of value magnitudes: in fact, as Sraffa (1960) was to demonstrate, no such ranking of methods of production according to 'factor-intensities', invariant with respect to distribution, could be made as it involved the reckoning of capital as a value magnitude.

In his introduction of the demand schedule, Marshall expressed some equivocation both in the text of *Principles* and, characteristically, in the footnotes and appendices. Unlike Jevons, who declared that the introduction of the utility-based demand was a break with earlier tradition, Marshall tried to present a semblance of continuity. He explained: 'Until recently, the subject of demand or consumption has been somewhat neglected' (*Principles*, 1920, p. 84). In the first edition (1890) he continued the text with the following sentence (dropped from the second edition onwards): 'The prominent place which consumption has received in the programme of the science has not been justified by any attempt to examine it carefully. Nor has this neglect been altogether accidental'; and to this was appended the footnote: 'James Mill indeed called a large part of his *Elements of Political Economy* by the title 'consumption', but it is really occupied almost exclusively with an inquiry into the principles of Taxation.' This indicates, we may observe here, that what dominated the analysis was the effects of changes in individual prices on consumption which were consequent upon, say, a tax, but that there was no generalized theory of demand, functionally linking demand to prices. Indeed, 'effectual demand' did play a significant role in their analysis so that the 'neglect' or 'absence of the demand factor' is to be understood only as the absence of a neoclassical demand function.

Marshall explains the 'comparative neglect' thus: 'For important as is the enquiry how to turn our resources to the best account, it is not one which lends itself, so far as the expenditure of private individuals is concerned, to the methods of economics.' He believed that 'The common sense of a person who has had a large experience of life will give him more guidance in such a matter than he can gain from subtle economic analyses ...' In fact, the three reasons that Marshall offers to explain the prominence acquired later by demand theory do not relate to this difficulty at all. The first is the growing belief that 'harm was done by Ricardo's habit of laying disproportionate stress on the side of cost of production when analysing the causes that determine exchange value'.[15] Secondly, the growth of exact mathematical habits of thought is mentioned and, thirdly, Marshall writes:

> the spirit of the age induces a closer attention to the question whether our increasing wealth may not be made to go further than it does in promoting the general well-being; and this again compels us to examine how far the exchange value of any element of wealth, whether in collective or individual use, represents accurately the addition which it makes to happiness and well-being. (*Principles*, 1920, p. 85)

It is this last question of welfare through price-guided resource allocation (which was not a question which concerned the classicals) that appears to have been important to Marshall. He was to construct the doctrine of 'maximum satisfaction', attained through the balancing of real costs and utilities by individuals. Thus the introduction of demand was an important element in the reductionist programme, seeking to demonstrate that efficient resource-allocation is achieved through the individual choices of the profit-maximizing producers and utility-maximizing consumers. The theoretical demand schedule was based not so much on observation as hypothetical attributes of demand behaviour and, if Marshall ultimately reduced consumption behaviour to utility calculus, despite his strong reservations (see below), it appears to have been dictated by the theoretical need for constructing such a demand schedule which in conjunction with the 'symmetric and opposite' supply schedule would yield the equilibrium prices and outputs.

Nevertheless, as in other instances, Marshall was not very comfortable with the break in tradition. He devoted quite a few pages to describing 'the variety of human wants, considered in their relation to human efforts and activities', where he was to make a verbal obeisance to civilization's 'desire for variety for its own sake', its 'craving for distinction and excellence', and its wants resulting from activities, habits and customs which were prompted by class distinctions, etc. He also gave an explicit warning against the tide sweeping in favour of the prominence of the 'demand' side.

> It is important still to assert the great truth on which they [the classicals] dwelt somewhat too exclusively: viz, that while wants are

the rulers of life among lower animals, it is to the changes in the form of effort and activities that we must turn when in search for the keynotes of the history of mankind. (1920, p. 85).

He was to repeat his warning,[16] maintaining that 'much that is of chief interest in the science of wants is borrowed from the science of efforts and activities'. But, as was characteristic of Marshall, he proceeded with his theory of demand – 'an elementary analysis of an almost purely formal kind'. Occasional warnings were given in short hints (e.g., in the Appendix on notes on statistics of consumption) referring to the importance of changes in incomes rather than prices in explaining changes in consumption. It is well to remember that the classical writers did indeed put more emphasis on the influence of income changes on demand than of the relative price variations.

Marshall's substantive contribution remained 'the purely formal kind'. For example, despite reservations, he proceeded to the construction of the notion of consumer's surplus. A rigorous extension of his theory of the doctrine of maximum satisfaction in the hands of Pigou[17] could not but expose the vulnerability of the theoretical construction. Similarly, in the case of the extension of Marshall's 'representative firm' into the 'equilibrium firm', Pigou drew out the rigorous consequences of what Marshall had left tentative and vague. The latter's biological analogies could not be integrated into his formal theoretical constructions which prompted Sraffa to conclude his debate with Robertson on the 'representative firm' thus:

> I am trying to find out what are the assumptions implicit in Marshall's theory: if Mr. Robertson regards them as extremely unreal, I sympathise with him. We seem to be agreed that the theory cannot be interpreted in a way which makes it logically self-consistent and, at the same time, reconcile it with facts it sets out to explain. Mr. Robertson's remedy is to discard mathematics, and he suggests that my remedy is to discard the facts. Perhaps I ought to have explained that, in the circumstances, I think it is Marshall's theory that should be discarded. (1930, p. 93)

It would seem, therefore, that the new theory of demand, constructing the demand schedule as symmetric and opposite to the supply schedule, moved away from the richness and variety of consumption behaviour. Moreover, the theory was not prompted by practical observation but by theoretical necessity. Akin to the redefinitions, modifications and increasingly restrictive assumptions that have accrued on the supply side, similar developments are occurring in the demand theory in the form of 'income effects', 'demonstration effects', 'hysterisis effects', 'process of learning', 'quality of life', etc.

The New Structure of Value and Distribution Theory
The marginalist theory thus created an altogether new structure for the explanation of value and distribution. Both relative prices of commodities

and prices of 'factors of production' resulted from the equilibrium between the forces of demand and supply which also determined, simultaneously with prices, the quantities of output and the (full) utilization of the factors. The theory assumed as its data the factor endowments, technological possibilities and preferences. In conceiving the existence of such an equilibrium, the theory had to stipulate appropriate restrictions on the supply-and-demand relations. *The theory needed to hypothesize properties of the system at the equilibrium position in terms of 'marginal' magnitudes of quantities and thus invoke hypothetical changes in the system. Further, these changes were supposed to be entirely governed by the economic principle of substitution. In particular, the substitution principle must so operate that 'well-behaved' supply-and-demand relations are generated.* In some cases (such as the prevalence of increasing returns) the difficulty was set aside by suitable assumptions or, in other cases, by hypothesizing particular conditions (such as the dominance of the substitution effects over income effects in demand).

The difficulty could not be avoided in the case of the demand function for capital. Capital which constituted heterogeneous produced means of production could not be conceived, as the neoclassical theory required, as a *magnitude* given independently of the distribution (i.e., of the rate of profit). The operation of the principle of substitution among 'factors' consequently failed to ensure the required demand function for capital, inversely relating capital-intensity to the rate of profit. These difficulties on the demand side were sufficient to demolish the explanation of the rate of profit, even while ignoring additional difficulties that could also arise on the 'supply side'. The difficulty arose not only in the more obvious case (which has been conceded more readily in recent controversies) in the versions of marginalist theory explaining distribution by means of an aggregate production function, à la J. B. Clark, but also in the general case of many commodities and general equilibrium. In the latter case, a measurement of capital endowment as a value magnitude is equally required (as in Wicksell) to make the assumption of capital endowment as a datum consistent with long-period equilibrium characterized by the uniform rate of profit (see Garegnani, 1960 and 1978). We shall not enter here into a detailed discussion of the subject, but may mention as germane to our theme of transitions in theory, the attempts of the Austrians and Fisher to resolve the question of the rate of profit. Some of the novel elements they introduced or highlighted within the overall structure of the marginalist theory have been used by later writers as a ground to introduce further radical conceptual shifts to a new notion of equilibrium (see below).

The Austrian Approach: The One-Way Avenue
The Austrian approach was characterized by two elements. First, the notion of the supremacy of demand, as reflected in the hierarchical ordering of commodities in relation to final consumption – the explicit one-way avenue of production. Essentially turning round the logic of the classical theory that the price of a commodity is built up from the

requisites of production, the Austrians derived the value of intermediate goods (and 'factors') from their contribution to final utility. Thus a 'time structure' entered into their valuation process. The second element was their attempt to reduce capital to invested land and labour which also introduced a 'time structure' in the depiction of their production process. However, a central question they addressed themselves to was the determination of the rate of profit within the supply-and-demand framework. While the reduction of capital to invested land and labour allowed them to avoid the use of capital as a value magnitude in the representation of the production possibilities (as Wicksell did), the requirement of having to represent capital endowment as a datum independent of distribution could not be avoided or consistently resolved by either Bohm Bawerk or Wicksell. Bohm Bawerk's attempt to isolate the period of production as a unit of time independent of distribution was simply a search for a proxy for capital-intensity. Sraffa (1960) demonstrated that such a measure could not be constructed, even in the case of capital consisting entirely of circulating capital.[18]

Extension of the Principle of Substitution to Intertemporal Analysis
It was, however, in Fisher that the attempt to represent all commodities and 'factors' as congealing 'events' or 'flows of incomes' was fully extended to supplant the notion of costs of production altogether, with each 'good' merely a depository of 'income flow' over time.[19] Fisher's view, like the Austrians, emphasized the subjective or 'psychological' elements in value[20] and treated time as 'the great independent variable of human experience'. Fisher insistently denies the existence of the 'cost of production in its objective sense and offers instead the principle of "present worth" which made the value of any article of wealth or property dependent on the future alone'.[21] He argued: 'When prices find their normal level at which costs plus interest are covered, it is not because the past costs of production have determined prices in advance, but because the sellers have been good speculators as to what prices would be' (1906, p. 188). Thus Fisher shifted all economic accounting to the future. Fisher's concern, however, like the Austrians', was with the explanation of the long-run rate of profit as the rate of return, and his attempt also met a capital-theoretic difficulty (see Pasinetti, 1969). *In terms of the arena of supply-and-demand relations, this view extended their operation freely into the future*. In fact, it was a complete reversal of the classical causation, as Fisher himself put it.[22] What needed to be anticipated here was to envisage the entire stream of future incomes and equilibrium as being established *through the substitution principle operating intertemporally*.[23]

Our focus in the above rapid review was on indicating how the demand-and-supply approach was successively extended so that it could be applied to economic activities and spheres of diverse kinds. Consequently, analytical symmetries were illegitimately imposed through choosing assumptions which were *not derived on the basis of historical observation, but were merely postulates required for the theory*. Not only was the choice problem of allocating given resources to alternative uses generalized to all spheres but the 'reductionist' programme was adopted simultaneously. With the theory of distribution co-opted within the relative pricing, the choice model was presented entirely in terms of individuals' intentions and decisions, and was presumed to generate consistent 'market' (collective) behaviour at the macro-level. The capital theory debate has brought out the fallacy of explaining the general rate of profit in terms of the supply-and-demand framework through merely inverting the choice-of-technique problem posed for the individual producer, for whom prices and wages are assumed to be parametrically given. Keynes, as is well known, exposed the 'fallacy of composition' when he questioned the theory's result that competitive equilibrium would lead to the equalization of savings and investment at full employment.

2 Altered Scope and Content of Concepts Within a Different Structure of the Theory

Apart from these important problems which the theory faced in preserving its internal consistency, the new structure of the theory connoted changes in the scope of certain central concepts now placed within a different structure. This has clouded a clearer understanding of the structure of classical theory, and the constructive role of Sraffa's *Production of Commodities* (1960), in particular. We shall discuss below, by way of illustration, two such notions: 'competition' and 'equilibrium'.

The Notion of Competition

To the classicals, competition signified mobility of capital and, to a certain extent, of labour, manifesting itself in a tendency towards uniformity of the rate of profit and wages. It was, however, allowed by Adam Smith that there could be a vector of rates of profit and of wages, with more or less stable differentials, not greatly or systematically affected by the movements of the economy. Furthermore, this uniformity was seen as a tendency since it was never implied that, in practice, one could observe the uniform rate of profit or that any individual industry could actually achieve it, just as it was not envisaged that the natural price would be attained actually and necessarily.[24] It was, in fact, through the restless movements of capital (investment) that the tendency would manifest itself.

With the shift to marginalist theory, with its choice behaviour extended to demand and the collective market behaviour rendered reducible to individuals' (quantity-adjusting and price-taking) choices, the characteristics attributed to competition became more stringent. The stipulation of a large economy with agents who have no influence on prices, have perfect knowledge of commodities and markets, have unrestrained access to them and who do not intervene directly in the choices of each other (i.e., no externalities) became the content of competition.[25] Such competitive conditions not only set the environment for the price formation of commodities, but also characterized 'factor-markets'. Given the availability of resources or factor-supplies, the working of competition would drive the economy towards full utilization as a consequence of the full play of competitive demand-and-supply forces. Adam Smith, in contrast, had no problem in recognizing a 'combination of masters' (the unequal bargaining strength of labour and capital), nor did Marx have any difficulty in allowing a fluctuating but permanent reserve army of labour. Faced with the reality of persistent unemployment, the neoclassical theory, attempting to synthesize Keynes, could only revert to imperfections and rigidities in the system as explaining deviations from the full employment equilibrium (see Garegnani, 1983b).

The Notion of Equilibrium

LONG-PERIOD POSITION IN CLASSICAL THEORY

Another important notion that was reinterpreted and acquired changed connotations is that of equilibrium. While, strictly speaking, 'equilibrium' is a misnomer in the context of classical theory, the notion of a 'long-period' or 'natural' position as an organizing concept is used in classical theory as much as in neoclassical theory (see Garegnani, 1976). The method lay in trying to identify relations which appear to be fairly persistent, so that they may be viewed as dominant tendencies at work in the economy.[26] Adam Smith's distinction between the 'natural' and 'market' price of a commodity illustrated the mode of analysing. The 'market price', or the actually observed price, could deviate from the 'natural price' which was defined as the price which is just sufficient to cover costs – namely, wages, rents and profits – all paid at their natural rates. Whenever the actual supplies in the market fell short of, or exceeded, the 'effectual demand' (itself defined as the quantities demanded by those who were willing to pay the 'natural price'), 'market prices' would deviate from 'natural prices', setting up a tendency for supplies to adjust to the 'effectual demand'. The 'effectual demand' was thus a state or a position of demand which could itself be seen as a central or average position of social demand.[27] A distinction was made between 'persistent' or 'stable' shifts in 'effectual demand', and 'temporary' deviations. When the former were identified, the position of the 'effectual demand' would be suitably altered. The 'natural price', or a long-period position, was thus obtained, given 'effectual demand', the dominant methods of production and wage. It was not essential that the actual observed positions of the system should comply exactly with this position. Thus, in actual practice, methods in use could differ from firm to firm: the actual rates of profits could also differ from firm to firm, or from industry to industry. It was required, however, that there would be underlying tendencies for the system to move towards the 'dominant' methods of production and towards uniformity of the rate of profit.

It was not necessary, therefore, to view the long-period position as a 'static' position or that it should be, in effect, attained. The distinction between a 'market' and 'natural' position was not made in terms of a temporal division, as such, and hence the use of a 'long-run position' for the latter could itself be misleading. The distinction was rather in terms of the character of causal forces and of their effects. For example, a tax on a commodity could have a 'temporary' or 'persistent' effect on its price and the quantities of it which were demanded or supplied. The effects would be considered permanent and affecting the 'natural position' of the system only if they invoked changes in the 'givens', that is, 'effectual demand', 'the dominant method of production', or the 'wage' (appropriately defined as constituting the basis for the 'natural position'). For example, the corn tariff became an important issue, affecting the 'natural position' of the economy since corn entered significantly into the 'natural wage' and also, under extended cultivation, connoted changes in the methods of production, following upon changes in output. The temporary effects could, in turn, be distinguished from the purely 'accidental'; the latter referring to short-lived causes, illustrated by Adam Smith's allusion to the sudden spurt of demand for black cloth in the event of the death of a queen. The effect of a drought could be 'accidental', 'temporary', or 'persistent', depending upon the nature of the output, the severity of the drought and its duration over production cycles and the nature of the consequent effects upon the methods of production and natural wage. The forces forming 'market values' were not considered suitable for exact analysis of a *general* kind: for the actual forces at work and the manner of adjustments they invoked or entailed could be historically diverse and specific, requiring concrete specification of the events. While 'accidental' causes were too fickle to be analysed at all, a short-period analysis of 'temporary' events was not ruled out. In the analysis of taxation, for example, Ricardo distinguished between cases when a tax on a commodity led to price changes of particular commodities without altering the general rate of profit, and those cases when it did alter the rate.[28] The former involved effects confined to changes in the conditions of a specific commodity and not affecting the natural position. Marx's analysis of the various circuits of capital and their failure to be co-ordinated, giving rise thereby to disproportionalities and periodic crises, illustrates the distinction he maintains between long-term tendencies and cyclical movements or irregularities. A 'short-period' realization crisis could arise through the temporary disjunction between sales and purchases due to the intervention of money, disrupting the continuous circuit of exchange. There could also be a 'long' period' realization crisis due to a chronic failure of demand consequent upon a very low or declining share of wages. The distinction, as illustrated here, between 'market' and 'natural' conditions and 'short' and 'long' periods appears to have been drawn on the basis of the qualitative nature of causes and effects, rather than on the basis of 'duration' of calendar time.

LONG-PERIOD EQUILIBRIUM IN THE SUPPLY-AND-DEMAND THEORY

With a different theory explaining value and distribution, the explanation of the 'long-period position' as 'long-period equilibrium' changed. What is germane to our immediate purpose, is to note first that Marshall's – or, for that matter, Wicksell's or Walras's – 'long-period equilibrium' was not a 'stationary state', as suggested by the recent associations of equilibrium with the latter concept. It was more akin to the classical notion, in that it was neither presumed that the economy was in equilibrium already, nor that equilibrium connotes absence of changes and, in particular, a zero rate of savings. As Robertson (1957, pp. 92–3) explains:

> 'Tends in the long run to equal' does not mean 'equals' ... We must not think of the 'long-run value' of a thing as something which will be attained after so many months or years and then stay put. It is more nearly legitimate to think of it as a norm around which actual values oscillate ... yet even that conception, though helpful, may be too clear-cut for application to a changing world. It may be that in such a world long-run equilibrium is *never* attained. It is the state of affairs which would be attained if all the forces at work had time to work themselves out.

Thus the notion of equilibrium did not imply that the economy would achieve equilibrium. However, the fact that it may never be achieved in practice was not considered sufficient to deny a tendency towards it. Robertson also noted a growing tendency towards mathematical formalization that tended to make concepts such as perfect competition more precise than Marshall had intended. Harrod (1948, pp. 6–8) also noticed some conceptual changes that have occurred: 'As an instance of the eroding process, tending to narrow down the static economics, taking the life out of it and departing widely from the intentions of its authors, may be cited the notion that it has to make such assumptions as perfect mobility, perfect knowledge and perfect foresight.' He notes the tendency to narrow the scope of statics by imposing even more numerous and rigorous restrictions on the alleged sphere and validity of the branch, 'making static assumptions so far reaching that a law based upon them seems incapable of having any application to the world of reality'.

However, this development seems to have been inevitable: *not because of the mathematical formalization*, as such, but because the logical difficulties which the theory faced were overcome by recourse to assumptions and axioms which were increasingly distant from observed reality. The early writings of Marshall maintained the significance of the classical distinction between 'temporary' and 'permanent' effects much more assiduously.[29] The new theory explaining prices, however, had a radically different structure. With the explanation of prices and outputs, as well as of distribution resting on the symmetrical influence of opposite and balancing forces of supply and demand, the 'causal forces' were now grouped into 'demand' and 'supply'. Marshall introduced 'a classification of problems of value by the periods to which they refer' (*Principles*, 1920, p. 378; see Bharadwaj, 1978b, Chapter 6 in the present volume). In elaborating the notion of equilibrium and emphasizing 'the great element of time' (*Principles*, 1920, p. 347), one of Marshall's important and explicit concerns was to interpret and limit this doctrine that the value of a thing tends in the long run to correspond to its cost of production' (p. 348), and to establish that 'every plain and simple doctrine as to the relations between cost of production, demand and value is necessarily false' (p. 368). He thus treated both Ricardo and Jevons as being at the extremities of his own position.

MARSHALL'S CLASSIFICATION OF 'PERIODS'

Marshall proposed a fourfold classification. First, in the case of 'market prices', supply is a fixed stock 'in sight'. Secondly, normal prices in the short period 'of a few months or a year', relate to the situation where supply adjustment is limited by what can be produced for the price in question, 'with the existing stock of a plant, personal and impersonal, in the given time'. Thirdly, long-period normal prices refer to the situation 'when supply can be produced by a plant, which can be remuneratively produced and applied within the given time'. Fourthly, while secular movements in normal prices are caused by 'the gradual growth of knowledge, of population and capital and in changing conditions of supply from one generation to another' (p. 368). While Marshall insistently refers to a broadly specified calendar period of time with regard to each classification, the distinctions rest on what conditions are imposed on the elasticity of supply, that is, what is held in *ceteris paribus*.

> In the relatively short period problem, no great violence is needed for the assumption that the forces not specially under consideration may be taken for the time to be inactive. But violence is required for keeping broad forces in the pound of *ceteris paribus* during, say, a whole generation, on the ground that they have only an indirect bearing on the question in hand. (p. 379, fn. 1).

In the illustrative example of the fishing industry (p. 369–70), Marshall refers to the accidental oscillations in 'market prices' due to weather conditions. The short-period 'normal prices' rest on the adaptability of supply to demand (given the existing capacity of fishing boats, number of sailors, etc.,), while the long-period 'normal price' is governed by 'different set of causes, with different results', with productive capacity and labour, as well as methods of production, suitably adjusting to the long-term demand conditions. All supplies are governed by expected demand, and the short-period utilization of capacity is influenced by the expectations concerning immediate changes in demand (which could also be expected to be short-lived), while decisions as to changes in productive capacity rest on long-term expectations of demand that take into account changes in income, population, tastes, living standards, etc. Once these different causes affecting supply (or, investment decisions) are classified, Marshall applies the same theory of supply and demand to trace their effects on price and quantities in each case. His reference to 'the period of time over which the forces work themselves out' is given no further analytical expression, since the process of the 'cause' producing the 'effect' is not analysed as a dynamic sequence. The differences in each case are entirely defined by the identification of different causes. That this distinction between 'short period' and 'long period' (with the former referring to the existing capacity and the latter to changes in productive capacity), as well as that between the short- and long-term expectations of demand, could be fruitfully used in the analysis of investment is evident from Keynes. Marx also distinguished between investment decisions pertaining to circulating capital (or to fluctuations in the short-term capacity utilization), and those concerned with 'machinery' or capacity-generating investments.[30] The two types of decisions could be influenced by different causal considerations. It may, however, be also noted that the causal structure of this part of Keynes's theory of output, particularly the multiplier process, is closer to the spirit of the classicals and bears an affinity to their separation of the analysis of prices and quantities.[31]

Marshall was concerned, however, with establishing that 'the general theory of the equilibrium of demand and supply is the Fundamental Idea running through the frames of all the various parts of the central problem of Distribution and Exchange' (p. viii), and probably, for that reason, insisted that there was no sharp analytical line dividing short and long periods.

> In both use is made of that paramount device, the partial or total isolation for special study of some set of relations. *In both opportunity is gained for analysing and comparing similar episodes ... and for ordering and coordinating facts which are suggestive in their similarities, and are still more suggestive in the differences that peer out through their similarities.* (p. 379, fn. 1, italics added).

The 'principle of continuity', which he staunchly advocated, was used by him, on the one hand, to argue that the element of time was continuous (and hence the short and long periods shade into one another by 'continuous gradation'). This was an aspect of his statical method'[32] which he considered noteworthy

> The forces to be dealt with are however so numerous, that it is best to take a few at a time; and to work out a number of partial solutions as auxiliaries to our main study. Thus we begin by isolating the primary relations of supply, demand and price in regard to a particular commodity. We reduce to inaction all other forces by the phrase 'other things being equal' ... In the second stage, more forces are released from the hypothetical slumber. (pp. xiv–xv).

On the other hand, Marshall saw the 'dynamical problem' becoming larger with changes in the conditions of demand and supply of particular groups of commodities coming into play; and, finally, reaching 'the central problem of Distribution among a vast number of different agents of production'. Thus 'fragmentary statical hypotheses are used as temporary auxiliaries to dynamical – or rather biological – conceptions' (p. xv). The analytical use to which Marshall puts his device of 'periods' in his 'statical' method is clear from the following examples. He argues that, *as a general rule*, the shorter the period which we are considering, the greater must be the share of our attention which is given to the influence of demand on value; and the longer the period, the more important will be the influence of cost of production on value' (p. 349). The reason he gives for this is that 'the influence of changes in cost of production takes as a rule a longer time to work itself out than does the influence of changes in demand' (ibid.). It is not clear, however, what 'time to work itself out' means in this context, nor why it should take a longer time, in general, in the case of changes in costs of production than of changes in demand.

The other example where the 'notion of time' is brought into use is to argue for the symmetric treatment of land, labour and capital. In the classical theory, the role that land, labour and capital play in the production process and the explanation of their revenues is different in each case. Marshall, while treating rent in the classical fashion (as 'not entering costs' and as a residual), treated efforts of labour and waitings of capital as entering, on par, into the costs of production. He attempted to bolster up the symmetry argument by the suggestion that 'the greater part, though not the whole of the distinction between Rent and Interest on capital turns on the length of the period which we have in view ...'. For land, labour and capital, though having peculiarities of their own in respect of supply and demand, could all be treated as 'fixed' or 'variable', depending upon the length of time; so that 'even the rent of land is seen, not as a thing by itself, but as the leading species of a large genus'(p. viii). Thus Marshall supported his claim that the Fundamental Idea of demand and supply 'runs through all frames' of exchange and distribution. Another instance when the statical theory of particular commodities was threatened, and Marshall recurrently reverted to the 'element of time' and 'limitations of the statical method', was the case of increasing returns. Neither his device of 'external economies' nor that of the 'representative firm'could eliminate the difficulty created by 'increasing returns' for the construction of a supply curve for the industry which was consistent with competitive equilibrium. (See 'Symposium on the representative firm', *Economic Journal*, vol. 11, 1930; and Bharadwaj, 1972, Chapter 7 in the present volume.)

As did the classicals, Marshall only used the long-period normal values for his analysis of distribution and investment of resources, etc. In fact, these were considered by him as 'dynamical extensions' of his statical method of determining prices of particular commodities. However, Sraffa's critique of Marshall's supply curve (1925, 1926), as well as of the representative firm (1930), demonstrated that Marshall's attempt to construct a 'normal supply curve' under statical assumptions, on the basis of the co-ordination of the laws of return, was not logically sustainable. He failed in his attempt to reduce thereby the Ricardian 'cost-of-production theory' of price to a special – and 'accidental' – case of his own. It also brought out clearly that the conditions impounded in *ceteris paribus* for the purpose, could not be so contained and that it would become necessary to consider the supply-and-demand conditions of all commodities simultaneously (Sraffa, 1926). With the theory of supply and demand moving into the general equilibrium, the theory of distribution could no more lie in the background, as it did in Marshall's theory of prices. The determination of 'factor prices' now appeared simultaneously with that of commodities in the theory of general equilibrium.

'THE ELEMENT OF TIME' AND 'DYNAMICAL METHODS' IN HICKS:
A SHIFT IN THE NOTION OF EQUILIBRIUM

The issue of 'the element of time' and 'dynamical methods' entered the centre of discussion when the explanation of the rate of profit within the general equilibrium framework encountered difficulties and was taken up by Hicks (1962) in *Value and Capital*, wherein he introduced a change in the notion of 'equilibrium' (see Garegnani, 1976). While the difficulty regarding capital arises from the structure of the neoclassical theory of value and distribution which requires capital as a datum to be measured independently of distribution, Hicks viewed the problem as one concerning 'method'; the error, in his view, being that the earlier neoclassicals had no general dynamic theory in which all quantities are properly dated.[33] Hicks saw Marshall's position as rather ambiguous:

> Although Marshall raises at least a part of the general dynamic problem, it is curious to observe how reluctant he is to abandon static conceptions even in dynamic analysis. Statics and dynamics are very little separated in his work: his dynamics are not made easier by running in terms of very static 'equilibrium' and by the fact that their central passage leads up to the introduction of that 'famous fiction', 'the stationary state'.

In the case of the Austrians, too, Hicks considers their hallmark to be the stationary state (1982, II, p. 287) which 'is a dynamic state where tastes, techniques and resources remain constant through time'. The crux of the dynamic theory, according to Hicks, lay in the fact that current supplies (and ultimately, demand too) are governed as much by expected prices as current prices, and the assumption of stationarity is made possible by ignoring the vital distinction between price expectations and current prices. It may be observed here that by shifting the onus on to 'method', Hicks bypasses the logical difficulties that the theory encountered, even in its 'stationary or static state' version. For example, Marshall's statical theory faced difficulties even before the question of passing from a statical to dynamical theory could be taken up. Secondly, the 'changelessness' that Hicks associates with the stationary state of the Austrians or of Walras appears to have been, as noted earlier, a product of attempts to render the theory logically consistent and rigorous by moving away from the original conception.

Initially, in *Value and Capital*, Hicks proposed the route of 'intertemporal equilibrium', wherein the analysis was in terms of plans and realizations during a single period within which prices were expected to be determined by the usual equilibrium analysis, that is, prices varied adequately in the period so that demands over the period would always be equal to the supplies over the period in terms of quantity. The windfall gaps between expectation and realization were to be entirely absorbed by price variations. Garegnani (1976, p. 30) argues that this shift in method appears to have been prompted by an erroneous identification of the weakness of the underlying theory with another difficulty – namely, the influence of expectations. He states:

> This difficulty over the determination of the quantity of capital is independent of the divergence between current and expected prices. The same need to measure the capital would arise if we wanted to determine the long period equilibrium while assuming that tastes and techniques and resources are not going to change in the future.

Hicks's solution appears to be to abandon the traditional *method*, while preserving the *theory* unaltered.

Hicks himself sees the limitation of this model in a very different light (1982, II, pp. 218–35). The model could work best only when there were two sorts of commodities – perishable goods and personal services – which could not be carried over in stocks and speculatively traded goods by merchants. Further, it needs to be assumed that while prices are fully adjusted at the end of the single period, they remain constant throughout the period, so that either the equilibrating forces work instantaneously or not at all. Hicks's self-critical remarks thus remain focused on the method. The entire onus is now on 'expectations', for which no objective basis is provided.

In his later work, Hicks adopts alternative 'methods of dynamic analysis' (Hicks, 1982, II, pp. 217–35). He identifies the problem of capital as mainly its longevity which inevitably brings in the element of time. Capital is created with the expectation of future returns in the minds of the investors and, once formed as fixed capital, the capital goods generate a flow of services over time. Hicks distinguishes two approaches to the dynamic problem: one based on the Lindahl–type, *ex ante/ex post* forward accounting, and the other based on stock/flow relations. In the first approach, expectations play an active role, with the deviations between *ex ante* and *ex post* quantities and prices directing the dynamics. In the second, the role of expectations is somewhat subdued and the accent is on the time structure of the relation between the stock of fixed capital and the flow of services. Hicks suggests that alternative methods of dynamic analysis may be appropriately adopted to suit the problem at hand, and may further be coupled with alternative assumptions regarding responses – one with flexible quantities and fixed prices, and the other with flexible prices and fixed quantities.

While this gives a neat taxonomy of methods, Hicks himself admits that 'these do not quite fit together into a single coherent whole' (ibid., p. 219). This disintegration of the supply-and-demand theory into separate methods appears to be an indirect admission of the failure of the theory which attempts to be all-comprehensive in its scope. What Hicks attempts to do is to salvage the theory through introducing special assumptions regarding the period over which the supply-and-demand relations are considered effective in establishing equilibrium, or regarding lags in the price-quantity responses. This shift to alternative methods does not in any way resolve the initial difficulty with capital in the theory of distribution. Expectations acquire new importance, although no new or objective basis is provided for them. The models also deal mainly with expectations about prices, while those that influence investment decisions appear mostly to relate to the general conditions of the state of the market and other systemic macro-level forces and were the ones predominant in classical discussions as well as in Keynes. The problems of dynamics of change, uncertainty and expectations are important dimensions of economic processes which every worthwhile theory must aim to capture. However, the question of paramount importance is the structure of the theory forming the foundation.

3 Structural Contrasts: 'Openness' of the Classical Structure

In contrast to the structure of the neoclassical theory of value and distribution, the structure of classical analysis keeps open the possibilities of allowing for a number of historical and social influences to enter the analysis. The broad methodological point may be put in the words of Sraffa, in the context of his critique of Marshall[34] which illustrates the meaning we may put on 'openness'.

> This first approximation ['cost-of-production theory' of the classicals, as Marshall called it] as far as it goes, is as important as it is useful: it emphasises the fundamental factor, namely, the predominant influence of cost of production in the determination of the normal value of commodities, while at the same time it does not lead us astray when we desire to study in greater detail the conditions under which exchange takes place in particular cases, for it does not conceal from us in fact that we cannot find the elements requires for this purpose within the limits of its assumptions. (1926, p. 187)

Unlike the marginalist theory (which, as we have seen, needed to presume a priori quantity-price relations in the form of the well-behaved, demand-and-supply relations generated through the active principle of substitution), no such strict relations need be presupposed in the classical theory.

More explicitly, the two important distinguishing features of the classical, or surplus-based, theory of prices which allow this openness may be underlined here. First, the theory separates, in the first instance, the changes in quantities and those in prices, in the sense that the output levels and composition, methods of production and the wage are given or determined prior to prices; whereas in the marginalist theory, all quantities and prices are determined simultaneously and within the same framework of relations.

This 'separation', as a first step, may appear unduly restrictive. On the contrary, it opens up the possibility of introducing a wider range of determinants and the real dynamics of the process of change; precisely because, thereby, the more complex, historically specific, institutional and social forces that govern changes (particularly in distribution, technology of production, and investment) can be introduced. While prices may, in turn, influence the quantities, it is recognized that there are even more significant factors directly influencing quantities that may be considered to operate fairly independently of changes in relative prices. This is illustrated, for example, in Adam Smith's treatment of the relation between the division of labour and the extent of the market; or in Marx's discussion of qualitative and quantitative changes in capital/labour relations, influencing, and being influenced by, technical change. Keynes's analysis of the multiplier could be said to follow the same approach. That wages (i.e., distribution) are influenced by various historical and social factors is amply evident from labour studies. A growing literature on the intricacies of the growth of technical knowledge, innovations, imitation and adaptation, etc., has over and over again demonstrated the importance of factors other than prices. The relationship between prices and quantities is asymmetrical in the force of their mutual determination, so that the relative prices of commodities may be derived uniquely on the basis of given quantities. We may even go a step further and state that the major influences that act upon the determination of investment, distribution and technical change are not confined to relative prices alone, but the real dynamics of economies is generated through the direct interactions among these. It is this openness of Marx's prices of production that enabled him to account for 'historical tendencies' in the domain of production, distribution and accumulation. At any 'observed' position of the economy – given wage, methods of production and the principle of surplus sharing among the capitalists (say, the uniformity of the rate of profit) – it was possible to know simultaneously the rate of profit, the value of the surplus and prices, and the corresponding distributive shares. Prices are thus seen to be conforming to the rules of production and distribution of surplus, appropriate to the particular mode of production.[35]

The second important distinctive feature of the classical structure is its view of production as a circular process. The one-way avenue of the neoclassical theory takes factor endowments as given. We have already noted the consequences of treating 'capital' as a given endowment in the theory of profit. Further, within this structure, the given endowments (along with the given preferences and technology) determine outputs. In the circular view, changes in output might as well determine the availability and utilization of resources. To note one of the analytical implications of this difference: in the neoclassical theory, prices not only play the role of allocating the scarce resources to different uses, but they also ought to lead to the full employment of resources. This indeed runs against the actual experience of capitalist economies.

Some Misinterpretations of Classical Theory
We may here refer briefly to some misinterpretations of the classical theory prompted by marginalist habits of thought. The idea that the classical theory of value is 'incomplete' and requires the demand side to be provided occurs repeatedly in critical writings (e.g., Samuelson, 1971 and 1978). Indeed, following Marshall, it has sometimes been suggested that the demand analysis was incipiently present in Ricardo (see Hollander, 1979).[36] On the latter, our discussion above had indicated the difference between the notion of effectual demand in classical theory and the demand schedule of the marginalist theory. Further, as Garegnani has argued elsewhere (Garegnani, 1982), the particular significance of the role that demand functions play in the marginalist theory arises solely from their explanation of distribution on the basis of the equilibrium between the demand and supply of 'factors'. In other words, that theory has to rely on the complement of demand schedule, which is no longer necessary in the classical theory where wages are given by historical and other forces from outside the price-schema.

Hicks (1979), too, imposes the marginalist structure on classical theory when he attributes a simple static model, relying on 'fixed technical coefficients', to Smith and Ricardo, and concludes that

> the range of problems to which such a model could be applied was nevertheless limited. For, in strictness it is only if there is just one original factor, into terms of which all costs are ultimately reducible (the 'labour theory of value') that the technical coefficients are sufficient to determine relative costs; if there is more than one factor, the relative prices of the factors must also play a part. (pp. 47–8).

Hicks then goes on to define those conditions on factor prices which keep factor-supplies from changing. All this is contrary to the way both Smith and Ricardo perceived the problem of distribution. In the classical theory the question of choice among known methods of production was not confined to the context of the changes in factor prices; nor were factor prices determined on the basis of the demand and supply of factors.[37]

A common misunderstanding in relation to Sraffa's *Production of Commodities* (1960) arises from his statement that his investigation is concerned with those properties of the system which do not depend upon changes in the scale of production or in the proportions of factors. This has tempted some to look upon the system as one which is invariant under these changes, and hence to attribute to it such assumptions as would render the system invariant within the general equilibrium theory. Accordingly, constant returns to scale are considered an essential assumption. The system of relations is also seen as a changeless, and hence a stationary, state. We have attempted to clarify in what way change is an essential requirement for the marginalist theory, but not for Sraffa. However, the fact that the propositions in the book do not depend upon change does not imply the assertion that no changes would or could follow.

In the circular view of the economic process that Sraffa endorses in the very title of his book, the condition of self-replacement is not identical with self-reproduction. It is only in the system without surplus that exact reproducibility occurs. Self-replacement refers to the viability of the system and does not indicate how the system would change in the next period. In fact, Sraffa takes an observed system of relations as given. When wages change, changes in other quantities may or may not follow. What Sraffa implicitly denies is the necessity of hypothesizing quantity-price responses, or of imposing conditions on the direction of these responses, for his derivation of prices and the rate of profit. Thus a change in wage may or may not induce a permanent shift to another method of production; even if it does, it may not be presupposed that the new method would replace a more (less) 'capital-intensive' method when the wage declines (rises). Similarly, not all changes in wage necessitate changes in output (composition or level). *It is not therefore denied that such changes take place, but it is not presumed that the scheme of relations determining relative prices is the exclusive and comprehensive domain to analyse changes in quantities.*

Sraffa's 'Return' to Classical Theory

Sraffa's 'return' to classical theory lies in his attempt to clearly delineate the structure of the surplus-based theory of value and distribution. In *Production of Commodities* (1960), he had a specific constructive goal – to identify and resolve some central problems in the basic structure of that theory, so that the approach could be shown to survive the carry-over from the labour theory of value to prices of production. A much-needed clarification was to demonstrate the inessentiality of certain appendages to the theory which had been adopted for momentary convenience, especially by Ricardo. Not only did these cripple the theory, but they also led it into deviant directions through easy misinterpretations. Some of these had already been discarded by Marx. For example, the 'population dynamics' to explain the subsistence wage in Malthus, which, with some hesitation, was used by Ricardo and subsequently criticized by Marx. Sraffa's 'given' and variable wage removed this association with the fixed subsistence wage, seen by some critics as a logical requisite of the classical theory.[38] Sraffa (1960) in his chapter on land shows how the classical view of rents could be divorced from the traditional 'law of diminishing returns', and thence from the 'supply schedule' based thereupon. We have seen how powerful the rent theory was in the original construction of marginalism. In fact, Sraffa shows, correcting the classicals, that differential rents as well as the identity of the 'no-rent' land depends on the rate of profit.[39] Similarly, the adherence to Say's Law, as in Ricardo, is no more to be seen as an essential feature of the prices of production, as indeed Marx expressly recognized.[40]

4 Conclusion

Our attempt in the above was to bring out the distinctive characteristics of the structures of the surplus-based classical theory and the marginalist theory of value and distribution, and to interpret Sraffa's 'return' to the classical theory as his being engaged in a dual task of criticism of the marginalist theory and clarification of the ground for the classical theory.

Notes: Chapter 10

This is a further amended version of the paper first presented at the Conference in Florence in 1983 on 'Sraffa's Production of Commodities after twenty-five years' and published in *Political Economy: Studies in the Surplus Approach*, vol. 1, no. 2 (1985) pp. 3–31. I am grateful to the participants at the Conference and to Professors Richard Arena and Harvey Gram for very useful discussions.

1 Although approaching similar conclusions, the various critiques have different foci and bases. A major thrust of criticisms – that were coincidentally voiced by three presidents of prestigious associations (Leontief, 1971; E. Phelps-Brown, 1972; and Worswick, 1972) – had been at the deficient observational basis and empirical support to assumptions in economic theory, their refutability and operational significance, as well as the limitations of econometric techniques employed to 'test' the validity of the theory. Another critique of 'fundamental Keynesians' (see Coddington, 1976) concerns 'the equilibrium method', which argues that the logical conditions defining the notion of equilibrium connote a state of affairs either unapproachable or unattainable, unless the economy is already in it (see Shackle, 1972). Joan Robinson returned to this theme repeatedly, contrasting history with equilibrium. Hicks has been engaged in developing 'methods of dynamics', wherein he is mainly concerned with modifications required in the demand-and-supply mechanisms in order to consider the element of 'time' (Hicks, 1982). Kaldor (1972), indicating the increasing arbitrariness of the assumptions imposed upon the theory by evermore precise cognition of the need for logical consistency, considers that the setback in economic theory started when 'value theory' took 'the centre of the stage'. This 'meant focussing on the allocative function of the market to the exclusion of the creative functions as an instrument for transmitting impulses in economic change'.

2   For a review of Sraffa's work, see Bharadwaj (1984, Chapter 13 in the present volume).
3   The problem appeared in Ricardo as the one of finding a measure of value, invariant with respect to a change in distribution; in Marx, it took the form of the 'transformation' problem. Sraffa's *Production of Commodities* focused on the resolution of this difficulty, which is situated at the very foundation of the classical theory.
4   Ricardo began his investigations, in part, dissatisfied with the explanation of profit given by Smith in terms of 'competition of capitals'. Marx criticized Ricardo for his 'neglect of constant capital' and his tendency to identify surplus value with profits. It was the controversy over the 'transformation problem' that was used by his critics to denounce the surplus approach. Recent attacks on the neoclassical theory have been prominently on their explanation of profit with the connected capital theoretic controversies. The capital theoretic critique also challenges the neoclassical theory of output and employment; prices and quantities being *simultaneously* determined within the *same* scheme of explanation in that theory.
5   Other pioneers of marginalist theory, like Jevons, stressed the break with the past. It is interesting to note that whereas this 'continuity' view has been revived in some recent discussions of the classicals (see Hollander, 1979; Hicks, 1979; Hicks and Hollander, 1977; and Samuelson, 1957, 1959, 1971, 1978, among others), wherein the theories of the classical writers, Adam Smith and Ricardo, have been viewed mainly as partial models of the later marginalist theory. Marshallian views have made their reappearance and have proved more long-lasting than was formerly believed.
6   On the constructive side of his work, Sraffa's editorial commentaries on Ricardo brought out in clear form the significant features of the surplus approach to value and distribution that was being developed in the classical theory. Sraffa helped dispel thereby a number of misinterpretations. (See Chapter 5 above)
7   Adam Smith considered the possibility of stable differentials in wages and profits, not greatly or systematically affected by advances in output so that a *vector* of rates (of profits and wages) could be envisaged.
8   The rate of profit, explained as the distribution of the total profits over the value of capital, necessitated the consistent measurement of heterogeneous aggregates and required the simultaneous determination of prices and the rate of profit, given wage (Sraffa, 1960).
9   See Garegnani (1960, 1984), Bharadwaj (1978a; and 1978b, now Chapter 6 in the present volume).
10 In other words, the nature of causal forces, as well as the pattern of their interaction, determining *quantities* could be diverse in historically specific cases. This is not to rule out the possibility of their abstract analysis, but to suggest a wider arena of causal forces and determination than we find in the supply-and-demand-based theories, where it is coterminus with the one determining prices.
11 See Sraffa (ed.), *Works*, IV; pp. 4–6.
12 Land was 'fixed' in supply to the society as a whole, while individual producers could vary the land under their command and its utilization.
13 The first tentative attempt to relate unit costs to output occurs in J. S. Mill (see Bharadwaj,1978b, Chapter 6 in the present volume; de Vivo, 1981) where, following the suggestion of Bailey, Mill seems to have adopted a classification of commodities with their own respective Law of Value.

14 For this reason, Wicksteed (1914) considered the extensive case a spurious case of 'marginal' analysis (see Sraffa, 1925, and 1960, pp. v–vi). The intensive margin also raised the question of what 'equality of a dose' and its 'marginal product' meant (see Bharadwaj, 1978a).
15 Ricardo's 'onesided emphasis' on costs of production and relative neglect of demand has been a favourite argument for those who see, in Ricardo, a partial resource-allocational model of general equilibrium. Hollander's recent attempts (Hollander, 1979) to attribute 'demand mechanisms' to Ricardo are critically discussed in Bharadwaj (1983, Chapter 4 in the present volume).
16 'There is a special need to insist on this just now, because the reaction against the comparative neglect of the study of wants by Ricardo and his followers shows signs of being carried to the opposite extreme' (1920, p.85).
17 Marshall expresses his grave concern about Pigou's overstepping the limits of the 'statical method' and shows awareness of the deeper troubles which he had skilfully tried to contain – and even conceal.
18 Hicks (1982, II, p. 98) quoting Sraffa, among others, points out that fixed capital cannot be reduced to invested land and labour. However, while mentioning this difficulty, he does not refer to the basic capital-theoretic difficulty that arises even in the case of circulating capital, which Sraffa poses. In fact, Hicks appears to pose the capital problem as one arising entirely from its durability (or, its stock dimension in a stock/flow relation), and therefore from its irreducibility to 'land and labour' (see pp. 241-3 above).
19 'All wealth and property imply prospective services or desirable events. It is the desirability of these future expected services which give meaning to all economic phenomena' (Fisher, 1906, p. 41).
20 'Wealth is wealth only because of its services: and services are services only because of their desirability in the minds of men and the satisfactions which man expects them to render ... It is only in the interim between the initial desire and the final satisfaction that wealth and services have place as intermediaries.' (ibid.).
21 'When values are considered, the causal relation is not from capital to income but from income to capital not from present to future but future to present' (ibid., p. 328).
22 See note 21 above.
23 Another method of extending the scope of equilibrium analysis over time was to envisage complete future markets so that each commodity with the specific time-suffix is treated as a separate commodity – a procedure adopted in Debreu (1959).
24 The following rather well-known passage from J. S. Mill (1871 [1909], p. 452) illustrates the argument: 'On an average of years sufficient to enable the oscillations on one side of the central line to be compensated by those on the other, the market value agrees with the natural value; but it very seldom coincides exactly with it at any particular time. The sea everywhere tends to a level: but it never is at an exact level; its surface is always ruffled by waves, and often agitated by storms. It is enough that no point, at least in the open sea, is permanently higher than another. Each place is alternately elevated and depressed but the ocean preserves its level.'
25 Morgenstern writes (1972, p. 1164): 'In identifying the economic phenomena certain primitive concepts and terms have to be used ... However, because of the freedom with which mind can move, it happens frequently that the relation with reality is lost, and that purely hypothetical notions

are introduced. In addition there is often a change in the meaning of words. Consider "competition": the common sense meaning is one of struggle with others, of fight, or attempting to get ahead, or at least to hold one's place ... In current equilibrium theory, there is nothing of this true kind of competition, there are only individuals, firms or consumers, given prices, fixed conditions, each firm or consumer for convenience insignificantly small and having no influence whatsoever on the existing conditions of the market (rather mysteriously formed by *tâtonnement*), and therefore solely concerned with maximising sure utility or profits – the latter then being exactly zero. The contrast with reality is striking.' It may be added that this disjunction with reality is not so much because of 'the freedom of mind' as the necessity imposed by the nature and structure of the supply-and-demand theory, explaining quantities and prices in general equilibrium.

26   Marx, more than any other economist, recognized the importance of structuring theory on the basis of abstractions drawn from historical observations. He made a distinction between 'qualitative' changes that occur in social formations and the 'quantitative' changes that occur within the bounds of a particular formation: The 'laws of motion' that propel these quantitative changes (and eventually transform them into a qualitative transition) were particular to the social formation or the 'mode of production'. Each mode of production is therefore characterized by the dominant relations and forms of production and its corresponding rules of surplus extraction, distribution and of exchanges. The 'prices of production' forms the rule of exchange under competitive capitalism.

27   As seen above, the classical, economists had a much wider notion of social demand based on 'wants' generated by 'efforts and activities' (as Marshall called them), by custom, tradition and habits, by class-composition of incomes and levels of income. In particular, they were conscious of the effect of the availability of commodities on demand. Marx, in particular, emphasized the interaction between production and consumption (Marx, 1857–8 [1973]).

28   Hollander (1979, p. 271) points to such a peculiarity, among others, in Ricardo and attempts to explain it on the basis of an attribution of an implicit assumption of identical factor-proportions. Hollander's interpretation of reading 'demand and supply based allocative mechanisms' in Ricardo is critically examined in Bharadwaj (1983, Chapter 4 in the present volume, pp. 77–110.): Ricardo's peculiarities are there explained along the above lines.

29   Marshall wrote to Edgeworth (1902): 'You know I never apply curves or mathematics to market values. For I don't think they help much and market values are, I think, either absolutely abstract or terribly concrete and full of ever-varying (though individually vital) side issues' (see Pigou, 1925, p. 435). Even later he wrote (Marshall, 1920, p. 349–50): 'The actual value at any time, the market value as it is often called, is often more influenced by passing events, and by causes whose action is fitful and short-lived, than by those which work persistently. But in long periods these fitful and irregular causes in large measure efface one another's influence; so that in the long run persistent causes dominate value completely.' An attempt to tone down this contrast was made, however, by devising a classification of markets, denying at the same time that there is any sharp line of division between 'short' and 'long' periods and asserting that, in all cases, price is governed by the relations between demand and supply.

30   Marx (1957), *Capital*, II, p. 262.

31 When the causal structure is complex, with sequential separation of the determination of interdependent variables, historical conditions and specificities can be introduced through comparisons of natural or normal positions, as indeed was done by the classical writers (and Keynes). The historical conditions enter into the determination of effectual demand, wage and methods of production.

32 Marshall's distinction between 'statical' and 'dynamical' must be seen as different from the usual 'statics' and 'dynamics', such as used by Hicks (1965). 'Statical' did not mean changeless, but implied that 'certain conditions remain the same'.

33 Hicks writes (1962, p. 116n) 'People used to be content with static apparatus, only because they were imperfectly aware of limitations. Thus, they would often introduce in their static theory "a factor of production", capital and its "price", interest supposing that capital could be treated like the static factors (cf. J. B. Clark's "free capital" and Cassel's "capital disposal"). That some error was involved in the procedure would not have been denied; but the absence of a general dynamic theory in which all quantities were properly dated made it easy to "underestimate" how great the error was.' Thus, in *Value and Capital*, Hicks sought to lay the foundation of dynamic analysis.

34 It is worth recalling here that the 1926 article was directed mainly against Marshall's scheme of determination of prices of particular commodities in his partial equilibrium framework, although the point made here is more general. Sraffa, keeping to Marshall's terminology, calls the classical theory of prices the cost-of-production theory. He warns explicitly against such a usage in his later work, *Production of Commodities* (1960).

35 Forewarning that analogies are dangerous if interpreted too precisely, we may use one here. The statement that a train is moving – obeying, no doubt, its laws of motion – implies that the wheels are on the tracks at each moment as it moves. It is a statement of compatibility or consistency. The prices of production state similarly the set of prices consistent with the rules of surplus generation and distribution. Using this analogy, we may say that the marginalist theory, in order to generate consistent prices, requires not only that the wheels are on the tracks but, additionally, that the tracks also turn in required directions (thus depending *essentially* upon hypothetical changes and hence having also to impose conditions, such as of convexity, on the feasible sets of choices).

36 On this, see Bharadwaj (1983, Chapter 4 in the present volume) for a detailed discussion.

37 Another misconception rests on treating the classical hypothesis of a *given* wage as being the fixed, subsistence wage so that, it is argued, the classical system of price equations was closed by determining the fixed wage through Malthusian population dynamics. Or else, it is maintained, the system would remain incomplete, requiring closure through introduction of 'demand' (Samuelson, 1971).

38 See note 37 above.

39 In this sense, under capitalist production rents become subordinated to profits, as Marx argued. Paradoxically, however, in the neoclassical theory an increasing temptation seems to be of treating capital as land.

40 It may be noted that Marx, too, comes to the realization problem sequentially separated from the problem of determination of prices, and that Say's Law is not implied in prices of production.

References: Chapter 10

Bharadwaj, K. (1972), 'Marshall on Pigou's *Wealth and Welfare*', *Economica*, vol. XXXIX, no. 153 (February–, pp. 32–46; Chapter 7 in the present volume.
Bharadwaj, K. (1978a), *Classical Political Economy and the Rise to Dominance of Supply and Demand Theories* (Calcutta: Orient Longman); Revised edition, 1986.
Bharadwaj, K. (1978b), 'The subversion of classical analysis: Alfred Marshall's early writing on value', *Cambridge Journal of Economics*, vol. 2, no. 3 (September), pp. 253–71; Chapter 6 in the present volume.
Bharadwaj, K. (1983), 'On a controversy over Ricardo's theory of distribution', *Cambridge Journal of Economics*, vol. 7, no. 1 (March), pp. 11–36; Chapter 4 in the present volume.
Bharadwaj, K. (1984), 'Piero Sraffa: the man and the scholar – a tribute', *Economic and Political Weekly*, vol. 19, no: 30–1 (August), pp. 1236–50; Chapter 13 in the present volume.
Böhm Bawerk, E. von (1891): *The Positive Theory of Capital*, ed. William Swart (London: Macmillan & Co).
Coddington, A (1976), 'Keynesian economics: the search for first principles', *Journal of Economic Literature*, vol. 14, no. 4 (December), pp. 1258–73.
Debreu, G. (1959), *Theory of Value* (New Haven, Conn.: Yale University Press).
De Vivo, Giancarlo (1981), 'John Stuart Mill on Value', *Cambridge Journal of Economics*, March.
Eatwell, J. L. (1982), 'Competition', in I. Bradley and M. Howard (eds), *Classical and Marxian Political Economy* (London: Macmillan), pp. 203–28.
Fisher, I. (1906), *The Nature of Capital and Income* (New York: A. M. Kelley).
Fisher, I. (1930), *The Theory of Interest* (New York: A. M. Kelley).
Garegnani, P. (1960), *Il capitale nelle teorie della distribuzione* (Milan: Giuffre).
Garegnani, P. (1976), 'On a change in the notion of equilibrium in recent work on value and distribution', in M. Brown, K. Sato and P. Zarembka (eds), *Essays in Modern Capital Theory* (Amsterdam: North Holland), pp. 25–45.
Garegnani, P. (1978), 'Changes and comparisons: a reply to Joan Robinson', mimeo; published in Italian in *Valore e domanda effetiva* (Turin: Einaudi, 1979).
Garegnani, P. (1982), 'The classical theory of wages and the role of demand schedules in determination of relative prices', paper read at AEA Conference.
Garegnani, P. (1983), 'Two routes to effective demand', in J. A. Kregel (ed.), *Effective Demand, Distribution and International Relations* (London: Macmillan), pp. 69–80.
Harrod, R. F. (1948), *Towards a Dynamic Economics* (London: Macmillan).
Hicks, J. R. (1962), *Value and Capital* (Oxford: Oxford University Press).
Hicks, J. R. (1965), *Capital and Growth* (Oxford: Oxford University Press).
Hicks, J. R. (1979), *Causality in Economics* (Oxford: Blackwell).
Hicks, J. R. (1982), 'Methods of dynamic analysis', and 'Time in economics', in *Money, Interest and Wages: Collected Essays on Economic Theory*, Vol. II, (Oxford: Blackwell), pp. 217–36 and 282–301.
Hicks, J. R., and Hollander, S. (1977), 'Mr Ricardo and the moderns', *Quarterly Journal of Economics*, vol. XCI (August), pp. 351–69.
Hollander, S. (1979), *The Economics of David Ricardo* (Toronto: Heinemann).
Jevons, W. S. (1871 [1971]), *The Theory of Political Economy* (Harmondsworth: Penguin).

Kaldor, N. (1972), 'The irrelevance of equilibrium economics', *Economic Journal*, vol. 82, no. 328 (December), pp. 1237–55.
Koopmans, T. C. (1957), *Three Essays on the State of Economic Science* (London: McGraw-Hill).
Leontief, W. W. (1971), 'Theoretical assumptions and non-observable facts', *American Economic Review*, vol. 11 (March), pp. 1–7.
Marshall, A. (1879 [1930]), *The Pure Theory of Foreign Trade. The Pure Theory of Domestic Values*, Series of Reprints of Scarce Tracts in Economic and Political Science, no. 1 (London: London School of Economics and Political Science).
Marshall, A. (1920), *Principles of Economics*, 8th edn (London: Macmillan).
Marx, Karl (1887 [1965]), *Capital*, Vol. I (London: Lawrence & Wishart).
Marx, Karl (1957), *Capital*, Vol II (London: Lawrence & Wishart).
Marx, Karl (1857–8), *Grundrisse. Foundations of the Critique of Political Economy* (Harmondsworth: Penguin in association with New Left Review).
Mill, J. S. (1871 [1909]), *Principles of Political Economy*, ed. W. J. Ashley (New York: A. M. Kelley).
Morgenstern, O. (1972), 'Thirteen critical points in contemporary economic theory: an interpretation', *Journal of Economic Literature*, vol. 10, pp. 1163–89.
Phelps-Brown, E. (1972), 'The underdevelopment of economics', *Economic Journal*, vol. 82, no. 325 (March), pp. 1–10.
Pasinetti, L. L. (1969), 'Switches of Techniques and the "Rate of Return" in Capital Theory', *Economic Journal*, vol. LXXIX, no. 315, September, pp. 508–31.
Pigou, A. C. (ed.) (1925), *Memorials of Alfred Marshall* (London: Macmillan).
Ricardo, D. (1817 [1951]), *Principles of Political Economy*, Vol. I and IV of *Works and Correspondence*, ed. by P. Sraffa (Cambridge: Cambridge University Press).
Robertson, D. (1957), *Lectures on Economic Principles* (London: Fontana).
Robinson, Joan (1959), *Collected Economic Papers*, Vol II (Oxford: Blackwell).
Robinson, Joan (1973), *Collected Economic Papers*, Vol. IV (Oxford: Blackwell).
Robinson, Joan (1980a), *Collected Economic Papers*, Vol. V (Oxford: Blackwell).
Robinson, Joan (1980b), *What Are the Questions and Other Essays* (New York: M. E. Sharpe).
Robinson, Joan (1982), *Essays in the Theory of Economic Growth* (New York: St Martin's Press).
Roncaglia, A. (1974), *Sraffa and the Theory of Prices* (New York: Wiley).
Samuelson, P. A. (1957), 'Wages and interest: a modern dissection of Marxian economic models', *American Economic Review*, vol. 57 (December), pp. 884–912.
Samuelson, P. A. (1959), 'A modern treatment of the Ricardian economy', *Quarterly Journal of Economics*, vol. 49, nos 1 and 2 (February and May), pp. 1–35 and 217–31.
Samuelson, P. A. (1971), 'Understanding the Marxian notion of exploitation: a summary of the so-called transformation problem between Marxian values and competitive prices', *Journal of Economic Literature*, vol. 9, no. 2 (June), pp. 399–432.
Samuelson, P. A. (1978), 'The canonical classical model of political economy', *Journal of Economic Literature*, vol. XVI (December).
Shackle, G. L. S. (1972), *Epistemics and Economics* (Cambridge: Cambridge University Press).

Sraffa, P. (1925), 'Sulle relazioni fra costo e quantità prodotta', *Annali di Economia*, vol. 2, pp. 277–328.

Sraffa, P. (1926), 'The laws of returns under competitive conditions', *Economic Journal*, vol. 36 (December), pp. 535–50.

Sraffa, P. (1930), 'A "criticism" and a "rejoinder" in the "Symposium on increasing returns and the representative firm"', *Economic Journal*, vol. 11, pp. 89–93.

Sraffa, P. (ed.) (1951 and 1955), Editorial introduction to *Works and Correspondence of David Ricardo*, Vols I and IV (Cambridge: Cambridge University Press).

Sraffa, P. (1960), *Production of Commodities by Means of Commodities: Prelude to a Critique of Economic Theory* (Cambridge: Cambridge University Press).

Steindl, J. (1982), 'The control of the economy', *Banca Nazionale del Lavoro*.

Worswick, C. D. N. (1972), 'Is Progress in Economic Science Possible?', *Economic Journal*, March.

Wicksell, K. (1934), *Lectures on Political Economy*, Vols I and II, translated from the Swedish by E. Classen and (ed.) Lionel Robbins (London: Routledge & Kegan Paul).

Wicksteed, P. H. (1914), 'Political Economy in the Light of Marginal Theory', *Economic Journal*, XXIV.

11
On the Maximum Number of Switches between Two Production Systems

In his *Production of Commodities by Means of Commodities* (1960) Piero Sraffa introduces a classification of commodities into 'basics' and 'non-basics': A commodity is called 'basic' to the system of production[1] if it enters, directly or indirectly, into every other commodity in the system; a commodity which does not do so is called 'non-basic'. Opinions have diverged as to the role and significance of this distinction. In the literature, production systems containing only basics are more in vogue.[2] In an article on Sraffa's book, Professor Newman (1962) proposes to 'abandon' non-basics, by omitting them from the system, in the interest of analytical simplicity; particularly, to avoid the possibility of negative prices which a system containing non-basics may give rise to (see Appendix below). However, the existence of non-basics is an objective property of a system and while non-basics may be ignored in a first approximation they will have ultimately to be taken into account. Other writers, while considering non-basics, have adopted, instead of this distinction between commodities, another classification based on an abstract property of the 'technology matrix' as being 'decomposable' or 'indecomposable'. A matrix is called 'decomposable' when by suitable interchange of columns and rows it can be reduced to the form $\begin{bmatrix} A_1 A_2 \\ 0\ A_3 \end{bmatrix}$ where A_2 and A_3 are square matrices and 0 is a zero matrix. A matrix which cannot be so reduced is called 'indecomposable'. Thus a system containing at least one non-basic has a decomposable technology matrix, while a system with all basics has an indecomposable one. However, as will be seen, *the basic/non-basic distinction, referring to commodities in a given economic system, uses directly more information about it and does so in a way that helps perceive the economic content of the distinction.*

This essay discusses a problem relating to 'reswitching of methods of production', an issue at the centre of a current controversy. A 'reswitch' in the methods of production is said to occur when, of two methods of production, one which has ceased to be the more profitable because of a change in the rate of profit becomes again more profitable than the other as the rate of profit moves further in the same direction. We shall take up here the more specific question of the maximum number of switches between two production systems, and incidentally note how part of the difficulty in the reswitching controversy arises from not taking into account the particular role played by non-basics.

We consider a situation where a number of commodities are being produced in annual cycles. Each commodity is produced by a separate industry, that is, there is no joint production. A system of production with a specified net output is composed of the methods of production for the commodities that form the net output as well as others which enter, directly or indirectly, into their production. There is one method for each commodity in a system. We then suppose that there is an alternative method for one of the commodities and an alternative system is formed characterized by the use of the alternative method for that commodity. The introduction of the alternative method could entail the use of new commodities while possibly dropping some others. The switch point between the two systems corresponds to the rate of profit at which the two alternative methods produce the commodity at the same price (i.e., at the switch point, both the wage rate and the prices of the commodities produced in both systems are equal). We deal in Section I with the case where each system consists only of commodities basic to it. In Section II we take up the case where the two systems also include non-basics and where they differ in the method for a commodity which is non-basic to both. We also examine there whether non-basics entering the value unit (in terms of which wages and prices are expressed) but not entering either of the alternative methods influence the number of switching possibilities, as is sometimes implied (see p. 265 below). A question that arises here concerns the conditions guaranteeing the positivity of prices in a system including non-basics. In this connection, we have reproduced, in the Appendix, letters[3] that were exchanged between Sraffa and Newman, following Newman's article, referred to above, which throw light on this point. In Section III we consider the advantages of the basic/non-basic distinction for the discussion of switching. Section IV contains the conclusions.

1 Production Systems Consisting of Only Basics

Consider a production system A involving m commodities, all basics. Suppose that for one of the commodities an alternative method of production is known which entails the use of some new commodities while possibly dropping out some others. Suppose the alternative production system formed by replacing the former method by the latter, call it system B, has n commodities all basics to it and that the two systems A and B have s commodities common to both; so that there are $(m-s)$ commodities used exclusively in system A and $(n-s)$ commodities used exclusively in system B. For convenience, we renumber the commodities so that $1, 2 \ldots s$ are the s commodities common to the two systems, $s + 1, s + 2 \ldots m$ are the $(m-s)$ commodities exclusive to system A and $m + 1, m + 2 \ldots m + n - s$ are the $(n-s)$ commodities exclusive to system B. A switch point from one system to the other would be found at the rate of profit at which the wage and the price of each of the s common commodities are equal in the two systems.

Assuming wages are paid at the end of each annual cycle we write the price equations for the two systems:

System A

$$
\begin{aligned}
(a_{11}p_{1a} + a_{21}p_{2a} + \ldots + a_{s1}p_{sa})\,\lambda \qquad & \ldots + a_{01}W_a = p_{1a} \\
(a_{12}p_{1a} + a_{22}p_{2a} + \ldots + a_{s2}p_{sa})\,\lambda \qquad & \ldots + a_{02}W_a = p_{2a} \\
\vdots \qquad \vdots \qquad \vdots \qquad \vdots \qquad & \qquad \vdots \qquad \vdots \\
(a_{1s-1}p_{1a} + a_{2s-1}p_{2a} + \ldots + a_{ss-1}p_{sa})\,\lambda \qquad & \ldots + a_{0s-1}W_a = p_{s-1a} \\
(a_{1s}p_{1a} + a_{2s}p_{2a} + \ldots + a_{ss}p_{sa} + a_{s+1s}p_{s+1s} + \ldots + a_{ms}p_{ma})\,\lambda + a_{0s}W_a &= p_{sa} \\
\vdots \qquad \vdots \qquad \vdots \qquad \vdots \qquad \vdots \qquad & \vdots \qquad \vdots \\
(a_{1m}p_{1a} + a_{2m}p_{2a} + \ldots + a_{sm}p_{sa} + a_{s+1m}p_{s+1a} \ldots + a_{mm}p_{ma})\,\lambda + a_{0m}W_a &= p_{ma}
\end{aligned}
\quad \text{(I)}
$$

where $p_{1a}, p_{2a} \ldots p_{ma}$ are the prices of commodities $1, 2 \ldots m$ and W_a the wage rate in system A and $\lambda = 1 + r$ where r is the rate of profit; a_{ij} $(i, j = 1, 2, \ldots m)$ and a_{0j} $(j = 1, 2 \ldots m)$ are the commodity input and labour coefficients respectively for system A. An analogous notation to represent prices and the wage rate in system B is adopted to write the price equations for system B. (Note that $i, j = 1, 2 \ldots s$, $m + 1, \ldots m + n - s$ and $a_{ij} = b_{ij}$ for $j = 1, 2 \ldots s - 1$.)

System B

$$
\begin{aligned}
(a_{11}p_{1b} + a_{21}p_{2b} + \ldots + a_{s1}p_{sb})\,\lambda + a_{01}W_b &= p_{1b} \\
(a_{12}p_{1b} + a_{22}p_{2b} + \ldots + a_{s2}p_{sb})\,\lambda + a_{02}W_b &= p_{2b} \\
\vdots \qquad \vdots \qquad \vdots \qquad \vdots \qquad & \vdots \\
(a_{1s-1}p_{1b} + a_{2s-1}p_{2b} + \ldots + a_{ss-1}p_{sb})\,\lambda + a_{0s-1}W_b &= p_{s-1b} \\
(b_{1s}p_{1b} + b_{2s}p_{2b} + \ldots + b_{ss}p_{sb} + b_{m+1s}p_{m+1b} + \ldots & \\
+ b_{m+n-ss}p_{m+n-sb})\,\lambda + b_{0s}W_b &= p_{sb} \\
(b_{1m+1}p_{1b} + b_{2m+1}p_{2b} + \ldots + b_{sm+1}p_{sb} + b_{m+1m+1}p_{m+1b} + \ldots & \\
+ b_{m+n-sm+1}p_{m+n-sb})\,\lambda + b_{0m+1}W_b &= p_{m+1b} \\
\vdots \qquad \vdots \qquad \vdots \qquad \vdots \qquad & \vdots \\
(b_{1m+n-s}p_{1b} + b_{2m+n-s}p_{2b} + \ldots + b_{sm+n-s}p_{sb} + b_{m+1m+n-s}p_{m+1b} + \ldots & \\
+ b_{m+n-sm+n-s}p_{m+n-sb})\,\lambda \; b_{0m+n-s}W_b &= p_{m+n-sb}
\end{aligned}
\quad \text{(II)}
$$

We need now to find out such values of λ at which $p_{ia} = p_{ib}$ $(i = 1, 2 \ldots s)$ when $W_a = W_b = W$[4]. We take $p_{1a} = p_{1b} = 1$ so that commodity 1 is chosen as *numéraire*. We have the problem of unequal numbers and different kinds of basics in the two systems (namely, commodities 1, 2 ... m in system A and 1, ... s, $s + 1$, ... $m + n - s$ in system B) which affect the wage/profit relations in the respective systems. We now introduce in system A, as non-basics, the commodities which are exclusive to system B and thereby augment the matrix;[5] let the matrix so augmented be called system A^+. Similarly we construct B^+ from system B. These would appear as follows:

$[A^+, A_0^+] =$

$$\begin{bmatrix} a_{11} & a_{21} & \cdots & a_{s1} & & & & & & a_{01} \\ a_{12} & a_{22} & \cdots & a_{s2} & & & & & & a_{02} \\ \vdots & \vdots & & \vdots & & O & & O & & \vdots \\ a_{1s-1} & a_{2s-1} & \cdots & a_{ss-1} & & & & & & a_{0s-1} \\ a_{1s} & a_{2s} & \cdots & a_{ss} & a_{s+1s} & \cdots & a_{ms} & & O & a_{0s} \\ a_{1s+1} & a_{2s+1} & \cdots & a_{ss+1} & a_{s+1s+1} & \cdots & a_{ms+1} & & & a_{0s+1} \\ \vdots & \vdots & & \vdots & \vdots & & \vdots & & O & \vdots \\ a_{1m} & a_{2m} & \cdots & a_{sm} & a_{s+1m} & \cdots & a_{mm} & & & a_{0m} \\ b_{1m+1} & b_{2m+1} & \cdots & b_{sm+1} & & & & b_{m+1m+1} & b_{m+n-sm+1} & b_{0m+1} \\ \vdots & \vdots & & \vdots & & O & & \vdots & \vdots & \vdots \\ b_{1m+n-s} & b_{2m+n-s} & \cdots & b_{sm+n-s} & & & & b_{m+1m+n-s} & b_{m+n-sm+n-s} & b_{0m+n-s} \end{bmatrix}$$

$[B^+, B_0^+] =$

$$\begin{bmatrix} a_{11} & a_{21} & \cdots & a_{si} & & & & & & a_{01} \\ a_{12} & a_{22} & \cdots & a_{s2} & & & & & & a_{02} \\ \vdots & \vdots & & \vdots & & O & & O & & \vdots \\ a_{1s-1} & a_{2s-1} & \cdots & a_{ss-1} & & & & & & a_{0s-1} \\ b_{1s} & b_{2s} & \cdots & b_{ss} & & & & b_{m+1s} & \cdots & b_{m+n-ss} & b_{0s} \\ & & & & & O & & & & \\ a_{1s+1} & a_{2s+1} & \cdots & a_{ss+1} & a_{s+1s+1} & \cdots & a_{ms+1} & & & a_{0s+1} \\ \vdots & \vdots & & \vdots & \vdots & & \vdots & & O & \vdots \\ a_{1m} & a_{2m} & \cdots & a_{sm} & a_{s+1m} & \cdots & a_{mm} & & & a_{0m} \\ b_1 m+1 & b_{2m+1} & \cdots & b_{sm+1} & & & & b_{m+1m+1} & b_{m+n-sm+1} & b_{0m+1} \\ \vdots & \vdots & & \vdots & & O & & \vdots & \vdots & \vdots \\ b_{1m+n-s} & b_{2m+n-s} & \cdots & b_{sm+n-s} & & & & b_{m+1m+n-s} & b_{m+n-sm+n-s} & b_{0m+n-s} \end{bmatrix}$$

where A^+ and B^+ are augmented matrices of commodity input coefficients and A_0^+ and B_0^+ are augmented matrices of labour coefficients. The switch point values of λ which satisfy the condition $p_{ia}^+ = p_{ib}^+ = p_i^+$ and $W_a^+ = W_b^+ = W^+$ are to be obtained by solving a vector of polynomial equations given by

$$[F_i^+(\lambda)] = [A^+ - B^+]\, \lambda\, [p^+] + [A_0^+ - B_0^+]\, W^+ = 0 \quad (1)$$
$$i = 1, 2 \ldots m + n - s.$$

where matrices A^+ and B^+ are both $(m + n - s) \times (m + n - s)$ and $p^+ = (1, p_2^+, p_3^+ \ldots p_{m+n-s}^+)$.

There would be as many non-zero elements in this vector as the number of differing methods of production in the augmented systems and in this case, therefore, there is only one polynomial to be solved, namely,

$$F_{(s)}(\lambda) = 0 \qquad (2)$$

In other words, it is sufficient to equate the price of the commodity s, the only commodity to have a different method of production in the two systems. We could solve for p^+ and W^+ in terms of λ in either of the two systems A^+ or B^+.[6]

From the system A^+, we can write:

$$p^+ = [p_{ia}^+] = \frac{[J_i^+(\lambda)]}{[g^+(\lambda)]} \text{ (2) and } W_a^+ = W_b^+ = \frac{f^+(\lambda)}{g^+(\lambda)} \qquad (3)$$

where $J_{(i)}^+(\lambda)$, $f^+(\lambda)$ and $g^+(\lambda)$ are of at most $(m + n - s - 1)$, $(m + n - s)$ and $(m + n - s - 1)$ degree in λ respectively. Hence the polynomial function in (1) can have at most $(m + n - s)$ roots and hence the maximum number of switches between the two systems is $(m + n - s)$. As a polar case, if the two systems A and B have only one basic commodity common between them, the maximum number of switch points would be $(m + n - 1)$.[7]

Of the number of possible switches thus obtained as an upper bound, the economically relevant number of switch points would be obtained only after excluding repeated counting of repeated roots, complex roots and those lying beyond the range $1 \leq \lambda \leq 1 + R$ where R is the lower of the two maximum rates of profit for the two systems.[8] Also, we consider only those situations in which all prices are positive.[9]

The case of the same basics in the two alternative systems which is often treated as 'general' (see, e.g., Bruno, Burmeister and Sheshinski, 1966) is seen to be only a particular case of the above more general formulation. With all n basics common to the two systems the maximum number of switches is seen to be only n. The assumption that the two systems have the same numbers and kinds of basics, while they differ in the methods of production, is extremely restrictive since it is unlikely that two different methods will use identical materials and tools.

The discussion of switching possibilities between two production systems has been usually conducted under the assumption that the two systems under consideration may differ in the methods of production for more than one (and up to all) commodities common to them. This has been described as the most general model; but, far from being a general case, this would be a very exceptional one.[10] Switches would occur between systems differing in the method of production for only one basic commodity common to the two systems. When more than one basic common to them is produced by a different method in the two systems, it is clear from the condition for obtaining the switch point set out in (1) above that a set of polynomial functions in λ of that number would have to have at least one common root. Such a condition would be fulfilled only as a fluke.[11]

2 Systems Including Commodities which Are Non-Basics to Both

The production systems discussed so far involved commodities which were basic to one or the other system. We now turn to those which include commodities that are non-basics to both. Even in such systems, when the two systems are characterized by a different method of production only for a *basic* produced in both, the switch points between the two methods for the basic (and hence the two systems) would be determined as in the earlier case using the augmented systems; the latter would include *only* the methods of production for the commodities which are basics to one or the other system. The methods of production for commodities which are non-basic to both systems can be ignored. We take up two cases where the methods of production of such non-basics may not be so ignored.

(1) If there are alternative methods of production for a non-basic there would be switches in the method of production for that non-basic as the rate of profit changes.[12] (Each of the basics has only one known method.)

(2) Non-basics may enter the value unit in terms of which prices and wage are expressed. It is evident that the non-basics could enter the price equations of the basics only indirectly in this way. If prices are expressed as functions of the rate of profit, the maximum degree of the price equation for a basic would be given by the number of commodities entering directly or indirectly into this value unit which includes non-basics. This seems to suggest that the maximum number of possible switches is also given by that number (see p. 262 below). We examine the question of whether the non-basics which enter the value unit, directly or indirectly, but do not enter, directly or indirectly, into either of the alternative methods between which switches are being considered, influence the switching possibilities. We first consider the question of the alternative methods for a non-basic.

Alternative Methods for a Non-basic
Suppose that one of the non-basics in a system A has an alternative method of production. When the alternative method is used, it might entail the use of some non-basics peculiar to itself while possibly dropping some others. Let us call the system characterized by the use of the latter method for the non-basic, system B. Suppose also that

commodity 1 (basic to both systems) is *numéraire*. We can follow the same procedure as on page 258 above and write the augmented systems A^+ and B^+ which would now include, in addition to the methods of production for commodities basic to at least one system, also those for non-basics to both which enter, directly or indirectly, into one or the other of the alternative methods of production for the non-basic in question. Such commodities as are non-basics to both systems and do not enter either of these alternative methods would not appear in the agumented systems. The augmented matrices would differ in only one row, namely, that representing the method of production for the non-basic with the alternative methods. The maximum number of switches for the two systems is given, as in the earlier case, by the dimension of the augmented matrix, that is, by the number of distinct commodities, basic and non-basic, without double counting, that enter in at least one of the alternative methods of production for the non-basic.[13]

Non-basic Entering Value Unit
Suppose that there are alternative methods of production for only a basic and non-basics enter the value unit. Further, that these are non-basics to both systems, the two systems differing in the method for the basic.[14] Would the non-basics entering the value unit affect the maximum number of switches between the two systems?

As a simple illustration we take production systems A and B, each with two basics (designated commodities 1 and 2 in system A and 1 and 4 in system B) and one non-basic (commodity 3 in both). They differ in the method for commodity 1. The non-basic is produced by the same method in the two systems and forms the value unit. Representing the two systems as below:

System A

$$(a_{11}p_{1a} + a_{21}p_{2a})\lambda + a_{01} W_a = p_{1a}$$

$$(a_{12}p_{1a} + a_{22}p_{2a})\lambda + a_{02} W_a = p_{2a}$$

$$(a_{13}p_{1a} + a_{33}p_{3a})\lambda + a_{03} W_a = p_{3a}$$

System B

$$(b_{11}p_{1b} + b_{41}p_{4b})\lambda + b_{01} W_b = p_{1b}$$

$$(b_{14}p_{1b} + b_{44}p_{4b})\lambda + b_{04} W_b = p_{4b}$$

$$(a_{13}p_{1b} + a_{33}p_{3b})\lambda + a_{03} W_b = p_{3b}$$

With $P_{3a} = P_{3b} = 1$, the switch points are to be obtained by augmenting A and B to A^+ and B^+ respectively, as discussed earlier, and by solving the following polynomial:

$$(a_{11}-b_{11}) \lambda p_{1a}^{+} + a_{21} \lambda p_{2a}^{+} + (-b_{41}) \lambda p_{4a}^{+}$$
$$+ (a_{01}-b_{01}) W_{a}^{+} = 0 \quad (4)$$

where P_{1a}^{+}, P_{2a}^{+}, P_{4a}^{+} and W_{a}^{+} are themselves polynomials in λ.

In this simple case we can make the following observations:

(1) If $a_{33} = 0$, the non-basic does not use itself in its own production, the polynomial in λ in (4) above has the maximum degree only three and hence the maximum number of switch points is only three.
(2) If $a_{33} \neq 0$, then $\lambda = 1/a_{33}$ happens to be the additional solution for λ. It should be noted, however, that at this value of λ, with the non-basic as the value unit, the prices of the basic commodities can no longer satisfy the positivity condition.[15]

The observations hold even if a composite commodity consisting of basics and non-basics (e.g., $q_1 p_{1a} + q_2 p_{2a} + q_3 p_{3a} = 1$ with q_1, q_2, q_3 constants) is adopted as a value unit. If there are non-basics which are required for the production of the non-basic that enters the value unit we can generalize the above observations. It would be found that:

(i) Such of the non-basics that enter directly or indirectly into their own production and enter, directly or indirectly, into the value unit would add to the number of possible solutions to the polynomial equation given by (4) above.[16]
(ii) However the solutions that are added on are the rate(s) of profit equal to the rate of reproduction for the separate non-basic or a group of interconnected non-basics, as the case may be. These switch points, however, would have to be ruled out for the following reasons. If the rate of reproduction of a non-basic (or a group of interconnected non-basics) is smaller than the lower of the two maximum rates of profit for the two systems, the condition regarding the positivity of prices at those switch points will not be satisfied. In fact, with the non-basic as a value unit and a rate of profit equal to its rate of reproduction, one obtains, as Sraffa shows (1960, app. B, p. 90–1) a 'formal' solution in which 'the price of every commodity is zero'. Thus the two production systems could 'formally' have a switch point which has to be ruled out since we consider only those switch points at which all prices are positive.

More importantly, such a value of the rate of profit at the switch point might well fall beyond the maximum rate of profit for at least one of the production sytems. A fuller discussion on this issue appears in the Sraffa–Newman correspondence which is reproduced in the Appendix below. Sraffa argues there that instances of a non-basic in the system having a rate of reproduction less than the maximum rate of profit for the system would be hardly met with and that the particular example of beans, a non-basic of that type, which he employed in Appendix B of his book had to be invented in order to establish that, with such a non-basic in the system, positivity of prices could not hold at a rate of profit equal to the rate of reproduction of that non-basic.

Propositions similar to (i) and (ii) above can be proved in the case where the commodity with the alternative methods is a non-basic, each of the other commodities common to the two systems having the same method. If there are other non-basics in the system, which, while not entering either of the alternative methods of production, directly or indirectly, enter the value unit, directly or indirectly, then such non-basics would not add to the maximum number of solutions for switch points between the two systems excepting in a formal way, as pointed out in (ii) above.

3   Significance of the Basic-Nonbasic Distinction

In the foregoing we have used the classification of commodities into basics and non-basics to discuss the question of switching possibilities between two systems. Another classification which has been used more frequently in current discussions is that of decomposable and indecomposable systems. However, given a production system, the classification of the commodities involved into basics and non-basics uses more of the available information about the system than does the classification of that system as decomposable or indecomposable. By stating that the system contains (or does not contain) non-basics we have already implied that the system is decomposable (or indecomposable). The classification of commodities into basics and non-basics would further inform us as to which commodities in that system give rise to its decomposability. For, by their very nature, the basics in the system can be identified as forming a wholly interconnected group (we shall call this system, formed by all the basics in the system, the Basic system), while the non-basics cannot do so since, while they require basics for their production, they are not themselves required in the production of the basics.

The additional information incorporated in the basic/non-basic distinction is relevant to the discussion of switching possibilities between systems since it directly leads on to a distinction between two types of switches which have different consequences. A switch in the method for a basic implies that the two systems (each characterized by the method that it uses for that basic) would have different Basic systems, each with a maximum rate of profit, different from that of the other. On the other hand, a switch in the method for a non-basic does not affect the maximum rate of profit of the system nor the prices of the basics, that is, the Basic system is not affected in any way by a change in the method for a non-basic. Another instance of the asymmetry between the two classes of commodities can be seen in this, that propositions concerning the switches in a basic (such as the maximum number of possible switches and the rate of profit at which a switch occurs) and the transition from one system to another that these switches imply can be derived from the consideration of the Basic system alone, ignoring the non-basics, while such propositions concerning a non-basic cannot be based on the consideration of non-basics alone.

It would seem that some of the confusion which arose from a paper by Levhari (1965), which concerned the decomposability of a system and its relevance to the reswitching of techniques, could have been avoided if the distinction between basics and non-basics had been taken into account. Levhari in his paper claimed to have demonstrated that if there are n commodities in a system and if the ith commodity ($i = 1, 2, \ldots n$) had k_i alternative methods of production (so that there are $\prod_{i=1}^{n} k_i$ possible systems of production) it is impossible that any one system of production should switch back as the rate of profit continues to move in any one direction. This claim was withdrawn later by Levhari and Samuelson (1966)[17]. They explained that Levhari's original paper had accepted the possibility of a decomposable system's reswitching as 'established without question' by Ruth Cohen, Joan Robinson and Sraffa, and it had attempted to show that such a reswitching could not happen in an indecomposable system. It should, however, be noted that Sraffa's demonstration of the possibility of reswitching was not limited to a decomposable case as Levhari had believed. When Sraffa takes the case of the alternative methods for a basic (having first considered briefly that of the alternative methods for a non-basic), his argument does not require the existence of non-basics in the system: the proposition concerning the possibility of reswitching of the basic holds whether the original system is decomposable or not. It is true that Sraffa makes a distinction between basic *uses* and non-basic *uses* but this distinction is introduced only in order to facilitate comparison between the alternative methods within the *same* system at rates of profit at which the two methods are not equally profitable, that is, away from the switch points. Each of the two commodities considered there (copper I and copper II) is basic to one or the other system. Off the switch point any comparison of the two alternative methods of producing copper at the prices of the system characterized by the use of copper I as basic, implies treating the method producing copper II as a non-basic in that system; the production matrix including *both* is decomposable.[18]

The case where two production systems have different basics, such as considered in Section I above, is a parallel instance where decomposability in the process of a comparison between the two systems arises. Each one of the two systems A and B appearing there is indecomposable, and yet a comparison of the two systems implies the use of augmented systems A^+ and B^+ formed by adding to each system, as non-basics, the commodities which are basics only in the other. As we have seen such non-basics peculiar to one or the other augmented systems of Section I have to be distinguished from the non-basics common to *both* systems considered in Section II. In general, when the switching possibilities for basics, involving a transition from one system to another with a different Basic system, are being discussed, non-basics to both systems can be ignored.[19]

As an illustration of how a failure to specify whether the commodity that switches is a basic or non-basic could be misleading, we may refer to Section III of the paper by Bruno, Burmeister and Sheshinski in the Symposium (1966, pp. 531–8). They first consider the 'canonical model' of Samuelson, with one capital good (which is basic) and one consumption good (which is non-basic) in each production system. While the capital good is different in the two systems, the consumption good is the same in both. The consumption good is *numéraire* and does not use itself in its own production. The authors state, correctly in this case, that there can be at most two switches. (There is only one commodity, the non-basic consumption good, which is common to the two systems, and the two production systems are characterized, therefore, by the non-basic being produced by a different method in each. As the non-basic does not use itself in either of these methods, the maximum number of switching points is only two.) After obtaining the sufficiency conditions for non-reswitching in this simple case they point out the difficulty of generalizing from these conditions to cases involving more than one capital good in a single method of production. It is here that the error creeps in when they state (p. 536): 'The latter fact [the difficulty of so generalizing] can be seen by considering a case with one consumption good and two capital goods where the prices are clearly equations of the third degree. Thus in general there may be three switching points.' In a production system with two basics and one non-basic, with the non-basic as *numéraire*, prices are not equations of the third degree in the rate of profit unless the non-basic uses itself as means of production (a condition not present in the canonical model). Further, we cannot conclude that the maximum number of switches between two production systems with two basics and one non-basic in each would be, in general, three. If following the 'canonical model' we were to assume that the two capital goods (basics) in each system were, in all, four different basics and that the non-basic did not enter its own production, the two systems have only one commodity, the non-basic, common to them; there are at most *four* switching points. If the two capital goods in each system were the same two basics and the two systems were characterized by a different method for one of the basics, the maximum number of switching points would be, at most, two. If the two systems had the same two basics, they differed only in the method for the common non-basic, and the non-basic did not use itself in any of the alternative methods, then the maximum number of switches would still be two. The maximum number of switching points would be three when the total number of *different* commodities entering, directly or indirectly, into at least one of the two alternative methods that switch is three.[20] No such condition is specified by the authors and it would seem that they arrived at the conclusion that the number of switches was, in general, three by counting the commodities in each system.

4 Conclusion

To sum up:

(i) At a switch point the adjacent production systems differ in the method of production for only one of the commodities common to them. The maximum number of switching possibilities between two such systems is equal to the number of distinct (i.e., without double counting) commodities entering, directly or indirectly, into the two alternative methods which respectively characterize the two systems. Thus if it is a basic to both systems which has different methods in the two systems, the maximum number of switches would be equal to the total number of distinct basics in the two systems together; if it is a non-basic which has different methods in the two systems, this maximum number is given by the total number of distinct basics in the two systems *plus* the number of distinct non-basics entering, directly or indirectly, in at least one of the methods for that non-basic.

(ii) The choice of the value unit does not affect the maximum number of switching possibilities. Non-basics which require themselves in their own production and which, while not entering, directly or indirectly, into the production of the commodity with alternative methods, do so enter the value unit, give additional formal solutions for switch points. These additional solutions would be ruled out for reasons given on p. 262 above.

(iii) The classification of commodities into basics and non-basics in a given system uses more of the available information about the system than does the classification of the system as decomposable or indecomposable. The additional information incorporated in the former distinction is essential for the discussion of switching possibilities between two systems.

Appendix

Professor Newman in his critique (1962) of Piero Sraffa's *Production of Commodities by Means of Commodities* (1960) raised the issue concerning the necessary and sufficient conditions for all prices to be positive in a production system which includes non-basics. These conditions (which he states in the article on p. 66) appear to him 'to have little economic significance'. His conclusion is that the presence of non-basics in the system 'will often not imply a positive price vector'. This question of the economic interpretation of these conditions and the treatment of non-basics were discussed in letters exchanged between Sraffa and Newman. I sought their permission, which they have kindly given, to publish the letters in full in this Appendix. I here summarize Newman's arguments as they appear on pp. 66–7 of his article.

Newman first establishes that for a system containing only basics, and in which 'labour consumes fixed levels of inputs irrespective of the rate of profit', there is always a solution giving a positive price vector and a positive rate of profit. He then considers a system which includes non-basics. He gives a simple illustration of a system consisting of only two commodities, iron and corn, where iron (designated commodity 1) is non-basic, and corn (designated commodity 2) is basic. With p_1 and p_2 as prices of iron and corn respectively, and r, the uniform rate of profit, the price equations in his example are:

$$(1 + r) \, 0.8 p_1 + (1 + r) \, 0.3 p_2 = p_1$$

$$(1 + r) \, 0.2 p_2 = p_2$$

$$0.2 p_1 + \quad 0.5 p_2 = 1$$

In this system if $p_2 \neq 0$ then $(1 + r) = 1/a_{22} = 5$ and at that rate of profit $p_1 = -5/4$ and $p_2 = 5/2$. Hence if $p_2 \neq 0$ the solution contains a negative price. If $p_2 = 0$, $p_1 = 5$ and $r = 1/4$. He concludes that 'in either case we have a contradiction of Sraffa's combined requirements that the system be in a self-replacing state and that profit rate be uniform'. Newman then states that the necessary and sufficient condition for such a production system having all positive prices is $a_{11} < a_{22}$ (where a_{11} and a_{22} are the iron-iron and corn-corn coefficients respectively). The economic rationale of this condition seems obscure to him. He poses the choice that either we must abandon one of Sraffa's assumptions (that there is a uniform rate of profit and that the system is in self-replacing state), or assume that non-basics do not exist. He favours the course of 'abandoning the non-basics'. He further adds that 'this choice is reinforced by the consideration that the question whether a good is non-basic is partly a matter of the degree of aggregation in the system'. He concludes that 'This result, that non-basics will often not imply a positive price vector, means that the rather heavy emphasis placed on such commodities by Sraffa [he exemplifies them by luxury goods] seems misplaced'.

The correspondence reproduced below centres on these issues.

Trinity College, Cambridge, England
4 June 1962.

Dear Professor Newman,

Thank you for sending me your excellent article on my book. I have read it with great interest and I am sure that it will prove illuminating to many who have been puzzled by my work.

There are naturally some points of disagreement. Among these I shall refer only to your criticisms (pp. 66–7) of my treatment of non-basic products. Have you not overlooked my Appendix B, to which the reader was referred to by a footnote on p. 28? It seems to say exactly the same thing as you say on p. 66. True, it says it in humdrum economic language, which is no doubt less elegant than mathematics. In this case, however, it has the advantage of making plain the economic circumstances which may give rise to a negative price for a non-basic, and which you find 'obscure' (p. 67).

Besides, it makes it obvious how rare (if any) such cases must be in the real world. If, e.g., the ratio of net product to means of production (R) in a basic *system* is 25%, it will be pretty hard to find a *single* commodity (whether basic or not) which requires the using up of more than *four* units of itself in order to produce *five* units of it in a year. I certainly failed to discover any faintly realistic example of this which I could use, and had to invent those 'beans'.

When you say such instances occur 'often' (p. 67) you must have been misled by your own example of a system consisting of a single basic and a single non-basic product – presumably concluding that $a_{11}>a_2$ is no less probable than $a_{11}<a_{22}$. In a real system, however, there is not one but a large number of basic products, and the ratio R resulting from the *system* which they form is practically certain to be much smaller than the own ratio of any one *separate* non-basic (or any of such small groups of interconnected non-basics as may exist).

You find a further ground for attacking the distinction between basics and non-basics in the supposition of its being 'partly a matter of the degree of aggregation in the system' (p. 67). Now aggregation is the act of the observer, whilst the distinction is based on a difference in objective properties. I have argued, for instance, that a tax on the price of basics will lower the general rate of profits for a given wage, whereas a similar tax on non-basics will leave the rate of profits unchanged. Surely, to answer this, one must prove the alleged consequence does not follow, instead of drowning the distinction through an appropriate degree of aggregation.

Thank you again for your article. If I may hope for more, it is that you will not really leave your reader to shift for himself in the maze of multiple-product industries.

Yours sincerely,
P. Sraffa

Department of Economics,
The University of Michigan,
Ann Arbor
8 June 1962.

Dear Mr Sraffa,

Thank you so much for your letter, and for your kind words concerning my article. It was a relief to learn that I had not badly misinterpreted your ideas, as I feared I might have done.

I can come half-way to meet your criticisms of my treatment of non-basics. I now think that there is some economic meaning to Gantmacher's conditions (p. 92) for the positivity of prices. Let us designate the reducible system $Ap = cp$ by

$$\begin{bmatrix} A_B & 0 \\ A_{BN} & A_N \end{bmatrix} \begin{bmatrix} P_B \\ P_N \end{bmatrix} = c \begin{bmatrix} P_B \\ P_N \end{bmatrix}$$

where A_B and A_N are the square 'internal' coefficient matrices for basic and non-basic goods respectively, A_{BN} is the (in general, non-square) matrix of coefficients of basic goods used in non-basic good manufacture, P_B and P_N are sub-vectors of the respective prices, and c is A's dominant latent root. Then we can consider A_B and A_N as themselves matrices like A, with dominant latent roots c_B and c_N respectively, and associated eq. 'rates of profit' r_B and r_N.

Then Gantmacher's necessary and sufficient condition for positivity of P_B and P_N may be expressed as $r_B < r_N$, i.e., the rate of profit in the basic system must be strictly less than the rate of profit of the 'internal' non-basic system. This seems to have economic meaning, though I am not sure about its significance. I confess that it does not seem to me to be obvious that we will usually have $r_B < r_N$, but I am open to argument. It seems to me that more empirical considerations would have to be brought in.

I would not have brought in the point about aggregation if I had not already made the earlier, and I think stronger, point. I do wonder a little about your mention of 'objective properties'. All we ever have is what we observe, or more strictly, what we classify. I personally find it difficult to think in terms of industries when considering production, and think more naturally of processes. For this reason, I think further discussion of this point would not be useful, since I imagine that we would both agree that the Part II analysis of processes is a considerable step forward. I have not thought about the role of aggregation in the latter context.

Your invitation to work on Part II of the book is very enticing. My free time is rather limited just now, and I suspect it will take much harder work than Part I. But I might steal time to work at it.

With best wishes.

Yours sincerely,
Peter Newman

Trinity College, Cambridge
19 June 1962.

Dear Professor Newman,

Thank you so much for your letter.

I am, of course, delighted, and grateful, that you can come half-way to meet me on the subject of non-basics, and I only regret to be unable to move the other half: I cannot yield an inch on this point!

You speak of a non-basic system and proceed to compare it with the basic system: I say that there is no such thing as a non-basic system. You also refer to 'the rate of profit of the internal non-basic system': again, I say there is no such thing.

It is in the nature (or, if you wish, the definition) of basic goods to be interconnected and form a system. It is, on the other hand, the peculiarity of non-basics to be unconnected with one another, and they are incapable of forming an independent system. At best, each of them can be formally treated as constituting a separate single-commodity system, with its own rate of profits: this rate (for each separate non-basic) can be compared with the rate of the basic system. It is a priori extremely unlikely that any individual rate will be smaller than that of the basic system, composed, as the latter is, of many products, all used directly or indirectly in one another's production. It has not been possible to find a reasonable case in reality in which the rate is smaller (and this is not a minute, hidden property that requires elaborate investigation for spotting it).

If I may go over the ground again. The immense majority of non-basics are not used in production, not even in their own production: so they do not even form individual systems. Some (mainly animals and plants) are used each in its own reproduction, and form individual systems. A few may be linked with one or two others, because of mixing, or cross-breeding, or if the length of gestation brings out the egg-hen dicotomy. And that is all.

The third class, which is the least numerous and may just be worth mentioning for the sake of completeness, is the source of all the trouble.

With many good wishes.

Yours sincerely,
P. Sraffa

Notes: Chapter 11

This essay was first published in Schweizerische Zeitschrift für Volkswortschaft und Statistik, No. 4 (December 1970), pp. 401–28. It was born out of some intensive discussions with Piero Sraffa on the basic-nonbasic classification. To him and Joan Robinson – then, at the centre of the reswitching controversy in Cambridge – and to Luigi Pasinetti and Pierangelo Garegnani, I owe my thanks for their helpful comments.

1. A system of production (alternatively, a production system) producing n commodities is a set of n production methods, one for each and each producing a single commodity.
2. The 'Leontief system' which is frequently used is one such system.
3. I am grateful to Professor Newman and Mr Sraffa for allowing me to publish these letters.
4. The condition regarding the equality of relative prices of the s commodities common to the two systems is equivalent to stating that the wage in terms

of any of them should be equal, at the switch point, in the two systems. A point of some interest to note is that, if we consider any two production systems differing in the method of production for more than one commodity common to them and express the wage and prices in the two systems in terms of some one of the commodities common to them, the relative prices for these common commodities in the two systems may not necessarily be equal at all the intersections of the wage profit curves for the two systems. The equality of the relative prices would have to be laid down as a priori condition to obtain the switch points among those points of intersections. But, see p. 259–60 and note 11 below.

5   We do so since, at a switch point, all the methods in both systems must be competitive.
6   Since $p_{ia}^+ = p_{ib}^+ = p_i^+$ and $W_a^+ = W_b^+$ either of the two systems can be so used.
7   A particular illustration of this is the result obtained by Joan Robinson and K.A. Naqvi (1967, p. 590) where they consider two production systems, one with wheat and iron as basics and another with wheat and aluminium as basics and obtain three switch points between them.
8   These switch points could also include such cases where, at the switch point rate of profit, the wage-profit curve for one system is tangential to that of the other wholly from above: that is, the same system continues to be the more profitable one on both sides of the switch point.
9   See p. 262 above.
10 Analytically there is no loss of generality involved in a procedure of successive consideration of production systems using a different method of production for only one of the commodities common to them as, given all possible systems of production, it could not lead to any different outermost boundary of wage/profit curves. Incidentally, it should be noted that whatever are the number of commodities produced by different methods in the two systems, the *maximum* number of switching possibilities will still be equal to the total number of distinct (without double counting) basics in the two systems together.
11 Alternatively, we could arrive at the same conclusion by observing that a system with m basic commodities (such as A above) has $(m + 1)$ unknowns $(m - 1$ relative prices, wage and the rate of profit) and m independent equations to solve them. Hence one more additional equation can be accommodated to make the system determinate, even though it does not bring in any additional commodity with its price. This additional equation would be the alternative method for one commodity in the system. If the alternative method brings in additional commodities there would have to be as many additional price equations. In our example above there are $(m + n - s)$ distinct commodities in the two systems together, and $(m + n - s + 1)$ independent methods would be needed to determine the prices, wage rate and the rate of profit. If more than one commodity in system A has a different method in system B the system of equations would be overdetermined.
12 However, the switches in the method of a non-basic have to be clearly distinguished from those for a basic, inasmuch as the former would not affect the relative prices of the basics in the system or the maximum rate of profit, whereas the latter do.
13 One may consider, as a curiosum, the case of a commodity basic to system A which, when produced by an alternative method, becomes itself a non-basic in system B, each of the other commodities having only one known method. This would, however, imply that the two systems would have no

commodities in common which are basic to both.

14 This needs some clarification: two production systems differing in the method of production for one of the basics common to them could have one or more commodities which are basic to one and not to the other. If wages and prices are expressed in terms of the 'standard commodity' of either one of the systems (for the definition of the 'standard commodity' see Sraffa, 1960, pp. 18–20) as Sraffa does (see ibid., p. 85) or in terms of any value unit involving commodities exclusively basic to one of the systems, the other system will have its prices and wage expressed in terms of a value unit involving non-basics to itself. These non-basics are, however, basics to the other system and hence enter, directly or indirectly, into the production of the basic (with alternative methods) in that system.

15 The price equation for the non-basic at $\lambda = 1/a_{33}$ gives in system A:

$$\frac{a_{13}}{a_{33}} p_{1a} + \frac{a_{23}}{a_{33}} p_{2a} + a_{03} w = 0.$$

With $a_{33} > 0$, $a_{13}, a_{23} \geq 0$ this cannot be satisfied for positive prices. See also p. 262 above.

16 Thus consider two non-basics in the above system (commodities 3 and 5) with the commodity 3 as a value unit and commodity 5 entering its production. We have the two systems differing in the method for commodity 1 as before. The price relations are given by (in system A):

$$(1 - a_{11} \lambda) p_{1a} - a_{21} \lambda p_{2a} - a_{01} W_a = 0$$

$$- a_{12} \lambda p_{1a} + (1 - a_{22} \lambda) p_{2a} - a_{02} W_a = 0$$

$$- a_{13} \lambda p_{1a} - a_{53} \lambda p_{5a} - a_{03} W_a = a_{33} \lambda - 1$$

$$- a_{14} \lambda p_{1a} + (1 - a_{55} \lambda) p_{5a} - a_{04} W_a = a_{35} \lambda$$

For system B coefficients in the first and second equations alone are different, the respective price equations being:

$$(1 - b_{11} \lambda) p_{1b} - b_{41} \lambda p_{4b} - b_{01} W_b = 0$$

$$- b_{14} \lambda p_{1b} + (1 - b_{44} p_{4b}) - b_{04} W_b = 0$$

The switch points for the two systems are obtained as before by solving for λ as in (4) above. The expression on the left-hand side of (4) gives, in this case, a common factor, a polynomial in λ of degree at most two and at most two additional values for λ (i.e., two more than would have been obtained if only basics formed the value unit). This common factor is $\{(1 - a_{33} \lambda)(1 - a_{55} \lambda) - a_{35} \lambda a_{53} \lambda\}$ which when equated to zero gives the value of $r = \lambda - 1$, equal to the rate of reproduction of the group of non-basics. It will be noted that if $a_{33} = 0$ and $a_{35} = 0$ (with $a_{53} > 0$, given) then $\lambda = 1/a_{55}$. This is the case when only commodity 5 of the two non-basics requires itself in its own production. Similarly, if $a_{33} > 0$ but $a_{35} = 0$ and $a_{55} = 0$ then $\lambda = 1/a_{33}$. In both cases the solution for λ gives a rate of profit equal to the rate of reproduction of the separate non-basics.

17 The Levhari Theorem (Levhari, 1965) was withdrawn (Levhari and Samuelson, 1966) when it was refuted conclusively by a number of writers (see Bruno, Burmeister and Sheshinski, Pasinetti, Morishima and Garegnani in the 'Symposium on paradoxes in capital theory', 1966).

18 Levhari's argument is based on the assumption that there are a number of alternative methods for producing each commodity and that each one of the possible systems of production consists of only basics. His statement on the non-reswitching of any one system of production seems to have been suggested by the conjecture that when there is a wide range of known methods for each one of the several commodities the *probability* that a number of methods should reswitch at the same point (i.e., the same system should return) would be very small. Levhari, however, claimed to have established rigorously the *impossibility* of such a reswitching, and this claim was certainly wrong.

19 We may conceive of a peculiar economic situation in which a nation consists of two or more separate economic communities having different customs and therefore, for instance, producing and consuming different kinds of food, etc. They are considered as forming a single statistical aggregate and therefore a single system. The production matrix for such a system would be 'completely decomposable'. (Mathematically, a square matrix A is called 'completely decomposable' when by identical arrangement of rows and columns it can be partitioned into $\begin{bmatrix} A_{11} & 0 \\ 0 & A_{22} \end{bmatrix}$ with A_{11} and A_{22} square.) In a completely decomposable system there are no basics, as no commodity enters, directly or indirectly, into the production of all commodities in the system. Such a system could be subdivided into the independent economies which are combined to form that system, and the commodities in each such economy classified as basics and non-basics to that economy.

20 With two basics and one non-basic in each system, the maximum number of switches would be three when:

(i) The total number of distinct basics in the two production systems together is three and (a) the two systems are characterized by the use of a different method for a basic common to them, or, (b) the two systems differ only in the method for the non-basic common to them and neither methods for the non-basic uses the non-basic. Or, alternatively when:

(ii) The total number of distinct basics in the two systems together is two; the two systems differ in the method for the non-basic and the non-basic uses itself in at least one of the methods by which it is produced.

Chapter 11: References

Bruno, M., Burmeister, E., and Sheshinski, E. (1966), 'The nature and implications of reswitching techniques', *Quartery Journal of Economics*, vol. lxxv, no. 4 (November) pp. 526–53.

Levhari, D. (1965), 'A nonsubstitution theorem and switching of techniques', *Quarterly Journal of Economics*, vol. lxxix, no. 1 (February), pp. 98–105.

Levhari, D., and Samuelson, P. (1966), 'The nonreswitching theorem is false', *Quarterly Journal of Economics*, vol. lxxx, no. 4 (November), pp. 518–19.

Newman, P. (1962), 'Production of commodities by means of commodities', *Schweizerische Zeitschrift für Volkswirtschaft und Statistik*, 98, pp. 58–75.

Paradoxes in Capital Theory: A Symposium in *Quarterly Journal of Economics*, vol. lxxx, no. 4, November 1966, pp. 503–83, with the following articles:

Luigi, L. Pasinetti, 'Changes in the Rate of Profit and Switches of Techniques', pp. 503–17.

P. Garegnani, 'Switching of Techniques', pp. 554–67.

David Levhari and Paul A. Samuelson, 'The Nonswitching Theorem is False', pp. 518–19.

M. Morishima, 'Refutation of the Non Switching Theorem', pp. 520–5.

Michael Bruno, Edwin Burmeister and Eytan Sheshinski, 'The Nature and Implications of the Reswitching of Techniques', pp. 526–53.

Paul A. Samuelson, 'A Summing Up', pp. 568–83.

Robinson, Joan, and Naqvi, K.A. (1967), 'The Badly Behaved Production Function', *Quarterly Journal of Economics*, vol. lxxxi, no. 4 (November), pp. 579–91.

Sraffa, P. (1960), *Production of Commodities by Means of Commodities* (Cambridge: Cambridge University Press).

12

On Effective Demand: Certain Recent Critiques

The aim of this essay is to raise 'some old-fashioned questions in economic theory' which appear to be critical for the direction that developments in the theory of effective demand is taking. The literature on 'the economics of Keynes', 'what Keynes really meant' – constituting revaluation, reinterpretations and extensions – is so voluminous that selectivity about the choice of the questions is unavoidable. There are no easy answers, or even definitively unique ones, especially at the present stage of theory. Nevertheless, the present company – containing Keynesian stalwarts – assures me that we should be able to sort out the grain from the chaff.

1 Resurgence of the Economics of Keynes

1.1 The common link in the resurgence of the economics of Keynes – its critical revaluation and attempts at reconstruction – is the opposition to the neoclassical synthesis which practically swept away a 'revolution' before it could settle down.[1] The counter-arguments to the *General Theory* (1936), (especially, to its claim of 'generality' and distinctiveness) soon formed themselves in the wake of its publication, Hicks (1937) initiating the 'Keynes and the Classics' debate with his now textbook-enshrined IS–LM exposition. The synthesis evolved in later writings, among the well-known landmarks being Modigliani (1944, 1963) and Patinkin (1965). In a generalized interdependent system within the neoclassical framework involving demand-and-supply relations for commodities, money and assets, the special Keynesian result of 'unemployment equilibrium' was seen to emerge from identifying one or the other assumption as 'crucial' which converted certain functions into constants or attached extreme values – of zero or infinity – to particular price elasticities or put restrictions on the form assumed by certain functions. For example, in Modigliani's version the crucial assumption for deriving the Keynesian result emerged as the rigidity of wages, more accurately 'a basic maladjustment between the quantity of money and the wage rate' (Modigliani, 1944, p. 225). Alternatively, the form of the money-demand function was stipulated to be such as to allow for a 'liquidity trap'. The conclusion was that Keynes's was not a 'general' theory; it was a special variant of the orthodox theory constructed by imposing restrictions which might be considered as arbitrary. It was partly conceded that Keynes's strong point was on the policy front: his acute and perceptive observations about certain facts of life, such as the rigidity of money wages, interest inelasticity of investment in certain ranges and the high interest elasticity of demand for money at certain junctures were acknowledged as crucial for policy purposes. These were peculiarities of the economic system – empirical propositions or specific forms of general relations, requiring testing and verification.[2] All this is a familiar story and we need not recount the details here.

1.2 While the shared ground is the opposition to the neoclassical synthesis, major differences arise among the critiques regarding the nature of Keynes's critique of the traditional theory and hence the characterization of the 'positive' and 'negative' elements in that critique. These differences are attributable essentially to the view that is taken concerning the logical validity of the neoclassical theory of value (i.e., prices) and distribution which ultimately lies at the foundation of the theory of accumulation. Assessments differ as to whether the economics of Keynes calls for a reconstruction – however 'radical' – of the orthodox (or, neoclassical) theory and hence the latter's preservation, albeit in a modified form, or whether Keynes's critique should be advanced to refute the neoclassical theory of distribution (and hence also of resource allocation), grafting the positive elements of Keynes's contribution on to an alternative structure. Understandably, the former view sees the limitations of the neoclassical synthesis in its eliminating those very insights of Keynes which, when incorporated, would enrich the neoclassical theory with possibilities of yielding theoretically more powerful results. Those holding the latter opinion, however, have seen the seeds of the compromise that led to the synthesis in Keynes himself;[3] arguing that the possibility of such a reabsorption was left open by Keynes because of the ambivalent and partial way in which he carried out his critique of orthodoxy. In the neoclassical theory, the full employment of labour (as of other resources) is a result that is reached by deduction from given premises and not a postulate;[4] Keynes's acceptance of the soundness of the theory in its resource-allocational aspects thus implied that his own explanation of unemployment could be eventually reduced to the identification of rigidities and imperfections of the system. Here, we are necessarily drawing a contrast between the two sets of critiques of the neoclassical synthesis on the basis of their position on the central issue of the theory of value and distribution. There are, of course, differences in particular aspects and viewpoints among those belonging to either set.

2 Reactions to the Neoclassical Synthesis: Neoclassical Reformulations

2.1 An important counter to the neoclassical synthesis has been presented by Clower (1965, 1967) and Leijonhufvud (1968 and 1969). It belongs to the first set of reactions I broadly set out, namely, those inspired by the need for reformulating the neoclassical theory on firmer grounds to accommodate Keynesian results. Their arguments are narrowly directed to show that Keynes's underemployment state can be explained independently of the 'liquidity trap', 'money illusion', 'wage rigidity', 'elasticity pessimism', or 'imperfections' in the system. Keynes's critique of traditional theory is seen not so much as directed against the basic structure of the theory but at the manner in which the processes of price-quantity formation are envisaged to work under large-scale decentralized decision-making in the Walrasian construction. Thus they argue that Keynes accepted and worked within the basic neoclassical assumptions of utility maximizing households, profit-maximizing firms, well-behaved preference orderings and production-possibility frontiers. Individual decision-making units – whether households or firms – respond normally to price incentives. Hence there is no money illusion. Thus the challenge which Keynes made to orthodoxy was neither to its basic theory of value and distribution, nor to the choice of primary categories of analysis, but was couched in terms of the price-signalling system that the neoclassical (i.e., Walrasian, in the context of the present authors) theory assumes. In the static general equilibrium system, it is presumed that the market-clearing vector of relative prices (whose existence is here presumed) is known by all transactors, and that each transactor adjusts to these parameters instantaneously so that the system simultaneously generates an optimal allocation of resources with their full utilization. It is argued by these authors that, while Keynes was willing to accept the efficacy of price incentives and price-responsiveness, his arguments can be construed to imply the denial of the price system disseminating appropriate information with sufficient efficiency to guarantee full employment. This is so, at least in the short run, which is their concern.

2.2 Putting the problem this way, the central question that Keynes faced appears to be the same that troubled general equilibrium theorists[5] – who is the auctioneer who can costlessly announce prices at which no actual trading takes place until the equilibrium market-clearing vector of prices is reached by *tâtonnement*? Furthermore, the auctioneer must succeed in establishing a new set of equilibrium prices whenever 'exogenous disturbances' (in tastes or technological possibilities) occur, and the infinite velocity of price adjustments is presumed in the establishment of the new equilibrium prices. Where assets are concerned, the price vector must have intertemporal dimension. In the absence of such an auctioneer or of the presumption of infinite velocity of price adjustments, it is argued, the effects of 'false trading' or of the divergence between 'realized' and 'planned' transactions become significant.[6] To Clower and Leijonhufvud, it is the trading that actually occurs at non-market-clearing prices and its consequences that is at the root of the Keynesian results. Expectations regarding the future, govern current transactions: it is 'the economic behaviour of the present under the influence of changing ideas about the future' (*General Theory*, 1936, p. viii) that was central to Keynes's investigations. These necessarily generate non-*tâtonnement* processes.

2.3 Concretely, how does this manifest itself? Drawing the illustration from the Keynesian discussion of the bond market, the authors argue: if there is a fall in the price of bonds, the risk-averting asset-holder, with inelastic price expectations, buys bonds on the expectation of a capital gain; if he expects the previous price to be 'normal'. In more general terms, the asset-owner, with a rise in the rate of interest, arranges his portfolio of assets so that, on balance, he moves towards a less liquid end of the asset spectrum. A fall in the rate of interest may only encourage bearish behaviour and money hoarding. A similar behavioural pattern is extended to the unemployed worker. According to this view, an unemployed worker forms, on the basis of his view of whether the current situation is temporary or not, an expectation about the possible wage he may secure. He searches for employment at the expected wage, weighing the present value of the income stream he can secure against that obtainable from the expected best offer. This expected best wage is a decreasing function of the length of his search. Thus the emergence of unemployment is to be ascribed to the reservation demand price on the part of the owner for the services of his asset, namely, labour.

2.4 Uncertainty, lack of sufficient information, is seen to generate cumulative, deviation-amplifying, system-wide consequences. The state of Keynesian unemployment is interpreted as emerging from the amplifying effects of initial disturbances occurring through a change in the long-run state of expectations (or equivalently, through a shift in the marginal efficiency of capital schedule) or a 'change in taste', altering the propensity to save or asset preferences. The 'deviation-amplifying' characteristic is considered a feature of a monetary production economy where money is the only commodity tradeable in all markets. Money plays the dual role of being the means of settling all payments, and as an asset that links the future with the present.

2.5 Clower emphasizes the distinctive character of the money economy in the possibility it generates of violating Walras's Law. Unlike a barter economy where commodity exchanges are coincidental, in a monetary economy exchanges are necessarily indirect and mediated through money. A distinction is made between the 'notional excess demands' based on the Walrasian solution involving the real transaction possibilities of the system, and the actual or effective excess demands – those which are backed by realized sales and hence effective purchasing power. A transactor desiring to increase his consumption of commodity i by supplying additional quantities of j, has first to realize money income through the sale of j so as to support his demand for i. In a 'disequilibrium' situation the sale of j may be frustrated. This, in turn, affects the realization of other transactions. It is only when the actual or realized sales and notional sales are equalized throughout, that the full equilibrium can prevail. When they deviate, the transactor will maximize his utility, subject to the effective purchasing power at his command and not to his 'notional' budget constraint and, then, not every household can transact (i.e., buy or sell) what it pleases if supply exceeds demand somewhere in the economy. When realized incomes appear as an independent variable in the market excess demand functions (or, when transaction quantities are introduced explicitly as constraints) traditional Walrasian formulation ceases 'to shed any light on the dynamic stability of a market economy' (Clower, 1965).

2.6 The consequences of an initial disturbance, accounted as a downward shift in the marginal efficiency schedule, are analysed as a chain of repercussions: given the general assumption of inelastic price expectations, the entrepreneurs would accumulate inventories rather than reduce prices in the face of a fall in demand. They would probably reduce the demand for productive services – labour, in particular. The consequence is augmented further by the unemployed worker 'searching' for a job at his reservation price, thereby withholding his services. The reduced wage incomes, and hence the effective purchasing power of workers, would eventually lead to a decline in their demand for commodities.[7]

2.7 A similar chain of effects is associated with a change in the propensity to save. An act of saving releases a command over general purchasing power without creating a specific demand for goods at any specific date in the future. In the absence of the information about the definite time profile, the equilibrium intertemporal price system is not 'revealed'. The fall in the interest rate, which would probably follow increased savings, may only encourage, through the operation of 'liquidity preference', money hoarding and encourage bearish behaviour on the bond market. Thus the fall in current consumption expenditure would not necessarily generate compensatory expenditure on investment goods. Thus, in this manner of explanation of the state of unemployment, it is the liquidity preference and/or the inelastic price expectations of transactors that take on the entire burden of explaining such a state the multiplier is seen essentially as an amplifier of disturbances.

2.8 Certain important questions arise from such a reappraisal of Keynes. To take up the more specific issues within the approach first: the explanation of unemployment in terms of a search procedure would seem to make the phenomenon appear to be voluntary. It is the reservation price that prevents the worker from accepting employment at a lower wage – as if such an opportunity were freely available. The view ignores that, in a Keynesian world, the number of men to be employed is decided by industrial firms (see Kahn, 1977, in a different context.) Secondly, in so far as the acceptable wage or the reservation price is supposed to decline as the search continues unsuccessfully, the consequence of the initial 'lack of information' is effectively the same as presuming a temporary stickiness in wages. Indeed, if the wage-earners do ultimately accept the lower 'equilibrium' wage, it is not clear why the 'neoclassical synthesis' does not come into its own with prices and quantities appropriately adjusted. The appeal then would probably be to the particular form of the money-demand function. It is not clear, therefore, how the reappraisal avoids relying upon 'wage-stickiness' or 'elasticity-pessimism', as it claims to have done.

2.9 The ambivalence concerning the nature of Keynesian unemployment – whether it is to be regarded as a phenomenon which is persistent and could continue even in the long period or as depicting temporary 'states of the system fairly close to full employment equilibrium' – is reflected in Leijonhufvud. He finds the basis of the multiplier itself in the 'illiquidity phenomenon'[8] (Leijonhufvud, 1969, pp. 43–4). The disturbance-amplifying effects of a multiplier would be stronger if the worker's consumption were guided by his current income rather than if he had assets to fall back upon or could sustain his consumption from falling, through borrowing, etc. The fact that workers' consumption is influenced by their current income would appear thus to be basically a reflection of their state of illiquidity. According to Leijonhufvud, both Keynes and the monetarists must consider the economy prone to disaster only when it is 'squeezed dry of its liquidity'. This situation is considered not to be a normal occurrence since transactors are usually possessed of buffer stocks. It is only when the consumption demand of the unemployed is in a large measure 'ineffective' that 'there will be latent multiplier effects of sizeable magnitudes for the policy maker to exploit' (ibid., p. 45). The case for fiscal measures for stabilization purposes, resting on their amplifying effects on effective demand, is thus weakened when the economy is fairly close to the full employment equilibrium – a case more commonly found in Leijonhufvud's view. With marginal flexibility in government net spending – a dose of pump-priming should help the system regain the full employment equilibrium.

2.10 While a description of the disequilibrium, non-*tâtonnement* process, amplifying disturbances and thus leading to unemployment, emerges from these attempts at providing microfoundations to Keynesian results, they have left a number of 'false trails'[9] and landed the theory into a state of theoretical uncertainty. The initial attempts were at construction of short-period Walrasian equilibria – whose existence depended upon tenuous conditions.[10] Apart from the fact that these early constructions failed to accommodate Keynesian unemployment equilibria, except by making them dependent upon price (particularly money wage) rigidities,[11] they left unexplained many parts of the *General Theory*, particularly, as Clower emphasized, those where choices of transactors depend on quantities as well as prices (particularly, the consumption function and demand for money). A solution that has been suggested in subsequent models to reconcile involuntary unemployment with equilibrium is to allow explicitly for situations wherein transactors must adjust their planned actions to the fact that they cannot sell as much labour as they would like to. That is, apart from the budget constraint, a constraint on the feasible supply of labour is imposed (both on the current as well as expected future supplies). Although under certain conditions, the short-period equilibrium (with a fixed money wage) of this 'non-Walrasian' variety may exist, the theoretical conditions for existence are very stringent indeed in terms of the expectational requirements and continuity of behavioural functions. As Hahn (1977) notes, it is not at all obvious that equilibrium would exist. Further, the question remains: *how do the transactors inform themselves of the 'quantity constraints' in the present period, let alone in the future periods*? On what basis do they form their expectations concerning these constraints which are to be taken as parametrically operative?

2.11   What we have is a description of the probable effects of, say, a fall in money wage when the economy is out of a 'short-run' unemployment, non-Walrasian equilibrium: a redistribution in favour of profits may not induce greater demand, if it is expected to be transitory; the workers, if they are in a relatively illiquid position, will curtail their demand for commodities; wages and prices may fall continuously; while real cash balances increase, they may fail to induce demand if the expectations concerning future price behaviour encourage hoarding of money or less liquid assets. First, it is not yet known where the 'sequence of states' of the economy leads to – whether it is a converging sequence at all. Hence no 'long-run' position can emerge. This uncertainty of the outcome is heightened when we realize that everything in this analysis depends upon the particular expectational hypotheses assumed. Equally disturbing is the loss of Keynes's 'macro-economic' insights, when it is becoming widely acknowledged that 'usable economics will have to be of some sort of macro character' (Hahn, 1977). In a scheme where any disturbance in the market triggers an amplifying effect in the market, where 'quantity constraints' are parametrically introduced without an explanation as to how they are generated and perceived, where much rests on 'expectations' formed subjectively by individual transactors, both the direction and causality of relations, as well as a judgement as to the relative strength and persistence of the stimuli, are lost altogether. It would seem that reconciling the Keynesian results within the Walrasian neoclassical theory has posed fundamental problems.

3   Pasinetti on *The Structure of Keynes's Theory*

3.1   Pasinetti (1974) opposes the 'neoclassical synthesis' because it introduces structural shifts which have obscured certain clearcut results that Keynes obtained, thus diminishing the thrust of his critique of the orthodox theory. Keynes's major breakthrough was to show that the equality between desired savings and the volume of investment is maintained by variations in the level of aggregate output and employment. While savings (and consumption) depend upon the level of income, savings is 'not a substitution of future consumption-demand for present consumption demand' (Keynes, 1936, p. 210) and cannot by itself stimulate investment. The volume of investment which an entrepreneur may undertake at any time is independent of the current level of income, but depends upon the expected outcome. The major thrust of Keynes's critique was against the equilibrating role of the rate of interest acting to equalize planned savings and investment in the orthodox theory. Pasinetti considers the Keynesian scheme to be causally ordered and deriving its efficacy in terms of powerful results from such a clearcut direction of causality. That is, the rate of interest is determined outside the sphere of output, on the basis of the demand for money and the exogenously given money supply, while, given the schedule of the marginal efficiency of capital, the rate of interest sets the level of investment. In the process of income determination, investment is thus the active element and changes in income (and employment) act to equilibrate savings and investment. Pasinetti is critical of Hicks (1937) for converting the Keynesian system into a generally interdependent one, and thus reinforcing the role of the rate of interest as equilibrating savings and investment, reducing thereby the basic contribution of Keynes to the liquidity-preference analysis.

> But this is surely a distortion. However important a role liquidity preference may play in Keynes's monetary theory, it is entirely immaterial to his theory of effective demand. What this theory requires, as far as the rate of interest is concerned, is not that the rate of interest is determined by liquidity preference, but that it is determined *exogenously* with respect to income generation process. Whether, in particular liquidity preference, or anything else determines it, is entirely immaterial. (Pasinetti, 1974, p. 47)

Pasinetti thus believes that the clearcut results of Keynes arise from a certain openness in the system due to the separation of the question of output determination from that of the rate of interest. This is at the root of Keynes's attack on the orthodox explanation of the rate of interest. 3.2 To the extent, however, that there is transaction demand and the finance motive enters in the demand for money, Pasinetti's causal ordering would not strictly hold. Nevertheless, the analytical advantage of separating output determination from the explanation of the rate of interest stressed by Pasinetti could be an important element in a theoretical reconstruction, retaining the positive contribution of Keynes's theory of effective demand. However, there has been a tendency to overemphasize causal ordering in attempts to differentiate Keynes from neoclassical writers (particularly, Walras), although Pasinetti himself does not do so. A particular kind of causal ordering, *in itself*, could not be considered a sufficient ground for favouring the Keynesian or any other formulation, even if such an ordering were indeed to hold. It may be more important to scrutinize the theory, specifying the relations and the mode of their operation rather than merely whether the underlying structure of causality is unidirectional or mutually interdependent. It is true that the more complex causality structures inevitably lose in their power of suggestiveness and sharpness of results. There is, however, more fundamental ground for dissatisfaction with the neoclassical *theory* – it faces a number of logical hurdles in satisfying norms of internal

ON EFFECTIVE DEMAND   283

consistency. To the exposure of these weaknesses, Pasinetti has himself made valuable contributions in the capital theory debates.

3.3   It is not surprising that, given Keynes's acceptance of the traditional theory in certain critical parts, attempts at reconstruction have proceeded in the direction of providing 'an anchorage in the fundamentals of our discipline'. A candidate for such an attempt is the consumption function (a macro-level conception to which Keynes attached considerable innovative significance but which is considered as an odd member) – an *ad hoc* construction, at best – as it is not generated from the usual utility-maximizing choice exercises performed by individuals in the conventional Walrasian models. The attempts at reformulation have not done justice to the variety of institutional, psychological and historical forces which Keynes stressed – many of them founded on a long-run perspective. His emphasis on the direct link between consumption and the level of output (income) and employment, and on the importance of income-distributional effects, kept open the possibility in the later post-Keynesian theory of explicitly dealing with functional distribution (wages and profits as distributive revenues) and the separate treatment of capitalists' and workers' consumption. The more interesting policy implications of the post-Keynesian analysis flow from such an extension. An important consequence of the 'Walrasation' of Keynes has been the complete shift to the micro-level entities as units of analysis, obliterating certain system-level causalities and influences present in Keynes. Although Keynes also operated in terms of individual households and firms as the basic unit, he could explicitly bring in certain system-level influences while discussing aggregate consumption behaviour, money-wage-level determination and the state of expectations. The attempt to derive Keynesian results in the decentralized framework has meant confining the analysis altogether to short-run phenomena, on the one hand, and to the behaviour of individual transactors under situations of uncertainty and influence of expectations, perceived basically in subjective terms, on the other. The micro-economics is left without any macro foundation.

4   *Garegnani's Appraisal of Keynes*

4.1   In the spate of controversy that followed the *General Theory* and its reabsorption into orthodoxy, its critical and constructive force has been greatly tempered. Garegnani has argued that Keynes's retention of certain elements of the traditional distribution theory rendered his critique weak and, in parts, unsustainable. Countering the traditional argument that changes in wages would lead to full employment, he accepted the 'first postulate' according to which wages must equal the marginal product of labour at a given level of employment, but rejected the second, that 'the utility of the wage when a given volume of labour is employed is equal to the marginal disutility of that amount of employment' (Keynes, 1936, p. 5). Garegnani comments: 'In doing so [i.e., accepting the first postulate], he accepts the conception of the process found in traditional theory' (Garegnani, 1978, p. 343). Further,

> The marginalist notion of a demand for labour elastic with respect to the real wage rate does not suffice to support the conclusion that competition among workers will lead to full employment. The *further* condition that investment adjusts to the changes in employment is also required ... Keynes's tendency in the *General Theory* was to consider this theory of interest as a further, unwarranted hypothesis that marginalist authors had introduced alongside the valid hypothesis concerning the variability of the proportions of factors of production in the productive process. (Garegnani, 1978, p. 343)

However, Garegnani points out, the theory of interest in the orthodox doctrine is part and parcel of their long-run theory of distribution and strictly dependent upon those marginalist hypotheses. That theory required the possibility of establishing an inverse relation between the volume of planned investment and the rate of interest. Now, the demand function for investment, negatively elastic with respect to the rate of interest, is ultimately founded on the demand function for capital, considered as one of the factors of production, which is taken to vary inversely relative to the rate of interest[12] – a proposition whose validity the capital theory debates have effectively challenged. Once the inverse relation of investment demand with respect to the rate of interest is accepted, as by Keynes, the efficacy of the rate of interest as an equilibrator of savings and investment would depend entirely upon the *extent* of sensitivity of the interest rate to the divergence between investment and full employment savings. Garegnani argues that Keynes's attack on the traditional theory was consequently directed more specifically against the latter proposition, namely, that the rate of interest varies with sufficient sensitivity to eliminate divergence between planned investment and savings at the full employment level.

4.2 The route that Keynes took was to construct an explanation of the rate of interest as determined proximately by monetary factors, that is, in terms of the demand for, and supply of, the stock of money. The rate of interest brings to equality, not the demand for and supply of savings, but the desire to hold money and the exogenously determined supply of money. Having thus determined the rate of interest, planned investment would depend upon the marginal efficiency of capital schedule and there is no necessity that the level of investment attained would be such as to equal the full employment savings. In a situation where planned investment falls short of planned savings, the equality would be ensured through the contraction of output. Keynes explicitly ruled out rigidity of wages as the basis of his result. The effect of a fall in money-wage rate depended upon its influence via the marginal efficiency of capital, the consumption function and the rate of interest. While the effect would be negative (in terms of employment) in the first two cases, Keynes argued that the effects via the rate of interest would be limited (as would it be in the case of open-market operations). The interest rate may not fall sufficiently if the reduction in money-wage rate is moderate, and may destroy the state of confidence if the reduction is sudden and sharp. Thus it is Keynes's critique of the traditional theory of interest rather than the hypothesis of money-wage rigidity that is crucial to his arguments. However, Keynes's liquidity-preference theory has been quickly absorbed within the neoclassical synthesis. The rate of interest, in such a synthesis, equates both the demand for and supply of money as well as savings. The Keynesian particular case is limited to the very low interest rates when the rate of interest can fall no further due to a decline in money wage, that is, the case of the liquidity trap. With a real wealth effect introduced at this stage, the argument would revert to rigidity of wages.

4.3 Garegnani (1978) discerns the source of ambivalence and contradictions in Keynes's theory in its composite character:

> A vision of the mode of operation of the economic system which is in radical conflict with the dominant theory, is imposed, as if by force, upon a conceptual basis which is, to a large extent, still the traditional one, thus giving rise to an inherently unstable compromise.

The novel and pathbreaking thesis of Keynes, that it is principally variations in the level of aggregate output that equilibrate savings and investment, is in conflict with the traditional marginalist *theory of distribution*. It is the way in which Keynes devised his critique that was responsible for denuding it of forceful results. Keynes accepted the traditional part of the theory in the two schedules of marginal product of labour and the marginal efficiency of capital, and turned his attack on the sensitivity of variations in the rate of interest to bring to equality savings and investment at the full employment level. The terms in which the critique was cast has also led to confining the theory to the short run. Garegnani's suggestion is that the recent controversies in capital theory, which have successfully challenged the logical validity of the neoclassical theory of distribution, could now be employed to argue that

> even if the rate of interest could be assumed to be sufficiently sensitive to divergences between planned investment and planned savings – there would not be sufficient ground for arguing that the rate of interest could ensure that the decisions to invest will adapt to decisions to save; nor would there be sufficient ground for arguing that aggregate demand will adapt to the level of production compatible with the full employment of productive resources available in the economy. (pp. 351–2).

And, this can be established without the obstacles of money and the state of expectations, which no doubt could be additional complications.

4.4 Further, the positive elements in Keynes need not be confined to the short period. The short-period problem of effective demand seeks to take account of forces operating upon the utilization of productive capacity and its consequent effects upon the state of investment, output and employment. The long-period problem concerns forces affecting accumulation (i.e., creation of capacity and investment). The centre of theoretical efforts in the 'economics of Keynes' appears to be the issue of whether there is an automatic tendency towards full employment in the short run (i.e., whether there is a short-run full employment equilibrium). If we accept – as many here would – that there is no automatic tendency towards full employment in a capitalist economy even in the long run, then we must recognize that there is an effective demand problem in the long run, too. Both Marx and Kalecki recognized a chronic tendency of the capitalist system towards involuntary unemployment – a tendency distinguishable from short-run cyclical fluctuations. To deal with the long-run problem, a necessity arises inevitably to specify the long-period theory of distribution and to link up the theory of output and employment with such a theory. The effective-demand principle need not necessarily be limited to short-run theory and investment. In the long, as well as the short, period, the level of investment could be treated as independent of the propensity to save.

4.5 Recent debates in capital theory which refuted the neoclassical theory of distribution would seem, then, to be of more than purely scholastic interest. They have exposed the structural weakness of that theory in explaining distribution and hence brought into doubt their characterization of capitalist production processes. The results of the controversy are not confined to the refutation of the analytical basis for the traditional explanation of profit but, furthermore, challenge the *long-run* explanation of output and employment, since it is the same analytical scheme of interdependent price-quantity relations that explains output levels, commodity and factor prices, as well as their rates of utilization. With the analytical basis of the long-run theory thus challenged, the theory has retreated into the study of the limited cases of 'pure exchange' and 'short-term equilibria', in order to avoid providing a consistent long-run theory of distribution. But, even in these limited pursuits, as Garegnani has argued,

> we should be moving on the dubious ground of wages and prices determined according to a short period analysis of the economy as a whole. In the course of such an analysis we would be faced by a multiplicity of factors, each of which may influence the demand for investment. We should thus have to take account of the disproportions between available equipment and the level of demand for products in each industry; the age structure of existing equipment and the connected irregular replacements, etc. (Garegnani, 1978, p. 347).

In the retreat to short-period analysis, the emphasis on expectations emerges. With productive capacities in individual producing units and industries adapted to various degrees to demand, and with varying expectations concerning the demand for their products, a definitive generalization could not be made regarding the nature of the macro-level, investment-demand schedule in relation to the rate of interest (i.e., regarding the direction of variation or the degree of responsiveness of the overall level of investment to the rate of interest).

4.6 A consistent theory of distribution is the central fulcrum to any analysis of accumulation. The present state of uncertainty of neoclassical theory – whether of short-period or long-period analysis – stems precisely from the loss of a consistent theory of distribution. This lacuna is felt all the more in the policy sphere, which is not our concern here. The recent revival of the classical political economy suggests that the surplus approach may provide an alternative foundation upon which a consistent theory of distribution and accumulation may be constructed. We shall consider some basic structural features of the approach which favours such a reconstruction below.

5 The Surplus-Based Approach

5.1 The surplus approach, developed in the hands of Smith, Ricardo and Marx, was concerned particularly with answering questions pertaining to the process of generation, distribution and accumulation of surplus in a competitive capitalist economy. We shall argue later that the approach is generalizable to a variety of historical situations, although these authors used certain abstractions pertaining to their particular historical stage of competitive capitalism. Prominent among these were the tripartite division of distributive revenues according to the three classes of landlords, capitalists and workers; and a tendency towards a uniform rate of profits, resulting from the capitalists' competitive struggle in pursuit of the maximum profit, and a uniform wage emerging as a result of the 'free' exchange of 'labour-power'.

5.2 An important analytical distinction was made between 'permanent' or persistent forces that act upon the system, and the transient influences that are accidental, sometimes unforeseen or possessing a random impact. It was maintained that the persistent tendencies (designated 'long-run' or 'natural') were the subject of theoretical analysis. 'Permanent' did not mean 'fixed', 'stationary', or 'invariant'. (A characteristic example is the distinction that was made between 'natural' and 'market' prices.) It was the tendencies of the system acknowledged as 'persistent' (e.g., the tendency towards a uniform rate of profit or a uniform wage) which were taken to be the basis of analysis of the problem of value, distribution and accumulation. A parallel concept of long-period equilibrium was constructed, for similar purposes, by the marginalists (Marshall, Walras, Wicksell). However, the *theory* that determined the long-period equilibrium in their case is different.

5.3 The need for a consistent explanation of natural price (or prices of production) arose in the classical theory as invariably connected with the question of the distribution of the surplus among the classes. The rate of profit was explained on the basis of given social output levels, given 'dominant' techniques of production and the real wage. A consistent set of 'natural prices' or 'prices of production', along with the natural rate of profit, emerged as a solution to this system (see Sraffa, 1960). Such an approach to distribution has certain features which we may note.[13]

(a) The 'given' wage allows a wide spectrum of social and historical factors to enter into its determination. Further, the system of price-and-distribution determination is open to considering, alternatively, the rate of profit as independently given (Sraffa, 1960), or introducing any other rule for surplus sharing[14], provided it is consistent with the rest of the system.

(b) Similarly, a 'given' level of social output does not connote fixity or stationarity. It underlines the fact that there are more complex historical forces affecting output levels and their composition which are not confined to the scheme of price-formation and hence for the purposes of price-determination, social outputs are taken as provisionally given. Thus Smith could talk of forces of technical change, division of labour, new commodities, changes in customs and habits while, at the same time, taking 'effectual demand' as a given, average position around which fluctuations might take place.

(c) Likewise the 'given' dominant methods of production does not imply that there is only a unique method in existence for each commodity, or that there is invariance of costs relative to the scale of output. Nor does this rule out technical change. A distinction was made between techniques in use, or 'known' techniques, and 'new' techniques not yet introduced. The 'dominant' method, among the methods in use, can itself be variously interpreted as the one most widely used (i.e., as producing the major share of output), or as the one in which new investments are taking place, or as the 'average' of all techniques in use. Given the spectrum of techniques actually is use, it is to be noted that not every change in technique adopted by an individual makes redefinition of *the 'dominant' technique* necessary.

(d) The fact that output, methods of production and the wage are 'given' for the derivation of prices does not rule out interaction among these factors. Indeed, the classical writers were explicitly concerned with such interactions between, say, the level of output and changes in techniques, or the speed of accumulation and the wage rate, or the wage and the methods of production. However, no rigid, functional links were forged between, for example, changes in output and costs of production, or changes in labour productivity and wages – as are found in marginalist analysis. Such rigid functional relationships stipulating the 'well-behavedness' of the relevant supply-and-demand relations constrain the analysis, and imply that only certain kinds of changes, and in preordained directions, could be compatible with the theory. In the surplus analysis no such general restrictive conditions are required, so that no logical difficulties arise internally to the theory from increasing returns, or from a positive relation between capital-intensity and the rate of profit, or between investment and the rate of interest.

5.4 This structure of relations thus has an openness which allows the introduction of specific historical factors and particularities of social relations. Unlike the neoclassical scheme, it is not encumbered by the needs of internal consistency to stipulate strict conditions on price-quantity relations. The openness also allows for cognizance of the macro-level forces directly, for example, the changing class-relations, forms and strategies of struggle, changing forms of control over the productive processes, the complex factors that enter the choice of technology by individual producers, and the forms of intracapitalist rivalry. These, no doubt, are significant forces affecting the pace of, and shaping the course of, accumulation.

5.5 Certain misgivings about the revival of the surplus approach must, however, be removed before considering an extension of that approach. An important misunderstanding that has been responsible for underrating its potentialities is Keynes's interpretation of the Say's Law controversy between Ricardo and Malthus. As Meek (1950–1), Dobb (1973) and Garegnani (1978, 1981) have clarified, the context and the terms of that debate were altogether different from that defined in Keynes's assault on Say's Law. No doubt, Malthus raised similar questions concerning the adequacy of total demand. However, he himself shared with Ricardo the crucial assumption of the identity of savings and investment, so that his arguments were internally inconsistent. That the content of that controversy was different is evident from the fact that Ricardo had no theory of the rate of interest as the price which equated supply of savings and demand for investment funds. Yet it was such a proposition that Keynes considered to be at the root of the fallacious position of his contemporaries. Further, Say's Law was not taken as a premise to deduce full employment as a consequence. In fact, underutilization of capacity and of labour could be quite consistent with the classical scheme. This was clear from Marx's notion of the reserve army of the unemployed as a persistent feature of the capitalist economy. Marx's criticism of Say's Law rested not on its implications regarding full employment, but in its simulating the logic of a barter economy, ignoring the interposition of money in the circuit of exchange, and ignoring thereby the implication of capitalist production for the realization of exchange value. That Marx could discard Say's Law without abandoning the scheme of 'prices of production' for the analysis of profit is proof enough that the law was neither an essential premise, nor an inevitable deduction of that scheme.

5.6 Another important misunderstanding arises from treating the prices of production scheme (particularly, as represented by Sraffa, 1960) as implying a 'stationary state', attributing to it an assumption of 'self-reproducibility'. Indeed (except for the preliminary chapter where Sraffa talks about a system without a surplus), no such assumption is involved. The general assumption he makes concerning the *self-replacing* system is merely a viability condition that is usually made without explicit statement. As no presumption is made regarding the subsequent utilization of surplus, the system remains open.[15] It should be possible to graft on to the scheme of prices such theories of output determination or of technical change as would not violate the internal consistency of the basic scheme; the advantage of the scheme being precisely that it would allow integrating a much wider set of determining forces without invalidating the logic of the system (cf. Eatwell, 1979).

5.7 A related objection pertains to the particular assumptions of the uniform rate of profit and given *real* wage. Reference is made to the fact that, historically, at no time have producers obtained the same rate of profit or has there been the same method of production in use for any commodity. Indeed, no classical writer ever maintained that such a uniformity was, or would be, achieved in practice. Statements to the contrary are more prolific. All their discussions regarding the tendency towards the uniform rate of profit (and the adoption of an optimum technique) were suffused with illustrations directly recognizing that there existed, in actual observations, differences among individual producers. Smith, as well as Ricardo, conceived of a vector of natural rates of profit (Smith, 1776 [1937], p. 160), with the differentials remaining stable with output movements (akin to their idea of historically obtained wage-rate differentials). Recognizing differences in actual or realized profit rates at any moment did not contradict the *tendency* towards levelling of profits such as to equalize the rates. This, as well as the uniformity of wages were the rules, so to say, by which the surplus was considered to be distributed. In a different historical situation the rules for distributing the surplus would indeed be different when a different stage of capitalist development exhibits a different characterization of capital/labour and/or intracapitalists' relations and a basis for a 'persistent' tendency is obtained to support the rule. Given the distributive rules, a set of consistent prices would emerge.[16]

Similarly, the assumption of a given real wage is also to be seen in the light of the historically specific situation in which the early classical writers postulated their observations. While 'given' does not necessarily mean 'fixed' or 'minimum subsistence', the variable that was socially manipulated and/or appeared as an historical datum was the wage rate. What is germane to our consideration is that the surplus approach allows the socio-historical determination of distribution (i.e., of either the wage or the profit rate).

5.8 Is the classical system based on the assumption of perfect certainty and foresight? These are indeed associated with steady growth models. The 'long-run' position of the classical theory does not rest either on perfect knowledge or error-free behaviour.[17] It takes account of the observed dominant characteristics of the system emerging as 'average' positions. It is not necessary, for example, that all producers are necessarily using the same method of production, or that all producers are actually realizing maximum profits or securing a uniform return on their capital. It is not essential that resources are fully utilized. The expectations of individual producers could well be unsatisfied. In fact, in the descriptive accounts found in Smith, Ricardo and particularly in J.S. Mill, of how the *tendency* towards the uniform rate of profit asserts itself, it is precisely the hope of gain and the fear of loss that induces movements of capital from one avenue to another, allowing for realization of outcomes which may diverge from those initially expected.[18] Disappointed individual expectations were, however, supposed not to affect the long-run 'average' position. If they did so systematically, a new central position (or long-run position) would be conceptualized. Marx's acknowledgement of the 'anarchy of competition' did not prevent him from deducing results about the more persistent tendencies of the system.

5.9 This brings us to another source of plausible misunderstanding in the context of the 'long-run'/'short-run' debate. The long-period position is a conceptual device for separating the more 'permanent' characteristics of the system from the more transient variations. Without such a benchmark in analysis, it is not possible to derive definite results, as was recognized by the classical writers and by the early marginalists (Marshall, Wicksell and Walras). Accepting the meaningfulness of the long-period position is not tantamount to denying the validity or relevance of any short-period analysis. The relevant questions are: (a) how is the short-period analysis to be related to the more persistent forces in the economy, and (b) what *theory* is used to explain the short-period as well as long-period positions.

5.10 The need to relate the short-period analysis to the long-period was recognized by the early marginalists, by Keynes as well as by Marx and Kalecki; although in each case, the theory that was used was different. Marshall was one of the first writers to 'periodize' markets into short and long periods, applying the same tool of analysis – supply-and-demand-based equilibrium – to various 'market' conditions (see Bharadwaj, 1978 b; Chapter 6 in this volume). However, he not only linked the conceptions of the short period to the long period, by successively releasing the conditions locked away in the *ceteris paribus* clause, but also maintained explicitly that the short-period forces were too fickle and fitful to support certain kinds of analysis. He did not, for example, advance any explanation of the rate of profit in the short period. Keynes, too, as Kregel (1976) argues, worked with alternative assumptions about the constancy of expectations and their effect on the system. Keynes mostly used the assumption of constant long-term expectations which allowed him to 'lock up' the effect of general expectations and uncertainty without assuming that they did not exist. He could then proceed to analyse the results of 'alternative, differing, given and constant states of expectations'; while admitting the possibility that particular individual expectations could be disappointed, The long-period expectations were assumed to be independent of such outcomes. Keynes could thereby attribute relative stability to the functional relations he used. Keynes's positive results on effective demand owed their power to his 'taming' the uncertainty and expectations to yield definite results. Although Marx presents no systematic theory integrating cyclical fluctuations with the long-run tendencies of the system, a distinction clearly emerges. For the latter analysis, Marx used his schemes of expanded reproduction; the realization crisis, for example, appears as a long-run phenomenon, while interruptions in financial and commodity circuits produce periodical disruptions (cf. the discussion in *Capital*, Vols II and III). Kalecki, too, was concerned with the relation between cycles and trend.[19] His models interrelating investment, profits savings and effective demand can produce either a cycle or a trend.[20]

5.11 Once the effective-demand problem is acknowledged, both in the short and long period (in the sense above in 4.4), it is necessary to recognize that the forces operating on the short-term capacity utilization and on the pace and direction of accumulation are not all the same or of the same persistence. Central to both analyses is the theory of distribution, which specifies the rules which govern the amount and distribution of surplus produced at any time. The theory of distribution brings out the 'inner connections' between the social classes and acts as the central fulcrum in the 'inherent mechanism of the economic dynamics' which works through the factors affecting the level of investment and the multiplier process. The dispute here is not so much about short period and long period being mutually exclusive, alternative methods. It is the neoclassical *theory*, having hopelessly floundered on the theory of distribution, that has receded to a conception of short-period equilibrium within that theory which has severed it from the long-period notions and has, simultaneously, reduced the long-period notions to sterile conceptions of 'steady growth'.

5.12 A certain misgiving also arises because of the confusion between long-period positions of the classical theory and stationary or steady-state models of neoclassical variety. Disappointed with the latter's performance, Joan Robinson (1979) has objected to the method of comparing long-run positions. Her objections to the ahistorical nature of stationary and steady-state analyses are relevant and powerful as criticisms of the theory that determines those long-period equilibria. Our discussion of the surplus approach should suggest that the 'openness' of the classical system allows for the introduction of historically specific characteristics (and changes in them) that are considered sufficiently definite to be abstractly postulated for analysis. In fact, it is only by comparing two or more different positions that definitive implications of historical changes in terms of their more significant effects on the system can be analysed. Marx adopted the same method when he analysed effects of accumulation using his departmental schema.[21] While there is no denying the need to incorporate real-world considerations and the fact that expectations and uncertainty are endemic in such situations, there is also the need to provide theoretical structures that lead to firm and meaningful results with real-world applications. It has been argued here that a firmer theoretical scaffolding may be available in the surplus theory which offers greater promise in this direction.

Notes: Chapter 12

This paper was presented at a conference held by the Centro di Studi Economici Avanzati at Udine in 1981, and first published in J. A. Kregel (ed.) 1983, *Distribution, Effective Demand and International Economic Relations* (London: Macmillan), pp. 3–27.

1 'After 1945', writes Joan Robinson (1971, p.ix), 'Keynes's innovations had become orthodox in their turn; now governments had to admit that they were concerned with maintaining the level of employment; but in respect to economic theory the old theology closed in again.'
2 Even on the policy side, the Keynesian gains are being increasingly threatened by the rise of the 'new monetarism'. The recent monetarist arguments – spearheaded by Friedman (1956, 1970) – have extended some of Keynes's own suggestions, particularly stressing money as an asset. In fact, the emphasis has been shifted entirely onto money as *one* among a variety of assets – financial, physical and human – yielding income which a utility-maximizing asset-owner chooses to hold, operating within his wealth constraint.
3 For instance, Joan Robinson (1971, p. ix) remarks: 'Keynes himself began the reconstruction of the orthodox scheme that he had shattered. "But if our central controls succeed in establishing an aggregate volume of output corresponding to full employment as nearly as is practicable, the classical theory comes into its own again from this point onwards ... It is in determining the volume, not the direction of actual employment that the existing system has broken down" (Keynes, 1936, pp. 378–9). He had been too much occupied with immediate problems to think very much about what the neoclassical theory (which he called classical) really entailed.'
4 The neoclassical theory, in all its variants, shares essentially the following structure. It assumes the primary resources, the technological transformation possibilities, and preference structures of individuals to be given. These are variously stipulated in the different variants of the theory. The substitution principle is assumed to operate in both commodity and 'factor' markets so that the individual consumers maximize utility, given consumption possibilities, commodity prices and the relevant budget constraints and producers maximize profits, given the transformation possibilities and prices, to yield 'normally behaved' demand-and-supply relations. Given the flexibility of prices and the operation of the substitution principle, the system would fully utilize resources in equilibrium.
5 Arrow has noted that if each transactor is a price taker, there is 'no one left over whose job it is to make a decision on price' (quoted in Leijonhufvud, 1968,p. 76). Hahn (1977) rightly points out, however, that 'the cliché' (that Keynesian economics is economics without the Walrasian auctioneer) is 'based on a muddle', which misinterprets *tâtonnement* as implying the existence of an auctioneer.
6 As Clower puts it '... we may reasonably assert that orthodox economics provides a general theory of equilibrium states – that is, an adequate account of the factors determining equilibrium prices and equilibrium transaction plans in a market economy ... Clearly, however, orthodox analysis does not provide a general theory of disequilibrium states: firstly, because it yields no direct information about the magnitude of *realized* as distinct from *planned* transactions under disequilibrium conditions; secondly, because it tacitly assumes that the forces tending at any instant to change prevailing

market prices are independent of realized transactions at the same moment (this includes as a special case the assumption, made explicitly in all 'tâtonnement', 'recontract' and 'auction' models that no disequilibrium transactions occur)' (Clower, 1965, pp. 275–6).

7   In the case of the worker, it is recognized that there would have to be a downward revision in the reservation price as the length of 'search' increases. His effective demand for goods, temporarily sustained on the strength of past savings or borrowings, must also ultimately decline.

8   Leijonhufvud favours, on grounds of empirical strength, Friedman's permanent income hypothesis and Modigliani-Brumberg-Ando's 'life-cycle' hypothesis as more satisfactory explanations of consumption behaviour than the Keynesian consumption function. The former suggest that the current income is less influential in the determination of consumption. Hence Leijonhufvud's interpretation of a strong multiplier as reflecting the state of illiquidity.

9   Hahn (1977) points out a number of misconceptions that have acquired currency in the growing literature such as the 'cliché cited in note 5 above. In the models of non-*tâtonnement* processes, allowing trading at false prices, no convincing explanation yet obtains as to how prices are actually changed, and the supposition that prices rise when there is positive excess demand (and fall, when it is negative) continues to be operative. The supposition could be far from correct. Hahn notes as another source of misunderstanding the idea that money, as such, has a special significance to the non-*tâtonnement* process in the existing short-period non-Walrasian equilibrium models and that it is basic to the emergence of the 'multiplier'. He argues that any non-reproducible asset would produce effects attributed to money *in these models*.

10 A short-period Walrasian equilibrium is defined to yield as a solution a set of current prices and associated expected prices at which every preferred plan of every agent on current markets is satisfied. For the existence of such an equilibrium, stringent assumptions regarding the nature of expectations are needed in addition to conventional postulates (see Arrow and Hahn, 1971). The stability of the intertemporal equilibria still needs to be established.

11 Keynes's view of the possibility of short-period unemployment equilibrium, it was believed, was due to his neglect of the effect of real cash balances on demand for current goods. Thus Keynesian theory, if it was about equilibrium, would have to rest upon wage rigidity, an assumption which Keynes did not make.

12 Garegnani (1978) argues that the two are related since the demand for capital goods as a stock and for capital as investment (a flow) are strictly related in theory.

13 A detailed treatment of the issues, summarized here, appears in Bharadwaj (1978a), Garegnani (1981) and Roncaglia (1978).

14 Definite rules for a non-competitive division of surplus among capitalists could be accommodated without difficulty.

15 That Sraffa concerns himself with 'properties of the system which do not depend on change' is not to be treated as equivalent to the proposition that the system is 'invariant' in its properties when change occurs, or that change is ruled out. It merely states that no presumption regarding change or changes of any particular kind are *essential* to the theoretical propositions contained therein. (Some implications are discussed in Bharadwaj, 1978a.) Such a position, in fact, permits the consideration of a greater variety of

changes, so long as they are consistent with the system. No presumptions regarding sequential changes are indicated a priori.

16 Reference could be made to Kalecki's attempt to link the micro, firm-level behaviour with the macro-functioning of the capitalist economy, constituted by workers, managers and rentiers bringing in system-level influences, like the nature of intracapitalist relations, working-class struggle, the structure of financial markets, the nature of the investment process operating under risk, the nature of technical progress and forces determining its pace, etc. Kalecki uses, on the one hand, firm-level behaviour in a setting of imperfect competition, and the Marxian departmental scheme, on the other, to deduce macro-level inferences. While many of Kalecki's formulations are incomplete they are indicative of the analytical richness of the broad approach.

17 Nor, in fact, does the long-period equilibrium in Walras, Wicksell, or Marshall rest on such a conception. However, in the marginalist theory full utilization of resources (capital and labour) are its deductions.

18 The investment behaviour of individual firms in a non-competitive environment may be influenced by other factors. With the emergence of more complicated organizational forms of producing firms and modes of financing, new factors have to be allowed for in planning of investment decisions and their realization. Here, again, Kalecki (1971) is much ahead of Keynes. Kalecki, taking note of the fact that a firm's ability to invest is affected by its own assets and the principle of 'increasing risk', attempted to evolve general rules of investment behaviour in a situation where firms have different economic strengths and enjoy differential access to financial markets. The 'risk' that Kalecki talks of is an objective organizational feature of the situation.

19 Considerable conceptual clarification would be required in interpreting Kalecki's use of 'short period' and "long period' in relation to the surplus approach as outlined above. In the usual discussions, the 'long run' is used in the neoclassical sense of long-period equilibrium and hence implying 'steady growth'. The 'long-period position' in the surplus approach, as stated above, does not connote full employment, nor does it imply balanced growth conditions. It only implies that certain observed features of the system (output levels and the methods of production) are taken to be provisionally given as representing the dominant characteristics and upon which the rules of surplus distribution are applied to yield the distributive revenues – profits and wages. Kalecki does, in fact, use such a rule when he assumes 'the degree of monopoly' as given in the 'short period'. Kalecki's theory as viewed from surplus approach requires separate treatment, not attempted here.

20 For a very insightful discussion see Steindl (1981).

21 Kalecki (1965) comparing econometric modelling and historical materialism, indicates a somewhat similar approach: '... in a special case where no changes in natural resources, productive relations and the superstructure affect the development of productive forces, the system will follow the path determined by an econometric model because the condition of relationships between the economic variables, not subject to change, is then fulfilled. In a more general case, the functional relationships alter under the impact of events in these three other spheres and the economic development is then a much more complicated process than that presented by an econometric model as it reflects the evolution of the society in all the aspects'. Steindl, in

a recent contribution (1981), proposes a way of integrating exogenous and endogenous causes of trend generated by innovations. 'The proposed marriage of exogenous and endogenous causes of the trend leaves ample room for the role of history while at the same time admitting that the impulses coming from outside are seized and molded by the inherent mechanism of the economic dynamics which acts through the multiplier and the distribution of income, through the accumulation of retained profits and utilization of capital equipment' (p. 46). A methodological similarity in handling historical changes in terms of logical models may be discerned in Steindl's proposals.

References: Chapter 12

Arrow, K. J. and Hahn, F. H. (1971), *General Competitive Analysis* (Edinburgh: Oliver and Boyd).

Bharadwaj, K. (1978a), *Classical Political Economy and Rise to Dominance of Supply and Demand Theories* (Calcutta: Longman Orient); Revised edition, 1986.

Clower, R. (1965), 'The Keynesian Counter-Revolution: A Theoretical Appraisal', in Brechling F. and Hahn F. (eds) *The Theory of Interest Rates* (London: Macmillan), pp. 103–25.

Clower, R. (1967), 'A Reconsideration of the Microfoundations of Monetary Theory', *Western Economic Journal* 6 (December), no. 2, pp. 1–9.

Dobb, M. H. (1973), *Theories of Value and Distribution Since Adam Smith* (Cambridge: Cambridge University Press).

Eatwell, J. L. (1979), *Theories of Value, Output and Employment, Thames Papers in Political Economy* (Summer).

Friedman, M. (1956) (ed.) *Studies in the Quantity Theory of Money* (Chicago: Chicago University Press).

Friedman, M. (1970), 'A Theoretical Framework for Monetary Analysis', *Journal of Political Economy*, 78(March/April), pp. 193–238.

Garegnani, P. (1976), 'On a Change in the Notion of Equilibrium in Recent Work on Value and Distribution', in M. Brown, K. Sato and P. Zarembka (eds) *Essay in Modern Capital Theory* (Amsterdam: North Holland), pp. 25–45.

Garegnani, P. (1978, 1979), 'Notes on Consumption, Investment and Effective Demand', Part I, *Cambridge Journal of Economics* 2, December 1978, pp. 335–53 and Part II, *Cambridge Journal of Economics* 3, pp. 63–82, March 1979.

Garegnani, P. (1981), *Marx e gli Economisti Classici* (Torino: Enandi).

Hahn, F. H. (1977), 'Keynesian Economics and General Equilibrium Theory', in Harcourt, G. C. (ed.), *The Microeconomic Foundations of Microeconomics* (London: Macmillan), pp. 25–40.

Hahn, F. H. (1980), 'General Equilibrium Theory', in *The Public Interest*, Special Issue, reprinted in Hahn F. (ed.) *Equilibrium and Macroeconomics* (1984) (Oxford: Blackwell), pp. 72–87.

Hicks, J. R. (1937), 'Mr. Keynes and the Classics', *Econometrica* vol. 5 (April), pp. 147–59.

Kahn, R. F. (1977), 'Malinvaud on Keynes', *Cambridge Journal of Economics*, 1, no. 4 (December), pp. 375–88.

Kalecki, M. (1964), '*Econometric Models and Historical Materialism*', in *On Political Economy and Econometrics: Essays in Honour of Oscar Lange* (Warsaw), pp. 233–8.

Kalecki, M. (1971), *Selected Essays on the Dynamics of the Capitalist Economy, 1933-70* (Cambridge: Cambridge University Press).
Keynes, J. M. (1936), *The General Theory of Employment, Interest and Money* (London: Macmillan).
Kregel, J. A. (1976), 'Economic Methodology in the Face of Uncertainty', *Economic Journal*, 86, no. 342 (June), pp. 209–25.
Leijonhufvud, A. (1968), *On Keynesian Economics and the Economics of Keynes* (New York: Oxford University Press).
Leijonhufvud, A. (1969), *Keynes and the Classics* (London: Institute of Economic Affairs).
Marshall, A. (1920), *Principles of Economics*, 8th edn (London: Macmillan).
Marx, K. *Capital*, vols. I, II, III (Moscow: Progress Publishers).
Marx, K. (1862–3 [1963–71]), *Theories of Surplus Volume*, Parts, I, II, III (Moscow: Progress Publishers).
Meek, R. L. (1950–1), 'Thomas Joplin and the Theory of Interest', *Review of Economic Studies*, 18, No. 47, pp. 154–63.
Modigliani, F. (1944), 'Liquidity Preference and the Theory of Interest and Money', *Econometrica*, 12 (January), pp. 45–88.
Modigliani (1963), 'The Monetary Mechanism and its Interaction with Real Phenomena', *Review of Economics and Statistics*, supplement, vol. 45, February, pp. 79–107.
Pasinetti, L. L. (1974), *Growth and Income Distribution* (Cambridge: Cambridge University Press).
Patinkin, D. (1965), *Money, Interest and Prices*, 2nd edn. (New York: Harper & Row).
Robinson, Joan (1971), *Economic Heresies* (London: Macmillan).
Robinson, Joan (1979), *Collected Economic Papers*, Vol. V (Oxford: Blackwell).
Roncaglia, A. (1978), *Sraffa and the Theory of Prices* (Chichester: John Wiley).
Smith, A. (1776 [1937]), *An Inquiry into the Nature and Causes of the Wealth of Nations* (ed.) Cannen, E. (New York: Modern Library, 1937).
Sraffa, P. (1960), *Production of Commodities by Means of Commodities: Prelude to a Critique of Economic Theory* (Cambridge: Cambridge University Press).
Steindl, J. (1981), 'Ideas and Concepts of Long Run Growth', Banca Nazionale del Lavoro, *Quarterly Review*, March.
Walras, L. (1953), *Elements of Pure Economics*, translated by W. Jaffe (London: George Allan & Unwin).
Wicksell, K. (1934), *Lectures on Political Economy*, translated by E. Classen and (ed.) L. Robbins (London: Routledge & Kegan Paul).

13
Piero Sraffa: The Man and the Scholar – A Tribute

1 Introduction

Piero Sraffa, a major economist of this century, died on 3 September 1983 in Cambridge. His writings, bearing evidence to his most meticulous and profound scholarship, have had considerable influence on theoretical developments in economics and have aroused controversies and debates in both mainstream neoclassical and Marxist theories that promise to persist for a while.

Sraffa's work as a scholar is so much integrated into his political and philosophical ideas and convictions, as well as his cultural and personality traits, that it is impossible to separate his work from the history of his times, the social and cultural milieu of which he was an active part and from his own qualities as an individual. The academic profession for him was certainly not an alienated world wherein he could indulge in specialized skills of intellectual gymnastics and jugglery. He was totally involved in theoretical work, reflecting an assiduous and uncompromising objectivity in the application of his razor-sharp reasoning; at the same time he remained deeply aware of the social, political and historical dimensions of economic theories.

As a scholar his range of interests was exceptionally wide. He had a deep and sensitive grasp of intellectual history, not confined to economics alone but ranging over philosophy, science, politics and history, particularly socialist ideas. A well-known and much respected bibliophile, with an intimate knowledge of antiquarian writings, he succeeded in building up one of the most valuable individual collections of rare manuscripts and books, particularly on political economy and socialist literature of the nineteenth and early twentieth centuries. His interest in these was neither merely speculative, nor for the sheer joy of possessing them. He quietly researched, spending long hours bringing many of them to life. He did not publish all of his findings but took immense delight in discovering clues and unearthing authentic information. His collection, presently housed at Trinity College, spans English, French, German and Italian works.

Sraffa was not, however, one of those scholars who can hardly breathe outside the ivory tower. His commitment to socialism, formed in his youthful years, remained unshaken and steadfast until the last, although his generation was one in which Marxists experienced tremendous vicissitudes – from the oppressive reign of fascism to the momentous and exciting event of the birth of the first socialist country. His qualities of intellectual depth and range, a warm and charming capacity for friendship, an admirable strength of conviction and honesty coupled with geniality, won him intimate friendships with contemporary personages such as John Maynard Keynes, Dennis Robertson, Wittgenstein and Mattioli, with whom he shared a variety of interests. But, above all, the association that profoundly influenced and shaped his life was that with Antonio Gramsci.

Born in 1898 at Turin, the only child of Angelo Sraffa, a well-established Professor of Commercial Law, Piero Sraffa grew up in a rather exceptional household, non-conformist in religion, open to socialist influence and congenial to intellectual development, under the fond care of the mother to whom he remained greatly attached. (His close friends admired the gentle regard with which Sraffa looked after her in her last difficult days.) He was, as a child, already exposed to a dose of internationalism, being taught a variety of European languages.

It was in his student days at Turin, during 1919–20, that he came into active contact with socialists and developed an association with Gramsci. He wrote anonymous commentaries in *L'Ordine Nuovo* which were already marked out by their lucid and forthright style as well as politically mature observations. In 1920, at the age of 22, Sraffa presented in Italian his doctorate on 'Monetary inflation in Italy during and after the war' (1920) which, as was the practice then, he had to debate with Luigi Einaudi and which he did with consummate skill. He was then in uniform, military service being compulsory for Italian youths. On the successful completion of his doctoral work, he was appointed to a professorship in the Faculty of Law at Perugia and subsequently to a Chair in Cagliari. It was at this time that he first visited England and met Keynes. Sraffa's current interest then was in monetary affairs and Keynes seemed to have been so impressed by the young man's knowledge and his understanding of financial affairs that he invited him to contribute an article on Italian banking affairs to the *Economic Journal* which he was editing. Sraffa's article on 'The bank crisis in Italy' (1922b) (see below for comments) was thus commissioned to appear in the 1922 June issue of the journal. The article was a well-informed, forthright exposure of the 'banking crisis' in Italy and the intricate involvement of the government and industry in financial affairs. Later, Keynes invited him to write a shorter article on the same theme for the *Manchester Guardian Weekly Supplement : The Reconstruction of Europe*, which he edited and which was published simultaneously in four languages. When published, Sraffa's article (1922a) caught the attention of Mussolini who expressed his strong disapproval to Sraffa's father and commanded that he should retract his opinions in print, failing which he was warned of the consequences. Piero Sraffa did not comply, responding that, since the article was based on verifiable facts, unless they were disproved there could be no ground for retraction. This would not have pleased Mussolini.

Sraffa, in the meanwhile, continued his active association with *L'Ordine Nuovo* and in its April 1924 issue wrote anonymously a letter (1924b), signed 'S', which critically assessed the strategy of the Italian Socialist Party in the light of the growing peril of fascism. It counselled against the strategy which would isolate the working class, insightfully recognizing the wider social basis and the pervasive form of control that fascism was rapidly gaining. It initiated a serious debate, Gramsci himself countering Sraffa's letter in defence of the official party position. Gramsci was to change his stand later. This exchange cemented the friendship between the two that was to strengthen with time and remained unbroken until Gramsci's death. It was a friendship that was to influence Sraffa's life greatly. It is believed that it was at Gramsci's suggestion that Sraffa turned to classical political economy as his abiding interest (particularly to Ricardo) from his previous preoccupation with monetary affairs. The role Sraffa was to play during Gramsci's sad and bitter last days in isolated captivity is well known. It is also recognized that it was due to Sraffa's constant and vigilant efforts and initiative that the *Prison Notebooks* could be saved and Gramsci could establish his surreptitious contacts with his political comrades outside. Sraffa's apparent political aloofness was an advantage in keeping access to Gramsci, as he alone was allowed to make regular, short visits to Gramsci in his confinement. We now have the fruits of that moving relationship between the two comrades in the letters which Gramsci wrote in his last days, expressing his anguish and desperation, and yet his irrepressible and indomitable hope and concern for the future of socialism.

With his interest having turned to the foundations of economic theory, Sraffa developed a penetrating critique of the, then sovereign, Marshallian particular equilibrium theory which was also gaining ground in Italy through its popularization by Panteleoni. This first appeared in an Italian article (1925), which was reworked in an abbreviated form with some important alterations for publication in the *Economic Journal* (1926), again at Keynes's instance (see below for comments). This article was to create a major impact on the Cambridge scene where, despite growing restlessness, Marshall's supremacy was unchallenged as yet, and was carried forward by Pigou, Robertson and others. It offered sufficient proof of the brilliant originality of the young Italian and so Sraffa was invited by Keynes to apply for a newly created Lecturership in Economics to which Sraffa was appointed from October 1927. Sraffa's continued presence in Italy had already become precarious under the fascist threat. Sraffa's lectures, which he delivered as a course in 'Advanced Theory', were prepared with his usual meticulousness and turned out to be both unorthodox and stimulating, with some original interpretations of the history of the theories of value and distribution. His attack on the neoclassical orthodoxy and the 'return' to the classical approach were already foreshadowed in them. For the young rebels in Cambridge,

Sraffa, although a contemporary, was already a 'progenitor of ideas'; to senior economists such as Keynes, Robertson and Pigou, he provided an unmistakable touchstone to try out their ideas, although his differences with them would be substantive. However, Sraffa temperamentally disliked holding forth to a captive audience in lecture rooms. He greatly enjoyed debates and discussions in smaller groups, but would retreat into silence in front of a larger audience. So unhappy was he with the prospect that he wished to renounce the lecturership. In any case, Sraffa at that time appears to have had no inclination or long-term plans to take up residence in Cambridge. In fact, until the last, he kept his Italian citizenship even at the risk of facing internment during the war as an Italian alien. (Incidentally, it was Keynes again who acted to obtain his release. The esteem in which the two held their friendship was revealed in many such incidents.) Keynes was, however, reluctant to let him leave and instead arranged a number of undertakings that would suitably engage his interests and energies: Sraffa was offered the Assistant Directorship of Research under which post he ran a seminar course for research scholars; he was appointed Librarian at the Marshall Library, the official position by which Sraffa designated himself among colleagues; and, above all, the editorship of the *Collected Works* (1951–73) of Ricardo, an edition planned by the Royal Economic Society. The last task, closest to Sraffa's own intellectual predilections, absorbed his energies for many years, culminating in a monumental edition in ten volumes, with an excellent index as the eleventh volume.

It was during these long years that, alongside the compilation of Ricardo's papers and providing editorial commentaries that were to give a definitive interpretation and significance to the materials, Sraffa laboured on his reconstruction of classical political economy, a work on its foundations. It emerged, in 1960, as a slim volume, *Production of Commodities by Means of Commodities*, which he subtitled *Prelude to a Critique of Economic Theory*.

Parallel to this work of reconstruction, Sraffa's critique of marginalist theory proceeded apace. Again, he chose to attack particular points of the theoretical base where the theory was most vulnerable, taking on the stalwarts among his opponents. It was Hayek's influential work, *Prices and Production*, that was to be such a target. Sraffa reviewed it most trenchantly and devastatingly in the *Economic Journal* (1932). The exchange that followed between the two was equally forceful (see below). Another issue that brought to the fore the fundamental methodological difficulties that the supply-and-demand-based theory faced in countering 'increasing returns', and the rather shifty device of the 'representative firm' used by Marshall to check the difficulty, opened up another battle front, in the symposium on the 'representative firm' in the *Economic Journal* (1930b), where the polemical skills of Robertson, Sraffa and Shove were fully employed.

For a scholar so fastidiously dedicated to intellectual pursuits, living the quiet, solitary and self-contained life of a Fellow in the precincts of a Cambridge college, Sraffa's publications are few and far between.

However, each work of his was seminal and marked a milestone in theory. Paradoxically, his articles appeared to concentrate on a narrowly limited, abstract issue in theory. And yet, in selecting the vantage point, the weakest but crucial link in the opponent's theory, he revealed his command over the theoretical terrain. In his critical works, he directed his attack to the heart of the matter. He also chose the best among the adversaries and applied the acid test of logical self-consistency to unmask evasive or slippery arguments. His style, particularly in the early work, was polemical but without verbosity, economical but conclusive in its arguments. Not only was there a succinct use of language, but there was also no yielding to a temptation to overkill. The critique would be a frontal attack on carefully chosen strategic points in the theoretical structure. No time would be wasted in offering all possible, subsidiary and peripheral criticism. It was this characteristic of a strong focus on essentiality and criticality of the strategic points in the critique that marked the choice of the target and the form of attack. This was to be his characteristic in discussions, too: while he would induce others to come up with their best arguments, he was a patient and careful listener – he himself would raise telling points in very short questions or brief observations. Wittgenstein is reported to have said that, after a discussion with Sraffa, he often felt like a bare trunk of a tree with its branches removed. It is also reported that it was a significant argument raised by Sraffa, illustrated through a gesture, that persuaded Wittgenstein to change his whole philosophical perspective. In a scholar with Sraffa's width and depth of knowledge this brevity and conciseness implies considerable self-restraint and modesty – a characteristic rarely found in the competitive academic sphere which encourages intellectual exhibitionism and where a writer is impelled to demonstrate to his readers all that he knows, or believes he knows.

For this reason, as well as his insistence on the utmost accuracy and objectivity, Sraffa was reluctant to publish or rush into print. This hesitation of his became almost legendary. While *Production of Commodities*, a slim volume, was in preparation over four decades, the Ricardo volumes needed Maurice Dobb's collaboration. Many a time Sraffa would prefer tackling even important criticisms made in print by other scholars in personal letters and conversations which he enjoyed immensely, the more engaging and controversial they were. He could never cease criticizing his own manuscript drafts – sometime violently rejecting them with a bold 'NO' in that clear hand. To his opponents, he was conscientiously objective. Every word, every footnote would be carefully read. It was not from intemperance that Sraffa wrote on Hayek, 'if Dr Hayek had taken as much pain in writing his book as his reviewer has taken in reading it ...'. Anyone who reads the editorial commentaries on Ricardo cannot but be struck by the relentless search for tracing out, collating and examining every bit of information and every strand of argument. It was probably these qualities of mind and scholarship which he shared with Wittengstein that brought them together despite their very diverse philosophical viewpoints and personality traits.

In discussions it would not be possible to gain Sraffa's easy concurrence on weak criticisms against Marshall or any other marginalist thinker whom he himself had forcefully attacked. In his obituary note on Panteleoni, which is remarkable for its ability to present a pen-portrait, Sraffa offered generous praise where due, in spite of the fact that Panteleoni was an ardent follower of Marshall and in politics held widely divergent opinions from his own. His objectivity, combined with uncompromising convictions, made his virulent polemics or devastating criticism bereft of arrogance and rancour, and gained him the appreciation and friendship of scholars with whom he had forcefully articulated differences.

Hard task-master as he was, with himself even more than with others, Sraffa was always a modest listener and possessed a sparkling sense of wit which, as Kaldor observes in a personal reminiscence, made the speakers feel 'cleverer, more clear-sighted and more amusing than they thought themselves to be. He combined modesty and reserve – he never tried to show himself superior by squashing an opponent in argument' (speech delivered at the Memorial Meeting at Cambridge on 19 September 1983). Warm and friendly, he was a keen observer of persons around him which would be revealed in a passing witty remark. He was, however, a very reserved person – rarely talking about himself, enjoying his regular, solitary, long bicycle rides in the countryside around Cambridge or annually visiting the mountains, sometimes in the company of friends but in later years most often alone.

2 The Major Thrust

Sraffa was continuously engaged in a simultaneous, two-fold task in economic theory. This was to develop a basic critique of the marginalist theory that had acquired dominance since the 1870s, and to elucidate and reconstruct the long-submerged approach to theory of the classical writers. The critical function was prominent in the 1925 and 1926 articles, the review of Hayek, and in his comment on increasing returns and the representative firm; while the interpretation of Ricardo involved delineating in clear terms the basic theoretical framework that was being developed in classical theory to explain the generation, distribution and accumulation of surplus. Both tasks demanded an astute understanding of the history of theory. It required, on the one hand, a clear perception of the conceptual and logical structure of alternative theories and, on the other, an appreciation of the transitions that occur in the dominant mainstream theory whereby one approach is abandoned, sometimes prematurely, and another established. The explanations for such transitions in ruling theories, in economics particularly, may not rest on the logical/analytical strength of the theories alone, but also in changing socio-historical conditions that lead to the nurturing of certain visions regarding the society's functioning. Sraffa did not subscribe to the Marshallian viewpoint that there was a continuous, unilinear development of theory from Smith to the marginalists. Importantly, Marshall claimed a close link between his theory and Ricardo's. Sraffa's view was that a fundamental shift in theory had occurred with Jevons and others developing the marginalist theory with a distinct structure of its own. The two key authors on whom Sraffa concentrated his attention were Marshall and Ricardo. Not only was Marshall contemporaneously important, a towering figure in Cambridge, but it was in his constructions, attempting to reconcile the classical theory with the newly forming marginalist theory, that all kinds of deviations and contradictions could be seen most clearly. Similarly, in Ricardo's continued attempts to explain distribution within the surplus framework, the bare rudimentary essentials of the problem of value-distribution were clearly perceived – and so also the origin of the logical difficulties that were to recur within that framework, whose unsuccessful resolution had led to a premature abandonment of the approach.

Sraffa chose also to focus on the problem of distribution – and hence of value. The earlier critique of Marshall was directed more towards relative price determination. Later on, his attention centred directly on distribution – particularly the explanation of the rate of profit – which is a base-level problem on which the theories of accumulation need to be securely founded. All economic theories concerning capitalist societies had been concerned, at their roots, with the explanation of the source and level of surplus (profits) and its utilization. Alternative theories had attempted to explain the nature, source and level of profits differently, and the search for a logically consistent explanation of profits was what impelled modifications, reformulations, or rejections of theories. It was apparently the 'failure' of the labour theory of value to yield a consistent explanation of relative prices and hence of the rate of profits – the so-called problem of transformation – that was offered, at an analytical level, as the ground for abandoning the classical and Marxian approach to distribution. Sraffa now sought to turn the tables: the neoclassicists' explanation of distribution was fundamentally erroneous. In the initial attacks on Marshall, Sraffa was to concentrate on demolishing the marginalist notion of supply schedules resting on the laws of returns within the particular equilibrium context. In his *Production of Commodities* the attack was squarely on the explanation of profit within the general equilibrium framework, as became evident through the capital theoretic controversies that emanated from that work.

3 The Published Writings of Piero Sraffa

Within the limitation of space, we shall briefly look at the major individual writings of Sraffa. Our intention is not to provide a detailed commentary – a task that would require much deeper study – but to give a flavour of the general tenor of his major published works.

'The bank crisis in Italy'
This article (1922b), replete with information on the financial affairs of the time in Italy and sketching 'the life, death and miraculous resurrection of the Banca Italiana di Sconto', brings out, in graphic terms, the alliance forged between the war-based industries, the financial companies and the Italian state. It reads like a complex detective plot. Banca di Sconto, formed through an amalgamation of series of small banks with varied organizational methods and backgrounds, was founded in 1915, the first year of Italy's entry into the war. It expanded at a very rapid pace, the major clientele for a new bank being the industries engaged in war supplies, which were booming with large profits and an assured government war demand. In fact, the Ansaldo Company of Genoa, one such major company which was the largest producer of armaments, obtained control of the Banca di Sconto through manipulation of the shareholders' votes. 'From thenceforward the fortunes of Banca di Sconto were indissolubly united to those of the Ansaldo Company and in fact the former followed all the vicissitudes of the latter up to the final common disaster' (p. 179). The Ansaldo Company's domain of activities expanded enormously in a very short time, extending to a number of affiliated companies. The story that follows is of the attempts of the Ansaldo Company and Banca di Sconto to find a solution to the twin problems: the necessity of relieving the bank of its burdensome engagement in a single company and the Ansaldo Company's colossal financial needs. The problem became aggravated by the occurrence shortly afterwards of the armistice which took away the war demand for production. Such production was in fact carried out at a high cost, Italy having no natural advantage in such production. The Ansaldo Company's attempt to 'storm' another bank to appropriate its control led to clashes with rival industrial groups and the banks linked to them.

The entire chain of episodes, picturesquely described in the article, reveals the various manipulations indulged in by concerned interests to rescue the bank from collapse and, when that occurred, the high drama that it culminated in, with creditors, financiers and the government all caught up in a series of battles, of mutual incriminations and high-handed illegal actions. Sraffa gives a fact-packed account of the developments, sketching a certain broad characterization of the contemporaneous Italian financial system. A close relation between banks and industry had developed. While the financing of industry was considered by the banks to be one of their legitimate major functions, namely, extending long-term credits to industrial concerns and often holding a large part of their share capital, the industries themselves were critically dependent upon bank finance due to the general paucity of capital and capital being generally shy to enter industry. This situation had developed into a serious one in many cases, where the banks had immobilized their funds in a single concern. In the Italian economic situation, with its preponderance of agriculture, lack of differentiation between traders and manufacturers, and dominance of foreign firms in trade, the banks could not have confined themselves to the orthodox, traditional function of discounting commercial bills whose flow was, in the circumstances, inadequate. This close interdependence had the consequence that the deposits of the Banco di Sconto were mainly drawn from its industrial customers – the very concerns that were financed by the bank. The bank's viability thus got closely linked with the fortunes of these firms.

The greatest danger of this dependence was the struggle for control – the bank attempting to control the firm in the interests of its own safety and to profit by its successes, and the industry attempting to make itself dominant by acquiring control of the bank. Rather than either party succeeding in obtaining full control, a more general pattern emerged: the elimination of opposition by the formation of large 'groups' of companies of the most varied kinds, concentrated around one or more banks, mutually related by the exchange of shares and the appointment of directors common to them. Further, within the 'groups' a few individuals gained control although, on their own, they possessed only a minor part of the shares. These groups acquired enormous financial and political power which they used to influence the government's domestic and foreign policies. Moreover, this entirely removed the industry from the control of the shareholders. The attempts of the state, Sraffa noted, to remedy these affairs through legal reforms and decrees had proved to be impossible and were total failures. Sraffa ends the article with a forthright censure: 'But even if these laws were not futile in themselves, what could be their use as long as the government is prepared to be the first to break them so soon as it is blackmailed by a band of gunmen or a group of bold financiers?' (p. 197). In the Italy of 1922 this statement was not just rhetoric. The band of gunmen were just as much present in the world of business as the group of bold financiers.

Reading Sraffa's article today, the doings of the bold financiers and the big 'groups' do not appear as 'mysterious activities'; they have now become the mainstay of large national and multinational monopoly operations. However, this article, written during the rising tide of fascism when the potent mixture of finance, industry and the fascist state was being formed, must have been one of the first revelations of the functioning of monopoly capitalism entering the stage of high finance.

The article demonstrated Sraffa's typical qualities as a scholar: the care with which facts were researched and marshalled, the complex web of economic, political and social interrelations analysed and related to the stage of economic development reached in Italy, and the logic behind the tumultuous series of events exposed in a neat pattern relating to the system. The short article is infused with a remarkable sense of history. It also has a boldness matched by competence. As noted earlier, the article's shorter version in the *Manchester Guardian Weekly Supplement* (1922a) hit its target, upsetting Mussolini sufficiently for him to demand its retraction. However, Sraffa was sure enough of his command over the facts to return the challenge.

Critical Writings on Marginalist Theory

In the 1920s Sraffa had already turned to a critical study of marginalist theory, the first expression of which was a long article in Italian (1925) on the relation between cost and quantity produced, that is, on the supply schedule of the marginalist theory constructed on the basis of co-ordinating the laws of returns. Sraffa was to argue that the marginalist theory of competitive value is inspired by the fundamental symmetry which is supposed to exist between the forces of demand and supply, and is based upon the assumption that the essential causes determining the prices of particular commodities may be simplified and grouped together so as to be represented by a pair of intersecting curves of collective demand and supply. It was the validity of this view – particularly as providing the basis for constructing the Marshallian supply schedule, one blade of a pair of scissors, in the context of particular equilibrium – which Sraffa examined thoroughly.

The 1925 article begins with a detailed examination of the hypothetical conditions that are assumed to give rise to tendencies towards increasing, decreasing and constant costs, and then scrutinizes within what limits, if at all, these would be co-ordinated to yield, in unison, a single 'law of non-proportional costs'. Sraffa points out, at the outset, that the notions of decreasing and increasing productivity arose in classical writings in diverse contexts; the former, a ground for an explanation of rents, became a part of the theory of distribution and did not enter into their theory of relative prices. The prime case was that of land, limited in supply for the whole economy; although the price of corn would be expected to rise with extended or more intensive cultivation, it was taken to affect all prices and not considered as providing a theory of relative prices. Increasing productivity was a phenomenon associated with the division of labour and general conditions of economic progress. It was only with marginalism that a supply schedule was envisaged, symmetric to, but independent of, the demand schedule, itself based on the 'universal law' of diminishing marginal utility. Such a supply schedule was constructed by co-ordinating the laws of returns to yield a systematic relation between output and the cost of production.

First, analysing the conditions necessary for the law of increasing costs, Sraffa demonstrates, using the example of land, how a certain misconception arises in considering the 'constant factor' as not susceptible either to increase or decrease in particular cases. If, however, the factor whose total maximum quantity is supposed to be constant is indefinitely divisible, and if only a part of it may be used in production, it is possible for the producer to choose such a combination of factors as to produce at constant costs. This possibility is all the more relevant in the case of an individual competitive producer who can buy (or sell) the land from others or put it to alternative uses. Decreasing productivity (or increasing costs) could occur only when the factor is used excessively, or its minimum level of use cannot be reduced further, that is, the factor is indivisible within the relevant limits.

The principle of declining productivity was generalized by the marginalists so as to be made applicable not only to all factors and branches of production, but also to envisage a symmetry in its operation with that of the 'fundamental psychological' law of diminishing marginal utility. The latter had roots, claimed Marshall, in the quality of human nature, while the former was rooted in the technical conditions of industry. 'Is it not strange', asks Sraffa, 'that two such heterogeneous elements as human nature and industrial technology bring about results so similar?' Not only that, but also to expect that such diverse technical conditions as characterize different industries should all result in a similar 'technical' outcome? The common element, Sraffa argues, lies not in any technical necessity but in a certain common axiom regarding human behaviour and an accompanying set of assumptions, construed similarly on the demand and the supply side. The assumptions are:(1) the universal prevalence of the principle of substitution, or the criterion on which economic choice rests, and (2) the feasibility of alternative combinations of variable and constant factors and of alternative uses of the variable factors, the alternative uses being independent of each other. Every decreasing productivity curve that has a general character is a 'descriptive' rather than a 'functional' curve (in Wicksteed's sense who, however, considered the case of 'extensive margins' to be 'descriptive' and that of 'intensive margins' to be 'functional' (see Wicksteed, 1914)). The uses to which successive doses are applied are arranged, dictated by the producer's own assessment of benefits and not due to material or technical necessity. Sraffa argues that the diminishing marginal utility principle is also analogously 'descriptive'. If we consider utility as the product and the goods consumed as the variable factors of production, the possibility of using different doses of *bene* to satisfy more urgent needs yields us the curve of diminishing marginal utility. There is no other 'psycho-physical law' that is at the root.

Technical and logical problems occur in presuming the possibility of the absolute ordering of the efficiency of doses. In the first place, the efficiency of a particular dose may not be independent of other preceding doses and may be affected by the sequence of their use. Secondly, a logical difficulty arises when the collective supply curve has to be constructed, the main problem being how the macro or collective equilibrium can be shown to be a consistent outcome of the series of individual equilibria arrived at independently in the case of individual producers. The particular equilibrium point of view assumes that the conditions of production (supply) and demand for a commodity can be considered, in respect of small variations, as being practically independent both in regard to each other and in relation to the supply and demand of all other commodities. This assumption becomes illegitimate when a variation in the quantity produced by the industry under consideration, sets up a force which acts directly not merely upon its own costs, but also upon the costs of other industries. A similar problem arises on the demand side, of aggregating individual demand curves into the collective demand curve. But, for that, it is sufficient to add up quantities of individual demands at any price, it being assumed that each individual's demand is determined independently of the demands of others. This does not apply to supply when a factor is limited in supply for the entire industry, but not to the individual producer. Either the individual producer uses so little of the factor that his cost of production is not affected by increasing output via the change in the price of the factor, or, if he is a substantive user and the price of the factor is affected by his increased demand, other producers utilizing the factor would be equally affected. Thus the supply schedule of the industry cannot be considered independently of the supply schedules of other industries, or of the demand for it as well as for others. These collateral effects are not a matter of 'the second order' to be ignored. It is no longer possible, without contradiction, to isolate the conditions required to obtain particular equilibrium. Only when the limited factor is entirely used in industry can the industry experience increasing costs without affecting other prices. This indeed could only be a minute class of commodities.

The same difficulty also arises in almost identical form in the case of increasing returns. Marshall himself recognized that a continued persistence of economies arising due to the possibility of spreading overhead charges and fixed costs over larger output (the 'internal economies') could not be compatible with competitive conditions. On the other hand, he had initially considered increasing returns as primarily arising from the general division of labour and social progress – economies which could not be attributed strictly to output increases of any one industry, and a situation where the cost advantages would affect industries generally. Such external economies could not be easily encompassed within the particular equilibrium analysis. It was in his *Principles* that Marshall introduced a compromise between 'theoretical rigour' and 'reality' by inventing a class of external economies, external to the firm and internal to the industry, which could be compatible with the individual producers' supply schedule exhibiting increasing returns. Again, such instances of economies would have been hard to come by.

Arguing on the ground that constant costs arise only when tendencies towards increasing and decreasing returns are finely balanced, Marshall (and his followers) held that the case of constant returns could arise only accidentally. The fact of the matter was that constant costs, in the Marshallian price determination, implied making the cost of production alone an effective determinant of value. Hence Marshall had interpreted Ricardo's theory to be this special case. Sraffa, having demonstrated the limitations on the valid domain of increasing and decreasing costs argued that 'reduced within such restricted limits, the supply schedule and variable costs cannot claim to be a general conception applicable to normal industries'.

The articles of 1925 and 1926 concentrated on the Marshallian supply schedule as a part of his particular equilibrium apparatus. Pointing out the logical weakness of the underlying notion of variable costs, Sraffa had suggested that the classical theory of the cost of production was to be preferred, and the premise of constant costs was much more suitable in normal cases. The emphasis here was on the question of the reconciliation of the particular equilibrium with the general equilibrium and the critique, therefore, was from within the power theory.

In his 1926 article – which was, in part, a summary in English of the 1925 Italian article – Sraffa advanced the idea of segmented competition where individual firms had limited monopoly and an elastic demand curve facing them. This idea was suggested as a possible way of tackling the close interaction between the costs and demands of various firms. The suggestions contained in the article were later developed into the theory of monopolistic competition in the hands of Joan Robinson and Joseph Chamberlin.

At this juncture, Sraffa appears to have been working towards a critique of marginalist theory within the Marshallian premises, the accent being on the theory of price determination of commodities. A critique of the general concept of the supply schedule in its role of price determination was also damaging to the complementary theory of distribution which regarded factor-pricing as only a part of the general price determination. It is in his book *Production of Commodities* that Sraffa was subsequently to address the problem of distribution directly, and to derive the critical implications of interdependent production against treating capital as a factor of production whose price was to be explained in terms of the equilibrium of demand and supply.

Incidentally, while the 1926 article was to stimulate research into the direction of monopolistic competition – not the direction that Sraffa himself would have been too enthusiastic about – , the deeper criticisms which were subtly expressed did not receive as much attention. One such subtle hint is found in a footnote in the 1925 article: Sraffa discusses there the methodological question regarding the validity of treating Marshall's supply schedule of an industry as independent both of its own demand curve and the supply curve of other goods. He notes that Marshall himself had emphasized the validity of the curves strictly within the neighbourhood of equilibrium. Sraffa points out, in the footnote, that Marshall's proposition is important not only because it excludes large variations in the quantity produced, but also because it allows – in fact, needs to allow – small variations. It is the positions on the curve in the vicinity of equilibrium which represent precisely the forces that will be set in motion if there is a movement away from it so as to re-establish the equilibrium. It is, in this sense, that Marshall's theory – and, in general, the marginalist theory – depends essentially upon change and requires restrictions to be placed upon the changes, *albeit* in the neighbourhood, in order that a state of equilibrium (its existence and stability) is obtained. Sraffa's criticisms of Marshall's derivation of, and reliance upon, increasing and decreasing costs was not merely that Marshall had, by convenient postulates, decided to ignore the 'second-order' repercussions of changes in the output of one industry on the costs and demands of others or, on its own demand, *but that these could not be considered as of 'second order' without logical contradiction*. The only way by which increasing or decreasing costs could be established was (a) in the increasing-costs case, by conveniently defining a factor or industry so that the 'limited factor' was exclusively absorbed by the industry, and (b) in the decreasing costs case, by limiting the 'externalities' to being entirely outside the firm, but totally internal to the industry. Sraffa's general critique concerning the essential dependence of the marginal theory on change and the need to stipulate a priori conditions on the form of these 'changes' (so as to ensure logical consistency) transcends the particular Marshallian context.

Another methodological point of a general nature to which we shall return later was concerning the choice between competing theories. In his 1926 article, Sraffa viewed the 'cost-of-production' theory, to use Marshall's vocabulary, of the classicals as a simple way of approaching the problem of competitive value:

> This first approximation, as far as it goes, is as important as it is useful; it emphasises the fundamental factor, namely, the predominant influence of cost of production in the determination of the normal value of commodities, while at the same time it does not lead us astray when we desire to study in greater detail the conditions under which exchange takes place in particular cases, for it does not conceal from us the fact that we cannot find the elements required for this purpose within the limits of its assumptions (p. 541).

This is a position on the role of theory and its domain that deserves deeper reflection.

Symposium on the Representative Firm (Economic Journal, 1930)
The symposium (1930) saw an attempt by Robertson to defend Marshall's construct of the 'representative firm' as a possible way of reconciling, within Marshall's framework, the equilibrium of the firm and increasing returns (and hence a 'partial rehabilitation of Marshallian orthodoxy on conservative lines', as Keynes introduced it). Expanding on the picturesque analogies of the trees in the woods of Marshall, Robertson had suggested that the 'representative firm' 'is no identifiable entity, with a continuing will and purpose of its own', so that 'All that is necessary is to be on one's guard against identifying it (the supply curve for the industry) with the cost curve of any firm whose name is to be found in the directory' (1930, p. 89). At different output levels, there could be a different 'representative firm'. This is how Robertson suggested overcoming the incompatibility of decreasing costs with a firm in equilibrium.

Sraffa took issue with Robertson's logic, the interpretation of which implied that each successive point on the supply curve of the 'representative firm' corresponds not only to a different quantity produced, but also to a different firm producing it. This approach could not reconcile the basic contradiction. Remembering that Robertson was dealing with a case where 'external economies' of every kind are supposed to be absent (so that an expansion of the industry cannot produce any such circumstances as favour large firms), the question yet unresolved remained: 'If the new firms can turn out a larger output at a lower cost than the old firms, why did they not come into existence before? Why in the new, and not in the old position of equilibrium?' (p. 92). In the exchange that followed Sraffa countered Robertson's reply point by point. An interesting part of the exchange – which throws light on Sraffa's methodological opposition and also illustrates the prose style of these two stalwarts – is noteworthy. Robertson writes:

> Mr Sraffa objects to my (and Marshall's) poetry, as I feared he would. But it does not require a sense of poetry, but only of human nature and of history, to refrain from asking – why slavery was not abolished or the Channel Tunnel built at the earliest moment at which the world would have been better for the change. (pp. 92–3)

Sraffa responds:

> Does stating that in equilibrium water in communicating vessels is at the same level, amount in effect to asking why rivers have not ceased to flow long ago? But I am not even stating as much. I am trying to find what are the assumptions implicit in Marshall's theory: if Mr Robertson regards them as extremely unreal, I sympathise with him. We seem to be agreed that the theory cannot be interpreted in a way which makes it logically self-consistent and, at the same time, reconcile it with the facts it sets out to explain. Mr Robertson's remedy is to discard mathematics, and he suggests that my remedy is to discard the facts; perhaps I ought to have explained that, in the circumstances, I think it is Marshall's theory that should be discarded. (1930b, p. 93)

It was clear to Sraffa that, despite Marshall's awareness of the importance of 'biological' methods and frequent references to real-life facts, particularly in his enticing analogies, the basic theoretical equilibrium framework that Marshall used was mechanistic; it was the problem of 'water in communicating vessels attaining the same level'. Its assumptions, implicit and explicit, were 'extremely unreal'. Sraffa was, furthermore, demonstrating that the theory was not even logically self-consistent and, in such a case, to dispute about the method was a diversion. Hence his summing up of the debate in the last sentence in the quote above.

On Hayek's Prices and Production

Hayek's four lectures delivered at the London School of Economics in February 1931 were published as *Prices and Production* in September 1931. It was most enthusiastically received at the LSE and won quick recognition, with most reviews considering it favourably as an analytically rigorous work attempting to deal with money within the Walrasian-Austrian framework. Keynes's *Treatise on Money* had also appeared and was reviewed by Hayek around the same time. A keen controversy was thus developing between the two rival schools of Cambridge and

London. Sraffa's review of the book appeared in the *Economic Journal* in March 1932, providing a jolt to the secured place the work was about to acquire.

As a staunch general equilibriumist, Hayek accepted without question the existence and uniqueness of competitive equilibrium established through the operation of the demand-and-supply forces and the ever-active principle of substitution that ensured its attainment. Not only does equilibrium exist in a non-monetary real economy but, whenever a disturbance occurs, a new equilibrium is rapidly established. The equilibrium so attained gives full sway to the voluntary decisions of producers and consumers, and forces are set against any interference with these decisions so that disequilibrium will not be tolerated for long. Given the inherent and inevitable tendency towards equilibrium operating in a real economy, all disequilibria and cyclical phenomena are to be ascribed to monetary factors. Thence Hayek investigates the characteristics of 'neutral' money, that is, a kind of money which leaves production and the relative prices of goods, including the rate of interest, 'undisturbed', exactly as they would be if there were no money at all. Hayek therefore first investigates the properties of the real system and the new equilibrium that it can attain when the decision to save is voluntarily made. In contrast, the situation is analysed when savings are 'forced' through external actions of banks lending credit to producers or consumers. Hayek ends by suggesting that the only 'neutral' money is a constant quantity of money (i.e., quantum of money multiplied by the velocity of circulation).

Sraffa acknowledges the definite contribution of the book in emphasizing the effects of monetary changes on the relative prices of commodities, rather than movements of the general price level on which attention until then had been exclusively focused by the quantity theory. The approach of isolating the effects of money on production and prices, via the adoption of the notion of neutral money (which, in Hayek, is tantamount to conceptualizing a non-monetary economy), could also 'have something to recommend', as it would allow a useful comparison between the conditions of a specific non-monetary economy and those of the various monetary systems. Such a comparison between a moneyless economy and various monetary systems, in terms of the effects of assumed cases of disturbances in equilibrium, would have been worthwhile as it would have revealed the essential characteristics common to every kind of money as well as their differences, and provided comparative merits of alternative policies.

However, Sraffa points out that Hayek completely forgets to deal with this task. He neither traces the repercussions of using any one monetary system, nor does he deal with money in any other role than purely as a medium of exchange. Hayek initially goes into a detailed exposition of the structure of a real economy, modelled along Austrian lines, with land and labour as the only means of production and all goods arranged into stages of production. Hayek assumes the structure to be triangular with the base representing output of consumer goods and the height representing the time elapsing between the first and the final stages of production. As in the Austrian theory, a positive relation is presumed to exist between the degree of round-aboutness of methods and their productivity, and an inverse relation between the former and the rate of interest. Hayek then traces out, assuming an initial equilibrium, the repercussions of a voluntary decision by consumers to change the rate of savings. The new equilibrium occurs at higher demand for capital, longer period of production, yielding ultimately a higher flow of consumption at lower prices. This situation is contrasted with 'forced savings' induced by the monetary policy (i.e., when the bank's lending rate falls below the natural rate, or when banks advance credits to producers). In such a case, producers are encouraged to lengthen the period of production without the 'real savings'. This leads to inflationary price rises as factors are bid away from the consumer-goods industries. The real consumption levels get depressed. However, this situation which is created through the extraneous intervention of banks cannot be perpetuated. The break operates either through the non-feasibility of continuing credit operations by banks, or due to the natural tendency for consumers to expand their consumption when their money receipts rise again. Thus cycles are caused when the natural movement of prices is disturbed by the movements of money supply or the extension of credit by the banking system. Hayek blamed the 'elastic' currency for recurrent disasters and favoured a constant or invariant money as being 'neutral'. In his view a money supply is not neutral, even if it keeps 'the general price level stable'. In fact, Hayek not only criticizes the neglect of relative prices by the quantity theorists, but also rejects the meaningfulness or the use of the 'general price level'.

While Hayek's criticism of the vagueness of the notion of a general price level (which was nothing more than one of many possible index numbers of prices) was well founded, Sraffa criticizes him for going further and rejecting 'not only the notion of the general price-level but every notion of the value of money in any sense whatsoever'. Sraffa notes that Hayek reduces the function of money to being a medium of exchange alone, ignoring that money is also a store of value, and the standard in terms of which debts, and other legal obligations, habits, opinions, conventions, in short all kinds of relations between men, are more or less rigidly fixed (p. 43). Regarding it purely as a medium of exchange 'deprives money of its essence' and it should then be inevitable, argues Sraffa, that when Hayek considers alternative monetary policies, money should be found to be 'neutral' and its effects identically immaterial in every case. But, paradoxically, 'Dr Hayek invariably finds, when he comes to compare the effects of alternative policies in regulating this emasculated money, that there is an all-important difference in the result, and that it is "neutral" only if it is kept constant in quantity, whilst if the quantity is changed the most disastrous effects follow' (p. 44).

The source of this paradox is more closely examined by Sraffa taking Hayek's analysis of the difference between 'voluntary' and 'forced' savings and their consequences. Hayek suggests that, in the former case, the changes brought about in the structure are permanent as they follow voluntary decisions of individuals; in the latter, they are 'forced' through inflation and therefore the consumers can be expected to re-establish the initial position as soon as inflation ceases and their freedom of action is restored. Sraffa, in this article, does not contest the existence or stability of equilibrium in the system but argues that the second situation of 'forced savings' could be equally stable. In the case of inflation, just as that of saving, the accumulation of capital takes place through a reduction of 'consumption'. Hayek's presumption that the economy would revert back to less capitalist methods and higher consumption levels can have no basis. Emphasizing the distributive implications of the inflationary process, Sraffa argues:

> One class has, for a time, robbed another class of a part of their incomes; and has saved the plunder. When the robbery comes to an end, it is clear that the victims cannot possibly consume the capital which is now well out of their reach. If they are wage earners, who have all the time consumed every penny of their income, they have no wherewithal to expand consumption. And, if they are capitalists, who have not shared in the plunder, they may indeed be induced to consume now a part of their capital by the fall in the rate of interest; but not more so than if the rate had been lowered by the 'voluntary saving' of other people. (p. 48)

Thus there could be no reversion to the previous position.

Further, Sraffa criticizes the asymmetrical reasoning which Hayek adopts in distinguishing between credits extended by the bank to producers and to consumers. Hayek holds, on the one hand, that the artificial stimulant of inflation, in the shape of producers' credits, cannot do any good. On the other hand, when consumers decide to save and additional credit is issued to them, he finds that it would frustrate the effects of saving or that, in short, inflation working through consumer's credit would be effective in decreasing capital. It is all the more surprising to have such asymmetry when one realizes that the producer's voluntary decisions are treated differently from the consumer's voluntary decisions. Summarizing this paradox, Sraffa writes:

> What has happened is simply that, since money has been thoroughly 'neutralised' from the start, whether its quantity rises, falls, or is kept steady, makes not the slightest difference; at the same time an extraneous element, in the shape of the supposed power of the banks to settle the way in which money is spent, has crept into the argument and has done all the work. As Voltaire says, you can kill a flock of sheep by incantations plus a little poison. (p. 49)

Sraffa's acute criticism of Hayek for confining the role of money to being only a medium of exchange and implicitly equating a 'neutral' money economy with a non-monetary economy is noteworthy.

Sraffa, in connection with Hayek's criticism of Wicksell, also stressed the point that a non-monetary economy could also be in disequilibrium, in contrast to Hayek's implicit notion that a divergence between the actual and the natural rate of interest is possible only in a monetary economy. Sraffa demonstrates that, in a barter economy, there could be as many natural rates of interest as there are commodities, and that each such rate will be equal to the equilibrium rate when the spot and forward prices coincide. Further, that 'under free competition, this divergence of rates is essential to the effecting of the transition [to equilibrium] as is the divergence of prices from the costs of production' (p. 50). Sraffa also rejects Hayek's criticism of Wicksell that the natural rate of interest could not both keep the price level stable and equate the demand and supply of capital in a growing economy. It is true that, in transition to a new equilibrium, there is no unique equilibrium rate of interest, but a weighted average of natural rates can be suitably defined using the same weights as for the general price level. This is, of necessity, not a unique average. In other words, for each composite commodity there is a corresponding natural rate that can equalize the purchasing power of savings and investment reckoned in terms of the composite commodity. Sraffa was also to point out that a non-monetary economy does not necessarily ensure a smooth transition to equilibrium through the matching of savings and investment. Resources need to be matched, and plans of consumers to save and those of investors to invest need to coincide so as to suitably direct resources from consumer goods to intermediate goods, and vice versa. Sraffa's critique was thus important in clarifying the nature of the problem of money and in dispelling the pure monetarist arguments that all disequilibria situations are created by money whose operation is analysed purely in terms of an extraneous intervention. At this juncture, we may note, Sraffa did not bring up his critique of the Austrian treatment of 'capital' as measured by the period of production although this was to appear prominently in *Production of Commodities* which was under preparation then.

Ricardo's Works and Correspondence
From the late 1920s until the 1970s Sraffa worked on the editing of David Ricardo's writings. In a certain sense, this arduous, monumental work epitomized his personal and scholarly qualities. His search for every detail of extant material on the life and works of Ricardo was remarkable for the perseverance and innovation with which the search was conducted in remote places and the farthest quarters wherever even a faint clue would lead to. The systematic collation of materials, skilful and imaginative methods of presenting them in print so as not to vitiate their authenticity and original context, and masterly editing with insightful and scholarly commentaries give the volumes an artistic, architectural quality. Sraffa himself went to great pains in selecting the format, type specifications and technical aspects of the printing, personally supervising every detail. The first volumes were published in 1951, in collaboration with Maurice Dobb. The last and eleventh volume, the *Index*, was published in 1973.

While the compilation itself was no minor task – many documents were discovered for the first time and published – it is in the interpretation of Ricardo that Sraffa's scholarship excelled. This was remarkable for its objectivity and the sense of history that makes the original texts stand out and speak for themselves, aided by Sraffa's comments. At the same time, in these brief comments, Sraffa reveals his deep knowledge and understanding of the contemporaneous intellectual environment and of historical events. Facts are meticulously collected, counterchecked and cogently presented with the utmost brevity. A unique piece in the eleven-volume set is the *Index* which is an excellent aid to Ricardo scholars as its approach is analytical and reflects Sraffa's command over the comprehensive *Works*.

It is in the introduction to Ricardo's *Principles of Political Economy* (*Works*, I) that Sraffa's genius comes out. With his characteristic agility and subtlety of logic he uncovers the bare foundations of the analytical structure underlying Ricardo's theory of value and distribution. The logical development of the surplus view of profit, emerging from the primitive corn model to the complexities of the capital problem encountered by Ricardo in his attempts at generalizing the surplus-based explanation of profit, is lucidly brought out. At every stage of this development, debates arose between Ricardo and his contemporaries, particularly Malthus. Sraffa helped to recover this correspondence from various quarters. With Sraffa's interpretation, the peculiarities of Ricardo's positions, the manner in which questions were raised and their resolution attempted, Ricardo's rather abstruse and apparently puzzling attempts to pursue that 'chimera of the invariant standard' – all these fall into a neater pattern. Sraffa takes care at every step not to overstate the case, not to impose constructions and interpretations that are at variance with Ricardo's more significant pronouncements. A masterly analytical ability and judgement, however, is exercised in detecting, sorting out and providing chains of reasoning that Ricardo himself, given the early stage and premature beginnings of the approach and of formal analytical techniques in economic theory, might have been confused about or was insufficiently aware of. Sraffa's attempt is to delineate the broad analytical framework that is compatible with Ricardo's main propositions so that, while a certain amount of discretion and abstraction is inevitably involved, it does not amount to fathering upon Ricardo theories of distinctly different tenor.

It is remarkable that Sraffa, an original thinker, should have been totally immersed in editing the works of a single scholar over an enormously long time. It is equally remarkable that the idea of working on Ricardo and classical political economy germinated in his early youthful period of political involvement. It would seem that Ricardo's place in the history of economic theory was crucial, not only for understanding the origins of marginalism that grew out of the deviant directions and subversions of classical political economy, but also for grasping the primitive (but, for that reason, transparently bare) structure of the distribution theory in those formative beginnings of surplus-based analysis.

A critique of economic theory, whether marginalist or of later developments in political economy, could start with a clarification of the core where the difficulties in the theory were exposed, unencumbered by sophistries or obfuscations. Marx was aware that a scrupulous study of scientific political economy – which he recognized as declining after Ricardo – was an essential preparation to launch his own ideas. Marshall, on the other hand, took pains to emphasize his lineal descendancy from Ricardo, succeeding, in the process, to subvert the classical theory through his 'generous' and 'sympathetic' interpretations.

That Sraffa's interpretation of Ricardo was not merely an exercise in the history of thought, purely of antiquarian interest, is obvious from the fact that, in recent times, the neoclassicists have found it increasingly pertinent to challenge his interpretations and revive the Marshallian 'continuity thesis' in order to depict Ricardo as a primitive general equilibriumist. Sraffa's work has thus stimulated a resurgence of interest in classical political economy, both on the part of those who support the continuity thesis and of those who acknowledge the essentially different structure and approach of classical theory. Maurice Dobb, a friend of Sraffa, contributed considerably to this revival of the surplus approach and collaborated with Sraffa in the editing of Ricardo's *Works*. Both were Fellows of Trinity where they enjoyed a long association and friendship.

Production of Commodities by Means of Commodities
The work of Sraffa which has triggered a still-continuing controversy is *Production of Commodities by Means of Commodities*, subtitled *Prelude to a Critique of Economic Theory* – a slim volume published in 1960 and in preparation from the 1920s. The book puzzled most readers by its rather unusual style, approach and brevity – debates starting from the title of the book onwards. While there was no disagreement about the rigorous logic that the book demonstrates, its motivation remained a mystery to many. It is, however, recognized that the work serves a dual purpose: first, to revive the classical approach to distribution and value by neatly identifying, formulating and resolving certain central logical problems in that theory. These problems, sometimes awkwardly formulated, had dogged the original Masters and had become one of the principal reasons for the premature abandonment of that theory. The second purpose is to expose the internal logical weaknesses of the marginalist theory that had acquired dominance, submerging the earlier approach.

It would not be possible here, given both the limitation of space and the state of the wide-ranging continuing debates, to deal at length with the approach, form and content of this work. Very briefly, on the reconstructive side, the book clarified the nature and form of the analytical difficulties encountered by the surplus explanations of profit in Ricardo and Marx, and suggested, implicitly, possible solutions to these problems. The construct of the 'standard commodity', as well as the simultaneous resolution of profits and prices within a multi-commodity system, are efforts in that direction. At the same time, Sraffa also demonstrates that the capital 'measurement' problem – which arises in the classical theory mainly because 'capital' constitutes 'competitively produced means of production' – also comes up, for the same reason, in the marginalist theory where it however takes a different form. The marginalist theory faces logical difficulties because the 'substitution' among factors induced by changes in factor-prices may not guarantee the inverse relation between factor-intensity and its price required for generating a consistent demand function for a factor. The debates on capital theory centred around the possibility of treating capital as a factor independent of distribution, or, in its more general form, of deriving a demand function for 'capital' with the requisite properties yielding an inverse relation between capital-intensity and the rate of profit. While the debate on capital was already taking place from the mid-1950s, the context of distribution theory appeared prominently in the post-*Production of Commodities* debates. This was initiated by David Levhari who asserted the impossibility of reswitching of techniques – a phenomenon discussed by Sraffa in his book as an obvious limitation of the marginalist explanation of profit – in a general equilibrium system. Levhari's claim was refuted by a number of authors in the Symposium on Paradoxes in Capital Theory (*Quarterly Journal of Economics*, 1966), vindicating Sraffa's criticism at the treatment of capital in marginalist theory. The objection raised against the marginalist treatment of capital could also be easily extended to the theory of international trade and growth, etc., where the principle of factor-substitution is used in determining relative prices, outputs and distribution.

Another major part of the much-needed clarification concerning the structure of the surplus-based theory was to demonstrate the inessentiality for it of certain specific propositions which were more like appendages, adopted for momentary convenience, especially in Ricardo. Not only did these cripple the advance of the theory and lead it into deviant directions through easy misinterpretations, but some of these features were precisely the one which the early marginalism picked out for elaboration and extension, The 'idea of diminishing returns on land', for example, which was borrowed by Ricardo from Malthus to explain rents was the one principle (apart from the principle of population) which Jevons chose to preserve as worthwhile, discarding unceremoniously the rest of Ricardo's theory. The idea of diminishing returns on land – which did suggest a possible relation between output and unit cost – was then generalized, as we have noted above, to provide the basis for the 'supply schedule'. Also, it was the diminishing returns on land that was to suggest an analogous proposition of diminishing utility on the demand side. That 'diminishing return' was not an essential element in the surplus-based theory emerged in Marx's criticism of Ricardo. Sraffa (1960), in his short chapter on land, the implications of which have yet to be developed, shows how the classical view of rents need not necessarily rest on the conception of 'the law of diminishing returns' or need not suggest necessarily any functional relation between output and cost, or even presume a unique rank ordering of lands according to productivity. In fact, correcting the classical writers, he shows that differential rents as well as the 'no-rent land' depend upon the rate of profit (or wages). Similarly, the notion, that the classical 'model' depended upon a fixed subsistence wage, constrained by the Malthusian population dynamics, and can work only under 'the iron law of wages', is shown to be wrong. The fixed or invariant wage hypothesis is a fifth wheel of the theory that could be easily dispensed with, as indeed Marx did. What is characteristic of the classical structure is the prior determination of wages by historical and social factors. Wages could very well change and, in fact, one of their major concerns was to trace out the implications of changes in wages. Sraffa goes even further and taking the wage as a variable, with wages partaking in surplus-sharing, he shows that variable wages can be accommodated within the classical theory without damaging the surplus-based explanation of profit. The variable wage was probably introduced by Sraffa to counter his opponents' argument that the theory was no longer relevant as wage-earners under advanced capitalism are 'property-owners' because they earn dividends.

Sraffa also implicitly demonstrates, by separating considerations affecting output (its level and composition) from price determination – or, put it more accurately, by not imposing functional links between output and prices – that the adherence to Say's Law in Ricardo is not an essential feature of the theory of distribution. Here again, Marx had already faulted Ricardo, developing his own analysis of accumulation and 'the realization problem', using the departmental schemes of prices of production. (We may note here that Marx also approaches the realization problem sequentially, having first developed his prices-of-production schemes.)

Another major contribution of the book, which largely remains to be explored – although significant beginnings have already been made – is the treatment of joint products which Sraffa uses to represent fixed capital. An immediate consequence which Sraffa derives is of reckoning accurately the depreciation of capital which, earlier, was settled either on the basis of accountancy practices (such as, the straight-line method, implying uniform efficiency through the life of the capital good), or through arbitrary assumptions (such as, one hoss-shay). Sraffa also demonstrates that depreciation of capital is only another aspect of capital valuation depending upon the rate of profit and the efficiency of the method in which the particular capital good is utilised, and not a pure 'technological datum'.

Because of its extreme brevity and terse and unusual character, the book has evoked a wide range of reactions, some crediting it with striking novelty and far-reaching implications and others viewing it as an extremely limited and partial framework which has arrived late on the scene by several decades. Sraffa himself called it a prelude and looked ahead to further extensions, if the foundations held. Staunch neoclassicists view it as a partial system (a Walrasian system operating under conditions of 'non-substitution theorems'), and many others as a stationary, unchanging system operating under constant returns to scale. Sraffa himself gives no hints as to how and where the system moves on to – no questions of the utilization of surplus are raised. Methodologically, he explicitly states that his immediate concern is the properties of the system which do not depend upon change. Erroneously interpreting this as invariance to change or changelessness, some have regarded Sraffa's analysis as restricted to a stationary equilibrium or, when extended, to signify steady states. There have been repeated charges about the ahistoricity of the exercise which appears then as merely abstraction-mongering.

This, as we have mentioned earlier, appears extraordinarily paradoxical for a scholar steeped in intellectual history as well as committed to a social and political philosophy. We may wonder whether the manner of presentation of this important prelude, in a basic, rudimentary form, has a deeper methodological motivation. We may venture to offer a suggestion with some plausibility. First, the extreme 'limitedness' that is ascribed to Sraffa's framework (which we may remind readers is no different from the 'prices of production' of Marx) perhaps originates from placing Sraffa's work within the moulds of thought of the dominant marginalist theory. That theory, as Sraffa mentions in his preface, *depends upon 'change'* (see comment above). Given the equilibrium method, the theory has gradually incorporated within its premises certain a priori relations between quantities and prices – 'change' being centred on the 'universal principle of substitution'. The marginalist theory of relative prices thus encompassed within its domain all spheres of economic activity and their movements through time. Indeed, there is a growing realization, especially among 'left Keynesians', that this theory of *equilibrium* in which 'change' nominally pervades – indeed which rests on a certain characterization of change – has grown inherently antithetical to all real history. The reasons lie, in our view, in the particular theoretical framework that the neoclassicists have used, and its ambitious scope extending to all facets of economic activity believed to be governed by 'universal' principles. (We have seen how Sraffa illustrated this with respect to the construction of the supply schedule and the analogous demand schedule.) It is pretentious pseudo-history that guises itself in the 'ever-present', restless principles of substitution acting as a vehicle of change.

In contrast, the classical approach which Sraffa revives appears to be more open. As Sraffa observed, speaking about the cost-of-production theory, that their theory had the advantage that 'it does not conceal from us the fact that we cannot find the elements required for this purpose [studying in greater detail the conditions under which exchange takes place in particular cases] within the limits of its assumptions' (1926, p. 187). The classical theory recognized the complexity and historical specificity that influenced distribution (wages), output levels and composition, social demand, the feasible and the employed methods of production and investment. All these could not be subsumed under the umbrella of price determination. (As noted in the Introduction, Chapter 1, above, the classical theory structures a 'separate' determination of prices and quantities in contrast to their simultaneous determination in the DSE theory within the same supply and demand framework.) However, this did not connote that the analysis of social consumption, of technical change, of the forces of accumulation and distribution (and their interactions) were unimportant or subsidiary. Indeed, it was precisely because due regard was to be paid to socio-historical factors in theorizing on these questions that they proceeded in short chains of reasoning. Probably the best way to broadly grasp this structure is to turn to Marx's treatment of these problems.

All said, it is true that Sraffa's mode of concise presentation has left considerable scope for alternative interpretations. However, it is only when his entire work is viewed as a unity that his methodological and philosophical standpoint emerges more clearly. Controversies on the efficacy of Sraffa's critique of marginalist theory and of his reconstructive efforts to return to the surplus approach are bound to continue.

4 Sraffa, The Bibliophile

A much less-known aspect of Sraffa's work relates to his passion as a book collector. As already mentioned, he succeeded in building up one of the largest individual collections in Europe. However, his joy was not only in owning antiquities. He continued throughout his life to work on old books, researching into their contents, authorship, dating, and so on. In 1938 he prepared an edition, along with Keynes, of Hume's *An Abstract of a Treatise on Human Nature*, with an introduction in which Sraffa established, with remarkable ingenuity, that the author of the abstract was Hume himself and not Adam Smith, as had been earlier maintained. (Keynes acknowledged in letters to friends that the entire work on the attribution of authorship, providing definitive evidence, was completely due to Sraffa's 'ingenuity'.) Sraffa had a very detailed knowledge of manuscripts and was well versed in the technical skills of historiographical research. He enjoyed it immensely, taking delight in discoveries which he however did not publish. For, as he said in a conversation, they were puzzles which once he had solved, he hardly felt like putting them down and depriving others of the exhilaration of discovery. He had a wide circle of contacts among connoisseurs, book collectors, librarians and archivists and was often, in turn, consulted on bibliographical matters and related research.

5 The Close of an Era?

Uncompromising in his convictions but truly modest, solitary but full of friendly generosity and warmth, Sraffa endeared himself to his close friends and was a pillar of strength to the younger students who were as much impressed by him as a person as a scholar. The passing away of Piero Sraffa soon after the death of Joan Robinson and of Maurice Dobb marks, as it were, the close of a memorable era in Cambridge history. However, it also marks the resurgence of classical theory and a prelude to new possibilities of explorations in our science.

Note: Chapter 13

This obituary article was first published in *Economic and Political Weekly*, vol. 19, no. 30–1 (August 1984), pp. 1236–50, and is reprinted here with minor revisions.

Piero Sraffa's Major Writings and References : Chapter 13

(1920), 'L'inflazione monetaria in Italia durante e doppo la guerra' (November) (Milan: Scuola Tipografica Salesiana).
(1922a), 'L'attuale situazione delle banche italiane', *Manchester Guardian Weekly Supplement: The Reconstruction of Europe* (7 December), pp. 694–5.
(1922b), 'The bank crisis in Italy', *Economic Journal*, vol. 32, no. 126 (July), pp. 7–29.
(1924a), 'Obituary to Maffeo Pantelleoni', *Economic Journal*, vol. 34, no. 136 (December), pp. 648–53.
(1924b), 'Problemi di oggi di domani', letter to A. Gramsci, published with Gramsci's reply in *L'Ordine Nuova*, 13 April; reprinted in A. Gramsci, *La construzione del partito communista, 1923–1926* (Turin: Einaudi, 1971).
(1925), 'Sulle relazioni fra costo e quantita prodotta', *Annali di Economia*, vol. 2, pp. 277–328.
(1926), 'The laws of returns under competitive conditions, *Economic Journal*, vol. 36, no. 144 (December), pp. 535–50.
(1930a), 'An alleged correction of Ricardo', *Economic Journal*, vol. 44, no. 40, pp. 539–44.
(1930b), 'A "criticism" and a "rejoinder" in the "Symposium on increasing returns and the representative firm"', *Economic Journal*, vol. XL, no. 157 (March), pp. 89–93.
(1932a), 'Dr Hayek on money and capital', *Economic Journal*, vol. 42, pp. 42–53.
(1932b), 'Rejoinder', *Economic Journal*, vol. 62, pp. 249–51.
(1938), D. Hume: *An Abstract of a Treatise on Human Nature (1740)*, ed. by P. Sraffa and J. M. Keynes (Cambridge: Cambridge University Press).
(1951–73), Editorial introductions to the *Works and Correspondence of David Ricardo*, edited by P. Sraffa, with the collaboration of M. H. Dobb: Vols I–X, 1951–5, and Vol. XI: *Index*, 1973 (Cambridge: Cambridge University Press).
(1955), 'Malthus on Public Works', *Economic Journal*, September.
(1960), *Production of Commodities by Means of Commodities: Prelude to a Critique of Economic Theory* (Cambridge: Cambridge University Press).
(1962), 'Production of commodities: a comment' (reply to Harrod's review), *Economic Journal*, vol. 72 (June), pp. 477–9.

Further References: Chapter 13

Gramsci, A. (1971), *Prison Notebooks* (London: Lawrence and Wishart).
Hayek, F. A. (1931), *Prices and Production* (London: George Allen & Unwin).
Keynes, J. M. (1930 [1958–60]), *A Treatise on Money*, 2 vols (London: Macmillan).

Levhari, D. (1965), 'A Nonsubstitution Theorem and Switching of Techniques, *Quarterly Journal of Economics*, vol. lxxxix, no. 1 (February), pp. 98–105.

Marshall, A. (1890), *Principles of Economics*, 8th edn, 1920 (London: Macmillan).

Robertson, D. H. (1930), in the Symposium on Increasing Returns and the Representative Firm, *The Economic Journal*, vol. xxxix, no. 1 (March), pp. 80–9 and 92–3. The symposium (pp. 79–116) introduced by J. M. Keynes (p. 79) contained the contributions also by Piero Sraffa (pp. 90–2 and p. 93) and G. F. Shove (pp. 94–116).

Wicksteed, P. H. (1914 [1934]), 'The Scope and Method of Political Economy', in L. Robbins (ed.), *The Commonsense of Political Economy* (London: Routledge).

Index

Anderson, John
  extracts from his note books on Smith's lectures 204, 211
Arena, Richard 247n
Arrow, K. J. 38n19, 293n5
Ashley, W. J. 65, 129n9, 156n8
Austrian approach
  one way avenue of production 282–3
  concept of hierarchical order of goods 187, 232–3; 'Time', measure of capital, independent of distribution 233
  shift to utility analysis 199, 232–3; supremacy of demand 232–3
  subsistence fund in 74n33, 199

Bacon, Francis 35n4
Bailey, Samuel 47, 49, 53, 56–7, 62, 65, 70, 71n1, 72n12, 72n19, 248n13
basics and nonbasics
  defined 255; objective property of the system 255
  significance of the distinction 10, 263–6; uses more of the available information than does the classification decomposable/indecomposable 263–6; different cases of switches of methods illustrated 256–66
Baumol, W. J. 71n4, 112, 118
Bohm-Bawerk, E. A. von 4, 74n33, 127, 233
Bentham, Jeremy 82–3, 150
Bharadwaj, K. 11, 14, 35n2, 41, 63, 65, 72n3, n8, 74n37, 108n64, 109n68, 120, 126, 128, 129n9, 132, 149, 157n13, 179, 192, 195, 208–9, 227–8, 237, 240, 248n2, n9, n13, 249n14, n15, 250n28, 251n36, 291, 294n15
Blaug, M. 43, 108n61, 118
Bortkiewicz, L. von 201n4, 212–14
Bosanquet, Charles 82–3, 103n13
Bowley, Sir Arthur 166
Bray, J. F. 71n6

Brougham, Henry 73n30
Bruno, M. 259, 265, 273n17
Burmeister, E. 259, 265, 273n17
Burton, J. H. 165

Cairnes, J. E. 74n33
Cannan, Edwin 107n54, 123, 211
Cantillon, R. 38n15, n17, 209
capital
  as hoarded or secondary labour (James Mill) 49–50; as accumulated produce of anterior labour (McCulloch) 59, as wages advanced 51, 139; treated as land 251n39; as 'present worth' (Fisher) 233, 249n19–n21
  fixed capital, effect of wage rise on relative values 70, 96–7; curious effect 70, 122; durability posing difficulties (Hicks) 249n18
  measure of 44, 49–50, 70, 96, 319; not independent of distribution 188, 199, 319; difficulties, in 70, 96, 103n7; of defining equal capital and equal value of products posed by Ricardo against Torrens (and McCulloch) 48, 96, 108n57
  proportion of, to population 51–2, 56, 60, 66, 138; *see* wages fund doctrine
capital theory debate
  demand function for capital not 'well behaved' 2, 8, 188, 199, 229, 232, 284; not confined to a critique of aggregate production function 199, 232; a priori ranking of method of production, independent of distribution, not tenable 229; reswitching of methods of production 10, 319; defined 255–7; the maximum possible number in alternative cases 256–66; *see* basics and nonbasics
  as a critique of neoclassical theory of value and distribution 2, 8, 10, 188, 199, 232–4, 241, 248n4, 286, 318–19; and of output and employment 10,

199–200, 248n4, 284, 286
Caravale, G. A. 128
Cassels, J. M. 127, 251n33
Catephores, G. 215
Chamberlain, Joseph 310
Chandrashekhar, C. P. 35n
Clark, J. B. 9, 135, 152, 156n2, n6, 232, 251n33
Clark, J. M. 119, 226
classical theories
   common basis shared by classical theorists despite differences 1, 15, 179–80
   surplus based approach 6, 41–2, 77, 80, 126, 183, 246, 248n6; *see* surplus
   structure of, of value and distribution 180–4; production as a circular reproductive process 6, 7, 27, 222, 244–6; scarcity implies non- or limited reproducibility 100–1; data of the system 7, 23, 25, 89, 98, 120, 126, 180–4, 192, 225, 287–8; given wages 25, 89, 181, 288, 290; given methods of production 25, 89, 182, 288; given social output (effectual demand) 25, 89, 130n12, 182–3, 288
   framework of choice and change in 6, 26, 223, 245–6; the concept of individual in the society in 4, 14–17, 19–21, 28, 34, 36n7, 210
   inter-relations among the data (quantity dynamics) 27, 98, 126, 288–9
   sequential separation of analysis of prices and quantities 7, 25, 27, 89–90, 181, 198, 225, 244, 251n31; 'openness' of 10, 26, 243–5, 248n10, 251n31, 289, 292
   distinctive placement of land, labour, capital and determination of their revenues 22–3, 39n24, 240
   whether demand side is absent in 127, 180–1, 191, 229, 245
   whether a subsystem of the later more general theory 5, 180, 191, 201n2, 225, 248n5
   whether relies on a single factor (corn or labour) 245
   certain misinterpretations of 245–6
Clower, R. 277–80, 293n6
Coddington, A. 247n1
Cohen, Ruth 264
Colson, L. C. 135, 145, 156n2
competition
   classical notion of 6; characteristics of 180, 224–5, 234; free competition 19; anarchy of 291
   neoclassical notion of perfect competition 6, 20, 234–5, 237;

atomistic competition 20; Morgenstern on 249n25
competitive capitalist economy 22, 224; characteristics of 6, 23
consumption
   theory of, in classicals 183, 198, 231; distinct from demand and supply theory 198, 231
   function 283–4
continuity in theoretical developments
   view supported by Marshall 3, 41, 77, 127, 129n8, 130n11, 134, 151–6, 190–1, 224, 318; by Hicks 248n5; by Hollander 77, 94, 102, 102n2, 248n5; by Samuelson 248n5; view scrutinized 134–5, 151–6; Shove on doctrinal continuity in Marshall 152; *see* divide in theories
   classical theorists as precursors of the neoclassical 3–5, 14, 35n2, 77, 116, 127, 192, 205; *see* classical theories, divide in theories
   supply and demand based analysis of resource allocation imputed to classical theorists 4, 77–8, 98–102, 108n62, 179, 192, 248n15, 250n28
   anticipations of general equilibrium theory read into classical theories 99, 207–8; special assumptions attributed to 5, 81, 95, 99–100, 180, 201n2, 245–6, 250n28; views questioned 27, 99–102, 208
   measurable motives and real costs imputed to classical theories 32–3, 39n23, 72n16, 151; this questioned 151, 209
   cost of production view of Ricardo (Marshall, Cassels, Stigler) 127, 191, 243; Ricardo aware of the essential role of demand in governing value but regards its action less obscure (Marshall) 127, 230; view contested 127, 131n18, 251n34; Smith praised for his decomposition exercise, pointing to Say and Walras (Schumpeter) 208; *see* value
cost of production
   resolved into capital or labour (James Mill) 47; difficulty of, expressed by Ricardo 45, 47, 71n11
   profits and wages constitute elements of (J. S. Mill) 66, 138–9; regulator of price 47, 139; synonymous with value (Ricardo) 131n18, 139; *see* value
Cournot, A. 146, 149, 156n3
Crotius 35n3

Debreu, G. 38n19, 249n23

INDEX 327

demand
  a desire to possess with the power of purchasing 88; where the power exists the will to purchase exists (Ricardo) 86, 88, also 104n25; Malthus's contrary view 88; limited only by production (Ricardo) 86–8; Malthus disagrees 86–8, also 105n33
  occasioned by accumulation as much as by consumption 88, 105n32; influence of income on demand 231
  effectual demand 4, 7, 23, 25, 27–8, 90, 100, 194, 228, 235, 250n27; factors affecting 25, 27–8, 100; distinguished from demand in the schedule sense 27–8, 35, 100, 194, 208, 228–9, 245
  whether present in or essential for classical determination of relative prices 5, 100, 104n27, 130n12, 180–1, 192–2, 201n2, 249n15, 250n28; and of the rate of profit 86–8, 104n27
demand and supply based equilibrium theories (DSE)
  structure of 26–7, 185–6, 293n4; one way avenue 7, 26, 222, 244–5; data of the system 7, 26, 185–6, 225, 232; given factor endowments 2, 4, 8, 185, 198–9, 245; given technology 2, 4, 185; given consumer's preferences 2, 4, 186
  framework of change and choice; potential change, a prerequisite 4, 7, 8, 26, 34, 222–3, 232; substitution principle, the mainspring of change 4, 7, 8, 26, 147, 186, 199, 232–3, 229, 243–4, 293n4; restrictive assumptions on choice sets 7, 8, 20, 26, 186, 229, 232, 234, 251n35; reductionist approach 224–5, 230, 233–4
  simultaneous determination of prices and quantities in 2, 7, 8, 10, 25–7, 223, 225, 231–2, 241, 244
  symmetrical treatment of factors and of their revenues 185, 187, 226, 240; of producers and consumers behaviour 7, 185; of demand and supply schedules 185, 228–31, 237
  dictatorship of relative price-based scarce resource allocational scheme 8, 26, 34, 145, 224–5, 230, 232, 234
  critique of, in terms of comparative structures of theories 3, 9, 222–3; see also capital theory debate, Dobb, M. H. and Sraffa, Piero
  critique of, on grounds of deficient observational basis 247n1; by fundamental Keynesians 247n1
De Vivo, G. 65, 248n13

divide in theories
  in 1870s 2–3, 41, 125, 178–9; whether in 1830s 178; distinctiveness of structure and approach of the two theoretical systems 1–7, 15, 25, 34–5, 115–18, 125–6, 196–200, 222–4, 247; reflected in Sraffa's work 130n11, 222, 246–7; upheld by Dobb 130n11, 178; Marshall's contrary view of continuity; see continuity in theoretical developments, Marshall, Alfred
  changing contents and roles of concepts 5–6, 10, 26, 34, 226–7; the notion of competition 6, 234–5; of equilibrium 6, 235–43; of effectual demand 27–8, 35; of resource allocation 8, 21, 26–9, 35; see demand, equilibrium
distribution
  of the produce among the revenue classes 6, 22–3, 30, 130n13, 206, 287; profits, rents, wages each determined along different principles 22–3, 30–1, 39n24, 240; division into profits, rents and wages, see profits, rents, wages
  whether prior to prices in classical theory 130n13, 196, 213
  problem of distribution treated before the value question (James Mill) 46, 47, 51–2, and in J. S. Mill 65
Dmitriev, V. K. 213–14
Dobb, M. H. 9, 11n3, 14, 65, 74n38, 111, 126, 129n3, 130n11, 157n14, 172n, 201n5, 219, 289, 302, 316, 318, 322
  his critique of theories in value and distribution; historically relativist character of theories in the choice of problems and modes of formalization 176–7; development of theory into two contending frameworks 178
  changing content and emphasis of the critique of supply and demand theory 179; early critique emphasizing conceptual shifts and their wider philosophical significance 186; replacement of the objective basis of classical theory by that in subjective utility 187; focus shifted from production to exchange, with the surplus notion disappearing 187–8; autonomous preferences of individuals, structure of market demand, independent of distribution 188; later critique of logical structure and internal consistency 187; draws upon the capital theory debate 188
  Marshallian bias in interpretation of classical themes in early writings

189–91; interpretation of Smith's supply and demand 192–5; of the logical structure of the two theories 196–200

effect of Jevonian revolution deeper than that of the Keynesian 178, 199–200

his major contribution to the revival of classical approach 211

Dunbar, C. F. 114, 116

Eatwell, J. L. 71n, 71n3, 108n64, 128, 179, 200n, 290

economic rationality, principle of 219

Edgeworth, F. Y. 148, 162, 250n29

effective demand
principle, in short and long run 285–6, 291–2; integrating the surplus approach with 291–2; notional and actual (effective) excess demand 278

Eltis, W. A. 28

equilibrium
condition of existence and stability 143, 145, 149, 174n20; of multiplicity 145, 149, 174n20

long period of equilibrium an organizing concept, similar to classical long run position explained differently 6, 235–7; whether connotes stationarity 237

equilibrium price, periodized into temporary, short period normal, long period normal and secular in Marshall 147–8, 238; *see* time

short period Walrasian equilibrium 294n10

shift in the notion of equilibrium (Hicks) 5–6, 241; intertemporal equilibrium 242, 294n10

versus history 247n1

see natural state (position)

equivalent exchange 212, 214

expectations
emphasis on, with retreat to short period 286; inhibits definitive generalizations regarding investment demand schedule 286–7; short and long period state of, Keynes's alternative assumptions 291

the form in which present in classical theory 290–1

subjective and objective basis of 243, 281, 291, 295n18; whether perfect foresight and certainty essential for long period position 290–1; the basis for a critique of the 'equilibrium method', position of fundamental Keynesians 247n1

fallacy of composition, exposed by Keynes 234

false trading 277

Ferguson, A. 35n4

Fetter, F. W. 74n38, 116

Fisher, Irving 160, 232–3, 249n19–n21

Foxwell, H. S. 71n6, 156n4

Friedman, M. 293n2, 294n8

Fundamental Keynesians 247n1

Gantmacher, F. R. 269

Garegnani, P. 9, 11, 43, 71n3, 74n36, 85, 93, 102n, 104n20, n22, 105n37, 107n51, 108n64, 121, 126–8, 130n13, 156n, 172n, 188, 213–14, 232, 235, 241–2, 245, 248n9, 270n, 273n17, 283–6, 289, 294n2, n13

Ghosh, Jayati 35n, 129n

Godwin, R. 71n6

Gordon, Barry 116

Gram, Harvey 247n

Gramsci, A. 299, 300

Gray, A. 71n6

Guillebaud, C. W. 155n

Hahn, F. H. 38n19, 281, 293n5, 294n9, n10

Hall, Charles 71n6

Harcourt, G. C. 35n, 102n, 126, 129n, 200n

Harris, D. 102n

Harrod, R. F. 237

Hayek, F. A. von 111, 301–3, 312
money in a real economy 313; effects of money on relative prices via the structure of production 314–15; basis in the Austrian theory of capital 313–14

Sraffa's critique of 313–16

Hicks, J. R. 245, 248n5, 249n18, 251n32, n33, 275, 282
element of time in 241–3; alternative dynamical methods, critique concentrating on method rather than on theory 241–3, 247n1; taxonomy of methods not forming a coherent whole 243

associates long period equilibrium with stationary state 241–2

period analysis (prompted by difficulty of capital) 241–2; inter-temporal equilibrium 242, 294n10; *see* equilibrium

Hirschman, A. O. 19

historical materialism
Scottish materialist interpretation (stadial view) of history 13–17, 35n4, 209–11; *see* Adam Smith; difference

from Marx's dialectical materialism 36n8
Hobbes, J. 54
Hobsbawm, Eric 178
Hobson, J. A.
  finds virtual confession of futility of marginalism in Pigou 159–60, 164, 166–7, 171, 172n2; Marshall's comment on 160, 164, 171–2
Hodgskin, Thomas 71n6
Hollander, J. H. 116, 123
Hollander, S. 5, 35n2, 71n3, 74n38, 77–86, 89–110, 128, 245, 248n5, 249n5, 249n15, 250n28
  his central proposition that Ricardo was throughout preoccupied with the link between the money price of corn, money wage and the rate of profit 78; in the pre-Essay correspondence 84–9; in the Essay and post-Essay period 91–8; contrasted with the line of development of Ricardo's theory of profit suggested by Sraffa 78, 81–98; position critically scrutinized 81–98
  imputes resource allocational mechanism to Ricardo borrowed from Smith 98–101; the position criticized 98–101; *see also* continuity in theoretical developments
Horner, F. 106n49
Howey, R. S. 156n4, n5
Hume, David 35n3, 37n9, 322
Hutcheson, F. 35n3, n4, 37n9
Hutchison, T. W. 116, 129n4, 130n13

interest
  not as equilibrator of saving and investment, which are identified in Smith and Ricardo 289
  theory of, marginalist 284; Keynesian 284; the rate of, determined outside the sphere of output in Keynes, a distinct causal structure (Pasinetti) 282
  divergence between the actual and the natural rate of interest, possibly only in monetary economy (Hayek) 316; as many natural rates of interest possible as there are commodities (Sraffa) 316; divergence of interests essential for effecting transition in equilibrium (Sraffa) 316

Jevons, W. S. 1–3, 118, 127, 134–6, 139, 142, 145, 153, 155, 178, 185–6, 196, 199, 226, 229, 238, 248n5, 304, 319
  considers Ricardo shunted the car of theory onto a wrong line 116; regards theories of population and rent as scientific in form and consonant with facts 156n9, 227; rent, a theory, distinctly mathematical, gives a clue to the correct mode of treating the whole science 156n9, 227
  Marshall's review of his Theory of Political Economy 156n3, n4
Joint product
  Pigou on costs in the case of 164; Marshall's comment 164–5

Kahn, R. F. 279
Kaldor, N. 8, 112, 247n1, 303
Kalecki, M.
  his attempt to link micro behaviour (of firms) with macro economic functioning 295n16; treats risk in investment decisions 295n18; short and long period in 295n19
Keynes, J. M. 8, 112–13, 129n2, 149, 156n4, 159, 177–8, 199–200, 218, 234–5, 239, 243–4, 275–86, 289, 291, 295n18, 299–301, 311–12, 321–2
  weakness of his critique of his predecessors 10, 276, 293n3; retains certain elements of neoclassical distribution theory, source of ambivalences in (Garegnani) 283–5; *see* neoclassical synthesis
  Pasinetti on the structure of causal orderings in the General Theory 282; output determination separated from that of interest 282
  variations in the level of output equilibriums saving and investment 285; his critique of the equilibrating role of interest 285; more significant than the wage rigidity hypothesis (Garegnani) 285; the capital theory critique refutes that role without the obstacle of money and the state of expectations (Garegnani) 285; *see* expectations, effective demand
Keynes, J. N. 143, 155n
Koopmans, T. C. 228
Kregel, J. A. 291, 293n
Kumar, Arun 35n

labour
  productive power of labour, a source of wealth (Smith) 22, 24, 37n11, 151; source of surplus value (Marx) 184, 201n4
  productive 24, 28–9, 156n7; unproductive labour 72n18; free labour, foundation of expanding production (Smith) 22; as a means for

measuring the productive potential of surplus (Smith) 24, 37n14, 195; productive employment of 28–9
as toil and trouble 54, 72n16, 195, 209; as disutility 151; as useful and abstract (Smith) 37n12, 22; as immediate (primary) and hoarded (secondary) in James Mill 49–50; immediate and accumulated (McCulloch) 59
division of labour, interaction with the extent of market (Smith) 7, 16, 21–2, 25
quantity of, as a measure of value; *see* value, measure of
natural and market price of labour 25; *see* wages

laissez faire
historical roots and context of the classical doctrine 18–20; the individual as a 'free agent' in 19–21; Smith's advocacy of, different from the Chicago School defence of competitive capitalism 205

land
as non-reproducible asset, fixed in supply for the economy 119, 182, 226, 248n12, 307; not fixed for an individual producer 248n12, 307; if variable in particular cases and indefinitely divisible, production at constant costs (Sraffa) 307
extensive and intensive cultivation of land, cases differentiated 226; declining productivity on, generalized as diminishing returns to all factors, including capital 226, 308; *see* laws of returns, rent

Landesmann, M. 129n
Lange, Oscar 219
laws of returns
increasing returns in classical theory, associated with division of labour, the general conditions of economic progress 227
increasing returns, contradicts Marshall's partial equilibrium framework 150, 191; irreconcilable with competition, difficulty for the equilibrium of the firm 227–8; problem of irreversibilities 149, 173n19, 174n20, 227; multiple equilibria 149–50; limitations of statical method 159–60, 167–9, 171, 240, 249n17; device of external economies 150, 162, 240, 309, 311; Marshall's attempted resolution, the representative firm 162, 231, 240–1, 311–12; monopolistic market

conditions as a way out 228, 310; assumed away in later neoclassical theory 8, 228, 232, 251n35
diminishing returns on land explains rent (distribution) but not price formation in classical theory 119, 226; generalized to the notion of variable returns and to all factors in marginalist theory 119, 139, 182; generalized to yield monotonic inverse relations between factor intensity and factor prices 119, 182
constant returns arise only accidentally (Marshall) 309; only under constant returns the ideal output (marginal supply price) and competitive output (supply price) coincide (Pigou) 159, 163, 166, 172n2
Marshall's coordination of, 139, 226–7; Sraffa's critique 227, 307–10

Lehmann, W. H. 36n7
Leijonhufvud, Axel 277, 280, 293n5, 294n8
Leontief, W. 247n1, 270n2
Lerner, Abba 219
Levhari, D.
on the impossibility of reswitching of techniques 264, 319; refuted 264, 319
life cycle hypothesis 294n8
Lindahl, Eric 242
liquidity preference theory 279, 284–5
liquidity trap 276–7, 285
Locke, J. 35n3, n4, 54
Lowe, A. 28
Luddites, the 46, 61

MacLennan, B. 200n
Mallet, J. L. 71n7
Malthus, T. R. 53–4, 58, 71n8, 72n18, 101, 103n6, n12, 104n27, 105n30, n31, n33, n35, n36, 106n41, n45, n49, n50, 107n51, 113, 116–18, 120, 125, 129n9, 138, 152–3, 184, 194, 209, 226, 246, 251n37, 289, 317, 319–20
his theory of rent, published simultaneously with that of West and Torrens 42–3, 92, 118; incorporated by Ricardo in his theory of profit 78
his theory of population 181, 190; meeting resistance and replaced by Neo-Malthusianism 46
wages, subsistence as physiological minimum for survival 190
debates with Ricardo (around Ricardo's Essay) 77; on effect of increase of capital on the rate of profit 78; basic principle in dispute, farmer's profit regulate the profits of other trades 42,

INDEX 331

78, 84–94, 104n21, 119, 128
critical debates on the Essay reflect the lack of a theory of relative prices of commodities 79, 90–4; neither grasp the sources of the difficulty 85–91; Ricardo confronts the difficulty, *see* profits
states the material (corn) ratio argument 85; and objects 85–6; wages not consisting of corn slone 85; controverts the determining role of agricultural profits 85; difference with Malthus explained by Ricardo to Trower (Letter of 8 March 1814) 85; many other circumstances, apart from a cheaper mode of obtaining food, increase profits with an increase of capital 85–6
the rate of production (the proportion of production to the consumption necessary) determined by the quantity of accumulated capital and not by the mere difficulty and expense of production corn 87, also 105n29
objects to a material rate of produce, independent of demand and the abundance of capital 87
rise of corn price stimulates demand and hence profits 86; Ricardo's position that determination of profits is independent of the issue of demand, recognized by Malthus 87
dearness of labour, following a rise in price of corn diminishes capital faster than revenue 86
when capital is scanty, profits are high 87; Ricardo argues, the state of demand for capital regulated by the difficulty of producting corn 87–8
every monied accumulation commands less labour and less produce 86; diminution of capital, a necessary consequence of import restrictions 104n28; cheaper corn imports affect real value of rents adversely 92–3; view opposed by Ricardo 93, 106n41
questions inverse relation between wages and the rate of profit 184
difficulty arises from different effects of an increase or diminution of capital on the land, manufactures and commerce, occasioned by the different nature of instruments employed 91
Malthus's measure of capital criticized by Ricardo for theoretical inadequacy, in Absolute value and Exchangeable value 97–8

Malthus-Ricardo controversy on Say's law, identity of savings and investment as in Ricardo 88; *see* Say's law
marginal supply curve
defined (Pigou) 166, 173n12; marginal supply price deviates from supply price except under constant returns (Pigou) 159, 161–4, 166–8, 173n16; Allyn Young's criticism 167–8; criticized also by Marshall 167, 171–2
Marshall, Alfred
upholds doctrinal continuity in theoretical developments 3, 5, 41, 77, 127, 129n8, 130n11, 134, 190–1, 224, 229, 318; his view contested 129n8, 134–5, 151–6
synthesizes classical and demand and supply theory 4–5, 114–15, 134, 153–5, 207; and subverts 5, 10, 127; Marshall's claim to the contrary 134, 152, 156n6; his Ricardianism questioned by Schumpeter 157n14
whether amongst the early pioneers of the marginalist school 134, 151, 155, 156n4
his early writings on value; link, with Mill and with Mill's version of Ricardo 134–6, 152–5; provides a fulcrum for his later writings 142–3; striking features of the Essay on value 143–51
equilibrium between demand and supply, the fundamental idea applied in distribution and exchange 239–40; on one sidedness of Ricardo's theory of value 191, 230, 237–8, 249n15; also of Malthus, Mcleod and Jevons 152
basis of demand curve in utility not developed in early Essay on value 145–6, 150; shift to utility based demand schedule 146–7, 150–2; treatment of demand symmetrical to supply 146–7, 228–31
treats conditions of normal supply less definite than that of demand 140, 146, 149, 157n13; difficulties with the supply schedule 149, 157n13, 168–70, 174n20, 179n19; *see* laws of returns, representative firm, time, supply schedule
element of time 152; his principle of continuity 147–8, 192, 239–40; classification of markets 143–9; and corresponding classification of values 147–8, 238–41; statical method stated 239–40, 251n32; limitations of 159–60, 167–9, 171, 240, 249n17

consumer's surplus 150, 166, 168, 170–1, 174n23, 231; producer's surplus 140, 168, 174n23; quasi-rents 139, 146
his Ms notes on Pigou's wealth and welfare 160–6; considers Pigou as over rating the possibility of the statical method 159

Marshall, Mary 148, 172n1

Marx, Karl 37n10, 38n22, 46, 65, 72n18, 73n24, 74n34, n38, 81, 116, 127, 178, 180, 200, 201n4, n5, 204–9, 211–19, 223, 236, 239, 246–7, 248n4, 250n26, n27, n30, 251n40, 286–9, 291, 298–9, 304, 318–22

original and radical reconstruction of political economy (within the surplus approach) 1, 3, 34, 41, 70, 126, 204, 216

Marx's openness in dealing with historical change 200, 223, 244, 250n26, 289, 292, 295n21; dialectical materialist interpretation of history 211; qualitative and quantitative changes 244, 250n26; modes of production and transitions 211, 215–17, 250n26; distinguished from the Scottish materialist school of history 36n8

the shared ground with Smith, Ricardo, the elemental, basic, structure of surplus approach to value and distribution 2, 3, 34, 77, 126, 205–6, 217, 287

critique of Smith: finds analytical inconsistencies and ambivalences 14–15, 29–34; criticize the adding up view 208; dual aspects in Smith, exoteric and esoteric 31–4, 206–7; dual views on value and revenue 29, 31–2; however, Smith praised for a twofold task 31–3

critique of Ricardo: neglect of constant capital 248n4; value not adequately distinguished from prices 131n6; Ricardo's procedure to derive the inverse wage-profit relation 131n16

criticizes identification of surplus value with profits in James Mill, McCulloch 51, 54–5

criticizes Malthusian population dynamics 246

on labour: labour power distinguished from labour 212; the labour process, a general depiction of production 215–16; reserve army of unemployed 181, 190, 235

organic composition of capital 214

on value: labour, not wages, create value 38n2; absolute surplus value 217; prices of production defined, distinguished from value 45, 212; Say's law not implied in price of production 247, 251n40; transforming values into prices 45, 81, 130n13, 184, 212–13, 248n13; *see* transformation problem

on wages: historically determined 181; influenced by capitalist's strategies 181; by the reserve army of unemployed 181, 190

profits as transformed surplus value 196, 212; origins of profits in exploitation 196, 212, 214; the rate of profit as total of surplus value(s) redistribution over total capital (c+v) 213

rents subordinated to profits 251n39

relation between wages and profits, the inner-connection of bourgeois society 213

interdependence among production, distribution, consumption and exchange (with primacy of production) in Grundrisse 181; dynamics of process of interaction and change 182–3, 244; Marx's analysis of effects of accumulation, method of comparison of long period positions 292

discards Say's law 289; realization crisis in the short period, due to interruptions in commodity circuits 292; and also in the long run (deficient demand) 292

Masson, D. 73n28

Mattioli, R. 299

maximum satisfaction
doctrine of, in Marshall 230; Pigou's extension of his conclusions on the question 159, 231; Hobson notes Pigou's virtual admission of the failure of marginalism 159–60, 171; Marshall on Hobson on Pigou 160; *see* Marshall Alfred, laws of returns

McCulloch, J. R. 41, 45–6, 48–9, 70, 72n14, n17, n18, n20, 73n22, n24, 96–8, 101, 103n13, n14, 131n6

adheres to Ricardo's doctrines initially 53, 72n14; later modified considerably 53, 72n15

on value 53–60; distinguishes between real and exchangeable value 54–5; adheres to labour value principle without qualifications 55–60; Ricardo's comment on 53

measure of value, different from cause of 57; shifting views on 'labour' 55–60; labour bestowed on capital or

INDEX 333

agent by which the commodity is
produced or quantity of labour
worked up in commodities 59; natural
agent or powers add nothing to value
60; differs from Ricardo on the
rationale of invariant standard 57
  on wages 60–1; actual level explained by
    the amount of capital relative to
    labour 56, 60; natural wage as the
    minimum necessary subsistence 60
  on profits, as surplus 61; as the result of
    sacrifice 61; questions the inverse
    relation between wages and the rate
    of profit on grounds of productivity
    changes 61
  on distribution, symmetry between
    capital and labour, profits and wages
    56, 61; views real cost of labour as toil
    and trouble 54, 72n16, n17; conflicts
    resolvable through fair legislation
    71n5; opposes Ricardo's altered stand
    on machinery of the third edition of
    Principles 51, 73n27
Meek, R. L. 9, 14, 35n2, n4, 36n6, 74n38,
  88, 126, 156n1, 157n14, 212, 289
  on relation of Smith's ideas to those of
    Marx 204–11; on the four stages
    theory of stadial development in
    Smith 204, 210–11; compared with
    Marx's sociology 211
  follows closely Marx's discussion of
    Smith 205–7; regards Smith as
    founder of the theoretical tradition
    starting from conditions of exchange
    207
  on transformation problem, *see*
    transformation problem
  distinguishes alternative theoretical
    approaches on the basis of
    explanation of price 218; not in terms
    of structures 218; the view examined
    218–19
Menger, C. 1
Milgate, M. 71n
Mill, James 30, 41, 46, 56, 60–1, 65, 69,
  71n11, 72n12, 79–81, 88–90, 94, 97–8,
  101, 103n8, 113–15, 118, 120, 122–3,
  129n9, 130n14, 229
  production and distribution treated
    prior to exchangeable value 46–7,
    51–2 (also in J. S. Mill 65)
  on exchangeable value 47–9;
    determined by quantity of labour
    47–8; whether affected by time 48–9;
    and by wage variations 49–50; cost of
    production ultimately and entirely
    regulates 47
  on labour, two species, primary and
    secondary, paid at separate rates
    49–50
  on capital, as secondary or hoarded
    labour 49–50; his criticism of Torrens
    and Bailey's objection to it 47–8,
    72n12
  on wages and profits 51–3; no reference
    to market and natural wage
    distinction 51; proportion of capital to
    labour determines the share of wages
    51–2; profits, a measure of quantity of
    hoarded labour 48–9; various
    meanings of the inverse relation, in
    terms of shares, vacuously true 52–3;
    in terms of 'quantities' and between
    share of wages and the rate of profit,
    necessity denied 52–3
  on distribution, symmetry between
    capital and labour, and profits and
    wages 51; identification of capital with
    savings 51; harmonious co-operation
    between labour and capital 51
Mill, J. S. 39n23, 41, 46, 63, 68–70, 74n33,
  n36, n37, 127, 129n9, 134–5, 142,
  145–6, 151–3, 157n14, 165, 192,
  201n5, 208, 228, 249n24, 291
  on value, accepts de Quincey's
    amendation of use value and its
    relation to exchange value 65, 136–7;
    cost of production view of prices,
    wages and profits determine value 65,
    139; three classes of commodities with
    distinct law of value for each 65,
    137–9, 248n13; the crucial third law
    provides ground for a supply relation
    between output and cost 138, demand
    as a ratio to supply replaced by
    demand dependent on prices 138
  on wages 66, 139, 156n7; debate with
    Thornton; *see* wages fund doctrine
  on profits, in part recompense for
    forebearance, risk and
    superintendence 66; as abstinence,
    following Senior 65–6, 139, 156n7;
    reformulates the inverse relation as
    between cost of production of wages
    and the rate of profits 66–7
Millar, J. 35n4, 36n5, n7
Mitchell, W. 18
Modigliani, F. 275–6, 294n8
Montesguieu, C. L. 35n3, n4, 36n5, n6
Morgenstern, O. 249n25
Morishima, M. 212, 215, 273n17

national dividend
  Pigou distinguishes between Marshall's
    and Fisher's definition of 160;
    Marshall's comment on 161

334 INDEX

natural state (position)
  analytical construction, based on historical observation 25; as an average state 23, 126, 290; illustrated by natural price 24–5, 31, 37n13, 235–6, 287; discoverable regularities in the form of permanent/stable tendencies 23, 37n13, 295n19; distinguished from market position, in terms of causal forces and effects 37n13, 235–7, 287
Naqvi, K. A. 271n7
Nayyar, D. 35n
neoclassical synthesis 178, 199, 235, 275–6
  seeds of compromise in Keynes 10, 276, 283–7, 293n3; opposition to 276, 281; neo-Walrasian critiques and reformulations 278–81
net product
  defined 120, 126, 201n3; see surplus; social and private, defined (Pigou) 161
Newman, P. 255–6, 262, 266–7, 269, 270n2 see basics and nonbasics
Newton, Isaac 35n4, 210
non-substitition theorem 201n2, 223
non-tatonnement process 278–81, 294n9

O'Brien, D. P. 72n14, 19n17, 73n25, 128

Panteleoni, M. 156n4, 300, 303
Pasinetti, L. L. 112, 214, 233, 270n, 273n17, 281–3
Patinkin, D. 275
Patten, S. 116, 118
Permanent income hypothesis 294n8
Petty, Wm. 1
Phelps-Brown, E. 247n1
physiocrats
  beginnings of political economy in France 1, 116, 126; Quesnay and Turgot combining social moralism with historical materialism 35n4
  surplus only in agriculture 23; additional productivity of land as rents, disputed by Ricardo 38n20
  notion of productive consumption in 120
Pierson, N. G. 152
Pigou, A. C.
  extends Marshall's argument on maximum satisfaction in *Wealth and Welfare*, 159, 170–1; see under Hobson, laws of returns; Marshall Alfred, maximum satisfaction
price
  of corn, regulates all prices (Smith) 30, 79–80, 82; view upheld initially by Ricardo 30, 79, 82–3, 86, 91, 121; later finds inconsistent with his theory of profits 30, 79–80, 106n47, 122–4; whether Ricardo considered increased money supply essential for the Smithian thesis 82–3, 103n15, n16
  regulated by quantity of labour necessary for production 24, 30, 38n22, 47–8, 53–4, 80, 95, 98, 122–3, 127–8
  natural price, defined 24–5, 27, 31, 99, 105n39, 131n18, 193–5, 201n, 225, 235; determinants of 27, 99, 136, 180, 225; distinguished from market price 5, 24, 27, 99–101, 180, 192–5, 201n1, 225, 235, 287
  market price 4–8, 24, 27, 136, 148, 180, 192–4, 225, 249n24; gravitation of market to natural price 5, 24, 27, 180, 193, 201n1, 225, 235
  distinctiveness of the classical notion of natural and market price 27, 192–4; from Marshall's 147–8, 154–5, 185, 192–3, 238–41, 250n29
  short period and long period normal (equilibrium) price 147–8, 154, 185, 192, 238–40, 250n29
  reserve price 140
  reservation price 279
Price, L. L. 156n5
principle of increasing risk 295n18
production system 255; defined 266, 270n1
productive consumption
  notion of 32, 183; refers to material means and sustenance of labour required for production 32, 120, 126
profits
  upon alienation (Steuart) 22; leavings of wages 37n14, 64–5; neither superior wage for management nor rent (Smith) 37n12; in part recompense for forebearance, risk and superintendence (J. S. Mill) 66; as abstinence (J. S. Mill following Senior) 65–6, 139, 156n7; arise not from the incidence of exchange but from the productive powers of labour (J. S. Mill) 66; the result of sacrifice (McCulloch) 61; constrained by conditions of production (Ricardo) 42, 88–9, 119, 184, 209, 212–13; theory of, within surplus approach 79–80, 104n20, 107n52, 120, 125
  theory of, Ricardo's corn ratio theory 4, 42, 79, 85–94, 106n48, 120; primitive agricultural form 4, 30; extension of corn to other necessaries, by analogy, in Pre-Essay correspondence and Essay 85–6, 90–1, 121; worked out

prior to the pamphlets on rents of West, Torrens and Malthus 42–3, 78, 92, 118–20; determined on no rent land 44, 119, 184, 212; depend upon wages 30, 42, 55, 120, 122, 139

whether profits of farmers regulate profits of all other trades, Malthus-Ricardo debate 42, 78, 84–94, 104n21, 119, 128; Sraffa's rational foundation of 79, 84, 92, 104n20, n26, 112, 120; disappears from Principles 78, 119, 128

generalization of the theory 42–3, 78–9, 93–4, 107n52; requires recourse to a theory of relative prices 84; significance not recognized in Pre-Essay Correspondence (Ricardo and Malthus) 42, 85, 90–1, 106n50; recognized later 43, 79, 92–4, 103n6, 120; Ricardo stopped by price, the turning point (Sraffa) 120; 'labour' replaces corn with adoption of general theory of value in Principles 44, 79, 107n52, 121, 184, 212

whether an independent cause (determinant) of value 139; Ricardo's difference with Malthus 131n18; Marshall's interpretation of Ricardo, cost of production view 127

whether lowered by tax 99; by restrictions on corn imports (Ricardo and Malthus) 87, 93

high when capital scanty (Malthus) 87; Ricardo's difference with Malthus explained to Trower 85–6

profits, the rate of
natural rate of 90, 108n66, 288; permanent factors influencing 89–90, 99, 105n30, 194, 201; market rate of, temporary factors influencing 89–90
uniformity of rates 92
determined by competition of capitals (Smith) 30, 32, 83–4, 122, 248n4; opposed by Ricardo 30, 84–98, 101, 248n4
determined by the proportion of production to consumption necessary for that production (Ricardo) 88–90, 105n29, n34
vary inversely with wages 42, 44, 47, 69, 99, 108n66, 120, 122, 125, 184, 212; transparently evident in the 'corn' and 'labour' value case 44, 69, 99, 120, 184, 212; obscured in the more general case 44, 69, 79, 91, 106n41, 184, 212; relation obfuscated in James Mill 50, 52–3, 69–70; in McCulloch 61, 69–70; in de Quincey 65

determined simultaneoulsy with prices 48, 101–2, 109n69, 126, 139, 196, 244, 248n8
determined in the wage-goods sector, given wages in kind (Bortkiewicz, Garegnani) 213–14
raised (lowered) by improvements (difficulties) in agriculture 78, 119, 105n34
Pufendorf, S. von 35n3

de Quincey Thomas 41, 46, 62–5, 73n28, n31, 136–7, 143, 228
on value, distinguishes between use and exchange value 62–3, 136–7; teleo logic (use) value as utility of a commodity to an individual in his own estimation 62–3, 137; places use value and exchange value on the same quantitative scale 62–3, 136–7; criticizes Smith's water-diamond paradox 62, 136–7; J. S. Mill adopts the view 136–7; Marshall extends 143; labour as regulator of value, without qualification 62; *see also* value; market and natural value, market value a technical concept 63
measure of value, search for, a chimera 62–3
on wages, no distinction between market and natural 63; four factors governing wages 63
profits, as leavings of wages 64–5
on rent, supports Richardo's theory on theoretical grounds 63–4, 74n31; opposes, on empirical 64
distributive relations harmonious 64

real cost
labour as 'sweat and toil', real cost view implicit in McCulloch 54, 72n17
doctrine of, development through Mill and Marshall 150–1, 208; in Marshall 187; view imputed to Smith and Ricardo by Marshall 72n16, 151, 208–9
real wealth effect 285
realization crisis 236, 292, 320
rent
theory of differential rent 31, 42, 226; allowed Ricardo to get rid of rent to isolate relation between wages and profits 119, 184, 192
as monopoly price (Smith) 31
does not enter price in Ricardo 31, 119, 240; sometimes treated as an element of price in Smith 31
extensive and intensive cultivation 226,

249n14; the intensive case generalized into variable factor proportions 226; marginal principle seen as underlying rent theory, extended to explain all factor returns 119, 226

leading species of a large genus 140, 240

quasi-rents 139–40

Consumer's rent in Marshall 136

the classical view of rents divorced form the traditional law of diminishing returns (Sraffa) 246–7, 319–20

representative firm 231, 240–1, 311–12; *see* Marshall Alfred, laws of returns

reserve army of the unemployed 190

Ricardians 3, 41

attempts at modifications and extensions obfuscated the structure of classical theory 3, 69–70; *see* McCulloch J. R., Mill James, Mill J. S., de Quincey T.

Ricardian Socialists

phrase coined by Foxwell 71n6; advocated radical reforms 46

Ricardo, D. 1–5, 9, 14–15, 24, 29–34, 38n20, 41–74, 77–109, 111–31, 134–9, 151–4, 157n14, 179–84, 190–2, 194–5, 198, 201n2, 204–9, 212–13, 216–18, 222–3, 226, 230, 236, 238, 241, 245–7, 248n3–n6, 249n15, n16, 250n28, 287, 289–91, 300–4, 316–19

his theory central to understand the logical foundations of classical political economy 111–12, 117; also the origins of later marginalism 111–12, 114–15

controversial interpretations of 115–16, 118, 126–8

on value, *see* value

on price, *see* price

on wages, *see* wages

on rent, *see* rent

on profits, *see* profits, profits, the rate of; controversy with Malthus on the determination of the rate of profit, *see* Malthus T. R., profits

on distribution, interests of landlords versus those of other classes in agriculture 42–3, 45; shift to a more open confrontation between labour and capital 45–6; *see* profits, the rate of

inverse relation between wages and profits; *see* profits

on machinery, altered position in the 3rd edition of Principles 46, 73n27, 101; injurious to the interests of workmen 61; opposed by McCulloch 61

Richard, A. 247n

Robertson, D. H. 231, 237, 299–301, 311–12

Robinson, E. A. G. 129n2, n5, 156n, 172n

Robinson, J. 9, 172n, 247n1, 264, 292, 293n1, n3

Roncaglia, A. 102n, 108n64, 126, 128, 294n13

Rosenberg, N. 19, 28

Samuelson, P. A. 5, 9, 112, 130n12, 201n2, 245, 248n5, 251n37, 264–5

Say, J. B. 109n67, 130n10, 138, 208–9, 217, 247, 251n40, 289

Say's law

in classical theory: Keynes' interpretation of Ricardo-Malthus controversy, questioned by Meek, Garegnani 289; not a premise to deduce full employment 289; Marx's criticism of, simulates barter economy 289; not an essential premise of prices of production 289

Scazzieri, R. 129n

Schumpeter, J. A. 14, 65, 116, 157n14, 179, 192, 204, 207–8, 217

Scientific political economy

attains its acme in Ricardo (Marx) 116; post-Ricardo decline of 3, 74n38

search behaviour 278–9, 294n7

self-replacing state

distinguished from self-reproducing in Sraffa's Production of Commodities 246, 289–90

Senior, Nassau 66, 139, 156n7

Seton, F. 212–13

Shackle, G. L. S. 247n1

Shaftsbury 35n3

Sheshinski, E. 259, 265, 273n17

Shove, G. F. 145, 150–4, 156n5, n12, 201n2

Skinner, A. S. 15, 36n5

Smith, Adam 1–5, 7, 9, 13–39, 54, 62, 72n16, 77–84, 86, 90–5, 100, 103n9, 107n53, 111, 115–16, 121–3, 126–8, 129n9, 131n18, 134–8, 142–3, 150–3, 179, 181–3, 190, 192–5, 201n1, n3, n6, 204–12, 217–20, 222–3, 227–8, 234–6, 244–5, 248n4, n5, n7, 287–8, 290–1, 322

as founder member of surplus based theories 13, 14, 33–4, 205–6, 209; opposition to mercantilism and their concept of surplus 18–19, 23, 195, 206; shift away from exchange relations 22, 195

method of theoretical history, stadial view of development 13–17, 31, 209–11; modes of subsistence,

hunting, pasturage, agriculture and commerce and transition 15–17, 211; *see* historical materialism
moral philosophy of 13–18, 21, 209–11; system of morality 14–17, 209–11; the twin perspective – moral and materialist 13–15, 209–11
system of natural liberty 18–19, 21–3, 209; natural order 15–19, 23, 37n9; Author of Nature 14, 17, 37n19; free individual in the society 4, 14–17, 19–21, 28, 34, 209–11; a moral being governed by a rational plan, inherent in nature 14; whether pursuit of self-interest ensures natural harmony 18–21, 210
invisible hand in 18, 20–1, 26, 37n9; contrasted with Walrasian auctioneer 4, 20–1
on value, *see* value
on wages, *see* wages
on profits, *see* profits, profits, the rate of
on rent, *see* rent
formulates concepts, categories in the context of accumulation 21–4, 34–5; the theory of output 28; ways of employing capital and the natural course of economic growth, agriculture, manufacture, commerce 28–9; interaction between division of labour and the extent of market, *see* labour
Sraffa, A. 299
Sraffa, Piero 3, 5, 9, 10, 44, 71n3, n10, 74n36, 78–81, 84–6, 89, 93, 95–6, 101, 102n2, n5, 104n20, n26, 105n38, 107n52, n54, 111–31, 150, 153–4, 172n, n1, 177, 179, 182, 191, 201n3, 214, 217, 222–9, 231, 234, 240–1, 243, 245–9, 251, 255–6, 262, 264, 266–8, 270, 272n14, 288–9, 294n15, 298–322
birth and childhood 299; early academic career and professional appointments 298–301; association with Gramsci 300; with Wittgenstein 302; with Keynes 299–301; appointment at Cambridge 300–1; commitmenty to socialism 298–9; the bibliophile 322
as a researcher 298; awareness of social, political and historical dimensions of economic theories 281; critical and constructive writings 111, 302–4, 307, 322; distinguishes two different structures of economic theories, classical and marginalist 246, 304; opposed to doctrinal continuity claimed by Marshall 303–4, 318
as a critique, of Marshallian theory 111, 117, 227–9, 300–1, 304, 307–10; on the presumed symmetry between the forces of demand and supply 228–9, 307–8; common axioms behind demand and supply schedules 228–9, 308; diminishing marginal utility and decreasing productivity curves, both descriptive 308; on the co-ordination of laws of returns in marginalist theory 227, 307; critique of Marshallian supply schedule, assumed independent of all other supply and demand schedules 191, 227, 241, 308–10; difficulties in the case of increasing and diminishing returns 227–8, 309; stringent requirement necessary for increasing/decreasing costs in Marshall 310–11; critique of the representative firm 231, 240–1, 311–12; *see* laws of returns, Marshall Alfred
on Hayek's Prices and production 314–16; favours comparisons between a moneyless economy and alternative monetary system to study effects of assumed cases of disturbances in equilibrium 313; Hayek criticized for dealing with money in no other role but of a medium of exchange 313–14; criticizes Hayek's presumption that the economy reverts to initial equilibrium after disturbance 315; criticizes asymetric treatments of effects of credit to consumers and to producers 315; multiple natural rates of interest for commodities possible in a barter economy, necessary for effecting transition to equilibrium 316; disequilibrium possible in a non-monetary economy 316; Sraffa's later critique of Austrian capital theory not present 316
as a reconstructive thinker 111; monumental edition of works and correspondence of David Ricardo with the collaboration of M. H. Dobb, on Keynes' suggestion 112–13, 129n2; as editor of works 11–15, 301–2, 316–17; provides rational foundation for theoretical propositions 3, 111, 114–15, 117, 119, 125, 317; on development of Ricardo's theory of profit 78–80; on the edition, Stigler 11–12, 129n3; Hutchison 129n4; on the preface to the works, E. A. G. Robinson 129n5
His production of commodities by means of commodities, dual

objectives pursued in 222, 318; reviving the classical stand point 10, 111–12, 126, 217–8, 222, 246–7, 300–4, 322

critique of marginal methods, focusing on the crucial problem of distribution 304, 319; change, a prerequisite for marginal theory 222–3, 226, 310–11

his investigation concerned with properties of an economic system, not depending on change 22–3; simultaneous determination of the rate of profit and relative prices, given methods of production and wage 318–19; see profits, the rate of; separate determination of prices and quantities 320; methodological advantage 321–2; see classical theory

on capital measurement problem 319; resolves a central difficulty in classical theory of distribution 318; notion of standard commodity 214, 318; implicit solution to the transformation problem 213–14, 248n3, 318–19; reswitching of methods 319; and the capital controversy 319; see capital theory debate; treatment of joint products in 320

on rent, demonstrates diminishing marginal returns, not essential element in classical theory 246–7, 319; differential rents as well as no rent land depend upon the rate of profit (wages) 247, 320

on wages, notion of variable wages, wages as a share of net national product 320

some misinterpretations 319–21; Sraffa system treated as a special case of general equilibrium 223, 320–1; as a stationary state 246, 289–90, 320–1; as an abstract intellectual experiment 223; whether constant returns to scale essential 222, 245–6, 320–1

standard commodity 214, 318

statics and dynamics

Hicks' distinction 251n33; distinguished from statical/dynamical notions of Marshall 251n33; taxonomy of methods of dynamics (Hicks) 243; see Hicks, J. R.

stationary state 237, 241, 246, 289–90, 292, 320–1

Steedman, Ian 156n, 200n, 215

Steindl, J. 295n20, n21

Steuart, J. 22

Stewart, D. 15, 35n4, 36n6

surplus

the basis of analysis in classical theory 6, 29–31, 41–2, 72, 80, 183, 195

or net product, total produce minus the requirements of productive consumption 126; arises in agriculture alone, in physiocrats 201n3; generalized to cover all production in Smith 23, 201n3; surplus netted for wages when paid in advance (Smith); wages and profits as shares of surplus, when wages paid post-factum (as in Sraffa and sometimes in Smith) 201n3

material rate of surplus, in corn 44, 79, 85, 120; see profits

size of 183

source of 184, 212; in labour, as surplus value (Marx) 214

measure of 23–4, 183–4

notion lost in demand and supply theory (Dobb) 187–8

supply schedule (curve)

supply functions not in classical theory 154, 183, 192, 226; Mill connects unit cost of production to output (in the third class of commodities) 65, 139; see Mill J. S.; Marshall's extension into a supply schedule 139, 146

normal short period and long period supply curve, Marshall's own doubts on 157n13, 228; particularly with regard to increasing returns 168–72; Marshall's true long period supply curve under increasing returns 170; Marshall's reservations on Pigou's use of long period supply curve 160; see laws of returns; Marshall, Alfred

Marshall's co-ordination of the laws of returns in the supply schedule, see laws of returns; Sraffa's critique; see Sraffa, Piero

curves of marginal supply price defined and used by Pigou; see marginal supply curve

Thomson, William 71n6

Thornton, W. T. 74n33, n37, 135–6, 140–2, 144, 151

Thunen, J. H. von 156n3

Thewatt, W. D. 28

time

reduction to dated labour 44–5; Ricardo's letter to McCulloch of 13th June 1820 154; whether indicates weakening of labour theory 59–60, 96–7, 130n13, 154; whether time, a separate cause of value apart from labour in Ricardo 96–7, 108n58, 124–5, 130n14, 154 time itself has no effect on exchangeable value (McCulloch) 59–60; time, the mere computation of annuity (James Mill) 48–9

Marshall's principle of continuity 152, 192; 'element of time' in classification of markets 137–40, 143–9; doubts on the stability of demand and supply function, difficulty due to 'element of time' 168–70, 173n19, 174n20; irreversibilities in production and consumption 169, 173n19, 174n20

element of time in Hicks; current supplies and demands governed by expected as much as current prices 241; shift from long to short period equilibrium 241–3; *see* statics and dynamics

prospective value: value of any article of wealth (present worth) dependent on future alone (Fisher) 233, 249n19–n21

time structure of the production process (Austrians) 233

complete future markets envisaged concurrently (Debreu) 249n23

Torrens, C. 42–3, 47–8, 58, 73n30, 92, 96, 98, 101, 108n56, 118, 130n14

transformation problem 130n13, n14, 184, 204, 211–12

deviation of prices from value recognized by Smith, Ricardo 184, 212–14

relation to Ricardo's search for an invariant standard 45, 81, 97, 130n13, n14, 248n3

Marx's faulty procedure corrected by later writers 213–16; implicit solution in Sraffa 213–14, 248n3; logical historical method applied to (Meek) 215; Marxian-Sraffian commodity models (Meek) 214; as a historical process; dubious 215

whether unnecessarily diversionary and misleading 215; analytical historical perspective on 215–16

trotter, C. 83, 103n17

Trower, H. 84–5, 104n21, 118

Turgot, A. R. J. 35n4, 210, 219

Turnbull, G. 35n4, 37n9

utility
the foundation, not the measure of value in classicals 100; rejection of utility governing value (Ricardo) 109n67, 217

not fully developed as the basis of demand curve in Marshall's early writings on value 146, 150; later adopted 150–1, 228–9

principle of diminishing utility, the basis of the demand schedule in Principles 228–9

water-diamond paradox resolved in total-marginal utility distinction 136–7

value
regulated by quantity, not value of labour 24, 30, 38n22, 47–8, 53–4, 80, 95, 98, 122–3, 127–8; but modified by different proportions of fixed and circulating capital 30, 44, 47, 57–8, 79, 122, 154; by greater or less durability of capital 30, 123, 154; by time elapsing before commodities are brought to market 154; by the rise or rall of wages 43–4, 53–4, 49–50, 79, 106n51, 116, 122–4; by the differences in the time pattern of embodied labour 48, 58, 154, 212; all reducible to time 79

labour embodied theory of value 24, 47, 49, 54, 57, 70, 81, 112, 115, 121, 123–4, 126–7, 184, 207–8, 218–19, 245; abandoned by Smith when stock accumulated and land appropriated 30, 122–3, 207–8, 212; Ricardo explains difference with Smith to Mill 30, 123; McCulloch on 57–60; discussion with Ricardo 57–9; analytical role of 184, 197–8, 216–17; role denied 127; an empirical principle (Stigler and Cassels) 127; Hollander upholds the view 81, 97–8, 107n53, n54, 128

synonymous with cost of production; a definition, not a theory 131n18, 139

adding up view, profits, rents and wages treated as both sources of revenue and of value 32, 38n16, n22, 122, 195, 208; Smith's original error and Ricardo's opposition to 30, 122, 131n18, 208; deficiencies of the view 30, 122, 193, 208

Absolute value and Exchangeable value, Ricardo's unfinished manuscript 57, 96, 108n58, 124, 130n14; absolute value distinguished from exchangeable value (Ricardo) 57

real and exchangeable value distinguished in McCulloch 54–5

value in use and value in exchange: value in use a necessary condition for a commodity to have value in exchange in Smith and Ricardo 100, 137; also depends on individual's estimation of its capacity to gratify subjective inclination in de Quincey, different from Smith and Ricardo 62–3, 137, 143; value in use as the extreme limit of value in exchange (de Quincey) 137; measure of use value in terms of the price an individual pays (de Quincey) 62–3, 137; extended by Marshall 109n68, 137, 143, 146

value, measure or standard of

Adam Smith's measure: labour embodied in the early and rude stage 24, 94, 184, 195; labour commanded after appropriation of land and accumulation of capital 24, 95, 183–4, 195; Ricardo's objection to labour commanded, no more invariant than corn or gold 24, 195

Ricardo's measure: corn 79, 184; quantity of labour embodied 79, 94–6, 107n52, 123–4, 184

invariant standard 4, 43–4, 127, 197–8; search for prompted by the theory of profit 43–5, 79–82, 124, 184, 198; properties of standard varies with the specific theory of value 45, 82, 96–7, 116, 123–4; produce of always the same quantity of labour (in ed, 1 & 2 of Principles) and produced with the medium proportions of the two kinds of capital (in ed. 3 of Principles) 44, 96–7, 107n54, 123–5, 128; variety of circumstances of production, difficulty in finding the mean proportion 57, 96–7, 108n58; no invariable standard found 57, 72n20, 97

theoretical measure, not an empirical concern of Ricardo 45, 97–8, 108n50, 124; treated as an empirical problem (Hollander) 81; as a chimera, disassociated from the theory of profit by Ricardians 45, 57

cause of value different from measures: in McCulloch 57; in de Quincey 62; in James Mill 50, 72n12; Ricardo close to identifying the problem of measure with that of law of value 72n21, 95–6, 109n56, 124

Viner, Jacob 13, 18–19, 35n3

Vulgar economy 3

vulgar elements in Smith's theory (Marx) 29

wages

in classical theory, determined outside the scheme of price determination 7, 26, 126, 181, 196, 320; given wages not necessarily fixed 89–90, 181, 190, 251n37, 288–90; not only subsistence 38n17, 181, 190, 320; customary wage 52; determination, contractual and conflictual 25, 38n18, 142, 181, 190

as material requirements of sustaining labour (Smith) 32–3, 195; as compensation for toil and trouble (Smith) 32–3, 195

price of wages 125, 105n38; natural rate of wages 25, 60, 63, 193–4; market rate of wages 60, 63; distinction not made in McCulloch and de Quincey 63

wages advanced; whether part of surplus (net produce) 201n3; *see* surplus

curious effect of rise of wages (Ricardo) 70, 122

effect of accumulation on wages (Smith) 7, 25–6, 32

wages fund doctrine

incipient idea of, in the determination of wages by relative magnitude of capital, stock and population (James Mill and McCulloch) 51–2, 56, 60

formulated in J. S. Mill 66, 73n32, 138; criticism of Thornton 138, 140–2; retraction from, by J. S. Mill 66, 141–2; Marshall on Mill-Thornton controversy 140–2; Cairnes' attempted reformulation 74n33; Marshall's synthesis 140–2, 190–1

subsistence fund in the Austrian theory (Bohm Bawerk) 74n33

wage rigidity

whether explaining unemployment equilibrium 276–7, 280–1, 284–5, 294n11

Walras, Leon 1–3, 108n62, 109n69, 134, 155, 156n2, 185, 201n2, 207–8, 217–18, 237, 277–83, 287, 291, 293n5, 294n10, 295n17, 312, 320

West, Edward 42–3, 92, 118

Weydemeyer, Joseph 36n8

Whitaker, J. K. 142, 156n

Wicksell, Knut 2, 185, 200, 232–3, 237, 287, 291, 295n17, 316

Wicksteed, P. H. 308

Winternitz, J. 212–13

Wittgenstein, Ludwig 299, 302

Wood-Cunningham, John 13

Worswick, V. D. N. 247n1

Young, Allyn 167–8

Author Index from Acknowledgements

Aitchison, Juliet xii
Bagchi, A. K. xi
Bhaduri, Amit xi
Bhushan, S. xii
Campus, Antonia xi
Chakravarty, S. xi
Chandra, N. K. xi
Dobb, M. H. xi
Eatwell, J. xi
Fries, Carole xii
Garegnani, P. xi
Ghosh, Jayati xii
Harcourt, Geoffrey xi
Harris, Donald xi

Kaldor, N. xi
Kurz, Heinz xi
McLennan, Barbara xi
Nell, Edward xi
Pasinetti, L. L. xi
Raj, K. N. xi
Robinson, Joan xi
Roncaglia, A. xi
Schefold, B. xi
Singh, Yashwant xii
Sraffa, Piero xi
Steadman, Ian xi
Sylos Labini, P. xi
White, Carolyn xii

DATE DUE